LAND RIGHTS OF INDIGENOUS PEOPLES IN AFRICA

With Special Focus on Central, Eastern and Southern Africa

Albert Kwokwo Barume

IWGIA Document 115
Copenhagen 2010

LAND RIGHTS OF INDIGENOUS PEOPLES IN AFRICA
With Special Focus on Central, Eastern and Southern Africa

Author: Albert Kwokwo Barume

Copyright: The author and IWGIA – 2010 – All Rights Reserved

Editorial Production: Marianne Wiben Jensen and Diana Vinding

Cover and layout: Jorge Monrás

Proofreading: Diana Vinding

Prepress and Print: Centraltrykkeriet Skive A/S
Skive, Denmark

ISBN: 978-87-91563-77-5

ISSN: 0105-4503

HURIDOCS CIP DATA

Title: LAND RIGHTS OF INDIGENOUS PEOPLES IN AFRICA
With Special Focus on Central, Eastern and Southern Africa
Author: Barume, Albert Kwokwo
Corporate editor: IWGIA
Place of publication: Copenhagen, Denmark
Publisher: IWGIA
Distributors:
Europe: IWGIA, Classensgade 11E, DK Copenhagen 2100 – www.iwgia.org
North America: Transaction Publishers, 390 Campus Drive, Somerset,
New Jersey 08873 – www.transactionpub.com
Date of Publication: 2010
Pages: 335
Reference to series: IWGIA Document Series, no. 115
ISBN: 978-87-91563-77-5
ISSN: 0105-4503
Language: English
Bibliography: Yes
Index terms: Indigenous peoples/Land rights/Legal frameworks/International jurisprudence
Geographical area: Central, Eastern and Southern Africa
Geographical code: 5200

**INTERNATIONAL WORK GROUP
FOR INDIGENOUS AFFAIRS**
Classensgade 11 E, DK 2100 - Copenhagen, Denmark
Tel: (45) 35 27 05 00 - Fax: (45) 35 27 05 07
E-mail: iwgia@iwgia.org - Web: www.iwgia.org

This book is dedicated to all African indigenous peoples who have lost or continue losing their ancestral lands

CONTENTS

Preface 10

Acknowledgements 15

List of Abbreviations..16

PART I
CONCEPTUALISING INDIGENOUS LAND RIGHTS
IN AN AFRICAN CONTEXT

I The Term "Indigenous"—An Evolving Concept.........................20
   The colonial meaning of the concept "indigenous" 21
   ILO Convention No. 107 23
   A modern understanding of the term "indigenous" 27

II Relevance and Applicability of the Concept "Indigenous"
    in an African Context 32
    Self-identification 34
    Non-dominant sector of society...39
    History of severe discrimination..43
    Land rights prior to colonization or to the occupation
    by other African groups 45
    Land-based culture 47
    Conclusion 47

III The Lands of Indigenous Peoples:
     Importance and Justification 51
     Land as the incarnation of culture.....................................51
     Right to lands and right to life 55
     Ancestral lands and indigenous languages........................60

IV Indigenous Peoples' Land Dispossession:
    Causes and Reactions...64

Main causes of land dispossession 64
African indigenous peoples' reactions to land dispossession 75

PART II
THE JUDICIARY AND INDIGENOUS
PEOPLES' LAND RIGHTS 85

V Indigenous Peoples' Land Claims in Kenya 86
    The Maasai and their land case 86
    The Ogiek and their land cases 91
    The Endorois and their land case 100
    Legal and policy landscape in Kenya relating to
    indigenous peoples' land rights 105
    Conclusion 120

VI Indigenous Peoples' Land Claims in Tanzania 123
    The Barabaig and their land cases 123
    The Maasai and their land cases 132
    Legal and policy landscape in Tanzania relating
    to indigenous peoples' land rights 138
    Conclusion 151

VII Indigenous Peoples' Land Claims in Southern Africa 153
    The Richtersveld community in South Africa
    and their land claim 153
    The San of Botswana and the Central Kalahari
    Game Reserve case 163
    Conclusion 173

PART III
INDIGENOUS PEOPLES' LAND RIGHTS IN
AN INTERNATIONAL AND AFRICAN PERSPECTIVE

VIII Characteristics and Foundation of
Indigenous Peoples' Land Rights 174
    Characteristics of indigenous land rights 175
    The foundation of indigenous land rights 184
    African jurisprudence 191

IX Constitutional Recognition and States' Practice Regarding
   Indigenous Peoples' Rights..196
      North America 196
      Latin America 204
      The Pacific and Asia...207
      Western Europe 212
      Constitutional provisions regarding indigenous
      peoples in Africa..214
      Conclusion 226

X Main U.N. Instruments and Mechanisms Relevant
   for Indigenous Land Rights 228
      The United Nations Declaration on the Rights
      of Indigenous Peoples 229
      Other U.N. declarations, conferences and summits 232
      U.N. mechanisms targeting indigenous peoples................234
      U.N. Human Rights Treaties...237
      ILO Convention No. 169 and indigenous
      peoples' land rights..251

XI Other Relevant Global and Regional Instruments 257
      The Convention on Biological Diversity.............................257
      The UNESCO Conventions 259
      The Geneva Conventions and other international
      humanitarian and criminal laws..262
      African legal instruments and institutions.........................266
      Multilateral Development Banks...272
      Major donor agencies targeting indigenous peoples.........278

XII General Conclusions and Recommendations..........................282
      Observations and recommendations 285

Bibliography...292

Useful Web sites..312

Index of Cited Court Cases and International Jurisprudence.........316

Appendices
1. African Commission on Human and Peoples' Rights:
   Advisory Opinion on the United Nations Declaration
   on the Rights of Indigenous Peoples..320
2. List of Treaties, Conventions, etc., adopted, signed
   and/or ratified by African countries...330

PREFACE

There are indigenous communities in Africa. These are communities whose ways of life were not taken into account by most post-colonial African policies, a historical injustice that has led to their particular severe marginalization, including dispossession of ancestral lands and inaccessibility to several rights and freedoms enjoyed by the rest of their fellow citizens. Within this human rights-related meaning of the concept "indigenous", understandably not all Africans can be considered as being indigenous. Communities such as the San of Southern Africa,[1] the hunter gatherers of African tropical forests and the pastoralists of arid lands in several parts of Africa call not for special rights but for redress of historical injustices and enjoyment of all rights on the same footing as the rest of their countrymen and -women.

In 2003, the African Commission on Human and Peoples' Rights (ACHPR) adopted a first ever Report on Indigenous Populations/Communities in Africa. This report highlights, among other things, the cultural uniqueness of African indigenous peoples and the historical injustices they have suffered, before making major recommendations to various stakeholders, including African States and Governments. By adopting this report, the African Commission has domesticated the issue of indigenous peoples' rights, and they can therefore no longer be labeled as western-oriented or copied human rights claims.

A main conclusion of the ACHPR report is that the protection of the rights to land and natural resources is fundamental for the survival of indigenous communities in Africa. Lands are, *all over the world*, central to indigenous peoples' demands because, more than constituting a mere source of income, ancestral territories are the basis for their livelihood, way of life, culture and existence as communities. Africa is no exception to this paradigm; on the contrary, ancestral lands remain for many African communities, and particularly those who self identify as indigenous peoples, sacred and embedded with spiritual or cultural values that cannot otherwise be protected and preserved.

---

1   San were formerly called Bushmen—and in Botswana, Basarwa—but these terms are considered by many as derogatory and have been replaced by the term San. San is a generic term and the distinct linguistic groups among the San designate themselves by their own name, as for instance, Khwe, Nharo, ‡Khomani, etc.

But the issue of indigenous rights to land and to the natural resources pertaining to their land has always been a complex and sensitive issue and indigenous peoples everywhere have for centuries experienced dispossession, forced removals and discrimination. This has also been the case in Africa, starting during colonial times where many indigenous peoples lost their land to European settlers and continuing up to this day, where they see their traditional lands increasingly being threatened, encroached on or expropriated for the benefit of conservation interests, agro-industries, commercial plantations, mineral exploitations, and other economic activities.

Indigenous peoples have not let this happen without reacting in some way or another. In some cases, as this book will show, they have even gone to court and filed their cases against the powerful, whether colonial authorities, governments or corporate companies.

And how has the judiciary dealt with this human rights thematic in Africa? As this book will show, defending the land rights of indigenous peoples in court has been a legal battle uphill with few successes since, even when the court has ruled in their favour, their rights have not always been restored. Why? What went wrong? What could have been done otherwise? What lessons can be learned from the land-related court cases indigenous peoples have filed in Africa? What issues should judges, lawyers and concerned peoples consider in order to better defend the land rights of indigenous peoples in African courts? These are some of the key questions that need to be put and which this book aims at answering.

In other words, the purpose of this book is to look at the issue of land and land rights in the context of Central, Eastern and Southern Africa. A special focus of the book is to analyse some of the land cases filed by indigenous peoples in order to draw some lessons learned and recommendations that may benefit indigenous peoples and their organizations in the future, but also help those who want to support their cause. In this regard, the book also intends to consider existing international legal frameworks relevant to the rights of indigenous peoples over their lands in order to see how African indigenous peoples can make better use of international law and existing jurisprudence to defend or protect their rights in courts.

This book stems from more than fifteen years of observations, research, analysis and interaction with indigenous communities in Africa. As a lawyer by training with a doctorate in international human rights law and a focus on indigenous peoples' rights, the author has also made an extensive reading of legal and non legal literature on the rights of minorities in general and of those of indigenous peoples in particular; he has carried out numerous interviews, visited indigenous communities, and participated in several regional/international meetings on indigenous peoples' issue. Two indigenous NGOs, the Ogiek Welfare Council (OWC) and the Community Research and Development Services (CORDS), based in Kenya and Tanzania, respectively, have contributed to the data collection.

The choice of law cases from Kenya, Tanzania, South Africa and Botswana as illustrations is justified by the fact that these countries have for long been at the forefront of the conflict between indigenous communities' claims to their ancestral lands and the demand for land created by the countries' free-market oriented economies coupled with emerging strong conservation interests. Furthermore, these four countries host indigenous communities that not only identify themselves as culturally dependent on their lands but have to a larger extent than in any other African countries chosen the judiciary as one of their main means of action to protect their ancestral lands.

This book does not aim at presenting a detailed account of the various human rights violations indigenous peoples suffer in Africa, a subject to which many publications have contributed and continue to contribute largely. It also does not present a complete list of land-related law cases filed by or involving African indigenous peoples.

Throughout, this book refers to one or a few indigenous peoples per country or per region as examples. Since the purpose of this book is not to present an overall picture of the peoples who in Africa identify themselves as indigenous peoples nor what human rights violations they face, the examples should not be understood as exclusive of non-cited peoples or communities who identify themselves as indigenous in the same country or region, or are recognized as such by the *Report of the African Commission's Working Group of Experts on Indigenous Populations/Communities*. Similarly, this book contains very little, if anything at all, on West and North Africa, a limitation due to the writer's lack of reliable information from these regions.

The book comprises three parts. Part I (chapters I to IV) is an introduction to the concept "indigenous", how it has evolved over the years and why it is relevant for Africa. Special focus is given to the issue of land—its importance for the well-being and survival of indigenous peoples; the process of land dispossession experienced by indigenous peoples and its multiple causes; and the reactions and strategies indigenous peoples have used to defend their land rights.

Part II (chapters V to VII) gives an illustrative presentation of the standard of protection of indigenous peoples' land rights in African courts and how it has evolved over the years. The few court cases from Kenya and Tanzania presented in this book reveal that, despite very early attempts in the 1900s by indigenous Maasai from Kenya to use courts as mechanisms of protection of their ancestral lands, judges every time failed the communities and ruled in favour of the settlers. In 1912, the East African Court of Appeal sheltered behind the theory of "act of State" to declare itself incompetent in dealing with the claims made by the Maasai that an eviction from their ancestral lands was illegal. Against all expectations, Kenyan and Tanzanian post-colonial judges continued on the same path, upholding almost every time the supremacy of written laws over customary tenures and on occasions making rather illogical rulings. In 1984, and after conclud-

ing that a defendant occupied unlawfully a disputed land, a Tanzanian High
Court found refuge behind the small number of the indigenous plaintiffs to argue
that restitution to a Barabaig indigenous community of land unlawfully lost was
no longer possible given that only a few individuals had appeared in court. More
recently (2000), a Kenyan High Court relied on an assumption that the Ogiek indigenous peoples had lost their ancestral way of life and therefore could no longer claim to have a culture that would not be able to survive outside their directly
traditional lands. Any excuse appears to be used by judges and governments to
avoid challenging government policies and redressing the historical injustices
suffered by indigenous peoples. Many cases are dismissed on various technicalities that judges always tend to find.

However, a trend of hope for a better judicial protection of indigenous peoples' right to land in Africa can be seen in two recent cases from Southern Africa.
In 2003, there was a first ever recognition of the concept of "aboriginal title" in
Africa when the Constitutional Court of South Africa ruled that the Richtersveld
community's customary land rights were not extinguished following the invasion of their lands by colonial and current South African State. Furthermore, this
court upheld that indigenous peoples' right in their ancestral territories included
also rights over natural resources such as minerals. A similar ruling, but not with
the same strong language, was made in 2006 by Botswana's High Court following an eviction of the San from the Central Kalahari Game Reserve (CKGR).

Part III (chapters VIII to XI) describes some of the specific features of indigenous land rights and takes on the questions "Is it really true that indigenous
peoples' rights to land are not arguable in African courts?" and "How could they
be argued in court?" In order to argue for indigenous land rights in a court case,
lawyers, judges and even communities need to comprehend the complexity and
the particular features of these rights. This is the purpose of chapter VIII, which
looks, among other things, at the collective aspect of indigenous land rights, and
how indigenous peoples' land rights therefore differ from the ordinary, modern
individual right of land ownership. It then presents a range of potential arguments as well as material that could be used to defend indigenous peoples' rights
to lands. For instance: is the concept "aboriginal title" applicable in Africa to the
extent of being relevant and arguable in court? If so, what are the theories or
principles behind this concept and are these principles applicable to the continent or arguable in courts? Did colonization and later the creation of modern
African States extinguish all pre existing land rights of traditional communities?
Have all indigenous African communities abandoned the fight and accepted that
their pre-existing rights were extinguished following the creation of states?

The three following chapters examine the main legal instruments that can be
brought into use for the protection of indigenous peoples' land rights. Chapter IX
gives a survey of how indigenous peoples' land rights are being provided for by
national constitutions in various countries around the world and how the consti-

tutions in African countries deal with the same issue. Chapter X and chapter XI analyse the various international legal instruments and mechanisms that have been developed over recent years, including the newly adopted U.N. Declaration on the Rights of Indigenous Peoples, and demonstrates that international law remains by far the best instrument available for the protection of indigenous peoples' right to lands in Africa. Most African States have adopted the U.N. Declaration and have ratified treaties like the International Covenant on Civil and Political Rights (ICCPR) and the International Convention on the Elimination of All Forms of Racial Discrimination (ICERD). But also other global legal frameworks like ILO Convention No. 169, the Convention on Biological Diversity, some of the UNESCO Conventions, the humanitarian laws or laws of war as well as the policies of international financial institutions, such as the Operational Policy 4.10 (OP 4.10) of the World Bank, contain norms that can be used in court to advocate for indigenous peoples' rights to lands. The African States have furthermore all ratified the African Charter on Human and Peoples' Rights, whose increasing use by indigenous peoples could be seen as linked to the adoption of the *Report of the African Commission's Working Group of Experts on Indigenous Populations/Communities*. A number of land-related communications by indigenous peoples are currently under consideration by the African Commission.[2] Finally, there are also inter-states organizations and even bilateral development partners to Africa that have adopted pro-indigenous policies which could be used to argue for indigenous peoples' land rights in courts.

The book concludes in chapter XII by looking at some of the lessons, which can be drawn from the various case studies and which are relevant to indigenous peoples as well as to their lawyers. On this basis, a number of observations and recommendations are listed.

It is the hope of the author that this book can fulfill to some extent the challenging task of providing judges, lawyers, scholars, researchers, lecturers, human rights trainers and activists, community leaders and communities themselves, with a range of supporting legal and multidisciplinary arguments and justifications that can be put to use in the protection of indigenous peoples' right to land in Africa.

---

2   One such communication was made by the Endorois (Kenya) in 2003. In May 2009, the African Commission responded by adopting a decision that found the Kenyan government guilty of violating the rights of the Endorois community by evicting them from their lands to make way for a wildlife reserve. This decision, which has subsequently been approved by the African Union in January 2010, creates a major legal precedent by recognising, for the first time in Africa, indigenous peoples' rights over traditionally owned land and their right to development. See African Commission Communication 276/2003, *Centre for Minority Rights Development and Minority Rights Group International (on behalf of the Endorois Community) v. Kenya* at www.minorityrights.org/download.php?id=748

ACKNOWLEDGEMENTS

This book was made possible thanks to assistance from the International Work Group on Indigenous Affairs (IWGIA), to whom I express all my gratitude. I am also immensely grateful to several persons who commented on the whole or parts of this book, particularly Diana Vinding, Marianne Wiben Jensen, Korir Singoei, Professor Philip Ngessimo Mutaka and Judith Bueno de Mesquita.

The Ogiek Welfare Council (OWC, Kenya), through Joseph Towett, and the Community Research and Development Services (CORDS, Tanzania), via Elifuraha Laltaika, provided invaluable data for this publication. I thank them together with several indigenous and pro-indigenous organizations, which invited me to several meetings, trips, discussions, trainings, seminars and conferences that became valuable sources of materials for this book. I want each and every one of them to know that I cannot thank them enough for their contribution, support and attention.

I am equally grateful to my beloved wife Dafina, my daughter Atosha, my son Yene and all the members of my family, alive and at eternal rest. Their immeasurable love and encouragements together with that of several friends lightened my way towards the accomplishment of this challenge.

Dr. Albert Kwokwo Barume

LIST OF ABBREVIATIONS

ACHPR	African Commission on Human and Peoples' Rights
ACP	African, Caribbean and Pacific (countries)
ADB	Asian Development Bank
AfDB	African Development Bank
ANCSA	Alaska Native Claims Settlement Act
APRM	African Peer Review Mechanism
AU	African Union
B.C.	British Columbia (Canada)
BCLR	Butterworth's Constitutional Law Reports (South Africa)
BCTC	British Columbia Treaty Commission (Canada)
BEAC	British East African Company
BIA	Bureau of Indian Affairs (USA)
BP	Bank Procedures (World Bank)
BWHC	Botswana High Court
CA	Court of Appeal
CAIP	Commonwealth Association of Indigenous Peoples
CAPRi	Common Agricultural Policy Regionalized impact
CARICOM	Caribbean Community
CAURWA	Communauté Autochtone du Rwanda
CBD	Convention on Biological Diversity
CCT	Constitutional Court of South Africa
CEMIRIDE	Kenyan Centre for Minority Rights and Development
CERD	U.N. Committee on the Elimination of Racial Discrimination
CESCR	U.N. Committee on Social, Economic, and Cultural Rights
CHRLD	Commonwealth Human Rights Law Digest
CHOGM	Commonwealth Heads of Government Meeting
CISA	Indian Council of South America
CKGR	Central Kalahari Game Reserve (Botswana)
COMIFAC	Commission des Forêts en Afrique Centrale
COP	Conference of Parties (CBD)
COPORWA	Communauté des Potiers du Rwanda (Rwanda's Potter Community)
CORDS	Community Research and Development Services (Tanzania)
CPR	Common property resources

CPSU	Commonwealth Policy Studies Unit
CV	Civil [case] (Tanzania)
DANIDA	Danish International Development Agency
DFID	(British) Department for International Development
DWNP	Department of Wildlife and National Parks (Botswana)
E.A.C.A	East African Court of Appeal
E.A.L.R.	East African Law Register
E.C.	European Commission
ECOSOC	U.N. Economic and Social Council
ECOWAS	Economic Community of West African States
EIDHR	European Initiative for Democracy and Human Rights
EU	European Union
FAO	U.N. Food and Agriculture Organization
FFP	Forest Peoples Programme (UK based NGO)
FIMI/IIWF	Foro Internacional de Mujeres Indígenas/ International Indigenous Women's Forum
FPIC	Free, prior and informed consent
GDP	Gross Domestic Product
GEF	Global Environment Facility
GIAHS	Globally Important Agricultural Heritage Systems
GPS	Global Positioning System
GTZ	Deutsche Gesellschaft für Technische Zusammenarbeit (German Agency for Technical Cooperation)
HC	High Court
HRC	U.N. Human Rights Committee
HWC	Human-wildlife conflict
IACHR/CIDH	Inter-American Commission on Human Rights/ Comisión Interamericana de Derechos Humanos
IASG	Inter-Agency Support Group (U.N.)
IBEAC	Imperial British East Africa Company
ICC	Indian Claims Commission (USA)
ICC	Indigenous cultural communities (Philippines)
ICCPR	International Covenant on Civil and Political Rights
ICERD	International Convention on the Elimination of All Forms of Racial Discrimination
ICESCR	International Covenant on Economic, Social and Cultural Rights
I.C.J.	International Court of Justice
ICSID	International Centre for Settlement of Investment Disputes
ICTR	International Criminal Tribunal for Rwanda
ICTY	International Criminal Tribunal for the Former Yugoslavia

IDA	International Development Association (World Bank)
IDB	Inter-American Development Bank
IFAD	The International Fund for Agricultural Development
IFC	International Finance Corporation
IHL	International Humanitarian Law
IIFB	International Indigenous Forum on Biodiversity
IIWF/FIMI	International Indigenous Women's Forum / Foro Internacional de Mujeres Indígenas
ILO	International Labour Organisation
IMF	International Monetary Fund
IPA	Indigenous Protected Area
IPACC	Indigenous Peoples of Africa Coordinating Committee
IPP	Indigenous Peoples Plan (World Bank)
IPRA	Indigenous Peoples' Rights Act (Philippines)
IWGIA	International Work Group for Indigenous Affairs (International NGO based in Denmark)
KADU	Kenya African Democratic Union
KANU	Kenyan African National Union
LCC	Land Claims Court (South Africa)
MDB	Multilateral Development Bank
MDGs	Millennium Development Goals
MGR	Mkomazi Game Reserve (Tanzania)
MIGA	Multilateral Investment Guarantee Agency
MPIDO	Mainyoito Pastoralist Integrated Development Organisation (Kenya)
NAFCO	National Agricultural and Food Corporation (Tanzania)
NAGPRA	Native American Graves Protection and Repatriation Act (USA)
NATO	North Atlantic Treaty Organisation
NBSAP	National Biodiversity Strategy and Action Plan
NCA	Ngorongoro Conservation Area (Tanzania)
NCAA	Ngorongoro Conservation Area Authority
NCHR	National Commission on Human Rights (Philippines)
NCIP	National Commission on Indigenous Peoples (Philippines)
NCSSD	National Conservation Strategy for Sustainable Development (Tanzania)
NEPAD	New Partnership for Africa's Development
NGO	Non Governmental Organisation
NZLR	New Zealand Law Reports
OAS/OEA	Organisation of American States / Organización de los Estados Americanos
OAU	Organisation of African Unity

OD	Operational Directive (World Bank)
ODA	Overseas development assistance
OEA/OAS	Organización de los Estados Americanos/ Organisation of American States
OP	Operational Policy (World Bank)
PAWM	Planning and Assessment for Wildlife Management
PC	Private Council (UK)
PRSP	Poverty Reduction Strategy Paper
SADC	Southern Africa Development Community
SCA	Supreme Court of Appeal (South Africa)
S.C.R.	Supreme Court of Canada
SCZ	Supreme Court of Zimbabwe
TANAPA	Tanzanian National Park Authority
TCWP	Tanzania-Canada Wheat Programme
TNRF	Tanzania Natural Resources Forum
Tshs	Tanzanian Shillings
U.N.	United Nations
UNCCD	U.N. Convention to Combat Desertification
UNCESCR	U.N. Committee on Social, Economic and Cultural Rights
UNDP	United Nations Development Programme
UNESCO	United Nations Educational, Scientific and Cultural Organization
UNHCHR	United Nations High Commission on Human Rights
UNICEF	United Nations' Children Fund
UNPFII	U.N. Permanent Forum on Indigenous Issues
UNPO	Unrepresented Nations' and Peoples' Organization
UNWGIP	U.N. Working Group on Indigenous Populations
USAID	United States Agency for International Development
VGDA	Village Grazingland Development Area (Tanzania)
VGDC	Village Grazingland Development Committee (Tanzania)
VLA	Village Land Act (Tanzania)
WB	World Bank
WD	Wildlife Division (Tanzania)
WGIP	U.N. Working Group on Indigenous Populations
WHO	World Health Organisation
WIMSA	Working Group of Indigenous Minorities in Southern Africa
WMA	Wildlife Management Area (Botswana)
WRM	World Rainforest Movement

PART I   CONCEPTUALISING INDIGENOUS LAND RIGHTS IN AN AFRICAN CONTEXT

CHAPTER I
THE TERM "INDIGENOUS" – AN EVOLVING CONCEPT

This chapter constitutes an indispensable starting point for anyone interested in the rights of indigenous peoples in Africa, a continent where the term "indigenous" is often misunderstood for various reasons, including an opinion that most Africans are indigenous to the African continent.

Etymologically, the term "indigenous" derives from the Latin word *"indigena"* made up of two words, namely *indi*, meaning "within" and *gen* or *genere* meaning "root".[3] In other words, the term "indigenous" refers to "born in", "something that comes from the country in which it is found", "native of", or "aborigine", in contrast to "foreign" or "brought in".

To reach its current understanding in international law, the meaning of the term "indigenous" seems to have evolved through several distinct phases. The first meaning of the concept, referred to hereafter as "the colonial meaning", can be considered as an alteration of the term's etymological understanding for colonial purposes. The second meaning of the term "indigenous" can be seen as having emerged in the aftermath of the creation of the United Nations and the decolonization process, and was confirmed by the adoption of ILO (International Labour Organization) Convention No. 107. Finally, it

---

3   Charles Annandale, *Home Study Dictionary* (London: Peter Haddock Ltd., 1999), p. 374. See also *Collins School Dictionary* (UK: HarperCollins Publishers, 1993), p. 370, and Longman *Dictionary of Contemporary English*, 3rd ed. (Harlowe: Longman, 1995), p. 724.

seems that the current understanding of the term "indigenous" is the result of the process starting with the Martínez Cobo study launched in 1972[4] that lead up to the adoption of ILO Convention No. 169 in 1989, as well as of subsequent efforts to develop the concept by—among others—the U.N. Working Group on Indigenous Populations (WGIP, established in 1982), the World Bank[5] (OD 4.20 in 1991 and OP 4.10 in 2004) and the African Commission on Human and Peoples' Rights (2003).

The colonial meaning of the concept "indigenous"

During the colonial era, the term "indigenous" was applied to all peoples found in colonized territories, regardless of whether or not they had been born there or were newcomers. Terms like "natives", "aborigines", "populations found on these territories", were used interchangeably. It is also interesting to note that the Berlin Conference of 1885, too, failed to make a distinction between people found in the various colonized territories.[6]

The earliest work of the International Labour Organization (ILO) similarly reveals that the colonial meaning of the term "indigenous" was slightly different from its etymological understanding. ILO was created along with the League of Nations in 1919 by the Peace Conference that followed World War I. On the basis of the understanding that achieving peace and security depended upon good standards of protection afforded to the social and economic needs of people, the League of Nations was meant to focus on peace and security, whilst the ILO addressed social and economic issues.[7] ILO's Constitution stated:

> Universal and lasting peace can be established only if it is based upon social justice ... and privation to large numbers of people [can] produce unrest so great that the peace and harmony of the world are imperiled ...[8]

---

4 The Martínez Cobo study was completed and adopted in 1986/7. Available online from the Web site of UNPFII: http://www.un.org/esa/socdev/unpfii

5 In 1982, the World Bank developed a policy statement on "Tribal People in Bank-Financed Projects". The World Bank has subsequently, in 1991, issued Operational Directive (OD) 4.20 on "Indigenous Peoples", which was replaced, in 2004, by Operational Policy (OP) 4.10. Available from the Bank's Web site: http://www.worldbank.org

6 General Act of the Conference of Berlin, February 26, 1885. Article 6 of the chapter on Freedom of Trade in the Basin of the Congo as well as several other dispositions contained in the Act refer to the populations found on the concerned territories by the colonial powers as "native" populations or tribes.

7 Clive Archer, *International Organizations* (London: George Allen and Unwin, 1983), pp. 3 and 11-18.

8 Preamble of the ILO Constitution. Available from http://www.ilo.org/ilolex/english/constq.htm

The issue of "indigenous" was one of the first to be dealt with by the ILO,[9] although it was not until 1936 that it adopted Convention No. 50 on the Recruitment of Indigenous Workers,[10] its first native-related instrument. By "indigenous", this convention meant as stated in Article 2(b): "workers belonging to or assimilated to the indigenous populations of the dependent territories of Members of the Organization and workers belonging to or assimilated to the dependent indigenous populations of the home territories of Members of the Organization."[11] This Convention and its *travaux préparatoires*[12] seemed to give a double meaning to the term "indigenous". On the one hand, in an understanding closer to the etymology of the term, ILO Convention No. 50 meant by "indigenous", those peoples who were natives, "born in non-independent territories", or, in other words, *"indigenous by origin"*. Delegates and government representatives mandated to draft this Convention thus made it clear that the convention was "dealing with the subject of native labour", and that if ratified, it would apply in particular to the African colonies, but also to other colonized territories. British delegates to these drafting sessions also said that ILO Convention No. 50 was expected to deal with populations of all the territories under its Colonial and Dominions Offices, such as Swaziland.[13]

On the other hand, ILO Convention No. 50 was also meant to apply to "workers ... assimilated to the dependent indigenous populations of the home territories of Members of the Organization",[14] even though such people considered as *"indigenous by assimilation"* might have come from somewhere else, as migrants or non-white settlers. In South Africa, for example, native or indigenous workers included: "(a) those who were engaged on the farms owned by Europeans; (b) the detribalized industrial workers in the towns; and (c) those who came out from the native reserves in the British Protectorates, Portuguese East Africa, Southern Rhodesia and Nyasaland".[15] With such an understanding, many Indi-

---

9   In 1921, the ILO conducted a study on indigenous workers and, in 1926, it established the Committee of Experts on Indigenous Workers.

10 ILO Convention No. 50 Concerning the Regulation of Certain Special Systems of Recruiting Workers—also called C50 Recruiting of Indigenous Workers Convention. For full text, see http://www.ilo.org/ilolex/english/convdisp1.htm

11 Convention No. 50 was drafted by the Committee of Experts on Indigenous Workers set up by the International Labour Conference, the governing body of the ILO, during its 31st session in 1926. The Committee was given the mandate of framing standards of protection of this specific category of workers. ILO Convention No. 50 appears to be the first indigenous-related text drafted by the Committee set up 10 years earlier. See International Labour Organization, *International Labour Conventions and Recommendations 1919-1951*, vol. I. (Geneva: International Labour Office, 1996), p. 277.

12 *Travaux préparatoires* (French for "preparatory works") are the official record of a negotiation.

13 International Labour Conference, "Proposed International Labour Obligations in respect of Non-self Governing Territories". Report IV(1), 29th session (Montreal, 1946), p. 11.

14 Ibid.

15 International Labour Conference, "Records and Proceedings", 19th Session (Geneva: International Labour Office, 1935), p. 414. The statement referred to was made by Mr. Bellinger, a Workers' adviser of the British Empire.

ans as well as many other Asian people were considered as assimilated to "indigenous workers". Colonized populations were indeed called indigenous not because they were natives of a land on which they were born but because they were under foreign domination.[16] Thus, the etymological meaning appeared to be broadened to include all non-westerners.

Having taken into account most of the suggested amendments, ILO Convention No. 50 was widely ratified by most big colonial powers.[17] Its understanding of the term "indigenous" prevailed up to the late 1950s,[18] when ILO Convention No. 107 was adopted with a new meaning for the term "indigenous".

ILO Convention No. 107

Towards the end of World War II, a change emerged in the attitude of colonial powers towards colonized populations because the latter contributed, among other things, to the war efforts but also because several colonial powers could no longer economically and militarily sustain the same presence overseas as before the War. This is the context in which ILO Recommendation No. 70 on Social Policy in Dependent Territories that enjoined its members to "promote the well-being and development of the peoples of dependent territories", was adopted in 1944.[19] Together with ILO Convention No. 82 concerning Social Policy in Non-Metropolitan Territories (1947),[20] these two documents could be regarded as having paved the way for further instruments concerning the well-being of populations in dependent ter-

---

16   Andrew Gray, "The Indigenous Movement in Asia", in *Indigenous Peoples in Asia*, edited by R.H. Barnes, A. Fray, and B. Kingsbury (Ann Arbor: Association for Asian Studies Inc., 1995), p. 37.

17   International Labour Conference, "Information and Reports on the Application of Conventions and Recommendations", Report III(I), 39th session (Geneva: International Labour Office, 1956a), p. 247: the United Kingdom ratified ILO Convention No. 50 on 22 May 1939 with reserve that it was not applicable to Aden, Bermuda, Cyprus, Falkland Island, Gibraltar, Malta, St. Helena and Zanzibar. Japan's ratification occurred on 8 September 1938 and it was said to be applicable to all the Pacific Islands that Japan had under its power from the League of the Nations' mandate. New Zealand's ratification occurred on 8 July 1947 and Belgium's on 26 July 1948.

18   The exact wording and meaning of the term "indigenous" were later referred to in ILO Convention No. 64 of 1939 on "regulation of written contracts of employment...", ILO Convention No. 65 on "penal sanctions for breaches of contracts of employment...", and ILO Convention No. 104 of 1955 abolishing the penal sanctions for breach of contract of employment. See http://www.ilo.org/ilolex/

19   ILO Recommendation No. 70 in its opening statements remarks that "the economic advancement and social progress of the peoples of dependent territories have become increasingly a matter of close and urgent concern to the States responsible for their administration". See in International Labour Organization, *International Labour Conventions and Recommendations 1919-1951*, vol. II. (Geneva: International Labour Office, 1996), p. 402. Article 1 of the recommendation stated that "...all policies designed to apply to dependent territories shall be primarily directed to the well-being and development of the peoples of such territories and to the promotion of the desire on their part for social progress".

20   For text of ILO Convention No. 82 (and others), see ILOLEX Web site at http://www.ilo.org/ilolex/

ritories. The United Nations Charter had also just been adopted (1945), stating, among others, "the principle of equal rights and self-determination of peoples".[21]

It was in such an environment that Resolution 275(III) by the U.N. General Assembly requesting the Economic and Social Council (ECOSOC) to carry out a "Study of the social problems of the aboriginal populations and other under-developed social groups of the American continent"[22] was passed in 1949.

None of the above mentioned documents contained anything on the meaning of the term "indigenous". The drafters of ILO Convention 107, however, could not avoid having to deal with the definition problem, since it built on previous work done by the Committee of Experts on Indigenous Labour and its report on the "living and working conditions of indigenous populations in independent territories".[23] At its session of June 1956, the International Labour Conference set up a Committee on Indigenous Populations,[24] with a mandate to analyse this report and to recommend a draft text on indigenous populations' rights. At the following session of the International Labour Conference, the Committee presented a draft text bearing the title: "Convention concerning the protection and integration of indigenous and other tribal and semi-tribal populations".[25] This Draft defined the term "indigenous" as:

[P]eoples who are indigenous because of some historical event such as conquest or colonization and who are still living in the tribal or semi-tribal form; and [on the other hand] people … whose social and economic conditions are similar to those of the people defined under the previous subsection.[26]

---

21 Article 1 of the Charter of the United Nations (1945).
22 U.N. General Assembly Resolution 275(III) of May 11, 1949. Available online at http://www. un.org/documents/ga/res/3/ares3.htm. See Dusan J. Djonovich (ed.), *United Nations Resolutions*, Series I, (New York, N.Y.: Ocean Publications, 1974), p. 264. It is said that the Study was never carried out because in order to do so, a request from all affected States was required and such a request was never made. See also S. James Anaya, *Indigenous Peoples in International Law*, (New York, N.Y., and Oxford, UK: Oxford University Press, 1996), p. 44.
23 International Labour Conference, "Living and Working Conditions of Indigenous Populations in Independent Territories". Report VIII(1), 39th session (Geneva: International Labour Office, 1956b).
24 The Committee on Indigenous Populations was set up on 7 June 1956 by the International Labour Conference. It was composed of 45 members, amongst them 30 Government members, 5 Employers' members and 10 Workers' members. The Committee grounded its work on studies on the conditions of indigenous populations in independent territories undertaken by the Committee of Experts on Indigenous Labour during its sessions of March 1951 and May 1954. It also received a great deal of materials and needed information from the responses of Governments to the questionnaire proposed by the Committee of Experts. See also in International Labour Conference, "Living and Working Conditions" (1956b), p. 3.
25 International Labour Conference, "Living and Working Conditions", Report VIII (1), (1956b).
26 International Labour Conference, "Protection and Integration of Indigenous and Other Tribal and Semi-Tribal Populations in Independent Countries", Report VI (1), 40th session, (Geneva: International Labour Office, 1957a), p. 3.

Ecuador welcomed this definition of the term "indigenous",[27] but the draft text presented by the Committee was not so well received by other conference delegates.[28] In relation to the meaning and the scope of the term "indigenous", numerous delegates accused the Committee of having gone beyond its original mandate. Discontented delegates argued that the term "indigenous" should not include social groups other than those recognized as the first inhabitants of independent countries.[29]

Other delegates proposed additional elements to be included in the definition of the term "indigenous". The United Kingdom's delegate, for instance, whilst objecting to the insertion of "other tribal and semi-tribal populations" in the scope of the definition of the concept "indigenous", recommended that the term "indigenous", should also include former immigrants.[30] Several other delegations took the view that "indigenous people" should be understood as those who had been reduced to poverty and social marginalization as a result of injustice and exploitation.[31]

Finally, it was agreed that the Convention would apply to:

a. descendants of people who inhabited the country at the time of conquest or colonisation, who lead a tribal or semi-tribal existence more in confor-

---

27 International Labour Conference, "Living and Working Conditions", Report VIII (2), (1956b), p. 10. The Government of Ecuador considered that "clauses (a) and (b) satisfactorily convey the social implications of the expressions 'indigenous people …'".

28 International Labour Conference, "Protection and Integration", Report VI (1) (1957a), p. 3.

29 International Labour Conference, "Records of Proceedings", 40th session (Geneva: International Labour Office, 1957b), p. 36. An Employers' delegate from Australia, for example, criticized the Committee saying that "instead of dealing only with the living and working conditions of these people, the Committee has changed the title and more important … considered the protection and integration of indigenous and other tribal and semi-tribal populations regardless of whether they were indigenous or not …".

30 United Kingdom proposed that the term "indigenous" refer to people "who retain their separate identities either by virtue of customs or traditions or as a result of special laws and regulation and whose social, cultural and economic conditions are in consequence substantially behind those of the rest of the population … For the purpose of this Convention, the term 'indigenous people' includes immigrants whose social and economic conditions are comparable to those referred to above …". See in International Labour Conference, "Protection and Integration", Report VI (2) (1957a), p. 10.

31 This was the view of Mr. Sabrosso, a Workers' delegate from Peru, who suggested that "indigenous people" be understood as those who have been reduced to poverty and social marginalisation as a result of the injustice and exploitation they have suffered. The Government of Honduras took a similar view stating that it was not necessary to speak of "conditions … prior to conquest or colonization …", because the concept "indigenous" should simply mean people living under lower social, economic and cultural status. The Brazilian Government's delegation suggested that the words "descendants of people who inhabited the country at the time of …" be deleted from the definition of the term "indigenous" because the question of who lived where and when could be a difficult one in some parts of the world. For the Government of Ceylon, the scope of the term "indigenous" should be wide enough to include "people whose main tribal characteristics have disappeared …".

mity with the social, economic, and cultural institutions of the period before conquest or colonisation than with the institutions of the nation to which they belong; or who are governed by special legislation; and

b. people with a tribal or semi-tribal structure whose social and economic conditions are similar to those of the people defined under (a).[32]

It emerges from these provisions that, once again, two meanings were attached to the term "indigenous": paragraph (a) brought into the meaning of "indigenous" the idea of *"indigenous by antecedence"* or origin; and paragraph (b) included within the scope of the Convention, people who would qualify as indigenous *"by similarity"*, meaning people who were not indigenous by origin but whose conditions of life were similar. However, in both cases, for people to be considered indigenous under ILO Convention 107, they still needed to be maintaining their "tribal way of life".

A Government of New Zealand representative and rapporteur of the Committee tried unsuccessfully to rally States to the inclusive approach in the definition of the term "indigenous", saying that "any single definition of the word "indigenous" would not satisfy more than a handful of people".[33]

Indeed, ILO Convention No. 107 did not get much support from former big colonial powers, which voted against it,[34] and they could have blocked it, if it had not received backing from delegates mainly from newly decolonised territories.[35]

However, by the mid 1980s,[36] "the paternalist language of Convention No. 107 [and its approach were said to have become] … unacceptable".[37] Its provisions, such as those of Article 2 that states, *"Governments shall have the primary responsibility for developing co-ordinated and systematic action for the protection of the populations concerned and their progressive integration into the life of their respective countries"*, were severely criticized. Consequently, ILO Convention No. 107 was revised and with this revision came a new understanding of the term "indigenous".

---

32 International Labour Conference, "Living and Working Conditions", Report VIII (2), (1956b), p. 9.
33 Ibid., pp. 42-43.
34 The United States, the United Kingdom, and Australia, among others, did not vote for this Convention.
35 The proposed convention concerning the protection and integration of indigenous and other tribal and semi-tribal populations in independent countries was adopted during the 26th Congress of the 14th session of the International Labour Conference. As a whole, it was adopted by 165 votes to 14, with 22 abstentions. See in International Labour Conference, "Records of Proceedings", 41st session (Geneva: International Labour Office, 1958), p. 417.
36 In 1986, the Committee of Experts on the Revision of the Indigenous and Tribal Populations Convention 1957 (No. 107) had already issued a report underlining the need for a partial revision of the Convention. See in International Labour Conference, "Partial Revision of the Indigenous and Tribal Populations Convention, 1957 (No. 107)", Report VI (2), 75th session (Geneva: International Labour Office, 1988a), p. 1.
37 International Labour Conference, "Records of Proceedings", 75th session, (Geneva: International Labour Office, 1988b), p. 32/1.

A modern understanding of the term "indigenous"

The need for protection of indigenous cultures, traditions, lands, and right to self-identification, together with the necessity to put in place mechanisms that would let indigenous peoples be consulted on issues that are important to them, can be considered as the leitmotiv behind the main amendments to ILO Convention No. 107 by its successor, ILO Convention No. 169 Concerning Indigenous and Tribal Peoples in Independent Countries.

With regard to the meaning of the term "indigenous", the drafting Committee of the new Convention suggested the following changes to ILO Convention 107:[38] Paragraph 1(a) of Article 1 of ILO Convention No. 107 was to be kept unchanged, apart from inserting the term "cultural" between the words "social" and "economic".[39] In paragraph 2 to Article 1, the Committee proposed that the words "members of tribal or semi-tribal populations" be deleted and replaced by either "peoples" or "populations". Finally, the Committee recommended the deletion of the entire paragraph 2 of Article 1 and its replacement by a statement on the principle of "self-identification".

The formulation of Article 1 of the new Convention (ILO No. 169) went through without major amendments.[40] However, the use of the term "peoples" in the definition of those to whom the Convention was meant to apply raised a major controversy, which was resolved by the adoption of a third paragraph to Article 1, stating that:

> *The use of the term "peoples" … shall not be construed as having any implications as regards the rights which may attach to the term under international law.*[41]

ILO Convention No. 169 was thus adopted to apply to:

(a) *tribal peoples in independent countries whose social, cultural and economic conditions distinguish them from other sections of the national community, and whose status is regulated wholly or partially by their own customs or traditions or by special laws or regulations;*

---

38 International Labour Conference, "Partial Revision of the Indigenous and Tribal Populations Convention, 1957 (No. 107)". Report IV (1), 76th session (Geneva: International Labour Office, 1989), p. 6.

39 Article 1(1a) of ILO Convention No. 107 speaks about, "*members of tribal or semi-tribal populations in independent countries, whose social and economic conditions are at a less advanced stage than the stage reached by the other sections of the national community, and whose status is regulated wholly or partially by their own customs or traditions or by special laws or regulations …*"

40 Amendments proposed by various delegates were minor, like the proposition by Norway to insert the terms "establishment of present States boundaries" before the word "colonization" in paragraph 1(b) of Article 1. This amendment was not adopted.

41 Article 1(3) of ILO Convention No. 169.

(b) *peoples in independent countries who are regarded as indigenous on account of their descent from the populations which inhabited the country, or a geographical region to which the country belongs, at the time of conquest or colonization or the establishment of present state boundaries and who, irrespective of their legal status, retain some or all of their own social, economic, cultural, and political institutions.*

However, it was emphasized in paragraph 2 that:

Self-identification as indigenous or tribal shall be regarded as a fundamental criterion for determining the groups to which the provisions of this Convention apply.

As one can see, the above Article 1, on the one hand, lists factors that could be considered elements regarding the scope of the term "indigenous" and, on the other hand, it emphasizes the principle of self-identification. Is this a contradiction? The Japanese Government delegates to the drafting sessions of ILO Convention No. 169 considered that there was an apparent contradiction between the two first paragraphs of Article 1 and argued that "the scope of the Convention [was] being ambiguous with the introduction of the notion of self-identification as a fundamental criterion".[42]

One should not read a contradiction in the combination of self-identification and the list of indigenous peoples' characteristics. An adviser to the Danish Government and, at the time, Rapporteur of the Drafting Committee, gave a hint of what the rationale might be behind this article. He made it clear that the drafters addressed the issue of which individuals are "indigenous" with an inclusive and comprehensive understanding. More specifically, he said that the Convention was meant to be a "significant expression of … concern for peoples who … suffered discrimination, injustice, dispossession and shameful treatment".[43]

This means that, contrary to the opinion that "ILO Convention No. 169 [has] succeeded in delimiting [its] scope of application", in terms of the persons it applies to (ratione personae),[44] it can be argued that what the drafters had in mind whilst outlining the provisions of paragraphs (a) and (b) of Article 1 was not to make a strict definition of the term "indigenous", but to offer guidance, to facilitate a better understanding of communities which could identify themselves as indigenous.

Andrew Gray, a well-known anthropologist and for many years Director of the International Work Group for Indigenous Affairs (IWGIA), shares the view

---

42   See in International Labour Conference, "Partial Revision of the Indigenous and Tribal Populations Convention, 1957 (No. 107)". Report IV (2A), 76th session (Geneva: International Labour Office, 1989), p. 13.

43   International Labour Conference, "Records of Proceedings", 75th session (1988b), p. 31/1.

44   See Siegfried Wiessner, "Rights and Status of Indigenous Peoples: A Global Comparative and International Legal Analysis", 12 *Harvard Human Rights Journal* 57 (1999), p. 112.

that the drafting Committee of ILO No. 169 did not define the term "indigenous". He makes indeed a useful distinction between "defining [indigenous] … and establishing procedures to exercise the right of self-determination". In other words, he does not understand the "guiding factors" as indirect definitions of indigenous, but as elements that help to comprehend which groups enjoy "the right of self-identification" protected by ILO Convention No. 169. Indeed, he argues that guiding factors must "be operational in order to serve international objectives and in particular to allow an understanding of the many different cultures; second, … [it must] be functional to allow participation of the indigenous peoples; third, … [it must] be flexible in order to be able to respond to new situations in the dynamic process of recognizing indigenous people's rights".[45]

Similarly, the opinion within the U.N. Working Group on Indigenous Populations is that a definition of the term "indigenous" would undermine the credibility of all the efforts made under the United Nations.[46] It is feared that "the diversity of the world's indigenous communities is such that no single definition is likely to capture the breadth of their experience and their existence, but may in fact exclude particular groups in its efforts to establish a defined category of indigenous peoples".[47] Indigenous communities themselves have also categorically rejected any attempt made by governments to define "indigenous peoples", stating that such matters "should be determined by the world's indigenous peoples themselves".[48]

This broad understanding of the term "indigenous", based upon guiding criteria combined with the principle of self-identification, is widely argued by numerous other international bodies. The World Bank, as discussed further in this book, underlines criteria such as attachment to ancestral territories or natural resources, being a culturally distinct community and the principle of self-identification.[49]

---

45 Andrew Gray, *Indigenous Rights and Development: Self-determination in an Amazonian Community* (Providence, R.I. and London: Berghahn Books, 1997), p. 15.

46 Erica-Irene A. Daes, "Standard-Setting Activities: Evolution of Standards Concerning the Rights of Indigenous People—Working Paper on the Concept 'Indigenous People'", U.N. Doc. E/CN.4/Sub.2/AC.4/1996/2, 10 June 1996, pp. 20-21 (1996a). Available online at http://www.unhchr.ch/Huridocda/Huridoca.nsf/(Symbol)/E.CN.4.Sub.2.AC.4.1996.2.En?Opendocument (1996a). See also David Weissbrodt, S. Garrigues and R. Kroke, "An Analysis of the Forty-Ninth Session of the United Nations Sub-Commission on Prevention of Discrimination and Protection of Minorities", 11 *Harvard Human Rights Journal*, 221 (1998), p. 243.

47 Tony Simpson, *Indigenous Heritage and Self-determination*, IWGIA Document No. 86 (Copenhagen: IWGIA, 1997), p. 22.

48 Statement by the Aboriginal and Torres Strait Islander Commission at the 14th Session of the U.N. WGIP re: A Definition of "Indigenous Peoples" - 28 June 1996. U.N. Doc. E/CN.4/Sub.2/1996/2/Add.1, paras. 153-154. Available online at http://cwis.org/fwdp/Oceania/96-13037.txt

49 World Bank, Operational Directive 4.20 on Indigenous Peoples, of September 17, 1991 refers to "indigenous" as including any group attached to ancestral territories or to the natural resources, self-identifying and identified by others as members of a distinct cultural group, etc. Accordingly,

In her Working Paper on the Concept "Indigenous People", Ms. Erica-Irene A. Daes, then Chairperson Rapporteur of the U.N. Working Group on Indigenous Populations, emphasizes the following guiding criteria: (a) priority in time, with respect to the occupation and use of a specific territory; (b) voluntary perpetuation of cultural distinctiveness, which may include the aspects of language, social organization, religion and spiritual values, modes of production, laws and institutions; (c) self-identification, as well as recognition by other groups, or by state authorities, as a distinct collectivity and; (d) an experience of subjugation, marginalization, dispossession, exclusion or discrimination, whether or not these conditions persist.[50] Ms. Daes insists particularly on factors such as "experience of subjugation, marginalization, dispossession, exclusion or discrimination … as essential if one is to comprehend the wide spectrum that the term indigenous could cover".[51]

The International Alliance of Indigenous and Tribal Peoples of the Tropical Forest insists upon another guiding element, namely the maintenance of practices and customs regulating the harmony between communities and the environment in which they live.[52]

The United Nations Declaration on the Rights of Indigenous Peoples does not define the term "indigenous" nor does it mention explicitly to whom it applies. This could be seen as one of its differences with previous instruments, including ILO Convention No. 169. Its Preamble does, however, state a number of main human rights violations that indigenous peoples tend to suffer from.

Concerned that indigenous peoples have suffered from historic injustices as a result of, inter alia, their colonization and dispossession of their lands, territories and resources, thus preventing them from exercising, in particular, their right to development in accordance with their own needs and interests.

One could consider these and similar provisions of the Declaration as guiding factors for identification of indigenous peoples.

The *Report of the African Commission's Working Group of Experts on Indigenous Populations/Communities* also enshrines the principle of self-identification and lists a number of characteristics. It states indeed that, "a strict definition of indigenous peoples is neither necessary nor desirable. It is much more relevant and constructive to try to outline the major characteristics, which can help us identify

---

this Operational Directive considers that "the terms 'indigenous peoples', 'indigenous ethnic minorities', 'tribal groups', and 'scheduled tribes', … are social groups with a social and cultural identity distinct from the dominant society that makes them vulnerable to being disadvantaged in the development process …".

50 Daes, "Working Paper on the Concept 'Indigenous People'", (1996a), para. 69. See also Erica-Irene A. Daes, "Paper presented at the Pacific workshop on the United Nations Draft Declaration on the Rights of Indigenous Peoples", Suva, Fiji, September 1996, p. 28 (1996b).

51 Daes, "Working Paper on the Concept of 'Indigenous People'"(1996a), p. 22.

52 International Alliance of Indigenous and Tribal Peoples of the Tropical Forests, *Indigenous Peoples, Forests and Biodiversity*, IWGIA Document No. 82 (London and Copenhagen: International Alliance and IWGIA, 1996), p. 100, but also pp. 76-7 and 80.

who indigenous peoples and communities in Africa are".[53] The Report also shows that the culture and ways of life of African indigenous peoples differ from those of dominant communities and that their survival depends strongly on access to ancestral lands.[54]

The Draft Declaration of the Organization of American States on the Rights of Indigenous Peoples can be regarded as also embracing this liberal understanding of the term "indigenous", since it only "defines the personal scope of the document, without, however, spelling out the meaning of the term 'indigenous peoples' itself".[55]

Several scholars have elaborated on this issue. James Anaya, for example, gives most emphasis to the issue of attachment to "ancestral lands in which [indigenous] live, or would like to live".[56] Patrick Thornberry speaks of an association with "a particular place, not an amorphous space".[57] In the same vein, Andrew Gray builds upon the fact that some continents can still experience "inter-groups domination", "relocations", "transmigration" and similar movements of peoples, to argue for a "pragmatic definition" that can be applied to all tribal, aboriginal and other groups, which consider their territorial base to be under external threat. He refers, for instance, to the case of more than three million non-native people relocated onto indigenous lands in West Papua by the Indonesian Government.[58]

Thus, despite the pressure for a formal definition by many Governments,[59] it remains almost unanimously accepted that self-identification should prevail on any other guiding factor.

But, how relevant and applicable are all these principles and norms of international law in Africa?

---

53 African Commission on Human and Peoples' Rights, *Report of the African Commission's Working Group of Experts on Indigenous Populations/Communities—submitted in accordance with the "Resolution on the Rights of Indigenous Populations/Communities in Africa" adopted by The African Commission on Human and Peoples' Rights at its 28th ordinary session*. (Banjul, The Gambia and Copenhagen: ACHPR and IWGIA, 2005), p. 87.

54 Ibid., p. 89.

55 Wiessner, "Rights and Status of Indigenous Peoples"(1999), p. 105.

56 Anaya, *Indigenous Peoples in International Law* (1996), p. 4.

57 Patrick Thornberry, *Indigenous Peoples and Human Rights* (Manchester: Manchester University Press, 2002), p. 37.

58 Gray, "The Indigenous Movement in Asia" (1995), p. 51.

59 Russell L. Barsh, "Indigenous Peoples and the U.N. Commission on Human Rights: A Case of the Immovable Object and the Irresistible Force", *Human Rights Quarterly*, 18, (1996), pp. 791-3 and 809.

CHAPTER II
RELEVANCE AND APPLICABILITY OF THE CONCEPT " INDIGENOUS" IN CENTRAL, EASTERN, AND SOUTHERN AFRICA

As already mentioned, the African continent has now domesticated the concept "indigenous peoples" with the adoption by the African Commission on Human and Peoples' Rights of the Report of its Working Group of Experts on indigenous populations/communities.

This chapter examines the applicability of the principle of "self-definition"[60] and other "guiding factors" regarding indigenous peoples in Africa, in general, and in some parts of the continent, in particular. It also touches upon the question of whether or not there should be a formal definition of the term "indigenous".[61] But it does not, unlike several other studies,[62] intend to come up with a working definition.

It is often asserted that "far too little is known of the indigenous groups in Africa"[63] or that "in Africa ... it is very difficult to come across communities which retain all their pristine tribal characters".[64] Others have even said that all Africans are indigenous to the continent. Overall opinions on indigenous peoples in Africa are diverse and on occasions contradictory, revealing that "Africa poses thorny problems of definition, because most Africans consider themselves to be indigenous peoples who have achieved decolonisation and self-determination".[65] The

---

60 Article 1.2 of ILO Convention No. 169 reads: *"Self-identification as indigenous or tribal shall be regarded as a fundamental criterion for determining the groups to which the provisions of this Convention apply"*.

61 For more on opinions on as to whether or not a definition of the terms indigenous is imperative, see Benedict Kingsbury, "Indigenous Peoples in International Law: A Constructivist Approach to the Asian Controversy", 92 *The American Journal International Law* (1998), p. 415ff.

62 Several studies, such as the Martínez Cobo Report, have their own working definition. See, e.g., the World Bank OP 4.20 (1991). See also Gray, "The Indigenous Movement in Asia" (1995), pp. 37-8.

63 Wiessner, "Rights and Status of Indigenous Peoples" (1999), p. 89.

64 Benedict Kingsbury, "Indigenous Peoples as an International Legal Concept", in *Indigenous Peoples in Asia*, edited by R. H Barnes, A. Fray and B. Kingsbury (Ann Arbor: Association for Asian Studies Inc., 1995), pp. 22-3.

65 Russell L. Barsh, "The World's Indigenous Peoples" (2000). Available at Calvert Investment Online at http://www.calvert.com/pdf/white_paper_barsh.pdf

South African judge Gildenhuys, in his ruling in the *Richtersveld* case, asked himself the question "whether the doctrine of indigenous title forms part of [South African] law" and answered that, to his "knowledge, [the notion of aboriginal title had] never been recognised in any reported court decision".[66]

The definition of the term indigenous by the Martínez Cobo Report to the U.N. Sub-Commission on the Prevention of Discrimination of Minorities (1986) has been criticised for, among other things, "potentially leaving out indigenous peoples in Africa, Asia, and other places that are oppressed by equally 'original' inhabitants of neighbouring lands that have now become the dominant groups of their society".[67]

Alfonso Martínez in his study on Treaties criticizes the Cobo Report for "tend[ing] to lump together situations that ... should be differentiated because of their intrinsic dissimilarities". According to him, "these dissimilarities hinge on a number of historical factors that call for a clear distinction to be made between the phenomenon of the territorial expansion by indigenous nations into adjacent areas and that of the organized colonization, by European powers, of peoples inhabiting, since time immemorial, territories on other continents". He goes on to say that "many representatives of what [is described] as state-oppressed groups/minorities/peoples in Africa and Asia have brought their case before the Working Group on Indigenous Populations for lack of other venues to submit their grievances" but in his view "post-colonial Africa and Asia autochthonous groups/minorities/ethnic groups/peoples ... cannot ... claim for themselves, unilaterally and exclusively, the 'indigenous' status in the United Nations context" but "should be analysed in other fora of the United Nations than those that are currently concerned with the problems of indigenous peoples, in particular in the Working Group on Minorities of the Sub-Commission on Prevention of Discrimination and Protection of Minorities." Martínez concludes that "the term 'indigenous'—exclusive by definition—is particularly inappropriate in the context of the Afro-Asian problématique and within the framework of United Nations activities in this field."[68]

As shown previously, ILO Convention No. 169, the U.N. Declaration and the Report of the African Commission on Human and Peoples' Rights provide for the principle of self-identification and a set of guiding factors for identification, which should be understood as elements to facilitate a better understanding of the situation of indigenous peoples. The most important are:

---

66 *Richtersveld and Others v. Alexkor Ltd. And Another*, 2001 (3) SA 1293 (LCC), p. 46.
67 Wiessner, "Rights and Status of Indigenous Peoples" (1999), p. 111.
68 Alfonso Martínez, "Study on Treaties, Agreements and Other Constructive Agreements between States and Indigenous Populations" (U.N. Doc/E/CN 4/Sub 2/1999/20, 22 June 1999), paras. 88, 90 and 91. Available at:
     http://www.unhchr.ch/Huridocda/Huridoca.nsf/(Symbol)/E.CN.4.SUB.2.RES.1999.22.En?Opendocument

- Self-identification
- Non-dominant status within a wider society;
- History of particular subjugation, marginalisation, dispossession, exclusion, or discrimination;
- Land rights prior to colonization or occupation by other African groups; and
- A land-based culture and willingness to preserve it.

Self-identification

The principle of "self-identification", as articulated in Article 1.2 of ILO Convention No. 169 and Article 3 of the U.N. Declaration on the Rights of Indigenous Peoples, recognizes to any community or peoples the freedom to define itself/themselves as "indigenous". In Central, Eastern and Southern Africa, numerous communities self-identify as indigenous peoples.[69] These include in Central Africa, the "Pygmies"[70] of the African tropical forests and the Mbororo. In Eastern Africa, there are the Hadzabe, Akie, Ogiek, Yaaku, Sengwer, Maasai, Samburu, Turkana, Barabaig, Pokot, Orma, Rendille, Karamajong, and numerous others. In Southern Africa there are the San, the Nama and the Himba. Representatives of these communities are active through various platforms such as the Indigenous Peoples of Africa Co-ordinating Committee (IPACC),[71] and at several regional/or international meetings on indigenous issues in Africa and world wide.[72] The following few illustrative examples show how these communities or peoples exercise this freedom.

The Central African indigenous hunter-gatherers, known generically as the "Pygmies" and estimated to be as many as 350,000, self-identify as indigenous peoples. In a letter addressed to the President of their country, the Batwa "Pygmies" of Rwanda not only state their aboriginal title over a number of forests, but also call upon their Government to address their claim to lands on the basis of ILO Convention No. 169 and other international instruments, which provide for

---

69 African Commission, *Report of the Working Group of Experts* (2005), pp. 15-19.
70 "Pygmy" is a generic term for a large number of indigenous groups living mostly in Central Africa. As some of these groups find the term derogatory and prefer to use their own names, it is now common to write "Pygmy" with inverted commas.
71 The IPACC was created in 1997 by a number of African indigenous peoples. This network of indigenous organizations includes among its members organizations representing the San of Southern Africa, the Batwa of Central Africa, the Maasai, the Barabaig and the Ogiek of Estern Africa, and the Tuareg and the Ogoni from West Africa. See Web site at http://www.ipacc.org.za/represent.html
72 In September 2001, for example, representatives from Maasai, Batwa, Ogiek, and several other communities that consider themselves indigenous took part in a conference on Indigenous and Protected Areas in Africa, held in Rwanda. Each one of these communities restated in its presentation its indigenousness as the basis for its land claims.

the rights of indigenous peoples.[73] Because of claiming indigenous status, the Batwa of Rwanda have experienced difficulties in their relationship with the Government, which considers the concept "indigenous" as a threat to national unity.

Not only Batwa representatives from Rwanda and Burundi, but also Mbuti, Bagyeli, and Baka representatives from the Democratic Republic of Congo and Cameroon have been regular attendants at the sessions of the former U.N. Working Group on Indigenous Populations, the U.N. Permanent Forum on Indigenous Issues, and the African Commission on Human and Peoples' Rights as well as at several other international gatherings. At the 16th session (1998) of the U.N. Working Group on Indigenous Populations, for example, members of the Batwa community from Rwanda and the Democratic Republic of Congo together stated that their communities consider themselves as the first nations of their respective countries,[74] an assertion that is widely accepted.[75] The consistent work of these groups at the United Nations level has made it possible that, in one of the final reports of the fifty-seventh session of the U.N. Commission of Human Rights, it was recommended that:

> The Governments of Burundi, the Democratic Republic of the Congo, Rwanda, and Uganda should recognize the Batwa as indigenous peoples and demonstrate their commitment to respecting that people's rights by fulfilling the obligations they had entered into under the African Charter on Human and Peoples' Rights and the International Convention on the Elimination of All Forms of Racial Discrimination. They should also ratify and implement ILO Convention No. 169 concerning Indigenous and Tribal Peoples in Independent Countries and support the adoption of the Draft Declaration on the Rights of Indigenous Peoples.[76]

The Mbororo is another community that identifies itself as indigenous. They are predominantly pastoralists and live in several African countries, notably Cameroon, Nigeria, Chad, and the Central African Republic. In all these countries, they ground their indigenous status on a particular way of life (nomadic or semi nomadic pastoralism) threatened by other communities' dominant way of life.[77] In

---

73 The letter was written by a member of the Batwa community of Rwanda and head of a platform of Batwa. See Web site of Héritiers de la Justice at http://www.heritiers.org/caurwaletpresi.html

74 See Web site of Héritiers de la Justice: http://www.heritiers.org/kapupugeneva.html

75 Jerome Lewis, *The Batwa Pygmies of the Great Lakes Region* (London: Minority Rights Group International, 2000), p. 6.

76 U.N. Commission on Human Rights, Summary Report, 57th Session (2001), para. 30. U.N. Doc. E/CN.4/2001/SR.15, 2 April 2001. Available at http://www.unhchr.ch/huridocda/huridoca.nsf

77 Albert Kwoko Barume, "Etude sur le cadre légal pour la protection des peuples indigènes et tribaux au Cameroun" (Genève: Organisation internationale du travail, 2005a), p. 25. See also the African Commission's *Report of the Working Group of Experts* (2005).

numerous national, regional, and international fora, this community has claimed to suffer particular discriminations related to its wish to maintain its way of life.

In Eastern Africa, the Maasai (estimated to number up to 500,000) self identify themselves as indigenous peoples to lands stretching over Kenya and Tanzania.[78] They could be considered as amongst the most active Eastern African communities with regard to claiming indigenous status and all this involves, including rights over resources. As early as 1912, the Maasai of Kenya were already in court to proclaim and protect their indigenous lands against the colonial Government. Despite ruling against the Maasai plaintiffs, the court recognized that they were sovereign over their lands.[79]

The Maasai have also used regional and international stages to proclaim their indigenousness. At the 1999 "Conference on Indigenous Peoples from Eastern, Central, and Southern Africa", held in Arusha (Tanzania),[80] a representative of the "Maa Development Association"—a Kenyan Maasai development organisation—stated: "The Maasai comprise some of the indigenous peoples of East Africa".[81] On the same occasion, a representative of the Maasai community of the Kiteto District in the Arusha area of Tanzania declared: "We are the people of South Maasai Steppes, we live on semi-arid land. We value our livestock and natural vegetation with relative resources ... we struggle to protect our land, which is home to all the habitats we know in our ecosystem".[82] Similarly, at a conference held in Kigali/Rwanda on Indigenous Peoples in Conservation Areas, representatives of Maasai communities living in the Ngorongoro area of Tanzania showed how their communities considered themselves as indigenous to the Serengeti.[83] Maasai representatives have also been regular attendants of numerous relevant gatherings, including the annual sessions of the former United Na-

---

78 In Kenya, the Maasai live in the areas of Narok and Kajiado in the southern part and Nakuru and Laikipia in the central part of the country, whereas the Maasai of Tanzania are found in the areas of Ngorongoro, Simanjiro, Kiteto, and Oldoinyo le Engai. The Maasai communities in Kenya and Tanzania are estimated to have some 155,000 and 330,000 members, respectively. See Web site of Maasai-Infoline: http://maasai-infoline.org/TheMaasaipeople.html

79 *Ol le Njogo and 7 Others v. The Honorable Attorney General and 20 Others*, Civil Case No. 91 of 1912 Court of Appeal for Eastern Africa [1913], 5 E.A.L.R. 70. Text of judgment (May 1913) available online at
http://www.geocities.com/olmorijo/land_case.htm

80 This conference was organized by PINGOs Forum—a Tanzanian umbrella organization for pastoralists and hunter-gatherers—and IWGIA.

81 Mary Simat, "The Situation of the Maasai Women", *Indigenous Affairs* 2/1999, pp. 39-39. Copenhagen: IWGIA.

82 Statement by Saruni Ndelelya representing Kinnapa Development Programme, a local non-governmental organization operating in the Kiteto District of Arusha in Tanzania, at the Conference on Indigenous Peoples of Eastern, Central, and Southern Africa, Arusha/Tanzania, January 18-22, 1999 (unpublished).

83 M. Kaisoe, and W. Ole Seki, "The Conflict between Conventional Conservation Strategies and Indigenous Systems: The Case Study of Ngorongoro Conservation Area" in *Indigenous Peoples and Protected Areas*, edited by John Nelson and Lindsay Hossack (Moreton-in-Marsh, UK: Forest Peoples Programme, 2001), p. 141.

tions Working Group on Indigenous Populations, the U.N. Permanent Forum on Indigenous Issues, and the African Commission on Human and Peoples' Rights, as reported by several documents.[84]

The Ogiek of Kenya, who number around 20,000 people, self-identify as indigenous to the Mau Forests, which they consider as their motherland and which they have occupied and used since time immemorial.[85] As noted before, they have been in court against the Kenyan Government on a number of occasions, each time claiming to be indigenous to the Mau Forest. In a Memorandum to the Kenyan Parliament dated July 1996, the Ogiek claimed to have a "birth right ... [on their] ancestral land in the Mau Forest".[86] Similarly, in 2000, they made a submission to the Njonjo Land Commission, in which they stated "our history has shown that we are environmentally friendly. Our land tenure system is also environmentally friendly ..." Referring to the Memorandum, they further asked the members of Parliament to "help us live in our ancestral land and retain both our human and cultural identities as Kenyans of Ogiek origin".[87] Like many other groups, the Ogiek are regular attendants of almost all indigenous peoples-related meetings and gatherings, occasions that they also use to claim their indigenous status.

In Southern Africa, the indigenous hunter-gatherers, known generically as the San and whose number is estimated at around 107,000,[88] live scattered over several Southern African countries but are, nevertheless, seen as constituting one culturally homogeneous community that considers the savannahs and semi-arid areas of Southern Africa, including most of the Kalahari, as their ancestral land.

The San have been rather vocal about their indigenous status and filed several land claims. In a case presented before the South African Government on the basis of the Land Restitution Act, the ‡Khomani San stated that they were the original occupants of the Kalahari and declared that "the San would cease to exist as distinct peoples unless a means is found to reverse the process that had evicted them from their lands".[89] The San living in Botswana have also attempted to have their indigenous status recognized and consequent rights to lands set aside for

---

84   Maasai representatives, for example, attended the 13th, 17th, and 18th sessions of the U.N. Working Group on Indigenous Populations. See reports of the U.N. Working Group on Indigenous Populations on the Web site of the United Nations High Commission for Human Rights: http://www.unhchr.ch/huridocda/huridoca.nsf/FramePage/WGPopulations%20En?OpenDocument&Start=1&Count=15&Expand=3.

85   Ogiek Welfare Council, Memorandum submitted to all members of Parliament, July 1996, Nairobi Kenya.

86   Ibid.

87   The Ogiek submission is available online at http://www.ogiek.org/report/ogiek-app1.htm. The Land Review Commission, known as the Njonjo Land Commission, was set up by the Kenyan Government in 2000 to assess, amongst other things, land claims by various communities. The Commission was named after its Chairperson, Charles Njonjo, member of the Kenyan Parliament.

88   African Commission, *Report of the Working Group of Experts* (2005), p. 16.

89   Roger Chennells, "The ‡Khomani San of South Africa", in *Indigenous Peoples and Protected Areas in Africa: From Principles to Practice*, edited by J. Nelson and L. Hossack (Moreton-in-Marsh, UK: Forest Peoples Programme, 2003), p. 276.

them.[90] San representatives have attended several sessions of the U.N. Working Group on Indigenous Populations and other relevant fora, on all occasions stating their indigenousness.[91] Since 1996, the San of Southern Africa have been represented by their own networking organisation, WIMSA (Working Group of Indigenous Minorities in Southern Africa), which coordinates the activities of elected San Councils in Botswana, Namibia and South Africa.

The Himba, a community that lives on lands stretching over northern Namibia, consider themselves as indigenous to these lands, which are affected by several development plans, including the building of a hydro-power dam.[92] Mr. Kapika, a local Himba leader speaking at a village meeting in 1995, stated, in relation to the Epupa Dam: "We do not want it. This is our land".[93] The following year, a group of members of this community addressed a letter to the Namibian Government re-stating their indigenous claim to the lands of the Epupa area: "The area which will be affected is the area where our households are, there are people living all over—it is impossible for us to give this land away! It is where the graves of our ancestors are—we cannot give this land away".[94]

The Himba have also claimed their status as indigenous at various regional and international gatherings. One of their representatives to a seminar on "Multiculturalism in Africa: Peaceful and Constructive Group Accommodation in Situations Involving Minorities and Indigenous Peoples" held in Arusha/Tanzania in May 2000, re-stated his community's indigenousness. Similar statements have also been made by Himba delegates at sessions of the United Nations Working Group on Indigenous Populations.[95]

The principle of self-identification is paramount for indigenous peoples and it appears to be upheld by States' practice in Africa. Indeed, as it will be shown later,

---

90 Robert K. Hitchcock, "Background Notes on the Central Kalahari Game Reserve and Ghanzi Land and Resources" (n.d.). See Web page of the Kalahari Peoples' Fund, http://www.kalaharipeoples.org/documents/ghanzi.htm

91 The San were represented, for example, at the 16th, 17th and 18th session of the U.N. Working Group on Indigenous Populations.

92 Andrew Corbett, "A Case Study on the Proposed Epupa Hydropower Dam", *Indigenous Affairs*, Dams, Indigenous Peoples and Ethnic Minorities, no. 3-4 (Copenhagen: IWGIA, 1999), p. 80. See also Web site of the International Rivers Network at http://www.irn.org/programs/epupa/articles.shtml

93 See Web site of the International Rivers Network: http://www.irn.org/pubs/wrr/9606/9606namibia.html

94 The full text of this statement by the Himba community to the Government of Namibia can be accessed on the Web site of the International Rivers Network, http://www.irn.org/programs/safrica/hear961031.html

95 Seminar on "Multiculturalism in Africa: Peaceful and Constructive Group Accommodation in Situations Involving Minorities and Indigenous Peoples" held in Arusha, United Republic of Tanzania on 13-15 May 2000. This seminar was co-organized by the U.N. Working Group on Indigenous Populations and the U.N. Working Group on Minorities and endorsed in resolution 1999/20 of the Sub-Commission on the Promotion and the Protection of Human Rights. U.N. Doc. E/CN.4/Sub.2/AC.5/2000/WP.3, 18 May 2000.

an increasing number of African countries tend not to require a formal definition as a precondition for addressing human rights violations facing such communities.

Non-dominant sector of society

One of the characteristics of indigenous peoples is that they belong to the non-dominant sector of society. There are a number of factors that may contribute to this situation, among others, their numerical inferiority, their ways of life and social organization, and their distinctive cultures. It should be noted, however, that indigenous peoples, as a matter of fact, sometimes constitute a majority but are nonetheless dominated by a minority group that controls the state apparatus and decides which rules and norms should apply in the country. This was, until recently, the case in Bolivia and still is the case in Guatemala.[96] Belonging to a non-dominant sector, therefore, also has to do with exclusion based on racial discrimination, cultural discrimination (customs, languages, religions, etc.) and the exercise of power (military, political, economic, etc.) by an economic and political elite, often the direct descendants of the colonizers.

Are all these factors relevant in the case of Africa?

Numerical non-dominance

The "non-dominant" guiding factor is often explained by the numerical inferiority of the indigenous peoples. With regard to Central, Eastern, and Southern Africa, this may have some bearing since most African indigenous peoples are numerically small in the countries in which they live, as illustrated by the following few examples.

In Central Africa, the "Pygmies" of the African tropical forests, which stretch over Cameroon, Central African Republic, Gabon, Equatorial Guinea, the Republic of Congo, the Democratic Republic of Congo, Rwanda, Burundi, and Uganda, are estimated to total 350,000,[97] whereas altogether these countries have a population exceeding 114.5 million people. In Rwanda, the Batwa make up about 0.4 per cent of the whole population, the two other ethnic groups (the Tutsi and the Hutu) making up the remainder of the national population estimated at approximately 7.3 millions.[98]

---

96 In December 2005, Evo Morales, who identifies himself as indigenous, became the president of Bolivia.

97 Virginia Luling and Justin Kenrick, "Forest Foragers of Tropical Africa. A Dossier on the Present Condition of the 'Pygmy' Peoples" (London: Survival International, 1998), p. 1.

98 See Web site of the Unrepresented Nations and Peoples Organization, UNPO: http://www.unpo.org/member/batwa/batwa.html

In Kenya, which has a population of over 29 million, the 2001 Population Reference Bureau's figures indicate that the Kikuyu make up 22 per cent of the population, the Luhya 14 per cent, the Luo 13 per cent, the Kalenjins 12 per cent, the Kisii 6 per cent, the Meru 6 per cent, "other Africans" 15 per cent, and the non-African (Asian Europeans and Arabs) 1 per cent.[99] As one can see, neither the Maasai (estimated to be 155,000) nor the Ogiek (estimated to be 20,000), are mentioned, possibly because of their significantly small numbers. Both the Maasai and the Ogiek are surely included in what the report calls "other Africans".

In Tanzania, with a population of over 36 millions, the Hadzabe are estimated to be not more than 1,500 people[100] and the Maasai some 330,000, whereas the Chagga ethnic group alone reaches the figure of about 1 million people.[101]

In Southern Africa, the San are estimated around 107,000 with approximately 50,000 San in Botswana, 40,000 in Namibia, 4,500 in South Africa, 1,300 in Zimbabwe, 9,700 in Angola and 1,600 in Zambia.[102] In all these countries, the San are numerically small communities. In the case of Namibia, for instance, they only represent 3 per cent of the national population, estimated at 1.7 million people.[103] The Himba of Namibia are believed to number some 15,000.

This numerical inferiority could explain why indigenous peoples are so often regarded as minorities,[104] a concept that has been much debated.[105]

---

99 See Web site of the Population Reference Bureau (PRB):
    http://www.prb.org/Articles/2008/kenya.aspx, (January 2008).
100 Andrew Madsen, *The Hadzabe of Tanzania: Land and Human Rights for a Hunter-Gatherer Community*. IWGIA Document No. 98 (Copenhagen: IWGIA, 2000), p. 14.
101 These Population Reference Bureau figures are from 2001. See on PRB Web site:
    http://www.prb.org/pdf/Tanzania_Eng.pdf
102 African Commission, *Report of the Working Group of Experts*, (2005), pp. 16-17.
103 CIA World Fact on Namibia. Available online at
    http://www.cia.gov/cia/publications/factbook/geos/wa.html
104 There exist several distinctions between indigenous and minorities. Indigenous communities are sometimes seen as a special category of minorities. See, for instance, Athanasia S. Akermark, *Justification of Minority Protection in International Law* (London: Kluwer, 1997), p. 20; and Will Kymlicka and Will Norman (eds.) in *Citizenship in Diverse Societies* (Oxford and New York: Oxford University Press, 2000). The latter two authors argue in their "Introduction" (pp. 18-24) that there are four types of minorities: firstly, "national minorities", which include stateless nations and indigenous peoples; secondly, "immigrant minorities", which include people with citizenship or rights to become citizens, people without rights to become citizens ("metics"), and refugees; thirdly, "religious groups", including "isolationist" and "non-isolationist" religious groups; and fourthly *sui generis* groups, which include "African Americans, Roma (gypsies), Russians in former Soviet states, etc." These various opinions, which consider indigenous peoples as a type of minorities, also reveal that the scope of the concept "minorities" has become so broad that it may no longer suit the special nature of indigenous peoples' claims and rights.
105 Several distinguished scholars have expanded on the issue of minority rights. See, for instance, Geoff Gilbert, "Minority Rights in Europe", *Netherlands Yearbook of International Law*, Vol. XXIII, 1992, pp. 69-74; Leslie Green, "Internal Minorities and their Rights", in *Group Rights*, edited by J.

However, it has also been argued that the term "minorities" cannot be regarded as being broad enough to provide protection for some groups that require particular attention, such as indigenous communities.[106]

Two factors could be considered as the main differences between "minorities" and "indigenous". First, minorities' rights are generally framed in individual terms,[107] whereas those of the indigenous are, or should be, worded in collective terms.[108] Minorities' rights are indeed individual rights that can be enjoyed or exercised as a group. Secondly, and perhaps more importantly, unlike minorities, the "indigenous" are characterised particularly by their strong cultural bond to their lands, without which they would not exist as a cultural entity and their lives would be in great danger. John Borrows calls this tie a "landed citizenship", which he defines as "loyalties, allegiance, and affection related to the land ... the water, wind, sun, and stars are part of this federation ... [Indigenous] teachings and stories form the constitution of this relationship, and direct and nourish the obligations this citizenship requires".[109]

Furthermore, minorities, either linguistic, ethnic or religious, are often identified with regard to a given state in which they are numerically small. Indigenous communities tend not to identify themselves with a given state but with a given and demarquable land within a state or region. Indigenous peoples claim their rights on the basis of social factors that existed long before the "state" as an institution. In other cases, indigenous peoples identify themselves with a whole region comprising different states. This is, for instance, the case of the "Pygmies" in Central Africa. In Eastern Africa, many Maasai continue to resist the Kenyan and Tanzanian Governments' efforts to try and integrate them, by holding two identity cards, because members of this community identify themselves more with their lands, which stretch over the two countries, than with the two states.

Baker (Toronto: University of Toronto Press, 1994), p. 105; Dave Ingram, *Group Rights* (Kansas: University Press of Kansas, 2000), p. 107. This last author distinguishes, for example, a gathering of individuals with "societal culture" from those without. With regard to the former, he refers to indigenous communities, whereas for groupings of individuals without a "societal culture" he refers to such groups as immigrants, refugees, guest workers, and former colonizers.

106 See, for instance, Henry J. Steiner and Philip Alston, *International Human Rights in Context* (New York: Oxford University Press, 1996), p. 1010.

107 Ibid., p. 80. Article 27 of the ICCPR is considered as protecting individual rights enjoyed as a member of a minority group. See also Peter Juviler, "Are Collective Rights Anti-human: Theories on Self-Determination and Practice in Soviet Successor States", *Netherlands Quarterly of Human Rights* 3/1993, p. 277: "The 1966 U.N. Covenants on Civil and Political Rights and on Economic, Social and Cultural Rights ascribe rights of self-determination to 'peoples' not to 'minorities'".

108 Article 14 of ILO Convention No. 169 on land rights speaks of "the rights of ownership and possession of the peoples concerned ..."

109 John Borrows, "Landed Citizenship: Narratives of Aboriginal Political Participation", in *Citizenship in Diverse Societies*, edited by W. Kymlicka and W. Norman (Oxford and New York: Oxford University Press, 2000), p. 326.

Non-dominant ways of life, societal model and other factors

In Africa, the non-dominant characteristic of indigenous peoples has also something to do with their ways of life as hunter-gatherers and pastoralists,[110] which
increasingly are threatened by the dominant way of life based on agriculture,
industrial farming and modern development. As Hugh Brody writes, "... then
came a revolution that transformed almost the entire surface of the earth: agriculture ... [so] any landscape that is not farmed is wild and therefore of little economic use".[111]

Agriculture is, however, not a mere act of tilling lands but also a way of life
that comes with numerous other social factors such as sedentary life style, accu-
mulation and storage of harvest, exclusive ownership and similar mechanisms.
This is what is happening in Central, Eastern and Southern Africa, where agriculture and large scale cattle farming, have become the dominant way of life and
threatens to extinguish all other ways of life including hunting, gathering and
nomadic pastoralism. Hunting and gathering as well as pastoralism are seen as
being detrimental to conservation efforts or as "backward" and uneconomical
ways of life that have no place in a "modern" world. As shown further on, apart
from a few countries like Ethiopia, the constitutions of most African States do not
protect land use and occupation by nomadic communities.

Governments and the international donor community give instead priority
treatments to agriculture and industrial farming, as well as to mining, the building of hydroelectric dams, the creation of national parks, and many other activities that are leading to the reduction of forests, bushes and grazing lands. Often,
this results in tensions, and sometimes even open conflicts, between sedentary
agriculturalists and nomadic communities.[112]

Pressure on grazing and forested lands also has to do with population growth
and land scarcity. An increase of agricultural production depends largely on both
the size of the cultivated land and the number of people working on it. As the
number of cultivators continues to grow, the problem of land shortage arises.
This often leads to a dispersal of community members in search of new areas
suitable for cultivation. Pastoralists and hunter-gatherers, on the other hand,
tend not to increase so rapidly in number. Pastoralists do not require much la-

---

110 It should be noted that indigenous peoples in many Latin American and Asian countries are of-
     ten small-scale agriculturalists and the characteristic of non dominance in these countries relates
     more to the discrimination and marginalization indigenous peoples are subjected to by main-
     stream society on account of their ethnic and cultural distinctiveness.

111 Hugh Brody, *The Other Side of Eden: Hunter-Gatherers, Farmers and the Shaping of the World* (Lon-
     don: Faber and Faber, 2000), pp. 120 and 149.

112 Ben Cousins, "Tenure and Common Property Resources in Africa", in *Evolving Land Rights, Poli-
     cy and Tenure in Africa,* edited by C. Toulmin and J. Quan (London: Department for International
     Development, International Institute for Environment and Development/Natural Resources In-
     stitute, 2000).

bour force to carry out their main subsistence activities (herding), and in the case of hunter-gatherers, the need for mobility and the availability of resources could be seen as one of the factors that encourage them to limit their numbers. Families thus avoid having several small children at the same time. Data has shown that while the Kenyan national population annual growth rate was 4 per cent, the growth rate of the Maasai and other pastoral people was approximately 2.2 per cent, or almost half of the national average.[113] The same phenomenon has been observed amongst the Hadzabe and the San of Tanzania and Southern Africa, respectively.

In the past, and as a result of their relative small numbers, pastoralists and hunter-gatherers did not often face the problem of land shortage. They also enjoyed larger areas of lands than their cultivator counterparts. Having the benefit of large and often fertile lands when many people are land-hungry has indeed contributed to the discrimination and land grabbing that indigenous peoples endure.

History of severe discrimination

This section does not depict all the types or forms of discriminations that indigenous peoples experience. It could also be argued that there are several groups, who, just like indigenous peoples, face severe discrimination and that discrimination therefore should not be considered as a characteristic particular to indigenous peoples.

So, what is noteworthy or particular about the discriminations indigenous peoples suffer from? With regard to the situation in Central, Eastern, and Southern Africa, it is a fact that mainstream societies look at them as "backward", "primitive", etc., and leave them only one option—to assimilate into the dominant culture, and in that process give up their ways of life, their culture, their language, etc., or, in one word, their identity. For instance, many African States in which "Pygmies" live believe that the education of indigenous children is a simple matter of getting these children away from their communities and getting them into modern schools where they can be educated just like other children.

Indigenous peoples tend to resist these measures and policies designed by their States to "civilise" them, and this struggle for their land-based cultural survival, their "societal cultures", often clashes with the interests of the States in which they live. In Andrew Gray's words, "indigenousness is an assertion by people directed against the power of outsiders",[114] including the power of the States. Most Kenyan and Tanzanian indigenous peoples, as well as several other indigenous peoples living in Central, Eastern, and Southern Africa consider their respective Governments to be outside powers established on their lands.

---

113 Shannon Kishel, E. Mcalpin, and A. Molloy, "The Maasai Culture and Ecological Adaptations". Mimeo. Denison University, Ohio. http://www.denison.edu/enviro/envs245/papers/Massai/Maasai2.html, Accessed December 10, 2003.
114 Gray, "The Indigenous Movement in Asia" (1995), p. 40.

The Ogiek indigenous peoples are in court against the Kenyan Government's policy, which aims first at de-gazetting the Mau Forest and then at dividing it into individually held land plots, a scheme that land-hungry communities, such as the Kipsigis, welcome. In Kenya, too, the Maasai community is resisting government policies of land individualisation. The Hadzabe and the Barabaig in northern Tanzania have sometimes resisted compulsory schooling of their children as well as the efforts made by their Governments to transform them into agriculturalists, considered to be the only rational way of life[115] or "legitimate occupancy" of land.[116] Actions taken by indigenous peoples in resistance to being "civilised" or assimilated range from open conflicts, legal challenges, lobbying at the international level against their States' policies, voluntarily ignoring the expropriation measures taken by the State by continuing to "clandestinely" use the contentious lands, burning down the resources on lands taken away from them by governments, etc.

In 2005, legal status was denied a Rwandan indigenous NGO, *Communauté des Autochtones du Rwanda* (CAURWA), on the grounds that their use of the term "autochtone" (indigenous) and their claim of cultural identity as Batwa indigenous peoples amounted to a breach of the Rwandan Constitution, which prohibits any act that may divide the Rwandan society along ethnic lines. The indigenous community-based NGO argued unsuccessfully that the term "Batwa" symbolized their cultural identity, which they wanted to maintain. In order to survive as an NGO with a legal status, CAURWA had eventually no other option than changing its name to *Communauté des Potiers du Rwanda* (Rwanda's Potter Community - COPORWA).

When indigenous peoples actively resist cultural assimilation policies and laws, dominant communities or the state apparatus tend to respond by violating and denying their rights in the name of national unity and similar principles. Unless a causal link is established between, on the one hand, indigenous peoples' resistance to cultural assimilation and, on the other hand, the particular discrimination and repressions carried out by dominant communities or the state apparatus, it is difficult to understand the distinctiveness of the discrimination that indigenous peoples tend to suffer from.

On numerous occasions, African officials have argued that indigenous peoples tend to auto-exclude themselves from modern life, national programs and policies. The "Pygmies" of Central African forests, the Mbororo, the Hadzabe, the San and numerous other communities are thus often accused of sidelining them-

---

115 Madsen, *The Hadzabe of Tanzania* (2000), p. 20, writes: "The objective of the Government became the transformation of these communities into what officials viewed as the more rational mode of life of sedentarised agriculture ..."

116 James Woodburn, "Indigenous Discrimination: The Ideological Basis for Local Discrimination against Hunter-Gatherers Minorities in Sub-Saharan Africa", *Ethnic and Racial Studies*, 20, no. 2. (1997), p. 350.

selves, of not taking their destiny into their own hands, as other Africans did with modernity after colonialism.

Obviously this "auto-exclusion thesis" developed by some African elites does not stand in front of realities as they manifest themselves in Uganda, for instance, where Batwa children, who dare attending primary school declared free for all, are ridiculed and subjected to mockery by other children because of looking filthy and being badly clothed. A pregnant Baka woman from Cameroon died after being denied medical attention by a nurse for being unclean.[117] The African Commission on Human and Peoples' Rights' Report on Indigenous Populations/Communities compiles numerous examples of particular discriminations suffered by indigenous peoples in Africa, including, for instance, the fact that some "Pygmies" are not considered to be citizens of the country in which they live.[118] But one of most recurrent discrimination and common to all countries is the denial that indigenous peoples enjoyed land rights prior to the formation of states—whether colonial or independent.

Land rights prior to colonization or to the occupation by other African groups

Indigenous peoples' land rights are grounded on immemorial occupation. People living on traditional lands and territories have strong cultural, historical and emotional connections to these lands and territories. Such lands have throughout time shaped the way of life of the communities involved. Without these lands, indigenous communities are unable to survive as cultural distinct entities.

As shown by international and a number of African jurisprudences, indigenous land rights are not proven by written modern land titles, but by testimonies and accounts of immemorial occupation and use. In order to prove indigenous peoples' land rights, it is often necessary to bring in not only the beneficiaries but also researchers, historians, anthropologists to testify, and to use archives and similar sources of historical information. This is because, in most African cases, indigenous peoples' land rights existed long before the current modern system of land ownership and written history.

Generally, the issue of "rights prior to colonization or occupation by other African groups"[119] raises the question of whether indigenous means "original" or

---

117 Barume, "Etude sur le cadre légal" (2005a).

118 African Commission, *Report of the Working Group of Experts* (2005), pp. 34-37.

119 Wiessner in his paper on "Rights and Status of Indigenous Peoples" (1999), p. 115, argues that, "Indigenous peoples are thus best conceived of as peoples traditionally regarded, and self-defined, as descendants of the original inhabitants of lands with which they share a strong, often spiritual bond. These peoples are, and desire to be, culturally, socially, and/or economically distinct from the dominant groups in society, at the hands of which they have suffered, in past or present, a pervasive pattern of subjugation, marginalization, dispossession, exclusion, and discrimination. …"

"prior" occupants. The interest for this analysis resides not in what each one of these concepts means, but rather how relevant they are in Central, Eastern, and Southern Africa. Are communities claiming indigenous status in these parts of Africa the original inhabitants of the lands they claim?

In many parts of Africa, people's movements have been less well documented than in other regions, to the extent that it is difficult to know who lived where and when. A further problem arises where the process of some communities being culturally overpowered by others is still taking place. Some have thus argued for the term "prior" in addition to "original".[120] In the Australian *Mabo* case, for instance, the term "prior" was chosen rather than "original", because, although the Meriam people[121] had been occupying the [contentious] Torres Strait Islands for generations before the first European contact, Justice Brennan, at the same time, also acknowledged that the original inhabitants of the islands were not the Meriam people, but probably Melanesian people who had come from Papua New Guinea.[122]

Andrew Gray similarly points out that the Chakma of the Chittagong Hill Tracts are not the original inhabitants of these lands, on which they settled after the Arakanese and Tripurans.[123] A recent study on Cameroon by the author of this book shows that Mbororo, living in that country, arrived from elsewhere too, but still claim indigenous status.[124] Nor are the Maasai the original occupants of their lands. Survival International reckons they arrived in the region known today as Maasailand (southern Kenya and northern Tanzania) around the fifteenth century.[125] Basil Davidson, on the other hand, believes that the Maasai reached Kenya long after 1545, establishing themselves along the Mount Ngorongoro near what is now Tanzania's border to Kenya.[126] The Himba are in the same way recorded to have originated from the Great Rift Valley in Central Africa around the fourteenth century A.D.[127] Not being the "original inhabitants", however, does not make the Maasai or the Himba less indigenous than the "Pygmies", the Hadzabe or the San, who are widely recognized as the first peoples of the African tropical forest, the forest around Lake Eyasi in northern Tanzania and the Kalahari, respectively.[128]

---

120 Gray, "The Indigenous Movement in Asia", (1995), p. 39.

121 The Meriam people live on Mer (or Murray) Island, one of the Torres Strait Islands, off the northern coast of Queensland, Australia.

122 *Mabo and Others v. The State of Queensland* (No. 2) [1992] 175 CLR 1, per Brennan J., at 2.

123 Gray, "The Indigenous Movement in Asia" (1995), p. 39.

124 Barume, "Etude sur le cadre legal" (2005a), p. 26.

125 See Web site of Survival International at http://www.survival.org.uk/index2.htm. Survival International is an international NGO that campaigns for the rights of indigenous peoples worldwide.

126 Basil Davidson, *Africa in History* (London: Phoenix Press, 1992), p. 148.

127 United States' Department of State, Bureau of African Affairs, Background Notes on Namibia. Available online at http://www.state.gov/r/pa/ei/bgn/5472.htm

128 Woodburn, "Indigenous Discrimination", (1997), p. 354. See also Woodburn, "The Political Status of Hunter-Gatherers in Present Day and Future Africa" in *Africa's Indigenous Peoples: "First Peoples" or "Marginalized Minorities"?*, edited by Alan Barnard and Justin Kenrick (Edinburgh: Centre of African Studies, University of Edinburgh, 2000), p. 3.

In other words, as far as the present situation in Central, Eastern, and Southern Africa is concerned, there are a number of communities, such as the "Pygmies", the San and the Hadzabe, whose indigenousness is argued, among other things, on the basis of being the original inhabitants of their lands. However, there are other communities, like the Maasai and the Mbororo, which are not necessarily the original inhabitants of their lands, but who have lived for so long (and prior to colonization) on a given land or region that their culture and way of life have become dependent on such lands.

Land-based culture

A land-based culture is also one of the main guiding factors that help understanding and identifying indigenous peoples. However, given the scope and weight of indigenous peoples' land rights, this issue will be dealt with in the next chapter.

Conclusion

From what has been discussed in this chapter, it emerges that there is no international binding instrument that indicates precise procedures to be followed by a community for declaring itself indigenous. Each community tends to exercise that freedom according to its national or regional context. In Central, Eastern, and Southern Africa, communities tend to proclaim their indigenousness through numerous means, including presentations and statements made at national, regional, international indigenous-related meetings as well as land claims, court cases and resistance against evictions, as further chapters will show.

At its fifteenth session, in 1997, the U.N. Working Group on Indigenous Populations concluded that a definition of indigenous peoples at the global level was not possible at that time, and that this did not prove necessary for the adoption of the Declaration on the Rights of Indigenous Peoples. It also said that the concept of indigenous must be understood in a wider context than only the colonial experience.[129]

In the process of adoption of the United Nations Declaration on the Rights of Indigenous Peoples, however, most of the African States—also designated as the "African Group"—objected to the principle of self-identification by saying that "the absence of a definition of indigenous peoples in the text creates legal prob-

---

129 U.N. Working Group on Indigenous Populations, Report of the WGIP on its fifteenth session (July-August 1997). U.N. Doc. E/CN.4/Sub.2/1997/14, para.129. Available at http://www.unhchr.ch/Huridocda/Huridoca.nsf/(Symbol)/E.CN.4.Sub.2.1997.14. En?Opendocument

lems for the implementation. It is therefore important that the Declaration's juris-
dictional clause defining the rights holders should be included in the text".[130]

The African Commission on Human and Peoples' Right appeased the worries
of African political leaders by underlining the principle of self-identification enshrined by ILO Convention No. 169, and stressing that "a strict definition of indigenous peoples is neither necessary nor desirable. It is much more relevant and
constructive to try to outline the major characteristics, which can help us to identify who the indigenous peoples and communities in Africa are."[131]

Unlike the situation on other continents where indigenous means first inhabitants as opposed to the colonizers and their descendants, in Africa the concept of
"indigenous peoples" refers to communities who have been long forgotten or
overlooked for the sake of post-colonial development programmes and projects
relating to, among other things, nature conservation, exploitation of natural resources, public infrastructure and industrial agriculture. These communities
have seen their ways of life being considered as backward, ridiculed and des-
tined to disappear. In each African country where they live, these communities,
whose way of life is negatively looked upon, are easily identifiable by the rest of
their fellow citizens and Governments. These peoples or communities are largely
hunter-gatherers and nomadic pastoralists whose methods of occupation and
use of the land have not been legally recognized and protected. In many African
countries, hunting, gathering and nomadism were not and are still not considered as being "civilized" and development-oriented ways of using the land. This
is not only because agriculture has become the main way of life, but also because
lands used by hunter-gatherers and other nomadic communities in most cases
look as if they are not occupied or are no-man's land *(res nullius)*. In the Americas,
Australia, and New Zealand, the concept of indigenous referred to peoples having been conquered, colonized, displaced, and even exterminated by the newcomers. In contrast, the colonization process in Africa appears to have been
somewhat less malignant. Nevertheless, here, too, people were subjugated and
displaced first by the colonial powers and later by post-independence mainstream societies. It is in response to these historical injustices suffered by a number
of African communities that the African indigenous movement should be seen.
The call to justice and equal enjoyment of all rights and freedoms by these communities goes via the human rights international framework called "indigenous
movement". This is indeed the human rights meaning of the term "indigenous"
in Africa, which therefore should be differentiated from its general meaning by
which each African can legitimately call himself or herself indigenous to the continent.

---

130 African Group, Draft Aide Memoire to the United Nations Draft Declaration on the Rights of
     Indigenous Peoples, New York, 9 November 2006. See also chapter X, this volume.
131 The African Commission, *Report of the Working Group of Experts* (2005), p. 87.

Belonging to a non-dominant sector of society, suffering from particular discriminations and having a land-based culture should not be regarded as elements of any formal definition of who are indigenous peoples in Africa, but as characteristics that help anyone to identify or understand those who consider themselves as indigenous.

It is therefore arguable that not all Africans are indigenous peoples, because, as understood in current international law, someone is indigenous in relation to a given, well-identified area of land.[132] This implies that an African community cannot be indigenous to the entire continent, not even to an entire country, but instead to a precise land that can be demarcated and seen as culturally important. There has to be a land to which a claimant community is culturally strongly attached. This is the situation also in Central, Eastern, and Southern Africa, where indigenous communities or peoples do not claim just any land or all lands of their respective countries. On the contrary, most African indigenous communities claim lands that are precisely identified, lands to which they can prove that they relate culturally. The San do not claim the whole of Southern Africa. Nor do the Bagyeli or the Batwa claim the whole of southern Cameroon or the entire national territories of Rwanda and Uganda. This human rights meaning of the term "indigenous" should therefore be distinguished from its general meaning on the basis on which each African could identify himself or herself as indigenous to the continent.

It should also be noted that most African indigenous peoples tend to use interchangeably the terms "communities" and "peoples". The African regional human rights system seems also to prefer the terminology "communities", rather than "peoples". It is argued that, whereas societies, organizations, clubs, and similar groupings are established by deliberate and voluntary actions of their members, communities "are groups based upon unifying and spontaneous factors essentially beyond the control of members of the group".[133] Communities are presented as entities that exist as cultural units,[134] and cannot be regarded as a mere aggregate of individuals. They are featured by a sense of belonging together, willingness to preserve "solidarity between them and sharing a common heritage and common destiny".[135]

The use of the term "communities" together with indigenous seems indeed more appropriate in Africa. Firstly, this concept implies the idea of culture, living together, sharing common values, and being willing to preserve a certain way of

---

132 Gray, "The Indigenous Movement in Asia" (1995), p. 36.

133 Nathan Lerner, *Group Rights and Discrimination in International Law* (Dordrecht: Martinus Nijhoff Publishers, 1991), p. 29.

134 Oliver Mendelsohn and Upendra Baxi (eds.), *The Rights of Subordinated Peoples* (Delhi: Oxford University Press, 1994), p. 120.

135 Patrick Thornberry, *International Law and the Rights of Minorities* (Oxford: Clarendon Press, 1991), p. 331; Lerner, *Group Rights* (1991). p. 32.

life, all of which are characteristics that appear closer to African indigenous peoples' claims. Secondly, the term "communities" is less politically charged than "peoples". It can be considered as appropriate for building up trust between indigenous communities and their States, since most African indigenous communities do not claim statehood, but autonomy, self-governance, and control over their lands and resources.[136] Thirdly, the term "communities" is unlikely to include any aggregate of individuals like the concepts "minorities" and "groups". There is also an emerging interchangeable use of the terms "communities" and "peoples" in various indigenous-related international human rights discourse, particularly on lands seen as the cornerstone of indigenous peoples' existence.

---

136 In Africa, there is not a single indigenous community which claims statehood. Neither do the Maori, nor the American Natives. Regarding Asia, Andrew Gray shows that with the exception of the people of East Timor, West Papua and Nagaland, most indigenous communities do not claim statehood nor use decolonisation as a legal argument. See Gray, "The Indigenous Movement in Asia" (1995), p. 55.

CHAPTER III
THE LANDS OF INDIGENOUS PEOPLES: IMPORTANCE AND JUSTIFICATION

This chapter focuses on the importance and role of ancestral lands, on how indigenous peoples' survival depends on these lands as it has always done, and on how philosophical and historical grounds lead us to believe that indigenous peoples' rights to ancestral lands survived the creation of current African modern States.

Land as the incarnation of culture

In international human rights law doctrine, culture is sometimes understood as being a "cluster of social, and economic activities, which gives a community its sense of identity".[137] The United Nations Human Rights Committee in a General Comment (1994) writes:

> 3.2   … To enjoy a particular culture may consist in a way of life which is closely associated with territory and use of its resources. This may be particularly true of members of indigenous communities …
>
> 7.   … Culture manifests itself in many forms, including a particular way of life associated with the use of land resources especially in the case of indigenous peoples. That right may include such traditional activities as fishing and hunting …[138]

---

137 Nigel Rodley, "Conceptual Problems in the Protection of Minorities: International Legal Development", *Human Rights Quarterly* 17 (1995), p. 59.

138 U.N. Human Rights Committee, General Comment 23, Article 27 (Fiftieth session, 1994a). Reprinted in Compilation of General Comments and General Recommendations Adopted by Human Rights Treaty Bodies, U.N. Doc. HRI/GEN/1/Rev. at 158 (2003). Available online at http://hrlibrary.ngo.ru/gencomm/hrcomms.htm. See also Raoul Wallenberg Institute, *Collection of General Comments or Recommendations adopted by U.N. Human Rights Treaty Bodies*, Vol. 1.: *Human Rights Committee* (Lund, Sweden: Raoul Wallenberg Institute, 2006), p. 69. Available online at http://www.rwi.lu.se/publications/books/treatycom.shtml

This Comment is usually seen as the most explicit legal linkage between indigenous peoples' right to lands and their culture.

It has also been said that "the survival of indigenous cultures throughout the
world is heavily dependent on protection of their lands"[139] because removals of
such communities from their lands often endanger not only their cultural values,
such as language, link to their ancestors, sacred sites, etc., but also the lives of
their members.[140] In her final report on the relationship between indigenous peoples and their lands, Ms. Erica-Irene A. Daes, then Chairperson Rapporteur of the
U.N. Working Group on Indigenous Populations, stated that the relationship between indigenous peoples and land has "various social, cultural, spiritual, economic, and political dimensions and responsibilities".[141] Indigenous peoples do
not indeed claim just any land, but lands which have cultural importance for
them.[142] For indigenous peoples, lands are not only for providing food, medicine,
fuel, grazing and browsing for livestock, fish and game, but also, and perhaps
more importantly, lands have "non-market values such as ... water retention,
inheritance value, aesthetic, shade, initiation sites, sacred areas, and the prevention of soil erosion, [which] are rated highly in [an indigenous] community".[143]

Indigenous peoples have indeed "a distinctive and profound spiritual and
material relationship with their lands".[144] They "view their relationship with the
land as central to their collective identity and well-being ... People and land and
culture are indissolubly linked ... [lands express] the rights of ... communities to
self-preservation ... The foundational right accorded to collective entities capable
of bearing rights would be meaningless without a right to the continued possession and enjoyment of their land".[145] Lands are simply "the raison d'être of [in-
digenous peoples'] culture".[146] That alien activities on indigenous peoples' lands
undoubtedly can threaten the "way of life and culture" of such peoples, has also
been emphasized by the Human Rights Committee.[147]

---

139 Will Kymlicka, *Multicultural Citizenship*, (Oxford: Clarendon Press, 1995), p. 43.
140 This was also stated in the *Delgamuukw v. British Columbia* [1997] 3 S.C.R. 1010 (Canada), which
       emphasized the special bond between indigenous peoples and their lands. For text of case, see
       http://www.canlii.org/en/ca/scc/doc/1997/1997canlii302/1997canlii302.html
141 Erica-Irene A. Daes, "Study on Indigenous Peoples and their Relationship to Land". Final Work-
       ing Paper by the Special Rapporteur to the Commission on Human Rights. U.N. Doc. E/CN.4/
       Sub.2/2001/21, 11 June 2001, para. 20. Available at
       http://www.unhchr.ch/Huridocda/Huridoca.nsf/(Symbol)/E.CN.4.Sub.2.2001.21.
       En?Opendocument
142 Ian Brownlie and F.M. Brookfield, *Treaties and Indigenous Peoples* (Oxford: Clarendon Press, 1992),
       p. 39.
143 Cousins, "Tenure and Common Property" (2000), p. 161.
144 Ibid.
145 Darlene M. Johnston, 1999, "Native Rights as Collective Rights: A Question of Group Self-Pres-
       ervation", in *The Rights of Minority Cultures*, edited by W. Kymlicka (New York: Oxford Univer-
       sity Press, 1999), pp. 193-4.
146 Barsh, "Indigenous Peoples and the U.N. Commission" (1996), p. 801.
147 See, for instance, the *Lubicon Lake Band v. Canada* case, U.N. Human Rights Committee, Thirty-
       eigth session (1990), Communication No. 167/1984, U.N. Doc. CCPR/C/38/D/167/1984 (1990),

"There is ample evidence of the "special connection between indigenous and the lands".[148] For example, during the proceedings of the *Mabo* case in Australia, several elders of the Meriam people were brought to testify on their community's immemorial occupation and cultural uses of Mer (Murray) Island. Similarly, in all the legal cases of the Barabaig against NAFCO (National Agricultural and Food Corporation) in Tanzania, numerous Barabaig elders were brought from their villages to testify why their lands were and continued to be culturally important for their survival as a community (see Part II of this volume). One of the lawyers, who acted for the plaintiffs, underlined the irreplaceable cultural value that these Tanzanian indigenous people accorded to their lost lands. With regard to sacred graves, various testimonies were recorded by Barabaig elders providing information that individuals who played important roles within this community were not buried in the same way as other community members. Their graves often took more than two years to build, as they required very special skills and a lot of materials because of their size and their cultural value. The areas, where these graves were located, were generally used by the Barabaig for seasonal gatherings. All these graves were bulldozed by NAFCO, against whom the Barabaig community later went to court.

Because sites such as graves have more than a symbolic value, the Maasai living within the Ngorongoro area close to the forest reserve of Karatu District (part of the Highlands of Tanzania) are challenging the ban which prevents them from gaining access to these forest lands. Not only are these lands important for grazing, particularly during the dry season, but also, and more importantly, the Karatu forests host grave sites and traditional medicinal plants.

Amongst the Mbendjele ("Pygmies") of Congo-Brazzaville, the forest plays a unique and paramount role:

> Women ... give birth to their children in the forest just outside camp. The forest inhabits the Mbendjele as much as they inhabit the forest. The forest is idealised as the perfect place for people to be. Every day Mbendjele conversations are obsessed with the forest, with different tricks and techniques for finding wild foods, about stories of past hunting, fishing or gathering trips, or of great feasts and forest spirit performances (*massana*) that occurred, or will occur in the near future. The forest links people to the past. Different areas in the forest are talked about in terms of the remembered ancestors that spent time there and the events that

---

para. 33. Mr. Bernard Ominayak, Chief of the Lubicon Lake Cree Indians, (Alberta, Canada), initiated the communication against the Canadian Government accused of having violated, amongst other things, Article 1 of the Covenant by allowing industrial companies to exploit the resources of the Lubicon Lake Band's traditional territory. The Communication is available at http://hrlibrary.ngo.ru/undocs/session38-index.html

148 Ian Brownlie, "Rights of Indigenous Peoples in Modern International Law", in *The Rights of Peoples*, edited by J. Crawford (Oxford: Clarendon Press, 1988), p. 4.

occurred. When Mbendjele die, they believe they go to another forest where *Komba* (God) has a camp. They will remain in *Komba*'s forest camp until they are told to take another path and are born into this world again.[149]

The Himba of Namibia believe that the construction of the Epupa dam on their lands will potentially inundate more than 160 of their ancestral graves.

> For the Himba, a grave is not just the location of the physical remains of a deceased person—it is a focal point for defining identity, social relationship and relationship with the land, as well as being a centre for important religious rituals. … Graveyards are usually located near a watercourse … [which makes these areas] heavily loaded with emotions, as the points where communities congregate, the starting point of annual cattle migrations.[150]

As put by Andrew Corbett, "the key point is not the physical fact of the graves themselves, but the connection between the graves, the family's history and the community's system of land tenure and decision-making".[151]

Similarly, an elder of the South African ǂKhomani San, who was interviewed during the process of reclaiming their ancestral lands from the South African Government, stated: "Without the Kalahari … we are nothing. In the Kalahari, we know where we belong, we know what to do with the land, we know who we are".[152] This is very much corroborated by what the author of this book saw and heard during his visit to San communities in the Kalahari, in November 2002.

However, the strong tie between indigenous communities' livelihood and culture with their lands should not be confused with the relation that we might all have, as members of the human race, to some resources, such as the ozone layer, marine life, international waters and similar resources. In her famous publication, *Governing the Commons: the Evolution of Institutions for Collective Action*, Elinor Ostrom uses the concept of "common property resources" (CPR), which is defined as resources used by many individuals in common and difficult to own.[153]

---

149 Jerome Lewis, "Forest People or Village People: Whose Voice will be Heard?" in *Africa's Indigenous Peoples: 'First Peoples' or 'Marginalized Minorities'?*, edited by Alan Barnard and Justin Kenrick (Edinburgh: Centre of African Studies, University of Edinburgh, 2001), p. 7.

150 Corbett, "A Case Study" (1999), p. 85.

151 Ibid.

152 Chennells, "The ǂKhomani San of South Africa" (2003), p. 278.

153 Elinor Ostrom, *Governing the Commons: The Evolution of Institutions for Collective Action*, Series Political Economy of Institutions and Decisions (Cambridge: Cambridge University Press, 1990), p. 1. The CPR concept considers resources such as air, coastal or marine life, ozone layer, and fishing stock as CPR simply because these resources are indispensable for the existence of human kind, and not because they shape a livelihood, a culture, or a way of life of a particular

Although this understanding of CPR could include the "collective lands of indigenous communities", one can see that the perception of the CPR, as resources "used by many individuals in common", gives the impression of insisting on "use" as the principal and main tie between the CPR and people.

This understanding of CPR seems not to underline the fact that, for indigenous communities, land is not just for use, but also and more importantly, land sustains their whole livelihood and culture. Furthermore, the indigenous communities also have a distinctive and profound spiritual and material relationship with their lands.[154] For indigenous peoples "their relationship with the land is central to their collective identity and well-being. … People and land and culture are indissolubly linked … [lands express] the rights of … communities to self-preservation. … The foundational right accorded to collective entities capable of bearing rights would be meaningless without a right to the continued possession and enjoyment of their land."[155]

Right to lands and right to life

Indigenous peoples' right to lands is so important that many have linked it with some aspects of the right to life. Many examples from Africa seem to corroborate this view. In the late 1960s, when the Batwa of eastern Democratic Republic of Congo were being expelled from their homelands—later to become the Kahuzi-Biega National Park—they numbered up to 6,000. In less than fifty years, these figures have approximately halved, due to the non-adaptation of these Batwa to any other type of lifestyle outside their forests.[156]

Before the beginning of their expulsion from the Mau forests in the early 1910s, the Ogiek of Kenya were also said to number far more than their current number, which is estimated to be up to 20,000 countrywide and 5,883 in the East Mau.[157] Forced to face a new way of life outside their natural environment, the life expectancy of the Ogiek has dropped drastically, as underlined by an Ogiek representative.[158]

---

community. Furthermore, damage to some of the CPR affects all communities, regardless of their way of life. We are all, as human beings, affected in the same way by the reduction of the ozone layer, deforestation, pollution and destruction of similar resources.

154 Ibid., p. 1.

155 Johnston, "Native Rights as Collective Rights" (1999), pp. 193-4.

156 Albert Kwoko Barume, *Heading Toward Extinction? Indigenous Rights in Africa: The Case of the Twa of the Kahuzi-Biega National Park, Democratic Republic of Congo*, IWGIA Document No. 101 (Copenhagen: IWGIA and FPP, 2000), p. 16.

157 J.K. Sang, "Kenya: the Ogiek in Mau Forest" in *Indigenous Peoples and Protected Areas in Africa: From Principles to Practice*, edited by J. Nelson and L. Hossack (Moreton-in-Marsh, UK: Forest Peoples Programme, 2003), pp. 114-115. Available from http://www.forestpeoples.org

158 Statement made by an elder Ogiek met at Nakuru, Kenya, during a training-discussion on the existing alternatives ways for an international action against the measures of the Government of Kenya with regard to the Ogiek's lands. More than 50 members of the Ogiek community took

Kenyan pastoralists such as the Maasai "feel especially attached to the land because they depend on its resources for the survival of the herds and people, and without it, they cannot survive especially since they do not also have the skill necessary for survival outside the pastoral sector".[159] Lotte Hughes (2006) gives a detailed account of the forced eviction of the Maasai from their ancestral lands and how it affected them.[160]

In Tanzania, the Government's attempts in 1927 and 1939 to settle the Hadzabe and make them give up their nomadic lifestyle, which the Government regarded as a cause for their non-integration into mainstream Tanzanian social life, led "to real disaster: outbreak of disease occurred and people died. In both cases the policy was abandoned quite quickly and the Hadzabe involved were allowed to return to their independent nomadic life".[161] Recent attempts to do the same or push the Hadzabe into a sedentary lifestyle have also been unsuccessful, as the Hadzabe often move out of the settlements as soon as they are moved in.[162]

The San population of the Kalahari also decreased as a result of their expulsion from their lands. Since the early 1900s, many were forced to leave their lands, most of which were transformed into large cattle farms and national parks, such as the Etosha Game Reserve in Namibia (1954),[163] the Central Kalahari Game Reserve (1961) in Botswana and the Kalahari Gemsbok National Park (1931)[164] in South Africa. One researcher notes that:

Today, the San of Southern Africa are the second largest population of former foragers in Africa. These peoples were the aboriginal groups who resided in an area stretching from the Congo-Zambezi watershed in Central Africa to the Cape. They once existed in relatively large numbers, with as many as 150,000 - 300,000 people dispersed widely in the region. Today, after centuries of conflict, genocide, assimilation and exploitation, they

part in this training organised by the Ogiek Welfare Council, a local NGO created by the Ogiek, and the Forest Peoples Programme (FPP), a British NGO working with indigenous peoples worldwide. The author of this volume contributed to this training as a facilitator.

159 Naomi Kipuri, "Indigenous Peoples in Kenya: An Overview". Available online at http://www.Whoseland.com/paper6, p. 4.

160 Lotte Hughes, *Moving of the Maasai: A Colonial Misadventure* (London: Palgrave Macmillan, 2006).

161 James Woodburn, "Minimal Politics: The Political Organisation of the Hadza of North Tanzania" in *Politics in Leadership: A Comparative Perspective*, edited by W.A. Shack and P.S. Cohen (Oxford: Clarendon Press, 1979), p. 249.

162 Madsen, *The Hadzabe of Tanzania* (2000), p. 20.

163 The Etosha Game Reserve was established in 1907 but the Hai//om San were first evicted in 1954.

164 The ‡Khomani San live in South Africa, in the southern area of the Kalahari. They were resettled when part of their lands was turned into the Kalahari Gemsbok National Park in 1931. This Park has since 1999 formed Africa's first transfrontier park with the Gemsbok National Park in Botswana under the name of the Kgalahadi Transfrontier Park.

number 100,000 people and can be found in six of the countries of Southern Africa.[165]

Whereas several experts[166] and UNESCO documents[167] therefore have used the
terms "ethnocide" and "cultural genocide" in relation to the forced removals of
indigenous peoples from their lands, there are no international instruments
which recognize that forced expulsions may amount to violations of the right to
life. Attempts to include the concept "ethnocide" into the scope of the crime of
genocide during the *travaux préparatoires* of the 1948 Convention on the Prevention and Punishment of the Crime of Genocide were unsuccessful.[168] Neither do
comments by the Human Rights Committee on the right to life refer to the expulsion of indigenous peoples from their culture-based lands.

The United Nations Human Rights Committee strongly—albeit implicitly—
hinted in the *Lubicon Lake Band case v. Canada* at a relationship between indigenous peoples' right to lands and the right to life of members of these communities. Considering the seriousness of the allegations made by the author of the
communication, Chief Bernard Ominayak, "that the Lubicon Lake Band was on
the verge of extinction, [the Human Rights] Committee requested Canada, under
rule 86 of procedures 'to take interim measures of protection to avoid irreparable
damage to [the author of the communication] and other members of the Lubicon
Lake Band'."[169] The Committee seems to have recognized that there is a connection between indigenous peoples' collective right to exist as a cultural entity and
the right to life of their members.[170]

The Inter-American Commission on Human Rights has also adopted a broad
understanding of the right to life in its decision on a number of communications, including the case of the Yanomami indigenous peoples, whose lands were affected by

165 Krystina Bishop, "Squatters on Their Own Lands: San Territoriality in Western Botswana", 31
    Comparative and International Law Journal of Southern Africa, 92, 1998, p. 14.
166 Julian Burger and Paul Hunt, "Towards the International Protection of Indigenous Peoples'
    Rights", *Netherlands Quarterly of Human Rights (NQHR)* 4/1994, pp. 413-4. See also Fergus McK-
    ay, "The Rights of Indigenous Peoples in International Law: A briefing paper for the Department
    for International Development" (unpublished, 2000), p. 7. Article 7(2) of the U.N. Declaration on
    the Rights of Indigenous Peoples states that *"indigenous peoples have the collective right to live in
    freedom, peace and security as distinct peoples and shall not be subjected to any act of genocide or any
    other act of violence, including forcibly removing children or the group to another group".*
167 UNESCO Declaration of San José on Ethno-Development and Ethnocide in Latin America (1981).
    See UNESCO, Meeting of Experts on Ethno-Development and Ethnocide in Latin America, Final
    Report, San José, Costa Rica (7-11 December 1981); and UNESCO, Meeting of Experts on the
    Study of Ethno-development and Ethnocide in Africa, Final Report, Ouagadougou, Upper Volta
    (31 January – 4 February 1983).
168 Burger and Hunt, "Towards the International Protection" (1994), p. 414. See also Maivân Clech
    Lâm, *At the Edge of the State: Indigenous Peoples and Self-Determination* (Ardsley, New York: Trans-
    national Publishers, Inc., 2000), p. 27.
169 U.N. Human Rights Committee, Communication No. 167/1984 *The Lubicon Lake Band v. Canada*
    (1990), para. 29.3.
170 Burger and Hunt, "Towards the International Protection" (1994), pp. 413-4.

a highway project promoted by the Brazilian Government. In response to allegations of violating Article 1 of the American Declaration of the Rights and Duties of Man regarding the right to life, the Commission ruled, amongst other things, that "invasion was carried out without prior and adequate protection for the safety and health of the Yanomami Indians, which resulted in a considerable number of deaths caused by epidemics of influenza, tuberculosis, measles, venereal diseases, and others".[171] In a similar communication before the Inter-American Commission on Human Rights, members of the Miskito indigenous people alleged that the Government of Nicaragua violated, amongst other things, their right to life and the right of their community to exist as a distinct cultural entity, by expropriating their lands.[172]

In its Report on the Situation of Human Rights in Ecuador, the Inter-American Commission on Human Rights likewise concluded that, in relation to indigenous peoples' right to lands, it is necessary to understand:

> ... [O]n the one hand, the essential connection they maintain to their traditional territories, and on the other hand, the human rights violations which threaten when these lands are invaded and when the land itself is degraded. ... For many indigenous cultures, continued utilization of traditional collective systems for the control and use of territory are essential to their survival as well as to their individual and collective well-being. Control over the land refers to both its capacity for providing the resources which sustain life and the geographical space necessary for the cultural and social reproduction of the group.[173]

More recently (May 2002), the African Commission on Human and People's Rights ruled that, regarding the destruction of Ogoniland by the Shell Petroleum Development Company, "the Federal Republic of Nigeria [violated amongst others] the right to life of Ogoni as articulated by] article 4 ... of the African Charter on Human and People's Rights", by allowing Shell to carry out a number of actions.[174]

---

171 Inter-American Commission on Human Rights, Resolution No.12/85, Case No. 7615 (Brazil), March 5, 1985. See OEA, Annual Report 1984-85, OEA/Ser.L/V/II.62 doc.10rev.1. October 1985.
172 During the 1980's political turmoil and the "Contra" war, in Nicaragua, several Miskito communities living on the Atlantic Coast of the country and on the border to Honduras became victims of forced relocation. Because they tried to resist, the Sandinista Government committed several human rights violations against the Miskito, including rape, murders and torture. In February 1982, the Miskito lodged their first complaint before the Inter-American Commission on Human Rights. See the IACHR's Report on the Situation of Human Rights of a Segment of the Nicaragua Population of Miskito Origin, OEA/Ser.L/V/II.62, doc. 26 of May 1984. Available at: http://www.cidh.oas.org/countryrep/Miskitoeng/toc.htm. See also Fergus MacKay, *A Guide to Indigenous Peoples' Rights in the Inter-American Human Rights System*, IWGIA Document No. 106 (Moreton-in-Marsh and Copenhagen: Forest Peoples Programme & IWGIA, 2002), p. 32.
173 Inter-American Commission on Human Rights, "Report on the Situation of Human Rights in Ecuador", OEA/Ser.L/V/II.96, Doc. 10 rev.1 (1997), p. 89.
174 This case was filed in November 1995, following death penalties carried out on nine leaders of the Movement for the Survival of the Ogoni People (MOSOP), a movement that fights for the

Recent jurisprudence, too, has several times linked the evictions of indigenous peoples from their lands with the right to life of these communities. Examples of this can be found in Malaysia, India and Colombia.

In *Kerajaan Negeri Johor & Anor v. Adong bin Kuwau & Ors*, a hunter-gatherer indigenous community of the Linggiu Valley in Malaysia alleged violations of, amongst other things, their right to life and lands following their Government's agreement with the Singapore Government to build a dam on their hunting and gathering lands. Citing a number of other cases in which the same view was upheld, the Malaysian Court of Appeal ruled that "the lower court made the correct finding as to liability. It is a well established principle that deprivation of livelihood may amount to deprivation of life itself".[175]

In the same vein, "Indian courts have interpreted the scope of the constitutional right to life expansively to forbid all actions of both State and citizen that disturb the 'environmental balance'."[176] This principle underpinned the ruling in *Indian Council for Enviro-Legal Action v. Union of India and Ors.*[177] This case involved a number of peoples inhabiting the village of Bichhri in Rajasthan, who alleged that the Government of India was violating, amongst other things, their right to life by failing to control and stop pollution caused by a local factory. The court built an argument on the constitutional right to life to order appropriate governmental regulatory measures.

In *Organización Indígena de Antioquía v. Corporación Nacional de Desarrollo del Choco*, "the Constitutional Court of Colombia held that the constitutional rights to life, work, property and cultural integrity of an indigenous community had been infringed upon ..." by the illegal cutting down of trees on their lands.[178]

In its recent decision on the Endorois case, the African Commission, too, found that the eviction of the Endorois from their traditional lands was a threat to their

---

rights of Ogoni communities in Nigeria. In June 2009, Shell agreed to pay US$15.5 millions in an out-of-court settlement of a legal action in which it was accused of having collaborated in the execution of the writer Ken Saro-Wiwa and eight other leaders of the Ogoni tribe.

175 *Kerajaan Negeri Johor & Anor v. Adong bin Kuwau & Ors*, [1998] 2 MLJ 158, (1998) 2 CHRLD 281. The Court of Appeal mentioned in its argument the following cases in which the same view was upheld: *R Rama Chandran v. The Industrial Court of Malaysia & Anor* [1997] 1 MLJ 145 (Mal FC), *Tan Tek Seng v. Suruhanjaya Perkhidmatan Pendidikan & Anor* [1996] 1 MLJ 261 (Mal CA) and *Hong Leong Equipment Sdn Bhd v. Liew Fook Chuan & Anor* [1996] 1 MLJ 481 (Mal CA) cited). See the Web site of Interights at http://www.interights.org/showdoc/index.htm?keywords=Malaysia&dir= databases&refid=2095.

176 Carl Bruch, *Constitutional Environmental Law: Giving Force to Fundamental Principles in Africa*, (Washington: Environmental Law Institute, 2000), p. 30. This publication gives also a long list of other cases in which the right to life versus environmental degradation was referred to by Indian courts. Text of publication available at the Web site of the Environmental Law Institute, http://www.elistore.org/reports_detail.asp?ID=527

177 *Indian Council for Enviro-Legal Action v. Union of India and Ors.*, 2000(5)SCALE286 See Web site of National Law School of India at http://www.nlsenlaw.org/waste-management/case-laws/supreme-court/indian-council-for-enviro-legal-action-v-union-of-india-uoi-and-or.2000

178 Bruch, *Constitutional Environmental Law*, (2000), p. 34.

rights to religious freedom and to culture, as well as a denial of their pastoralist way of life.[179]

So if the right to land of indigenous peoples is so closely and directly linked to the right to life of indigenous individuals, it is therefore arguable that this right to land could be considered as non derogatory, meaning it cannot be suspended even in a situation of a state of emergency, when a State can strike a fair and just "relationship between a particular objective and the administrative or legislative means used to achieve that objective".[180]

The linkage of land to the right to life of indigenous peoples is of key importance. Another important linkage is the linkage between indigenous peoples' ancestral lands and their languages.

Ancestral lands and indigenous languages

For indigenous peoples, as shown by the above few examples, lands are "intimately related to its holders' identity, of which it is an essential component".[181] The usage of indigenous languages is an important part of this identity. As noted by Kymlicka,

> Modernisation involves the diffusion throughout a society ... of a common culture, including standardized language, embodied in common economic, political, and educational institutions, one of the most important determinants of whether a culture survives is whether its language continues to be used.[182]

In most parts of the world, indigenous languages are endangered. This is especially the case of those languages that have no script (the case of 80 per cent of all languages in Africa!). This is, among other reasons, the consequence of national language policies. In post-independence Tanzania, the main political objective was to create a nation with "a system of generalised identification ... a unified education system and a unifying language".[183] This was also the case in Botswana, where Setswana is the only local official language.

---

179 See ACHPR Communication 276/2003 (2009) and chapter V, this volume.
180 Gránne De Búrca, "The Principle of Proportionality and its Application in the EC Law", in *Yearbook of European Law*, vol. 13, edited by A. Barav and D.A. Wyatt (London: Clarendon Press, 1982), pp. 105-150.
181 L.P. Delville, "Harmonising Formal Law and Customary Land Rights in French-speaking West Africa, in *Evolving Land Rights, Policy and Tenure in Africa,* edited by C. Toulmin and J. Quan (London: Department for International Development, International Institute for Environment and Development/Natural Resources Institute, 2000), p. 116.
182 Kymlicka, *Multicultural Citizenship* (1995), p. 111.
183 Woodburn, "The Political Status of Hunter-Gatherers" (2000), p. 6.

In some cases, there appears to be a striking and strong link between the expulsion of indigenous peoples from their lands and the disappearance of their languages. At the same time, however, there are also indigenous peoples around the world who have lost their languages but still hold on to their lands, and inversely, there are those who have retained their language but lost their lands. Examples of both can be found among indigenous peoples in Central, Eastern, and Southern Africa.

The "Pygmies" of the Ituri region, in the north-west of the Democratic Republic of Congo, and to some extent the Mbendjele of Congo-Brazaville, as well as the Baka of the east of Cameroon, still live on most or at least part of their lands and have maintained their language. The Baka of Cameroon call God *Komba*, spirit *molili*, a soothsayer *nganga*, witch *ndoki*, village *mboka*, and animal *nyama*.[184] These terms and countless others are not just similar but almost identical in meaning and even spelling amongst the Mbuti of the Ituri region of the Democratic Republic of Congo, and the Mbendjele Yaka of northern Congo-Brazzaville.[185] What these striking resemblances between the languages used by three indigenous peoples living thousands of miles from each other could suggest is that these communities once had one common language that has survived, despite being separated from one another, following the division of Africa into modern States. According to the French anthropologist, Serge Bahuchet, the "Pygmies" of the African tropical forests were not much affected by the colonial system because of their nomadic life style.[186] This could explain why, despite having their lands divided into different countries, these peoples maintained their language.

Although the Maasai have lost most of their lands, they have retained their Maa language. The Maasai, however, have actually never been forced to integrate into other communities. Whether in Tanzania or in Kenya, every time the Maasai were moved out of their lands, they were allocated another piece of land, although smaller and less valuable.[187] One could argue that this is one of the reasons why their language has survived.

---

184 Daniel Boursier, "Réflexion sur l'évangélisation des Baka", *Univers Vivant* No. 396 Novembre-Décembre 1991, pp. 26-7.

185 Lewis, "Forest Peoples or Village Peoples" (2001a), pp. 61-69.

186 Serge Bahuchet, "Les pygmées changent leur mode de vie", *Vivant Univers* No. 396, Novembre-Décembre 1991, p. 5.

187 See M.M.E.M. Rutten, *Selling Wealth to Buy Poverty: The Process of the Individualization of Landownership Among the Maasai Pastoralists of Kajiado District, Kenya, 1890-1990.* (Saarbrüchen - Fort Lauderdale: Verlag Breitenbach Publishers, 1992), pp. 173-200. The author shows consistent evidence of different actions by colonial and post-colonial Kenyan authorities consisting in moving Maasai from one place to another. Tundu Lissu, in his paper "Policy and Legal Issues on Wildlife Management in Tanzania's Pastoral Lands: The Case Study of the Ngorongoro Conservation Area", *Law, Social Justice and Global Development, (LGD)* 2000 (1), p. 1, comments on various treaties between the Maasai and Tanzanian authorities. As in Kenya, Maasai were moved to new lands every time their ancestral lands were needed by the Government. Lissu's paper is available online at:
http://www2.warwick.ac.uk/fac/soc/law/elj/lgd/2000_1/lissu/#a8.1

The British anthropologist James Woodburn points out that, because the Hadzabe of Tanzania have remained on their lands until recently, and the fact that they have kept their distance, both socially and culturally, from neighbouring groups, this could be regarded as the reason why their language is seen as "wholly unintelligible to their neighbours".[188]

On the other hand, there are indigenous peoples who have been expelled from their lands and scattered in different directions and have subsequently lost their languages. The communities that appear to have been most affected in this way are the hunter-gatherers. These communities' numeric inferiority and the prejudices, from which they suffer on the part of other communities, could be considered as the main reasons why their languages tend not to survive "integration" into other communities.

For instance, in the eastern part of the Democratic Republic of Congo, where the Batwa have been completely expelled from their lands, most members of these hunter-gatherer communities now speak either *Mashi*, *Kitembo* or *Kihavu*, which are the languages of the main ethnic groups into which the Batwa were forced to integrate.[189] The situation is the same in Rwanda, where the Batwa, although they argue that, at one time in history, they had their own language, today speak *Kinyarwanda*, the language of the main ethnic groups, the Tutsi and Hutu.

Members of the Ogiek people, who, in pre-colonial times, moved southwards from what is now known as Kenya and into Tanzania, also lost their original language and currently speak a dialect that is closer to the language of their neighbours, the Maasai.[190]

As victims of, and trying to hide or escape from prejudices, hunter-gatherers are often ashamed to speak their own languages. This was, for example, the case with the ‡Khomani San of South Africa: "Adults and children alike were ashamed of being San, and in a trend repeated by other hunter-gatherer peoples the world over, they increasingly assumed the ways and languages of their oppressors". Consequently, "the old language spoken by the San [fell] ... into disuse ... [and] was prematurely declared to be officially dead in 1970".[191] Today, it is estimated that there are far less than a thousand people who can still speak *N/u*, (name of the traditional ‡Khomani San language), without which it would not have been possible for the San

---

188 Woodburn, "Indigenous discrimination" (1997), p. 251.
189 M. Kapupu, "Etude du milieu des pygmées voisins du Parc National de Kahuzi-Biega, zones rurales de Kabare et Kalehe". A study commissioned by the German Agency of International Cooperation (GTZ), 1996, p. 8.
190 Sang, "Kenya: The Ogiek in Mau Forest" (2003), p. 115.
191 Chennells, "The ‡Khomani San of South Africa" (2003), pp. 278-279. One San elder interviewed during the reclaiming process stated: "My mother did not teach me N/u language because she was ashamed to speak it. I want to make sure that all the young people can learn the language, and can know that they own the Kalahari, where we all came from".

activists and community members to establish the different waterholes, hunting areas, ritual places, etc., which, once put together, established the San rights over the Kgalagadi Transfrontier Park of South Africa.

CHAPTER IV
INDIGENOUS PEOPLES' LAND DISPOSSESSION: CAUSES AND REACTIONS

Despite their cultural importance, the lands of indigenous peoples continue to be encroached and alienated. This chapter looks at the main causes of these dispossessions and how African indigenous peoples tend to react.

Main causes of land dispossession

Agriculture as central for national economies

As pointed out by Hugh Brody, agriculture has transformed the entire Earth to the extent that any unfarmed land is considered as being of little economic use.[192] Most Governments focus on modern development paradigms at the expense of traditional ways of production, and Africa is no exception when it comes to considering agriculture as central for national economies. In many cases, local communities, including indigenous peoples, are forced out of their lands without due compensation to make way for cultivation. The U.N. Committee on Social, Economic, and Cultural Rights (CESCR) reached the conclusion that "many activities undertaken in the name of 'development' have subsequently been recognized as ill-conceived and even counter-productive in human rights terms".[193] Or, as Chris Jochnick puts it: "Human welfare and the environment have been increasingly left to the vagaries of market, with Government playing almost second role in trying to ensure a basic level of welfare for their populations".[194]

---

192 Brody, *The Other Side of Eden* (2000), pp. 120 and 149.
193 CESCR, General Comment No. 2 (on Article 22). U.N. Doc. E/C.12/1990/23 (1990), para. 7. Available at http://hrlibrary.ngo.ru/gencomm/epcomm2.htm. See also Chris Jochnick, "Confronting the Impunity of Non-States Actors: New Field for the Promotion of Human Rights", *Human Rights Quarterly*, 21 (1999), p. 78.
194 Jochnick, "Confronting the Impunity" (1999), p. 64.

The need for economic growth, free movement of capital and, as highlighted by Samir Amin,[195] control and access to natural resources, have become the overriding objective for many States. This explains partly why most Central, Eastern, and Southern African States have declared themselves to be the sole owners of all land, including lands belonging to indigenous communities. "The States continue to hold legally defined *de jure* ownership rights over land … in much of rural Africa, while rural communities and individuals exert *de facto* rights which are partly defined in terms of customs and partly by ongoing adaptations of practices and rules to changing circumstances".[196]

Generally, the land claims of States are grounded on the assumption that lands used or occupied by communities are unoccupied, poorly developed, or vacant.[197] These are generally lands belonging to communities with a nomadic lifestyle whose use and occupation of lands are almost invisible. These communities are mostly hunter-gatherers and pastoralists.

In the 1960s and early 1970s, agricultural lands in Kenya and Tanzania were put under strong government control. In Kenya, the opening of the "White Highlands" of Kenya and the introduction of settlement schemes, which gave African cultivators access to land bought from departing European farmers, confirmed that the post-colonial development paradigms did not depart from an agricultural system type, and in 1973, the Rural Lands (Planning and Utilisation) Act No. 14, enabled the Government to bring all communities into cultivation. In Tanzania, a socialist-type of land policy known as *Ujamaa* was introduced in the late 1960s, and cultivation was considered to be the mode of subsistence "capable of generating growth from the [country's] own resources, while, at the same time, benefiting the majority of the people".[198] Many saw in the *Ujamaa* policy an attempt to transform all communities into cultivators.[199] People were moved into villages to work on common lands and expected to achieve a quota of cash crops.

---

195 Samir Amin, "The Challenge of Globalisation: Delinking" in *Facing the Challenge: Responses to the Report of the South Commission*, edited by the South Centre (London: Zed Books, 1993), p. 133.

196 Cousins, "Tenure and Common Property" (2000), p. 169.

197 Ibid., p. 155. Bernard Cousins also shows (p. 166) that, as far as land use in African rural areas is concerned, there is a clear shift from rule to practice in the analysis of land rights and tenure in Africa. It is not always what the law says, but what the practice is: "Despite efforts in many parts of rural Africa to clarify land rights and regulate processes of allocation … and transfer, access to resources remains subject to contest and negotiation. Access has continued to hinge on social identity and status, and hence on membership of groups and networks …"

198 See Ringo Tenga, "Legislating for Pastoral Land Tenure in Tanzania: The Draft Land Bill" (1998a), p. 3. Available online at http://www.whoseland.com/paper8.html; see also A.S.Z. Kiondo, "Structural Adjustment and Land Reform Policy in Tanzania: A Political Interpretation of the 1992 National Agricultural Policy", in *Agrarian Economy, State and Society in Contemporary Tanzania*, edited by P. G. Forster and S. Maghimbi (Aldershot: Ashgate Publishing Co., 1999), p. 44.

199 Rodger Yeager and Norman N. Miller, *Wildlife, Wild Death: Land Use and Survival in Eastern Africa* (Albany: State University of New York Press, 1986), p. 24.

The focus on agricultural land has been further illustrated by the fact that the majority of land legislation enacted in both Kenya and Tanzania has been in relation to cultivated lands. In Kenya, more than 15 laws on cultivation lands have been adopted against less than five on conservation lands; in Tanzania, more than 24 major laws related to land cultivation have been enacted from 1923 to 1999, against less than 10 on other types of land. The Strategic Plan for the Implementation of the Land Acts of 2005 clearly reflects that the Government of Tanzania is committed to modernize the agricultural sector and make land an important commercial asset and one of its conclusions is that "pastoralists have to be given land and told to settle (*meaning nomadic tradition has to stop)".[200] More recently, the Poverty Reduction Strategy Papers (PRSPs) of Cameroon, Congo, Rwanda, Uganda, and several other African countries clearly indicate the central role to be played by agriculture in national economies.[201]

The focus on agriculture and large scale encroachment of the lands of indigenous peoples by farmers has thus prevented most African Governments from paying attention to other ways of land use, including hunting, gathering and pastoralism.

Perpetuation of pre-colonial land control by individuals and Governments

Pressure on Kenya to liberalize the agricultural land market was mostly grounded on the failure by the settlement schemes and group ranches to kick-start national production. The Tanzanian *Ujamaa* policy was declared a failure because of its inability to increase the production of agricultural products such as cotton, tobacco, pyrethrum, and other cash crops.[202]

As shall be seen in the Kenyan and Tanzanian case studies on land laws and policies (Part II of this book), options of individual land holding tend to affect negatively land rights of indigenous peoples. The 1999 Tanzanian land laws show striking similarities with their Kenyan counterparts, which have not been amended for more than thirty years. For example, under the Kenyan 1968 Land (Group Representatives) Act and the Land Adjudication Act, an individual member of a "group ranch" could apply for a legal delimitation of his or her plot of land and consequently for an individual title. Similarly, under the 1999 Tanzanian Village Land Act, a village member can apply for an individual registration of part of the

---

200 United Republic of Tanzania, *Strategic Plan for the Implementation of the Land Laws, SPILL* (Dar es Salaam: Ministry of Lands and Human Settlements Development, 2005), p. 14.
201 All PRSPs can be found on the World Bank's Web page: www.worldbank.org/prsp
202 G. M. Fimbo, *Essays in Land Laws of Tanzania* (Dar es Salaam: University of Dar es Salaam Press, 1992), p. 10.

land of a given village. In both cases, the most feared consequence is that, once individually registered, such part of the village land or group ranches can then be alienated at will by its owner, even to outsiders.[203] Both mechanisms provide indeed for a gradual individualization of community lands.[204]

Furthermore, under both systems, lands are managed and administered by elected members of the villages or members of the ranches, and the Government keeps enormous powers of control and directive over these managing bodies. As Karuti Kanyinga puts it, in neither country the powers over lands are vested in community institutions.[205]

Looking at the whole continent and beyond the Kenyan and Tanzanian cases, it can be rightly argued that the post-colonial African leaders "failed to foresee the traps and snares that lay ahead ... They accepted the colonial legacy—whether of frontiers or of bureaucratic dictatorship—on the rushed assumption that they could master it".[206] The independence of most African States was underpinned, amongst other things, by a legal setting meant to perpetuate and protect the interests and property rights of the former colonial powers, foreign companies and investments.[207] This was done through the introduction of the Bill of Rights into the constitutions of the newly independent states:

> In the late fifties and early sixties when the colonies were nearing independence, the issue of Bill of Rights came to the fore. It was raised by the very Powers that had been suppressing it for years. But this time there was a good reason for it. The colonisers were leaving. The colonised were ascending into power. What of the property taken over during the whole period of colonialism by nationals and companies of the colonial powers? This had to be protected. Therefore the issue of the individual rights, especially the rights to own private property and state protection of the same, became one of the main topics of discussion on independence.[208]

Commenting on constitutional changes in post-apartheid South Africa and Uganda, Issa G. Shivji argues that constitutional changes amongst African States often result from a need for these States to "re-establish their credibility with the West-

---

203 Issa G. Shivji and Wilbert B.L. Kapinga, *Maasai Rights in Ngorongoro, Tanzania* (Dar es Salaam: Hakiardhi (The Land Rights and Resources Institute, 1998), p. 100.

204 Ibid., p. 101.

205 Karuti Kanyinga, *Re-Distribution from Above: The Politics of the Land Rights and Squatting in Coastal Kenya* (Upssala, Sweden: Nordiska Afrikainstitutet, 2000), p. 53.

206 Davidson, *Africa in History* (1992), p. 181.

207 Issa G. Shivji, "The Right of Peoples to Self-Determination: An African Perspective", in *Issues of Self-Determination*, edited by W. Twining (Aberdeen, Scotland: Aberdeen University Press, 1989b), p. 19.

208 Legal Aid Committee, *Essays in Law and Society* (Dar es Salaam: Faculty of Law, 1985), pp. 12-3; see also Shivji, "The Right of Peoples" (1989b), p. 19.

ern World",[209] and guarantee individual rights[210] so as to protect the interests of colonial masters. It can be seen, indeed, that most constitutions of African post-colonial States strongly protect individual ownership of land and very few provide for collective ownership of community lands, on which extractive industries and protected areas have been or are being implanted.

Strong conservation interests

The objective of developing a tourist industry has led large land tracts used by nomadic communities to become protected areas. In Tanzania for example, in 1961, at the time of independence, Tanzania had one national park, one conservation area and a number of reserves.[211] In 2007, the country had the highest percentage of protected areas in East Africa, namely 37.7 per cent of its territorial area.[212] A powerful Ministry of Natural Resources and Tourism has been created to oversee the work of various conservation institutions, including the Wildlife Division (WD); Tanzania National Park (TANAPA); Ngorongoro Conservation Area Authority (NCAA) and the Forestry Division.[213] "Between July 1990 and August 1993, the number of investment projects approved in the country was 80 in tourism, 58 in agriculture, and 41 in natural resources".[214] In 1994, tourism contributed up to 7.5 per cent of the Gross Domestic Product (GDP) and provided up to 25 per cent of total foreign exchange earnings.[215] More recent figures (2007-2008) indicate that "that the contribution of Travel & Tourism to Gross Domestic Product was 9.7 per cent

209   Issa G. Shivji (ed.), *State and Constitutionalism: An African Debate on Democracy*, Southern Africa Political Series (Harare, Zimbabwe: Southern Africa Printing & Publ. House, 1991), p. 27.

210   H.W.O. Okoth-Ogendo, "Constitutions without Constitutionalism: Reflections on an African Political Paradox" in *State and Constitutionalism*, edited by I.G. Shivji (1991a), p. 4.

211   United Republic of Tanzania, *Report of the Presidential Commission Inquiry into Land Matters*, (Dar es Salam, Tanzania and Uppsala, Sweden: Government of the United Republic of Tanzania/ Ministry of Lands, Housing and Urban Development, and the Nordiska Afrika Institutet, 1994), Vol.1, p. 263.

212   According to the United Nations Environment Programme /World Conservation Monitoring Centre (UNEP/WCMC), protected areas in other East African countries cover the following percentages of the territorial area: Uganda: 26.09, Ethiopia: 17.54, Kenya: 12.15, and Eritrea: 3.9. See UNEP/WCMC's Web site at http://www.unep-wcmc.org/wdpa/mdgs/index.cfm

213   David Bourn and Roger Blench, *Can Livestock and Wildlife Co-Exist: An Inter Disciplinary Approach* (London: Overseas Development Institute and the Environmental Research Group Oxford, 1999), p. 10.

214   C.S.L. Chachage, "Land Issues and Tanzania's Political Economy", in *Agrarian Economy, State and Society in Contemporary Tanzania*, edited by P.G. Forster, and S. Maghimbi (Aldershot: Ashgate Publishing Co., 1999), p. 67. Many investors are foreign companies like, e.g., the United Arab Emirate Safaris Limited, and their interests have sometimes resulted in the eviction of pastoralists (see chapter VI).

215   Halvor Wøien and Lewis Lama, *Market Commerce as Wildlife Protector? Commercial Initiatives in Community Conservation in Tanzania's Northern Rangelands*, Pastoral Land Tenures Series (London: International Institute for Environment and Development, (IIED), 1999), p. 9.

... and export earnings from international visitors and tourism goods were expected to generate 31.7 per cent of total exports".[216] Tourism was already in the 1990s becoming the second largest foreign exchange earner after agriculture.[217] At a certain time, Tanzania was making an annual amount of about US$1.3 million on entry fees and concessions in the Serengeti National Park alone.[218]

As for Kenya, there are now 291 protected areas covering approximately 12.15 per cent of the national land area,[219] and, according to Kenya's Ministry of Tourism, tourism accounted in 2007 for 10 per cent of the GDP, making it the third largest contributor to Kenya's GDP after agriculture and manufacturing.[220] The conservation sector has emerged as having the potential of becoming Kenya's largest earner of foreign exchange, and it is already today Kenya's third largest foreign exchange earner after tea and horticulture. Tourism has been identified as one of the key drivers in achieving the goals of the government's Vision 2030. [221]

This same trend of promoting conservation interests has also led to forced evictions of pastoralists in Tanzania, such as in the cases of Mkomazi and Usangu Plains, and to what happened, in November 1970, when the homelands of the Batwa of the Kahuzi-Biega forests, in eastern Democratic Republic of Congo, were gazetted as a National Park without their prior and informed consent.[222] Nor did, for example, the Maasai of the Ngorongoro Conservation Area in Tanzania, the Bagyeli of Cameroon, the Hadzabe of Tanzania, the Batwa of Uganda and Rwanda, the ‡Khomani San of South Africa, get consulted in relation to the creation of the Serengeti National Park, the Amboseli National Park, the Campo Ma'an National Park, Ngorongoro Conservation Area

---

216 World Travel and Tourism Council, at http://www.wttc.org/eng/Tourism_Research/Tourism_Satellite_Accounting/TSA_Country_Reports/Tanzania/, 12 December 2008.

217 J. Kweka, "Tourism and the Economy of Tanzania: A CGE Analysis". Paper presented at the CSAE Conference on .Growth, Poverty Reduction and Human Development in Africa, 21 - 22 March 2004, Oxford, UK. Available at: http://www.csae.ox.ac.uk/conferences/2004-GPRaHDiA/papers/1f-Kweka-CSAE2004.pdf

218 Lucy Emerton and Iddi Mfunda, "Making Wildlife Economically Viable for Communities Living around the Western Serengeti, Tanzania", Evaluation Eden Series, Working Paper No.1 (London: International Institute for Environment and Development (IIED), 1999), p. 17. Available online at: http://www.iied.org/pubs/

219 According to UNEP/WCMC, http://www.unep-wcmc.org/wdpa/mdgs/index.cfm, 12 December 2008.

220 Ministry of Tourism (Kenya) at http://www.tourism.go.ke/ministry.nsf/pages/facts_figures, 12 December 2008.

221 J. Mwanjala, "An Overview of Wildlife and Tourism Management in Kenya". Paper presented on behalf of Kenya Wildlife Service at the 3rd International Institute for Peace through Tourism (IIPT) African Conference on Peace through Tourism, held in Lusaka – Zambia, February 6th-11th, 2005; Ministry of Tourism (Kenya), http://www.tourism.go.ke/ministry.nsf/pages/facts_figures, 12 December 2008.

222 Barume, *Heading Towards Extinction*? (2001), p. 70.

and the Mgahinga and Bwindi National Parks, the Nyungwe Forest, the Kgalagadi Transfrontier Park, respectively. In all these cases, community land rights were ignored as if they had never existed. And most of the conservation areas in these countries are under regimes according to which human habitation or use of these lands by communities are prohibited.[223]

Strong logging and mining interests

In numerous other cases, indigenous peoples' lands are conceded to private or public business, including farming, fishing and logging companies.

For many countries of Central Africa, the logging sector has become one of the main sources of national income. According to the figures of the United Nations Foods and Africulture Organisation (FAO), in Cameroon, for example, with an annual production of more than 2.5 million cubic meters of timber, the forestry sector is the State's third source of hard currency (after agricultural and petroleum exports). It accounts for 8.9 per cent of the GDP.[224] In the Republic of Congo, the forestry sector produces about 1.5 million cubic meters per year and employed in 1999 almost six times more people than the oil sector.[225] With an estimated 125 million hectares of forest, forecasts estimate that logging with an estimated potential production of 6 million cubic meters a year could contribute significantly to the Democratic Republic of Congo's economy.[226] A regional forestry policy known as the 1999 Yaoundé Declaration, with an action plan called *Plan de Convergence*, states clearly that within the framework of the fight against poverty, Congo Basin countries intend to derive as much revenue as possible from forestry. This was restated in the final communiqué of the Heads of States Summit held in Brazzaville in February 2005.[227] Accordingly, most Congo Basin countries have recently passed on new forest laws (in 1994 in Cameroon, in 2000 for the Republic of Congo,in 2002 for the Democratic Republic of Congo and in 2008 in Central African Republic), which clearly reveal the Governments' intentions to derive a revenue at any cost from logging concessions.

A number of indigenous peoples' lands are also rich in minerals, including gold, diamonds, and coltan. This is the case of the CKGR in Botswana which is

---

223 Emerton and Mfunda, *Making Wildlife Economically Viable* (1999), pp. 3-5.

224 U.N. Food and Agriculture Organisation (FAO), Forest sector and forests: Cameroon country profile, see: http://www.fao.org/forestry/57478/en/cmr/

225 FAO, Forestry Department, see:
     http://www.fao.org/documents/show_cdr.asp?url_file=/DOCREP/003/X6778F/X6778F06.htm

226 Albert Kwoko Barume, "Le nouveau code forestier congolais et les droits des communautés forestières". Paper presented at the Workshop on the Implementation process of the Forestry Code of the Democratic Republic of Congo, Kinshasa 17-19 November 2003, Working Group on Forests and Rainforest Foundation, p. 3. Available online at http://archive.niza.nl/docs/200501181516531833.pdf.

227 See COMIFAC's Web site: http://www.comifac.org/accueilfr.htm

reported to be rich in diamonds and from which the San were recently expelled. Similar situations occur in South Africa, Namibia, Tanzania, Kenya and numerous other African countries. The mineral known as coltan, used in the mobile phone industry, is exploited on Batwa's ancestral lands, now a national park (Kahuzi Biega), in the Democratic Republic of Congo. Another project to exploit more than 50 million cubic tons of cobalt/nickel in the middle of Cameroon's tropical forests[228] will surely affect ancestral lands of indigenous Baka ("Pygmies") people. Oil exploitation will also increasingly affect land rights of African indigenous peoples as the continent continues its exploration efforts pushed by world powers in search for market diversification. Lands of the Bagyeli in Cameroon were also used for the construction of the Tchad-Cameroon oil pipeline.

Nation-state building

Unlike other continents, where the civil rights movement emerged in a context of relatively long-established independent States, against which victimized communities and groups were reacting, in Africa this human rights movement emerged simultaneously with the decolonisation process.[229] Consequently, the ideals and ideas that were behind this movement were "hijacked" by the new post-colonial African political elites. These elites wrongly assumed that the idea of "self-identity", cited amongst other principles of this movement, referred to states as formalized at the 1885 Berlin Conference and that the term "peoples" meant states.[230]

It emerged indeed that the post-colonial African political affairs were underpinned by two objectives, which in fact could not ever have prompted a human rights culture or a strong civil society. Firstly, in the name of national unity, considered as an antidote to the danger of "tribalism" leading to secession, the new

---

228 See on Web site of the cobalt mining company, the Geovic Company: http://www.geovic.net

229 The year of independence for the following Sub-Saharan countries (in alphabetical order) is: Angola (1975), Benin (1960), Botswana (1966), Burkina Faso (1960), Burundi (1962), Cameroon (1960), Congo DR (1960), Republic of Congo/Congo Brazzaville (1960), Ivory Coast (1960), Djibouti (1977), Equatorial Guinea (1968), Eritrea (1993), Gabon (1960), Gambia (1965), Ghana (1957), Guinea Bissau (1973), Guinea (1958), Kenya (1963), Lesotho (1966), Liberia (1847), Madagascar (1960), Malawi (1964), Mali (1960), Mauritania (1960), Mauritius (1968), Mozambique (1975), Namibia (1990), Niger (1960), Nigeria (1960), Rwanda (1962), Senegal (1960), Sierra Leone (1961), Somalia (1960), South Africa (1910), Sudan (1956), Swaziland (1969), Tanzania (1964), Togo (1960), Uganda (1962), Zambia (1964) and Zimbabwe (1980).

230 At what is known as the 1958 Accra First Conference of Independent African States, the post-colonial new African leaders stated "We, the African States assembled here in Accra, in this our first Conference, conscious of our responsibilities to humanity and especially to the peoples of Africa, ... affirm the following fundamental principles ... respect for the sovereignty and territorial integrity of all nations". The same line of understanding or using, indistinctively, the terms "nations", "peoples" and "states" was later also taken by the U.N. General Assembly's Resolution 1514 (XV) of December 14, 1960 on decolonization.

political leaders in Africa opted for nation-states policies.[231] Promoting the identity of communities was regarded as an obstacle to national unity and a source of instability. Thus "it became a ... strategy of the new Governments to subsume the national self-determination rights of ethnic groups into the rhetoric for the betterment of all ... and national unity".[232] In other words, "nation-building thus became the overall task of the newly independent countries", which intensified chauvinism and oppression of or discrimination against ethnic groups, such as the Hadzabe, the Maasai, the "Pygmies", and several other groups that attempted to claim an identity of their own.[233]

Thus, unlike America where the civil rights movement boosted civil society, in Africa the "democratic revolution aborted"[234] and the destruction of civil society became an approach taken by many dictatorships imposed upon the continent after independence.[235] Since then, the African "neo-colonial State has tended, for its own reproduction, to usurp and obliterate the autonomy of civil society and therefore the very foundation of democracy".[236] This behaviour has meant that the first generation of leaders of the newly independent African States failed to "recognise how damaging the division of Africa into modern states [by the colonial system] was to the identity of many peoples".[237] Julius Nyerere, president of Tanzania from 1961 to 1985, for example, warned against any attempt to try to redesign the African map.[238] Consequently, they furthered the "balkanization" of several communities, such as the "Pygmies", the San, the Maasai, the Mbororo and other peoples who found themselves living in several different states. [239]

This acceptance of the colonial legacy by the political elite of the newly independent African States was furthered by the militarization of the continent's politics. As noted by Eboe Hutchful, "it is estimated that between January 1956

---

231 Shivji, *State and Constitutionalism* (1991), p. 31; Shivji, "The Right of Peoples" (1989a), p. 35.
232 Lerner, *Group Rights* (1993), pp. 128-130.
233 Ernest Wamba-dia-Wamba, "Discourse on the National Question", in *State and Constitutionalism*, edited by I. Shivji (1991), p. 60; Shivji (ibid.), p. 33. Shivji elaborates also on the impact of the building of "nation-states" on national struggles and self-determination. Citing the cases of Rwanda, Burundi, Ethiopia, Tanzania, Sudan, and Nigeria, he underlines the oppression and discrimination that characterized most post-colonial Sub-Saharan African States in dealing with the cultural identity of their communities. Eritreans, Tigreans, Oromos, and Somalis are all communities that were denied their identity by the political leaders of Ethiopia. The Katangese community of the Democratic Republic of Congo was denied its right to self-determination.
234 Issa G. Shivji, *The Concept of Human Rights in Africa*, (London: CODESRIA Book Series, 1989b), p. 5.
235 Shivji (ed.), *State and Constitutionalism* (1991), p. 39.
236 Shivji, "The Right of Peoples" (1989a), p. 5.
237 Barume, *Heading Towards Extinction?* (2001), p. 24.
238 Davidson, *Africa in History* (1992), p. 184.
239 The "Pygmies" are found in Gabon, Central African Republic, Democratic Republic of Congo, Rwanda, Burundi, and Uganda. The San live in Botswana, South Africa, Namibia, Angola, Zambia and Zimbabwe as a result of the division of southern Africa into states. The Maasai live in Kenya and Tanzania and feel that they belong to the same community that existed before the Berlin Conference of 1885. The Mbororo are found in several African countries including Cameroon, Central African Republic and Nigeria.

and the end of 1985 there were sixty successful coups".[240] However, these coups did not resolve the ever-existing friction and divergent interests that characterized the relation between States and communities.[241]

The current African political leaders cannot be seen as being in a position to do better than their predecessors in relation to indigenous rights. Most current Central, Eastern, and Southern African political leaders tend to compensate "their economic weakness and political instability by denying their peoples the right to struggle and organize in opposition, protest, and revolt".[242] Other African leaders simply deny the existence of social and economic problems,[243] and therefore do not attempt any sort of "redistributive policy".[244] However, knowing deep down that they are failing their people, including indigenous communities, most current African political leaders live in fear of radical democratic tendencies or civil societies' call for justice, land restitution, to the extent that they could be described as "men concerned primarily with power and self-interest, not with real people facing real problems in the World".[245] Thus land rights of several social groups are often contested since States do not seem ready to abandon the doctrine of state ownership.[246] In other words, most "land laws in Africa ... are products of politics ... They have been enacted by and are directed at benefiting the ruling group in each country" and never the communities.[247]

Pressure/support from international donors

Pressure from international donors can sometimes also contribute to loss of lands by indigenous peoples. In both Kenya and Tanzania, overseas development assistance (ODA) and the World Bank have played and continue to play an important role in the conceptualization, design, and implementation of these countries' land laws and policies impeding on native communities' land rights. International donors have not only been pressing for the liberalization of land ownership, but also providing important support for new laws, reforms, and projects, which are blamed for the continuing assault on an already weak and almost non-

---

240 Eboe Hutchful, "Reconstructing Political Space: Militarism and Constitutionalism in Africa", in *State and Constitutionalism,* edited by I. Shivji (1991), p. 183.
241 Ibid., p. 187.
242 Shivji, "The Right of Peoples", (1989a), p. 103.
243 Davidson, *Africa in History* (1992).
244 Alicia Puyana, "New Challenges for Developing Countries", in *Facing the Challenge: Responses to the Report of the South Commission,* edited by the South Centre (London: Zed Books, 1993), p. 285.
245 Noam Chomsky, "World Orders, Old and New", in *Facing the Challenge: Responses to the Report of the South Commission,* edited by the South Centre (London: Zed Books, 1993), p. 140.
246 Delville, "Harmonising Formal Law" (2000), p. 121.
247 Patrick McAuslan, "Only the Name of the Country Changes: Diaspora of European Land Law in Commonwealth Africa", in *Evolving Land Rights and Tenure in Africa,* edited by C. Toulmin, and J. Quan (London: DFID/IIED, Natural Resources Institute, 2000), p. 92.

existent system of protection afforded to native communities' land rights. In Kenya, as will be shown later (chapter V), the strong criticisms and pressures that
led to the gradual abolition of the group ranches came from, among others, the
World Bank, which argued that the scheme was preventing other Kenyan
groups from acquiring land in Maasai districts and thus not promoting a liberal
use of land.[248] The current privatisation process that the land sector is undergo-
ing in this country could be regarded as strongly supported by these international financial institutions and donors.[249] In Tanzania, Ringo Tenga shows that
"what cannot be masked is that the World Bank and the IMF are at the centre of
the stage" of land reform in Tanzania. "Now the British Overseas Development
Administration [today known as the British Department for International Development (DFID)], has come in to complete the task of assisting in drafting a
new land code of (or for) Tanzania",[250] providing not only the funds but also the
human expertise.[251]

In a number of cases, donors' support to Governments continues even when
violations of indigenous peoples' rights are taking place. In the conservation sector, accounts by Bourn and Blench attest that:

> Tanzania has received a wide range of donor support for wildlife conser-
> vation since 1990, and increasing emphasis has been given to involving
> local communities in the process, and exploring ways in which the benefits
> of maintaining wildlife can be equitably shared. GTZ has been active in
> and around the Selous, and the EU in the Serengeti and Ngorongoro re-
> gion; and DFID in and around the Ruaha. USAID supported the Planning
> and Assessment for Wildlife Management (PAWM) project in the early
> nineties.[252]

In Kenya, similar supports from ODA and World Bank have been ever-present in
numerous projects including fencing National Parks and trying to provide alternative arrangements for communities depending on these areas. Such was the
case in 1977, when the Bank provided funds for a pipeline project that aimed at
channeling water out from springs located inside the fenced Amboseli National
Park to Maasai communities, whose only watering resources were those springs
to which they no longer had access. After the end of the project and having func-
tioned for some years, the system broke down for lack of maintenance and fuel

---

248 Rutten, *Selling Wealth* (1992), p. 476.
249 Kanyinga, *Redistribution from Above* (2000), p. 50.
250 Tenga, "Legislating" (1998a), p. 6.
251 The two Tanzanian Land Acts were drafted by Patrick McAuslan, a law scholar and expert in
     land laws. He has worked in numerous land related legal reforms in many developing countries
     on behalf of various foreign development agencies, such as the British DFID.
252 Bourn and Blench, *Can Livestock and Wildlife Co-exist?* (1999), p. 11.

and the conflict between the Maasai community and the Park re-emerged.[253] Whatever might be said about this World Bank project, it did not solve the fundamental problem, namely the fact that Maasai people are prevented from enjoying part of their ancestral lands.

The focus on agriculture as pillar of national economies, the protection of individual ownership of lands, strong conservation, logging and mining interests as well as the need for nation-state building and pressure from the donor community emerge as main causes of indigenous peoples' land dispossession in most parts of Africa. In other words, States, extractive industries and conservation agencies, three of the world's most powerful actors, battle the world's most vulnerable, poor, and powerless communities, namely, indigenous peoples. Yet, most indigenous peoples in Africa have not given up on their lands lost to outsiders. On the contrary, they appear to have developed a range of reactions against their dispossession.

African indigenous peoples' reactions to land dispossession

"They took the land on paper, but the land on the ground is ours."[254]

Indigenous communities in Central, Eastern, and Southern Africa appear to react to these state-led land dispossessions in two major ways: through immediate reactions and through long-term strategic reactions.

Immediate reactions

Amongst the most common immediate reactions of Central, Eastern, and Southern African indigenous communities to their land dispossession are "clandestine" use and occupation, often sustained by small-scale violent actions.

The Batwa of the Kahuzi-Biega Forest in eastern Democratic Republic of Congo continue to enter and use the resources of the forest despite the Government's interdiction to do so. Quite often, Batwa are arrested, detained and "subjected to brutal and inhuman treatments in order to deter them from entering the Park".[255] In 1995, tens of hectares of the Kahuzi-Biega National Park were burned down, obviously by people who were reacting to their expulsion from their lands.

---

253 Ted Cheeseman, "Conservation and the Maasai in Kenya. Trade off or Lost Mutualism" (n.d). Available online at: http://www.environmentalaction.net/aa_kenya_policy.htm

254 Statement by an elder Maasai of Iloodoariak/Kenya, cited by Sammy Oleku Ole Roore in "The Iloodoariak Land Scandal", in *Pastoralists in the Horn of Africa*, Minority Rights Group Report of a Workshop on Social and Economic Marginalisation, 8-10 December 1998, Nairobi-Kenya, p. 6.

255 Barume, *Heading Towards Extinction?* (2001), p. 82.

The Batwa of the Nyungwe Forest in Rwanda have continued to use these forests clandestinely, despite the Presidential Decree of March 13, 1992 that made "clandestine" use of forest a criminal offence.[256] The Nyungwe Forest Conservation Project that is essentially funded by the American organization Wildlife Conservation Society also has a strong anti-poaching policy. Those who are caught within this forest are fined up to 5,000 Rwandan francs (an equivalent of more or less US$10). This amount of money is almost unaffordable for most of the Batwa. In 1997, hundreds of hectares of this forest were mysteriously burned down by unidentified people.

In Uganda, the Batwa are forbidden to enter into the Bwindi National Park. However, "the majority ... still use it for vital subsistence and religious activities. They risk imprisonment or fines if caught but their dependence on forests is so fundamental to their way of life that they cannot be expected to stay away from it. The Batwa still collect honey and seasonal vegetables, lay traps for small game, collect herbal medicines and other forest products (vines for ropes, bamboo, etc.) and visit ancestral sacred sites for rituals and to make offerings. According to park officials, it has proved impossible to prevent the Batwa from using the forest despite the military guards and regular patrols."[257]

The Hadzabe of the Yaeda Chini and Meatu District areas of Tanzania are also regularly arrested and harassed for hunting on lands that they consider being their homelands, but which now belong to private hunting companies.[258] The Hadzabe from the area northwest of Balangida are also often arrested and detained on the same grounds of hunting illegally on lands which they consider theirs, but which are now exploited by the Robin Hurd Hunting Company.

The Ogiek in Kenya, too, rely on continuing use and occupation of their lands, the Mau Forests, despite the risk of being arrested, detained, and even tortured. A member of the Ogiek community met during a fieldwork visit confirmed cases of rape of Ogiek women by forest guards, as a means to force their husbands to leave their lands. Cases of burning down parts of the Mau forests have also occurred. But no-one knows whether this is because of the frustration of the Ogiek community.

The San also continue to use and live in the Central Kalahari Game Reserve (CKGR) despite several evictions by the Botswana Government. Similarly, their

---

256 The Presidential Decree of 1992 makes a reference to the provisions of Article 446 of the Rwandan Penal Code, which prohibits cutting of protected trees and other resources.
257 Penninah Zaninka, "The Impact of (Forest) Nature Conservation on Indigenous Peoples: The Batwa of South-Western Uganda; A Case Study of the Mgahinga and Bwindi Impenetrable Forest Conservation Trust", in *Indigenous Peoples and Protected Area in Africa: From Principles to Practice,* edited by J. Nelson and L. Hossack (Moreton-in-Marsh: Forest Peoples Programmes, 2003), p. 182.
258 Madsen, *The Hadzabe of Tanzania* (2000), pp. 73-5. Andrew Madsen gives accounts of frequent arrests and even imprisonments of Hadzabe for allegedly hunting on lands conceded to private hunting companies, such as the Tanzania Game Trackers Ltd.

Namibian fellows continued to "clandestinely" use lands taken away from them by the Government for conservation purposes.[259]

However, in comparison with other communities, hunter-gatherer communities rarely resort to violence. It is argued that hunter-gatherers do not often react violently to the loss of their lands because they only constitute small groups and because of their political insignificance combined with the lack of strong political institutions capable of organising a strong resistance.[260]

While indigenous pastoralists communities also react with "clandestine" use and occupation as immediate answers to actions aimed at preventing them from using or occupying lands that they believe to be theirs, they sometimes resort to violence. This happens when they are confronted with aggressive game wardens and law enforcers trying to hinder their herds' access to life sustaining resources, such as grazing and water.

Several cases of such violent confrontations have taken place in Kenya and Tanzania. In Kenya, clashes involving Maasai are principally based on land and water but also express the Maasai's deep frustrations over being repeatedly betrayed by broken promises. A case in point is the conflict around Amboseli National Park. When the Amboseli Game Reserve was gazetted as a National Park in 1974, the Maasai were offered a number of benefits as compensation for moving out of the Park. These benefits included: guaranteed access to water supplies, compensation for tolerating wildlife, increased infrastructure (i.e., schools, clinics), and direct benefits from tourism. The Government, however, failed to provide the Maasai the promised long-term benefits. For example, the pipeline worked for only a couple of years due to lack of maintenance, wildlife fees became sporadic and stopped after 1981, and direct benefits were almost non-existent.[261] In 1981, Maasai reacted by illegally entering the park, spearing animals in protest and spearing the PVC pipeline in hopes of getting some water.[262]

Clashes between Maasai and Kikuyu communities are relatively frequent. This happened, for instance, in January 2005, in the central Rift Valley when youths from the two communities fought using machetes, spears, bows and arrows and clubs. At least 15 people were killed. Many more were injured and thousands of people fled their homes. Evidence suggests that the clashes were mostly a result of competition for dwindling water for livestock. "The bone of contention is the use of River Ewaso Kedong whose volume of water has been reduced drastically because of the current drought. The Maasai, who live downstream, claim their neighbours upstream, the Kikuyu, are using the river water

259 James Suzman, *Minorities in Independent Namibia*, Minority Rights Group International Report (London: MRG, 2002), p. 24.
260 Woodburn, "Indigenous Discrimination" (1997), p. 352.
261 Leela Hazzah and Stephanie Dolrenry, "Coexisting with Predators". Paper presented at Nature, Wildlife, People – A symposium on wildlife protection and people's livelihoods, September 2007. Accessible online at http://www.india-seminar.com/2007/577.htm
262 Cheeseman, "Conservation and the Maasai in Kenya" (n.d).

for irrigation, thereby complicating the drought situation for them and their livestock."[263]

The same factors have been cited as major causes of friction among communities living in the arid northern and eastern districts of the country. Disputes over grazing and water also occur between different groups of indigenous pastoralists. This is for instance, the case in Northern Kenya, where there have been a number of violent conflicts between, among others, the Turkana and the Samburu.[264]

In Tanzania, confrontations have taken place in the Northern Highlands Forest Reserve (NHFR) in the Ngorongoro Conservation Area (NCA), where in March 1997, for instance,

> [A]n armed squad of NCAA's game wardens raided Nainokanoka herdsmen who were grazing their herds of cattle in that part of the forest which forms Irkeepusi Village. Three herdsmen were severely assaulted and beaten with the iron ends of their own spears while their *'sime'* (machete) were used to slash their herds of cattle with. Some 15 herds of cattle belonging to nine villagers were either killed, maimed or lost in the ensuing stampede. Maasai warriors mobilised immediately for war against the NCAA game wardens. A potential bloodbath was only averted after the intervention of the Maasai *Laigwanak*, the District Commissioner and the Member of Parliament for Ngorongoro District.[265]

But conflicts over land use or water resources may also pit Maasai against farmers. In December 2000, violent clashes between Maasai cattle herders and farmers in Morogoro Region,

> … left 31 people, mostly women and children, dead. The clashes between Maasai nomads and farmers … had been in progress since the end of October, but worsened during four days of fighting. … The 8 December attack was in revenge for the killing of two Maasai tribesmen and the slaughtering of 35 cows by the farmers … The combination of revenge and sheer anger at the confiscation of their herds compounded a conflict over land use to which there is no clear solution in sight.[266]

---

263 Navaja Ole Ndaskoi, quoting *The East African*, January 24, 2005 in "The Roots Causes of Maasai Predicament". Available online at http://www.galdu.org/govat/doc/maasai_fi.pdf (n.d.), p. 17.

264 See, for instance, James Bevan, "Armed Violence in African Pastoral Communities." Report commissioned by the Government of Kenya, the Swiss Confederation and UNDP (2007). The report gives an overview of land disputes that have developed into violence and looks at some of the root causes. Available online at http://www.genevadeclaration.org/pdfs/pastoral.pdf

265 For a more detailed account of this incident as well as of other similar incidents in the NHFR area, see Lissu, "Policy and Legal Issues" (2000).

266 IRIN Central and Eastern Africa – Weekly Round-up 50, 9-15 December 2000. Available online at http://iys.cidi.org/humanitarian/irin/ceafrica/00b/0028.html

Long-term strategic reactions

In addition to the various immediate reactions to their land dispossession, the indigenous communities of Central, Eastern, and Southern Africa appear to have developed long-term strategies for reclaiming their lands. These counter-attacking strategies could be grouped into three categories, as the following few illustrative examples show. The first two approaches (legal challenge and lobbying advocacy) appear to take a strategy whereby educated members of indigenous communities act on behalf of their fellows to challenge States. In contrast, the third approach (revival of community's history) could be considered as a strategy that consists of first mobilizing communities' belief in their land rights and culture, before making collective claims for the lands in question.

Legal challenges

This approach consists of legal challenges or court cases filed by indigenous communities against their Governments or private companies. To date, such cases have been filed mainly in Kenya, Tanzania, South Africa and Botswana and they will be specifically discussed in Part II of this book. If successful, a legal challenge can lead to the titling of indigenous peoples' lands.

Lobbying and advocacy

There are indigenous communities in Central, Eastern, and Southern Africa that have opted for the lobbying and advocacy approach. This approach consists of rallying as many influential actors as possible to their cause, and getting the injustices they suffer from put on the agendas of national and international debates.

The Bagyeli of Cameroon, for example, went to Washington where they had an opportunity to discuss the possible impact on their way of life of the planned oil pipeline between Chad and Cameroon.[267] Following a meeting with World Bank officials, the Bagyeli representatives called upon the Bank to make sure the following arrangements were made before the beginning of the project:

---

267 The 665 miles long oil pipeline from Chad to Cameroon was approved by the World Bank in June 2000. The World Bank provides up to US$240 million of the US$3.5 billion needed for the whole project.This Project has been subject to much criticism from indigenous communities because they felt that their existence is threatened by this pipeline. For more about this project and its implication on indigenous communities, see the Web site of the Forest Peoples Programme (FFP): http://www.forestpeoples.org/briefings.htm

a. full participative consultations with the Bagyeli communities are carried out again, by a team independent of the local elite, in a culturally appropriate manner so that the Bagyeli are fully informed of the negative and positive impacts of the pipeline;

b. the Cameroonian Government is educated about the general situation of Pygmies in Cameroon;

c. the Cameroon Government formally regularises the land tenure situation of Pygmies and allocates land to them;

d. measures are put in place to combat the inequalities which exist between the Bantu and the Pygmies, facilitate access to schooling, health services, and help Pygmies to obtain official documentation such as birth certificates and identity cards.[268]

The World Bank postponed its final decision on the project for a few weeks after this submission by the Bagyeli community before reactivating the whole process. In November 2002, a World Bank's inspection panel was finally sent to Cameroon for a fact-finding mission. Later on, the project was implemented, an Indigenous Peoples Development Plan was adopted and a number of corrective measures, even though regularly criticized, were put in place.

The lobbying and advocacy approach has also been adopted by the Batwa of Rwanda. Early in 2001, a member of this community addressed an open letter to the president of Rwanda, raising a number of issues particularly affecting his community and calling upon the Government of Rwanda to provide a special protective regime for the Batwa.[269] The Batwa community of Rwanda also hosted the first African conference on "Indigenous Peoples and Protected Areas in Africa: from Principles to Practice", which was held in Rwanda in September 2001. Attended not only by several representatives from international lobby and support groups for the cause of indigenous peoples but also by highly placed local government officials,[270] this conference served the Batwa of Rwanda to raise the profile of their situation. Since then, the Batwa of Rwanda have been active on several advocacy fronts including the Peer Review mechanism of NEPAD, the African Commission on Human and Peoples' Rights and similar relevant international fora.

---

268 Letter by the representative of the Bagyeli indigenous community to the World Bank. See on Web site of World Rainforest Movement, at http://www.wrm.org.uy/alerts/june00.html

269 See the full text (in French) of the letter written by a representative of the Batwa community of Rwanda to their President on the Web site of Héritiers de la Justice: http://www.heritiers.org/caurwaletpresi.html

270 In addition to more than 50 representatives of indigenous communities from Rwanda, Burundi, Uganda, Democratic Republic of Congo, South Africa, Cameroon, Kenya, and Namibia, the conference was attended by representatives from the Swedish Society for Nature Conservation, the World Wildlife Fund, and the Forest Peoples Programme.

Due to the conflict that affects the Democratic Republic of Congo, Batwa communities living in this country have not been very active at the national level. Instead, they appear to seize every sub-regional, regional, and international opportunity to put forward their case of land dispossession. Together with their Rwandan counterparts, they are trying to organize a network of Batwa indigenous peoples living in Central African countries.

The Ugandan Batwa, who were expelled from their lands, now known as the Mgahinga and Bwindi National Parks famous for hosting the mountain gorillas, also use the lobbying and advocacy approach in their struggle for regaining control over their lost lands. The "Mgahinga and Bwindi Impenetrable Forest Conservation Trust" was created by the Ugandan Government with a World Bank's grant of more than US$4 million. One of the duties of this Trust is to support the Batwa community through a number of projects. Since 1995, when the Trust became operational, most of the current efforts by Ugandan Batwa to regain control over their lands and its resources have focused on trying to get the World Bank to understand their case, as well as getting involved in the activities and objectives of the Trust as much as possible.[271]

Despite being established on lands and resources over which the Batwa of Uganda claim indigenous land rights, the Trust did not for a long time have one single member of the Batwa community on its Management Board, which is mainly composed of representatives from the Government, the tourist industry, and even other local communities.[272] However, in an attempt to try to get the Batwa involved in its activities, the Trust organized in 1999 a workshop which, for the first time, involved more than five Batwa. In September 2000, 101 acres of land were bought outside the limits of the Parks by the Trust for the Batwa community. The Trust has also built a number of schools attended by a few Batwa children. However, despite all these dispersed efforts, most Batwa feel that the Trust does not work in their interests and that the World Bank's funds instead were used to enable the Government to enforce their eviction from their traditional lands.[273] Consequently, the Batwa of Uganda continue contacting Uganda's major donors such as the World Bank, the USAID, and the Dutch Government, some of which are also non-voting members of the Trust and lobby for their case.[274] One result has been that the Dutch embassy in Kampala, for example, has

---

271 Zaninka, "The Impact of (Forest) Nature Conservation" (2003), pp. 11-5. See also IWGIA, *The Indigenous World 2005* (Copenhagen, Denmark: IWGIA, 2005). Available on http://www.iwgia.org

272 The Trust Management Board is composed of nine (9) voting members, with one member from each of the following governmental bodies: Uganda National Park, the Forest Department, the Wildlife Clubs of Uganda, CARE (an international development agency), the Institute for Tropical Forest Conservation, the Ugandan Tourism Association, and one representative from the Districts of Kisoro, Rukungiri, and Kabale.

273 Zaninka, "The Impact of (Forest) Nature Conservation" (2003), p. 15.

274 Ibid., p. 11. The USAID and the Dutch embassy in Kampala are amongst the non-voting members of the Trust.

agreed to fund the representation and participation of the Batwa in the work and institution of the Trust.[275]

In Kenya, and due to the numerous obstacles that their court cases have been facing, (see chapter V in Part II) the indigenous Ogiek community appears now to combine the legal avenue with a lobbying and advocacy approach. It has, for example, set up an electronic mailing list that helps dispatching information and updating the members of their lobbying and support network on any development relating to their claims. In 1995, 21 elders of the Ogiek community met with the Kenyan President, Mr. Arap Moi, on the issue of their lands. The Ogiek addressed a memorandum on the same issue to the Kenyan parliament in July 1996. More recently, the Ogiek and numerous other indigenous communities in Kenya have been involved in the process of consultations aiming at a constitutional revision. Lately, Maasai representatives went to Washington to lobby the World Bank to stop funding the Magadi Soda mine in Kenya.

Indigenous peoples in Tanzania have been active in key policy processes such as the development of the new Draft National Land Policy and the National Policy and Action Plan on Human Rights. Indigenous peoples have equally attempted to influence policy processes with a bearing on pastoral livelihoods in Tanzania through pastoralist and hunter-gatherer umbrella organizations. East African indigenous peoples are also increasingly using the media in their advocacy work, producing, for instance, radio programmes.

In 1997, two traditional leaders of the Himba community in Namibia toured Europe, visiting Germany, Belgium, Great Britain, Norway and Sweden. In all these countries, they met not only with grass roots campaign groups interested in hearing what impact the Epupa Dam would have on Himba communities but also with various political leaders.[276] Similar lobbying activities have been undertaken by the San, travelling, for example, several times to the USA to raise awareness of their situation in the CKGR.

Revival of the community's history

Thirdly, and as stated earlier, unlike the two first approaches that use top-down strategies, some indigenous communities have opted for a bottom-up strategy. This approach consists, for a community, of first reconstructing its historical values such as culture, social structures, ancestral land use and language, before challenging the State with their claims.

This seems to be the case of the ‡Khomani San of South Africa who, after realising that, as in most African countries, including South Africa, the laws do

---

275 Zaninka, "The Impact of (Forest) Nature Conservation" (2003), p. 12.
276 See http://www.earthlife.org.za/campaigns/other/epupa.htm

not state for the principle of aboriginal title, convinced themselves that "a strategy to reclaim land would need to be more creative than a direct legal challenge". The ‡Khomani San also believed that legal challenges could be costly, confusing, divisive, lengthy, and thwarted by the lack of independence that affects many African judiciaries.[277]

In 1996, the San decided to launch their claim to their indigenous lands and to base it on a multidisciplinary research and cultural reconstruction, which was made possible thanks to a systematic recording, from the few remaining San's elders, of their cultural values and the different sites used, occupied, and owned by the community. The research also compiled resources relating to the San language, reconstructed the San's genealogic lines, and re-created or restored the lost sense of pride in being San.[278]

Through these efforts, the community members came to believe in their right to the lands, and thanks to the technology of GPS (Global Positioning System) they were able to make their own maps of these lands. Once all these elements were assembled, the ‡Khomani San then confronted the South African Government with their demand to have their aboriginal lands given back to them. At first, this San community was given 40,000 hectares of farmlands outside the Kgalagadi Frontier Park, and in March 1999, the Government of South Africa, recognizing the rights of the ‡Khomani, awarded them in addition 25,000 hectares in the southern part of the Park, as well as commercial and symbolic rights in and to the remainder of the Park.[279]

Numerous other indigenous communities in Central, Eastern, and Southern Africa have been working on awareness raising as an advocacy tool, but the ‡Khomani San's approach continues to be considered as quite special given the length of its process, the anthropological materials it generated and its outcome.

In concluding terms, it appears that depending of the national socio-political context an indigenous community might prefer legal challenges to advocacy or combine both. However, indigenous communities should keep their options open and be ready to switch from one strategy to another every time the context changes or the original strategies do not work. In fact, numerous indigenous communities are combining several strategies for claiming back their ancestral lands' right.

One could argue that research and land titling are other strategies used by indigenous peoples. Indeed, some indigenous organizations use research and data collection as a way to strengthen their advocacy work. This is for instance

---

277 Chennells, "The ‡Khomani San" (2003), p. 274.
278 Ibid. Chennells writes: "It was decided to base the ‡Khomani land claim upon a solid bedrock of practical research, which would not only establish and confirm the ancient rights of the San to the land in question, but at the same time, the history and culture of the San community ..."
279 According to a personal communication by one of the San leaders who took part in the negotiation process, the community intends to use their regained lands for various activities, including eco-tourism, camping trails, tourism lodge and permanent settlement.

the case in Burundi, where the Batwa organization has undertaken a comprehensive land rights survey to document the deplorable land rights situation of the Batwa people in Burundi. A leading Batwa organization in Rwanda has undertaken similar work. But generally, such research is carried out as a tool for lobbying, strengthening a legal challenge or demonstrating either pre-existing land rights or highlighting human rights situations of indigenous communities.

Similarly, land titling could be a result of either a lobbying, legal challenge or a community revival strategy. This is for instance the case of some pastoralist organizations in Tanzania, which based their land titling claims on the provisions in the Village Land Act. This land-titling approach has been successfully pursued in Latin America; in Africa, however, so far, this has not been the case since the legal framework is generally not conducive to such activities.

PART II   THE JUDICIARY AND INDIGENOUS PEOPLES' LAND RIGHTS

This part presents and analyses court cases from Kenya, Tanzania, South Africa and Botswana, as examples that illustrate, on the one hand, an old fashioned or colonial-like approach that continues to deny indigenous peoples the right to their ancestral lands; and on the other hand, a new trend where judges are willing to adapt modern laws to local cultures and to draw on international jurisprudence.

The few cases referred to in this book are mere illustrations of attempts by African indigenous peoples to involve judges in their quest for justice on lands. This does not mean there have not been other court cases filed by indigenous peoples relating to others rights.[280]

The court cases are grouped regionally. The presentation of the various cases is divided in four sections dealing respectively with background facts and the claimants' arguments, the defendants' core legal points, the ruling and reasoning of the court and some concluding observations on the result and impact of the court case.

In the case of Kenya and Tanzania, which are the main focus of this Part II, the cases are followed by an analysis of the legal and policy landscape in the two countries in relation to indigenous peoples' land rights.

---

280 See, for instance, the Web site of the Kenyan Maasai NGO, Mainyoito Pastoralist Integrated Development Organisation (MPIDO) at http://www.mpido.org/prog.html

CHAPTER V
INDIGENOUS PEOPLES' LAND CLAIMS IN KENYA

This chapter illustrates the legal battle of Kenyan indigenous peoples by presenting a number of land-related lawsuits filed by Maasai, Ogiek and Endorois. It also provides the general legal, social and political context of these cases.

The Maasai and their land case

The Maasai are indigenous peoples living in both Kenya and Tanzania and their total population is estimated to be 500,000.[281] The Maasai are pastoralists and have a semi nomadic lifestyle. In Kenya, the Maasai, who are estimated to number 150,000, claim large areas of the Rift Valley, including Laikipia, as part of their ancestral lands.

Ol le Njogo and 7 Others v. The Honorable Attorney General and 20 Others. Civil case No. 91 of 1912 (5 E.A.L.R. 70), also known as the colonial Maasai case

Background facts and claimants' arguments

On 10 August 1904, a treaty, to become known as the Anglo-Maasai treaty, was signed between the Chief Lybon Lenana,[282] on behalf of the Maasai community, and Sir Donald Stewart, on behalf of the British Crown:

---

281 See Web site of the Maasai Association at http://www.maasai-association.org/welcome.html
282 The *lybon* is the ritual and spiritual leader of the Maasai; his authority is based on his mystic and medicinal/healing powers.There are some inconsistencies with regard to the spelling of the name of Chief Lybon Lenana. *Lybon* (plural form: *lyboni*) is sometimes spelled *laibon, loibon, olaibon* (in plural: *loiboni, oloiboni, olaiboni),* and Lenana (which is the spelling used in the Agreement as reproduced on the Web page of the Kenyan Coalition for Constitutional Reforms) is sometimes spelled Olonana (see, e.g., Rutten, *Selling Wealth,* 1992).

We, the Undersigned, being the Lybons and Chiefs (representatives) of the existing clans and sections of the Masai [sic] tribes in the East Africa Protectorate, having this 9th day of August, 1904 met Sir Donald Stewart, His Majesty's Commissioner for the East Africa Protectorate, and discussed fully the questions of a land settlement scheme for the Masai, have, of our own free will, decided that it is for our own best interest to remove our people, flocks, and herds into definite reservations away from the railway line, and away from any land that may be thrown open to European settlement.

We have, after having already discussed the matter ... given this matter every consideration, and we recognise that the Government, in taking up this question, are [sic] taking into consideration our best interests.

Now we, being fully satisfied that the proposals for our removal to definite and final reserves are for the undoubted good for our race, have agreed as follows:

That the Elburgu, Gekunuki, Loita, Damat, and Laitutok sections shall remove absolutely to Laikipia. ...

...

And by the removal of the foregoing sections to the reserve we undertake to vacate the whole of the Rift Valley, to be used by the Government for the purposes of European settlement. Further, that the Kaptei, Matapatu, Ndogalani, and Sigarari sections shall remove into the territory originally occupied by them to the south of Donyo Lamuyu (Ngongo), and the Kisearian stream. ...

...

In addition to the foregoing, Lenana, as Chief Lybon, and his successors, to be allowed to occupy the land lying in between the Mbagathi and Kiserian Streams from Donyo Lamuyu to the point where both streams meet. ...

...

In addition to the foregoing, we asked that a right of road to include certain access to water be granted to us to allow of [sic] our keeping up communications between the two reserved areas, and further, that we be allowed to retain control of at least 5 square miles of land ... whereat we can carry out our circumcision rites and ceremonies, in accordance with the custom of our ancestors.

...

We ask, as a most important point in this arrangement, that the Government will establish and maintain a station on Laikipia, and that officers whom we know and trust may be appointed to look after us there.

In conclusion, we wish to state that we are quite satisfied with the foregoing arrangement, and we bind ourselves and our successors, as well as our people, to observe them.

We would, however, ask that the settlement now arrived at shall be enduring so long as the Masai as race shall exist, and that European or other settlers shall not be allowed to take up land in the settlement. ...[283]

According to this agreement, about 11,200 Maasai were moved across the railway,[284] away from their ancestral lands in the Rift Valley and confined in two reserves. One reserve was in Laikipia in the northern highlands, the other in the south on the border with German East Africa/Tanzania. This last reserve was divided in two located in the Narok and the Kadjado areas, respectively.[285] The evacuated lands were immediately occupied by hundreds of white settlers.

Despite the fact that, in 1904, both parties had agreed that *"the settlement now arrived at shall be enduring so long as the Masai as race shall exist and that European or other settlers shall not be allowed to take up land in the settlement"*, a few years later, in 1911, the British colonial authorities then administering Kenya broke their promise and managed to conclude another treaty with a number of local Maasai leaders. As a result of this new agreement, the "northern" Maasai were moved again, at gunpoint, from Laikipia to an extended Southern Maasai Reserve. Upward of 20,000 people and at least 2.5 million livestock were moved between 1911 and 1913.[286]

Unhappy with this second treaty and acting on their behalf as well as on that of all the other Maasai of Laikipia, some members of the Maasai indigenous community decided to file a lawsuit before a Kenyan High Court, claiming that having not signed the 1911 treaty they were still bound by the 1904 treaty and, thus, still entitled to Laikipia. They argued that the 1911 agreement was "obtained under duress and is further not binding as it has not received the approval of the tribe". Furthermore, the plaintiffs claimed that the 1904 and 1911 signed documents were mere agreements and not treaties.

The plaintiffs asked the court to declare void and null the 1911 civil agreement for breaching terms of the previous one concluded in 1904. They further argued that this second agreement was concluded with individuals who did not represent the Maasai as a tribe. The suit named as defendants three colonial officials including the Attorney General, R.M. Combe, as well as twenty Maasai men who had collaborated with the Government, among them Segi, the Maasai Paramount Chief. The defendants were accused of having conspired to cause both physical and economic suffering on the Maasai resulting from the forced move.

---

283 For text of treaty, see Web site of Coalition for Constitutional Reforms (CCR) – Kenya: http://www.ccr-kenya.com/Resources/53.html

284 The newly completed Uganda-Kenya railway.

285 See Lotte Hughes, "Rough Time in Paradise: Claims, Blames and Memory Making Around Some Protected Areas in Kenya". *Conservation and Society* 5, no. 3 (2007), pp. 307–330. Available online at http://www.conservationandsociety.org/cs-5-3-307.pdf

286 Ibid.

Defendants' core legal points

The Attorney General of the then colonial power argued that treaties were acts of States and therefore not disputable in Protectorate courts. In fact, the colonial Government argued that the Maasai people constituted a nation and therefore the agreements were not mere civil contracts but treaties or "acts of States", which cannot be disputed in a municipal court. It thus avoided any debate on the facts.

Ruling and reasoning of the court

The High Court judge ruled in favour of the colonial Government by dismissing the case on technicalities. He supported the Attorney General's argument that treaties are acts of States and therefore cannot be dealt with in Protectorate courts.[287]

> [T]he other parties to this agreement were persons whom the Commissioner and the Governor, acting on behalf of the Crown, chose as representatives of the Masai Tribe with whom the Crown could enter into such agreements. The Masai tribe as living within the limits of the East Africa Protectorate are not subjects of the Crown, nor is East Africa British territory. But East Africa, being a Protectorate in which the Crown has jurisdiction is in relation to the Crown, a foreign country under its protection, and its native inhabitants are not subjects owing allegiance to the Crown but protected foreigners, who, in return for that protection, owe obedience.
>
> …
>
> In my opinion, there is here no legal contract as alleged between the Protectorate Government and the Masai signatories of the agreements, but the agreements are in fact treaties between the Crown and the representatives of the Masai, a foreign tribe living under its protection….
>
> …
>
> Now, are the acts of defendants complained of by the plaintiffs Acts of State?
>
> The answer to this is, in my opinion, contained in my finding that both the agreements are in fact treaties. For it follows from that finding that there was no such contractual relationship as alleged between the parties, and that in this action the plaintiffs are seeking by means of the court to enforce the provisions of a treaty. The Paramount Chief himself could not bring such an action, still less can his people
>
> …

---

287 *Ol le Njogo and 7 Others v. The Attorney General and 20 Others*, Civil Case No. 91 of 1912, 5 E.A.L.R. 70. Available online at http://www.ccr-Kenya.com/Resources/53.html

As regards the plea of duress and the want of approval of the tribe to the second agreement, as affecting its validity, it is not within the competence of this court, having held the agreement to be a treaty, to consider its validity as affected either by the pourparlers before its signature or a want of authority on the part of the signatories.

...

I hold therefore on the issue before me that the acts of the defendants complained of by the plaintiffs are in fact Acts of State, which are not cognisable by a municipal court.

The Crown, acting through its Commissioner, first made one treaty with the Masai, and subsequently acting through the Governor modified that treaty by another, and I cannot do better than to adapt to the present case the concluding words of Lord Kingstown in giving judgement in the Privy council in the case of Secretary of State for India v. K. B. Sahaba (XIII Moore 22*): "It may have been just or unjust, politic or impolitic, beneficial or injurious, taken as a whole, to those whose interests are affected. These are considerations in which this court cannot enter. It is sufficient to say that even if a wrong has been done, it is a wrong for which no municipal court of justice can afford a remedy".*

The action is dismissed with costs.

This decision by the High Court was confirmed in appeal by the Eastern African Court of Appeal (E.A.C.A.). This court ruled indeed that the protectorate was a foreign country; that the Maasai remained foreigners to the colonial power and as a tribe they amounted to a nation with whom treaties could be made.

Concluding observations and results/impact of the court cases

The rulings by the two courts have been much criticised for the dismissal of the case on technicalities. It is believed that any debate on the core issues raised by the plaintiffs could have had a different outcome[288] and one can see why the colonial Government did not want to go that way. The "Act of State" argument by both courts, which led them to rule that the 1904 and 1911 agreements were treapties and not mere civil contracts, is equally very disputable. Patrick McAuslan[289]

---

288 Even officials within the Colonial Office were uneasy about the case and the 1913 judgment. One of them went as far as concluding that he could not imagine the Privy Council supporting the judgment if it was brought before them on appeal. See Robert M. Maxon, *Struggle for Kenya: The Loss and Reassertion of Imperial Initiative 1912-1923* (Madison, N.J.: Fairleigh Dickinson University Press, 1993), pp. 64-65.

289 Patrick McAuslan, "Land Law and the Making of British Empire", in *Modern Studies in Property Law*, edited by Elisabeth Cooke (London: Hart Publishing, 2007), pp. 258-9.

wonders what element of sovereignty the Maasai remained with during colonial time, but says that ruling that the Maasai remained a sovereign nation was the only way the courts could take "refuge [behind the] British colonial constitutional doctrine of act of State". How could the Maasai remain sovereign over their lands when the Crown Land Ordinance of 1902, had already transformed all Kenyan communities into mere tenants of the Crown? This question reveals that the courts' reasoning was legally flawed, lacked logic and to some extent was dishonest.

The Maasai were given leave to appeal to the Privy Council in Britain, then highest Court of Appeal in the whole British colonial empire. But no such action was taken in time. It is believed the plaintiffs faced a financial problem and could not raise enough resources in time to finance such costly procedures that required travelling to Britain. Even if the plaintiffs had had the necessary resources, the same defendant Government was still the one to make the arrangements for such travels.

The Ogiek and their land cases

The Ogiek are indigenous peoples living in Kenya and they are estimated to number up to 20,000 countrywide and around 6,000 in the East Mau Forest, which is situated in Eastern Kenya.[290] The whole Mau Forest is made up of seven forested areas—South West Mau (Tinet), East Mau, Mau Narok, Transmara, Maasai Mau, Western Mau and Southern Mau. The Mau Forest, considered by the Ogiek as their ancestral lands, covers more than 250,000 hectares and provides more than 40 per cent of the Kenyan supply of fresh water.[291]

Joseph Letuya, Patrick Kibet Kuresoy and Others v. The Attorney General, The PC Rift Valley Province, Rift Valley Provincial Forest Officer, District Commissioner of Nakuru, Wilson Chepkwony, Director of Forest. Miscellaneous Civil Application No. 635 of 1997

Background facts and claimants' arguments

In the early 1990s, the Government of Kenya started allocating individual land plots to non Ogiek in and around the Mau Forest, on land the Ogiek consider as their ancestral lands. Large numbers of non Ogiek presented as landless were

---

290 Sang, "Kenya: "The Ogiek in Mau Forest" (2003), pp. 114-5. See also Kai Schmidt-Soltau, "Indigenous Peoples Planning Framework for the Western Kenya Community Driven Development and Flood Mitigation Project (WKCDD/FM) and the Natural Resources Management Project (NRM)", Final Report. (Nairobi: Republic of Kenya, 2006), p. 143.

291 Albert Kwoko Barume, "Indigenous Battling for Land Rights: The Case of the Ogiek of Kenya", in *International Law and Indigenous Peoples,* edited by Joshua Castellino and Niamh Walsh (Boston: Martinuus Nijhoff Publishers, 2005b), pp. 365-392.

being settled on the disputed lands. Following these land allocations, some members of the Ogiek indigenous community started being forcibly evicted. The Ogiek found that these actions by the Government amounted to a violation of their customary rights in the disputed land. So, on 25 June 1997, Mr. Joseph Letuya and twenty-one other Ogiek individuals filed a case in the High Court of Kenya against a number of government representatives, namely the Attorney General, the Provincial Commissioner of the Rift Valley Province, the Rift Valley Provincial Forest Officer, the District Commissioner of Nakuru, Wilson Chepkwony, and the Director of Forestry. The disputed lands are commonly known as the East Mau Forest and were gazetted against the wish of the Ogiek.

The plaintiffs argued that the allocation of their ancestral lands to individuals who were strangers to their community infringed their constitutional rights. They requested the court to declare that:

1. The right to life—protected by section 71 of the [Kenyan] Constitution —of every member of the Ogiek community in Mau Forest, including the applicants, has been contravened and is being contravened by forcible evictions from the parcels of land in the Mau Forest and pretended settlements by the Rift Valley Provincial Administration.

2. The eviction of the Ogiek community from their land in Mau Forest by the Rift Valley Provincial administration is a contravention of their right to protection of law, and their right not to be discriminated against under sections 77, 81 and 82 of the Constitution.

3. The pretended settlement scheme under which the Rift Valley Provincial Commissioner, the Forest officer and the Nakuru District Commissioner are allocating land to persons from Kericho, Bomet, Transmara and Baringo Districts in the Mariashoni location, Elburgon division and Nessuit location, Njoro division, Nakuru district occupied by the applicants ... [is in breach of] the Agriculture Act and the Forests Act and is null and void.[292]

The applicants underscored also that they had lived in the East Mau Forest since time immemorial, long before the creation of the Kenyan State and that their livelihood derived from it.

> Before the birth of our nation, our ancestors were living in the Mau Forest as food gatherers and hunters. Upon the introduction of the colonial rule, our ancestral land was declared a forest. Since that declaration of our ancestral land as a forest, members of our community have led a very precarious life which has been deteriorating.[293]

---

292 *Joseph Letuya and Others v. The Attorney General and Others,* Miscellaneous Civil Application No. 635 of 1997.
293 Ibid.

Furthermore, the plaintiffs requested from the High Court an order or injunction restraining the respondents or the Government of Kenya from any further allocations on the disputed land.

Referring to the legal basis of their claims, the plaintiffs contended that:

1. Section 71 of the Constitution guarantees every one the enjoyment of the right to life which includes protection of one's means of livelihood as the Supreme Court of India has held in *Olga Tellis v. Bombay Municipal Corporation* (1996) AIR 180 (S;)
2. Sections 78 and 82 of the Constitution protect each community's right to live in accordance with its culture;
3. The international human rights jurisprudence recognises the right to development of the disadvantaged sections of the political community like the Ogiek and that this right has been and is being contravened.[294]

Defendants' core legal points

Local officials argued that the Government had decided to carry out a settlement scheme on the disputed lands so as to address the problem of land shortage faced by numerous other Kenyans. It was also argued that the disputed land was part of public land on which the Ogiek had no special right. The defendants, who were beneficiaries of the contested allocations, argued that they had lawfully acquired rights to the disputed land.

Ruling and reasoning of the court

On October 25, 1997, the High Court responded favourably to one of the applicant's demands with an order that there should be no further allocation of the debated lands until the suit had been heard and determined.

After the court's order of 1997, there came no further action, not even a further hearing as the case kept being postponed. This until 30 January 2001, when the Minister for Environment made the following announcement in the press:

In accordance with the provisions of section 4(2) of the Forests Act, the Minister for Environment gives twenty eight (28) days' notice, with effect from the date of the publication of this notice, of his intention to declare that the boundaries of the Eastern Mau Forest will be altered … [by] approximately 35,301.01 hectares. …

294 Ibid.

This notice, published in the Official Gazette on 16 February 2001, concerned primarily the land subject of the court case filed by the Ogiek. The size of the disputed land was to be reduced with up to more than 35,000 hectares, which were to be put to other uses by the Government. This was considered by the plaintiffs as a breach of the 1997 High Court's decision that ordered the Government not to take any further action on the disputed land until the matter was concluded in court. Thus, in March 2001, the Ogiek plaintiffs asked the same court (High Court of Kenya) to quash the Gazette notice published by the Minister for Environment and to order that no action be taken on the basis of this Gazette notice. The plaintiffs argued that:

> (1) the said Gazette Notice of 2001 is a blatant violation of the order of the High Court of 1997; (2) the said Gazette Notice has in the circumstances of this case no legal basis; (3) the respondent, both in his capacity as a citizen of Kenya and a Minister in the Government of Kenya, is bound at all times to respect, obey and uphold orders of this honourable court; (4) the said Gazette Notice is a contempt to court by the respondent.[295]

Since then, no other judicial decision has been taken in this case despite numerous attempts by the Ogiek to activate the process. In the meantime, the Government has continued with forced evictions of communities, including Ogiek communities, in the area. A common 2007 report based on investigations by several international and national NGOs, notably Amnesty International, the Centre on Housing Rights and Evictions, Kenyan Land Alliance, Hakijamii Trust and Kenyan National Commission on Human Rights, concluded that,

> Incidents of forced evictions have been reported in different areas of the Mau Forest since 2004, affecting thousands of families. ... The cases of eviction in Mau Forest, discussed in this report, reveal a failure by the authorities to abide by international human rights and standards in respect of evictions. The notice provided was inadequate and confusing and there was no consultation with residents or effort to find an alternative to evicting them from their homes. None of the evictions was carried out on the basis of a court order; on the contrary, a court injunction halting evictions was ignored.[296]

In July 2008, Kenya's Prime Minister established a "Task Force on the Conservation of the Mau Forest Complex" to look into the Mau question. The Task Force

---

295 Ibid.
296 Amnesty International et al., "Kenya Nowhere to go: Forced Evictions in Mau Forest". Briefing Paper, May 2007. Available online at:
     http://www.asiapacific.amnesty.org/library/Index/ENGAFR320062007?open&of=ENG-398

published its report in March 2009, recommending, among other things, that all settlers be evicted from the Mau complex as soon as possible. Kenya's parliament adopted the report in September 2009 and it is feared that many of the Ogiek people will now be evicted from the Mau Forest.

Concluding observations and results/impact of the court case

1. This case represents one of the best illustrations of delays being used as tactics by a Government against indigenous peoples' court cases on lands. In this case, a Government buys time to engineer new actions and assaults on the disputed lands. This is also a case that could be taken to international mechanisms such as the African Commission on Human and Peoples' Rights given that the unwillingness of the judges and collusion with the Government seem apparent.

2. The major lesson drawn from this case is the relevance of asking for intermediary measures, similar to the Court Order that the Ogiek plaintiffs asked and obtained from the Kenyan High Court, in order to stop the situation from worsening as the court case proceeds. Even if it apparently did not prevent the Kenyan Government from further actions, asking intermediary measures are highly recommendable in similar cases.

Francis Kemei, David Sitienei and Others v. The Attorney General, the PC Rift Valley Province, Rift Valley Provincial Forest officer, District Commissioner Nakuru. Miscellaneous Civil Application No. 128 of 1999

Background facts and claimants' arguments

This court case was initiated by ten plaintiffs representing 5,000 other members of the Ogiek community of the Tinet Forest in south western Mau Forest, one section of the lands the Ogiek peoples claim as their ancestral lands and on which they have lived since time immemorial.

After being declared and gazetted as Forest Reserve during colonial time, there were numerous unsuccessful attempts in the early 1990s to evict the Ogiek from the disputed lands. Even when the Government managed to evict some, they returned into the forest almost immediately. According to the Forests Act (Cap 385), no cutting, grazing, removal of forest produce or disturbance of the flora is allowed in such natural reserves, except with the permission of the forest authorities. It is also prohibited to be found in a forest area between 9 p.m. and 6 a.m. Similarly, it is strictly prohibited building within a gazetted forest.

In 1999, the Government of Kenya through the District Commissioner issued a 14 days ultimatum. A few days later, the ultimatum was followed by another order to vacate the disputed lands or risk a forceful eviction by the Government.

In prevention of such a strong action by the Government, ten members of this Ogiek community decided in June 1999 to challenge the threat of eviction in court. In so doing, the plaintiffs, who managed to also represent 5,000 other members of their community, alleged that they depend, for their livelihood, on this forest since they are primarily food gatherers, hunters, peasants farmers, bee-keepers and their culture is associated with this forest where they have their residential houses. They argued that their culture is basically concerned with the preservation of nature so as to sustain their livelihood and that the Tinet Forest was their ancestral land on which they depend for physical and spiritual survival. On these grounds, as developed further in their affidavits, the plaintiffs asked the court to declare that:

1. Their eviction from Tinet Forest by the Government contravenes their rights to the protection of the law, to not be discriminated against, and to reside in any part of Kenya;
2. Their right to life has been contravened by the forcible eviction from the Tinet Forest;
3. The Government compensate the plaintiffs; and
4. The defendants pay the costs of the suit.

Defendants'core legal points

The respondents presented their defence argument around four main points. They claimed and argued that:

1. The plaintiffs were not the genuine members of the Ogiek community and that they had not been living in Tinet forest since time immemorial.
2. The plaintiffs had entered illegally in the Tinet forest, after the Government had shelved its plan to degazette this forest as it was considered one of the main water catchments. Since then, the Government has been trying to have the plaintiffs evacuate this protected land.
3. Rights and freedoms enshrined in the Constitution are subject to limitations designed to ensure that their enjoyment by individuals does not prejudice the rights and freedoms of others or public interests.
4. The plaintiffs were not landless as they claimed to be. That, in fact, since colonial time, members of this community had been resettled with other Ogiek.
5. The eviction was not discriminatory, as all illegal occupiers of the disputed lands would be asked to leave. It was also argued that the plaintiffs were no longer depending on forest resources

Ruling and reasoning of court

In March 2000, the High Court made an interesting starting point:

> *These people do not think much of a law which will stand between them and the Tinet Forest. In particular, of the Forests Act, they say ... that it found them there in 1942 when it was enacted.*

This reasoning could have led the High Court to develop an argument for an aboriginal title, showing that the rights of the Ogiek indigenous peoples to the disputed lands were ancient with respect to government measures. Unfortunately, the court did not go that far; it ruled against the plaintiffs by firstly attacking the community's alleged environmentally-friendly culture:

> *Whilst in their undiluted culture, the Ogiek knew their environment best and exploited it in the most conservational manner, they have embraced modernity which does not necessarily conserve their environment. As we have just said, they cannot build a school or a church house, or develop a market centre, without cutting down a tree or clear a shrub and natural flowers on which bees depend, and on which bee-hives can be lodged, from which honey can be collected, and from which fruits and berries can be gathered.*

Secondly, in disagreement with the plaintiffs' argument of a violation of their right to life in case of their eviction, the High Court judges made reference to an Indian case that they did not find compelling when applied to the Ogiek case:

> *We were referred to the Indian case of* Tellis and Others v. Bombay N Municipal Corporation and Others *[1987] LRC (Const) 351, on the first point concerning the right to life as one of the constitutional fundamental rights. It was a case of the forcible eviction of pavement and slum dwellers in the city of Bombay, India. When we read the case, we found its main thrust on this point to be that, although the right to life was a wide and far reaching right, and the evidence suggested that eviction of the petitioners had deprived them of their livelihood ... the Supreme Court of India ... found and decided and concluded that Bombay Municipal Corporation were justified in removing the petitioners, even though these pavement and slum dwellers were probably the poorest of the poor on the planet Earth. ...*

> *[The] Tellis case is not, therefore, helpful to the present applicants. The applicants are not the poorest ... records show that they by themselves or by their ancestors were given alternative land during the colonial days, and such alternative land for Tinet Forest was compensated. All along they have had a fair opportunity to come*

to the court to challenge the many evictions that have gone on before, but they have never done so till this late.

Thirdly, the High Court judges disconnected land ownership from untroubled land use and occupation:

> *To say that to be evicted from the forest is to be deprived of the means to livelihood because then there will be no place from which to collect honey or where to culti-vate and get wild game, etc., is to miss the point. You do not have to own a forest to hunt in it. You do not have to own a forest to harvest honey from it. You do not have to own a forest to gather fruits from it. This is like to say, that to climb Mount Kenya you must own it; to fish in our territorial waters of the Indian Ocean you must dwell on, and own the Indian Ocean; to drink water from the weeping stone of Kakamega you must own that stone; to have access to the scenic caves of Mount Elgon you must own that mountain. But as we all know, those who fish in the Lake Victoria do not own and reside on the lake. ... there is no reason why the Ogiek should be the only favoured community to own and exploit the sources of our natural resources, a privilege not enjoyed or extended to other Kenyans.*

The judges went on arguing that:

> *If hunting and gathering in a territory were in themselves alone to give automatic legal proprietary rights to the grounds and soils we hunt and gather upon, then those who graze cattle nomadically in migratory shifts everywhere according to climatic changes would have claimed ownership of every inch of every soil on which they have grazed their cattle. ...*

The High Court avoided confronting the plaintiffs' argument built upon the the-ory of aboriginal title and survival of customary land right following succession of powers and sovereigns as presented in the Australian *Mabo* case. The unease of the High Court is very obvious. Firstly the judges argued to have not been provided with the necessary materials and arguments by the plaintiffs:

> *We have missed the opportunity to closely analyse the whole law of our land, stat-utes and customary laws were not argued for, and the case was presented within the narrow limits of the forest legislation and the extra-curial struggles and resis-tance of the people who had been removed from the place and relocated elsewhere. Although we were denied the opportunity by lack of full and any serious argument on, and analysis of, the various relevant land statutes, customary law rights, and common law, we read the Mabo case, but found that the material facts in it, and which led to the propositions of principle there, cannot be fairly likened to those obtaining in the instant case.*

Secondly, the High Court judges argued that, contrary to the plaintiffs in the *Mabo* case, the respondents were nomadic and therefore not able to establish long lasting use and occupation of a given land, implying thus that only sedentary life style could generate rights over lands:

> *The applicants there* [in the *Mabo* case] *had a culture and rights sharply different from those of the applicants in the instant case. Theirs was a life of settled people in houses in villages in one fixed place, with land cultivation and crop agriculture as their way of life. They lived in houses organised in named villages, and one would be moving from one village to another. Land was culturally parcelled out to individuals, and boundaries are terms of known landmarks. Gardening was of the most profound importance to the inhabitants at and prior to early European contact. ... In that kind of setting, those peoples' rights were to the land itself. Our people of Tinet Forest were concerned more with hunting and gathering, with no territory fixity. They traditionally shifted from place to place in search of hunting and gathering facilities. ...Whether a people without fixity or residence could have proprietary rights to any given piece of land, or whether they only had rights of access to hunting and gathering grounds—whether a right of access to havens or birds, game, fruits and honey gives title to the lands where wild game, berries and bees are found—were not the focus of the arguments in this case; and the material legal issues arising from the various land law regime were not canvassed before us as they were in the Mabo case.*

The High Court judges concluded then by stating that,

> *The pre-European history of the Ogiek and the plaintiffs was not presented ... in court* [*and that nothing showed*] *early history to ... confer them with any land rights. ... For these reasons the Court dismisses all prayer sought. ... In the context of this case, we know no safer ways for this country and for these litigants, than dismissing this case with costs to the respondents.*

Concluding observations and results/impact of the court case

1. The High Court made a questionable assumption that most Ogiek people have moved away from traditional way of life and embraced modernity. This unfunded assumption was made in order not to accept the plaintiffs' arguments that their indigenous way of life was threatened of extinction and that they could not survive outside their ancestral lands, the Tinet Forest.
2. The High Court refused to be dragged into international jurisprudence. The Ogiek's lawyers referred indeed to a court ruling in India that linked

an eviction with a violation of the right to life of the evictees. The community's lawyers also referred to the Australian *Mabo* case and argued for an aboriginal title of the Ogiek that survived the transformation of the lands in dispute into a forest reserve. On both occasions, the High Court simply argued that the facts and the contexts were different from the situation in Kenya.

3. What is very particular and obvious in this case is the High Court's effort or apparent deep belief that a nomadic life style over a land cannot be considered as source of legal rights. It was explicitly argued, for example, that *"if hunting and gathering in a territory were in themselves alone to give automatic legal proprietary rights to the grounds and soils we hunt and gather upon, then those who graze cattle nomadically in migratory shifts everywhere according to climatic changes would have claimed ownership of every inch of every soil on which they have grazed their cattle"*. Had it been a case by agriculturalists that had established large farms and habitations on the disputed land, would a similar reasoning and conclusion have been made?

4. What would have happened if the Richtersveld case in South Africa (see chapter VII of this book) had already been ruled upon by the Constitutional Court of South Africa? In this case, the Constitutional Court recognized the notion of aboriginal title in Africa as argued by the lawyers of the Ogiek. This underlines indeed the importance of international law and standards.

5. This case also reveals that despite having the law on their side and even being defended by competent lawyers who grapple very well with international standards, indigenous peoples are in most cases denied justice in Kenya.

On 19 October 2001, the disputed forest land was degazetted by Notice No. 148 published in Kenya Gazette Legislative Supplement No. 147 of 2001. Once again, in March 2005, the plaintiffs went to the same High Court and requested an "Order of prohibition to prohibit the Respondents, their agents, servants and/or officers from preparing, processing and/or issuing title deeds in respect of [the disputed land]". The case is yet to be heard and decided upon. In the meantime, some of the plaintiffs continue to live on their lands.

The Endorois and their land case

The Endorois are an indigenous pastoralist community depending on livestock, including cattle, sheep, and goats. Their estimated population is 60,000. Like many other pastoralist communities in Kenya, the Endorois have traditionally occupied and used large areas of the Baringo District in Rift Valley and sometimes roamed as far north as to the Laikipia plains.

The problems of the Endorois started in 1973 when part of their lands, namely the Mochongoi Forest, was gazetted as a state forest, causing a loss of large grazing areas for the Endorois community. The disputed lands are found around Lake Bogoria, known previously as Lake Hannington, in the Rift Valley province. The lake and its surroundings were gazetted in 1973 as the Lake Hannington Game Reserve, and when the lake's name changed to Bogoria in 1978, re-gazetted under the name of Lake Bogoria Game Reserve. The Lake Bogoria is known for its geysers, boiling pools, hot springs, flamingos and pelicans. The surrounding area, which together with the lake constitutes the Game Reserve, protects Kenya's remaining herd of greater Kudu.

Following these gazettements, an estimated 400 Endorois families were displaced after receiving a compensation, which many have disputed or considered inappropriate.[297]

William Arap Ng'asia & 29 Others suing on the behalf of over 43,000 Other Members of the Endorois Community v. Baringo County Council and Koibatek County Council (1997-2000). HC - Nakuru, Miscellaneous Civil Application No. 522 of 1998

Background facts and claimants' arguments

In August 1997, William Arap Ng'asia and Others lodged with the High Court at Nakuru a Miscellaneous Civil Application No. 214 of 1997 (dated 4 August 1997) for leave to file a representative constitutional reference case on behalf of the Endorois Community's 43,000 members and against the Baringo and Koibatek County Councils. Leave was granted and the substantive application was filed as High Court Miscellaneous Civil Application No. 522 of 1998.

The applicants claimed that they were "peasant nomadic pastoralists residing on trust land areas peripheral to the Lake Bogoria Game Reserve ... [that] all the lands within these boundaries were what the British Colonial Administration after 1895 called Endorois location".[298] They went on to state that "their ancestral land parcel of approximately 30-50 km radius around Lake Bogoria was set aside by the defendants to create Lake Bogoria Game Reserve sometime in 1973". The plaintiffs highlighted also the cultural value of the disputed land, including leaking sites for livestock, medical plants that grow around the lake and spiritual sites for traditional ceremonies. They stated that "Lake Bogoria was formed

---

297 See Cynthia Morel and Korir Singoei, "Matter: Right to Land, Case 151, Kenya 1" (Applied Human Rights Association (AHRA), July 2004). Available online at
    http://www.ilsbu.com/cases_page/default.htm.
298 *William Arap Ng'asia & 29 Others v. Baringo County Council and Koibatek County Council,* HC - Nakuru, Miscellaneous Civil Application No. 522 of 1998.

when, due to inequities and sins of some clans and families of the community, the ground sunk with them one night after a heavy rain, hence the lake was formerly known as Lake Hannington. The families that survived the tragedy of the lake formation are the present day Endorois of Kapsaragi and Kapsogomo".[299]

Due to a procedural error, the application had, however, to be withdrawn and the applicants to subsequently seek—and be granted—fresh leave to commence a representative suit on behalf of the Endorois community. The Miscellaneous Civil Case No. 183 of 2000 thereafter proceeded to the High Court of Kenya at Nakuru on 19 August 2000.[300]

The plaintiffs requested from the High Court:

1. A declaration that the land around Lake Bogoria is the property of the Endorois community held in trust for their benefit by the County Council of Baringo and the County Council of Koibatek …
2. A declaration that the County Council of Baringo and County Council of Koibatek are in breach of trust fiduciary duty to the Endorois Community because of their failure to utilise the benefits accruing from the game reserve to the benefit of the community …
3. A declaration that the applicants and the Endorois community are entitled to all the benefits generated through the game reserve exclusively and/or in the alternative the land under game reserve should revert to the community under the management of Trustees appointed by the community …
4. An award of exemplary damages arising from the breach of the applicants constitutional rights.

Defendants' core legal points

The two defendants, namely Baringo and Koibatek County Councils, argued that the disputed lands had been gazetted as a game reserve, and that according to Sections 114 and 115 of the Kenyan Constitution, Trust Lands are vested in County Councils.

Ruling and reasoning of the court

In 2002, the High Court ruled against the plaintiffs despite recognising them as customary residents of the disputed lands. The judges grounded their ruling against the applicants firstly on the mechanisms of Trust Lands' management as provided for by the Constitution and secondly on compensation allegedly paid

299 Ibid.
300 See Morel and Singoei, "Matter: Right to Land" (2004).

to communities when the Lake Bogoria and surrounding lands were gazetted as game reserve.

As expressed by the judge:

> *Lake Bogoria Game Reserve is gazetted in accordance with the provisions of the relevant Acts and especially under Wildlife (Conservation and Management) Act cap. 376, Laws of Kenya … Section 114 of the Constitution is an interpretation section which defines what is a Trust Land under the Constitution. Section 115 vests Trust Land on County Councils and section 117 makes provisions for the County Council to set apart an area of Trust Land for certain purposes but it can only do so in accordance with an Act of Parliament. …. Both sections 115 and 117 have a proviso. The proviso is to the effect that no right, interest or other benefit under African Customary Law shall have effect for the purposes of the Act so far as it is not repugnant to any written law… .*

By so arguing, the judges aimed at showing that the disputed lands were legally under the defendants' management and that no customary law can be accepted to overrule such a written law. The judges also argued that the *"law does not allow individuals to benefit from the natural resource simply because they happen to be born close to that natural resource"*.

Furthermore, the judges argued that legal procedures for compensation were strictly respected at the time of events and that if the plaintiffs did not agree with the compensation scheme, they should have appealed, which they did not do.

> *The applicants have admitted in affidavits that, when the disputed land was set apart for use as a game reserve, meetings were held and compensation paid… It was upon the applicants and other residents who were affected to make use of their right of appeal and appeal against the award of compensation …. We note that none of the claimants appealed…. It is now too late to complain.*

Having so argued, on 19 April 2002, the High Court judges concluded that they:

> *[H]ave considered all the relevant material placed before [them] and [they] have come to the inevitable conclusion that this application is unfortunate and cannot succeed… The application dated 19th August 2000 is dismissed in its entirety with costs to the respondents.*

Concluding observations and results/impact of the court case

1. Right from the start, the High Court declared primacy of written laws over customary norms as a strategic move to undermine all further argu-

ments of the plaintiffs based on immemorial customary use and occupation of the disputed lands. The ruling therefore logically listed a number of legal procedures that were followed in declaring the land in dispute a game reserve.

2. The ruling against the plaintiffs was also grounded on the fact that they did not appeal against the compensation given to them at the time of eviction. It was argued that if the plaintiffs had not been content with the compensation, they should have appealed, which they did not do. Logically, it was assumed that the plaintiffs were happy with the compensation since they did not complain and that it was now too late to do so. Whether or not these statements are correct and fair, the fact is that any indigenous community unhappy with compensation measures should appeal against them immediately. Accepting some kind of compensation and later arguing the contrary will always undermine claims.

3. In 2003, the Endorois people, assisted by the Kenyan Centre for Minority Rights and Development (CEMIRIDE), took the case to the African Commission on Human and Peoples' Rights under the provisions of Article 55 of the African Charter on Human and Peoples' Rights. The Endorois [the complainants] were seeking a declaration that the Republic of Kenya was in violation of the African Charter's Articles 8 (right to freely practice their religion), 14 (right to property), 17 (cultural rights), 21 (right to natural resources and in case of spoliation, the right to the lawful recovery of property as well as to an adequate compensation) and 22 (right to development). They were also seeking restitution of their land with legal title and clear demarcation as well as compensation for the loss the community has suffered through the loss of property, development and natural resources, as well as the freedom to practice their religion and culture. In 2004, the African Commission issued an Urgent Appeal to the Government of the Republic of Kenya, requesting it to stay any action or measure in respect of the subject matter pending the decision of the African Commission. During its 40th Session in 2006, the Commission declared the Endorois case admissible and in accordance with rule 111 of its internal regulations. In 2009, the Commission issued its findings, namely that Kenya [the Respondent State] is in violation of the above mentioned Articles of the African Charter; that the Endorois are an indigenous community and a distinct people, sharing a common history, culture and religion and having a status, which entitles them to benefit from the African Charter's provisions protecting collective rights. The Commission therefore recommends, among other things, that the Respondent State (Kenya) recognize "the rights of ownership to the Endorois and restitute Endorois ancestral

land".[301] This case shows that a representative suit can be successfully filed with the African Commission on Human and Peoples' Rights.

Legal and policy landscape in Kenya relating to indigenous peoples' land rights.

During colonial times

Unlike Tanzania that for many years was a territory under mandate and under the control of the League of Nations, Kenya never had an independent eye overlooking the management of the colony, and this lack of international control has had a significant impact on the situation in Kenya in general and on the land tenure system in particular.

In 1885, Kenya became part of a British dependency that included Zanzibar and Uganda and was under the charter of a private company, the British East Africa Company (BEAC), soon to become the Imperial East Africa Company (IBEAC).[302] In 1895, the British Foreign Office took over what now became the East African Protectorate. In 1920, Kenya was declared a Crown Colony, while Uganda and Zanzibar remained protectorates until independence in 1962 and 1963, respectively.

Caring for the land rights of African communities was never a priority in Kenya. The Kenyan colonial system was designed to settle Europeans and other foreign farmers on indigenous peoples' lands, as was the case in South Africa, New Zealand, Australia, and many other places where this type of colonial system operated. [303] The highlands (later to be designated as the White Highlands) were

---

301 ACHPR Communication 276/2003. Besides the findings and recommendations already quoted, the Commission furthermore recommends that the Respondent State (i.e., Kenya) ... b) ensure that the Endorois community has unrestricted access to Lake Bogoria and surrounding sites for religious an cultural rites and for grazing their cattle; c) pay adequate compensation to the community for all the loss suffered; ... f) engage in dialogue with the Compainants for the effective implementation of these recommendations and g) report on the implementation of these recommendations within three months from the date of notification. The Communication was adopted by the AU assembly in January 2010. For more information on the case, see http://www.minorityrights.org/download.php?id=748

302 The BEAC (from 1888 the IBEAC) was created in 1885, as a commercial private company with the mandate to help the British Government open up East Africa and gain control of the interior up to the head water of the Nile through either treaties or conquests. See also R.L. Tignor, *The Colonial Transformation of Kenya*, Series: Eastern African Studies (Princeton, New Jersey: Princeton University Press, 1976), p. 16; Kanyinga, *Re-Distribution from Above* (2000), pp. 34-5; Rutten, *Selling Wealth* (1992), p. 171.

303 This was not the case in Uganda, where malaria and sleeping sickness in the beginning kept white settlers away. Later, the British authorities stated as a principle that Uganda should remain an African state with several semi-independent monarchies and a large African farming community producing cotton, coffee and tea for export.

the most sought after areas, due to their pleasant climate and agricultural potential.[304]

In order to control Uganda, at the time seen as a strategic country due to its command of the Nile's headwaters, the British Government considered it important to secure the new protectorate's access to the sea and enormous resources were consequently injected into Kenya through various projects, such as the building of the first railway line linking the interior of Kenya and Uganda with the port city of Mombassa. But by the turn of the century, the European "scramble for Africa" was over and the British Government no longer had the same strategic interests in Uganda. Understandably, the issue of "how to develop sufficient local export production to generate freight revenues to make the railways pay and tax revenues to support the developing state apparatus" became compelling. The railway, at the same time, provided adequate communication for the development of inland freehold and long-term leasehold land grants for ranch development by white farmers.[305] The Foreign Office decided to make Kenya pay part of the bill by making it a settlement colony.[306]

Following the arrival of the settlers in Kenya, communities became either squatters or confined to native reserves.[307] In both cases, communities enjoyed a severely limited "right of occupancy" over their lands. A colonial agent, quoted by Okoth-Ogendo, stated:

> I am afraid that we have got to hurt their (the communities) feelings, we have got to wound their susceptibilities and, in some cases, I am afraid we may even have to violate some of their most cherished and possibly even sacred traditions if we have to move communities from land on which, according to their own customary law, they have an inalienable right to live, and settle them on land from which the owner has, under that same customary law an indisputable right to eject them.[308]

---

304 H.W.O. Okoth-Ogendo, *Tenants of the Crown: Evolution of Agrarian Law and Institutions in Kenya* (Nairobi, Kenya: African Centre for Technology Studies, 1991b), p. 8.

305 See J. C. Ng'ethe "Group Ranch Concept and Practice in Kenya with Special Emphasis on Kajiado District", Available online at http://www.fao.org/wairdocs/ILRI/x5485E/x5485e0t. htm. See also Bruce Bernan, *Control and Crisis in Colonial Kenya: The Dialectic of Domination*, (London, Nairobi, Athens, Ohio: Currey, Heinemann Nairobi, Ohio University Press, 1990), p. 50; Tignor, *The Colonial Transformation of Kenya* (1976) p. 18; Okoth-Ogendo, *Tenants of the Crown* (1991a), pp. 7-9; Kanyinga, *Redistribution from Above* (2000), pp. 35-6; Rutten, *Selling Wealth* (1992), p. 173.

306 See Kanyinga, *Redistribution from Above* (2000), p. 35, and Bernan, *Control and Crisis* (1990), p. 51.

307 Okoth-Ogendo, *Tenants of the Crown* (1991b), p. 53. The term "reserve" meant land set aside by the colonial system for dispossessed indigenous peoples. These lands were later called "Trust Lands". See also Smokin C. Wanjala, *Land Law and Disputes in Kenya*, (Nairobi: Oxford University Press, 1990), p. 3; Rutten, *Selling Wealth* (1992), pp. 176-7.

308 Okoth-Ogendo, *Tenants of the Crown* (1991b), p. 58.

Settlement policy was based on a number of assumptions, including that "an excessive livestock population was destroying the vegetation and soil",[309] that "customary systems of land tenure [were] inimical to the goals of increasing agriculture output and rural income",[310] and that the traditional economy was to be "transformed in order to take forward the process of modernisation".[311] In other words, the colonial system was determined to write off pre-existing customary land tenure, regarded as an obstacle to making the Protectorate profitable. Between 1903 and 1906, 60,000 acres of Kikuyu land were taken over by white settlers,[312] and by 1926, European settlers had acquired a total of 463,864 acres, three times more than in Tanzania.[313]

The Kenyan colonial system achieved such enormous results in such a short period of time because of the use of violence. "Punitive expeditions" were carried out to crush any native resistance against the settlement schemes.[314] Apart from the Maasai community, which entered into several treaties with the colonial authority,[315] which meant that they had to abandon their traditional homelands, other communities were facing "the effect of the ... military strength in a series of campaigns, called euphemistically ... punitive expeditions, which were designed ... to punish dissident African groups".[316] Some of these expeditions resulted in more than 1,500 victims.[317]

Furthermore, following the enactment of the Native Authority Ordinance 1902, the mechanisms of designation and the functions of traditional chiefs were significantly modified, with an impact on the system of land administration. Kenya became administratively divided into provinces, districts and locations, without consideration of pre-colonial sociological settings. Provincial Commissioners took charge of the provinces, the District Commissioners were responsible for the districts, and the chiefs were in charge of the locations.[318]

These "headmen [or native chiefs] were not worthy individuals who commanded respect in their local areas",[319] and native chiefs eventually came to look

---

309 Tignor, *The Colonial Transformation* (1976), p. 10.
310 Jack Glazier, *Land and the Uses of Tradition among the Mbeere of Kenya*, (Lanham, MD: University Press of America, 1985), p. 2.
311 Ibid.
312 See Rutten, *Selling Wealth* (1992), p. 174, and Tignor, *The Colonial Transformation* (1976), p. 326. According to Tignor, by 1959, "nearly 780,000 acres of land [in the Kikuyu District of Kiambu-Limuru alone] had been consolidated out of a total of 999,000 acres of fragments farmed under the traditional tenure system".
313 Tignor, *The Colonial Transformation* (1976), p. 25.
314 Ibid., pp. 20-21, Rutten, *Selling Wealth* (1992), p. 171.
315 For a more elaborate account, see Okoth-Ogendo, *Tenants of the Crown* (1991b), p. 30, See also Rutten, *Selling Wealth* (1992), pp. 181 and 464.
316 Tignor, *The Colonial Transformation* (1976), p. 21.
317 Ibid.
318 Section 2 of the Trust Land Act, CAP. 288. For text, see http://www.kenyalaw.org/kenyalaw/klr_app/frames.php
319 Tignor, *The Colonial Transformation* (1976), p. 42.

more like "salaried public servants directly accountable to the District Commissioner"[320] than trustees of a traditional way of life and customs. Their new functions included recruiting labour, keeping roads clean, maintaining public order, and collecting taxes. Kanyinga argues that "the imposition of new forms of administrative authorities and the subsequent concentration of powers in the institutions of indirect rule, particularly that of the chiefs, undermined the traditional and customary structures of land administration, thereby shaking the basis for social and political security, and of a secure land tenure system itself. The economic organization was similarly disrupted … Political unrest developed as land problems intensified".[321]

The Kenyan Crown Land Ordinance of 1923 declared most lands "Crown Land" on the assumption that "Africans owned land only in terms of occupational rights and that the chiefs and heads of clans did not hold any sovereignty over their land".[322] As pointed out by Maini, the rationale behind this argument was that "there did not exist a valid custom by virtue of which … tribes … either collectively or by individual members, can assert a right of ownership over or alienate land".[323] Accordingly, the Ordinance extended the scope of the term Crown Land to include "all lands occupied by the native tribes and all land reserves for the use of any members of any native tribes".[324] Unlike the settlers, who could hold titles of "conclusive evidence" of absolute and indefeasible proprietorship,[325] communities were recognised with a "right to occupation" on reserves, becoming thus "tenants at the will of the Crown".[326]

By end of the 1920s, Kenyan communities' grievances over lands had reached a peak. The reserves had become congested and incapable of responding to the needs and claims of communities; at the same time, the high number of squatters on settlers' farms led to a review of labour regulation, which occasioned more displacements or evictions from settler farms and therefore more unrest in the reserves and the White Highlands.[327] Realizing the political explosiveness of the situation,[328] the colonial authority made an attempt to diffuse these tensions by

---

320 Glazier, *Land and the Uses of Tradition* (1985).

321 Kanyinga, *Re-distribution from Above* (2000), p. 33.

322 Okoth-Ogendo, *Tenants of the Crown* (1991b), p. 11. Okoth-Ogendo shows that, the Foreign Office, whilst still considering all "unoccupied lands" as belonging to the indigenous peoples, requested an expert legal view on the issue. On December 13, 1899, the view from London was that Her Majesty had power of control over "waste and unoccupied land" in protectorates and that, if Her Majesty considered it appropriate, could declare such lands "Crown Lands".

323 Krishan M. Maini, *Land Law in Eastern Africa* (Nairobi: Oxford University Press, 1967), p. 27.

324 Ibid., p. 15.

325 Section 23 of the Kenyan Crown Land Ordinance No. 26 of 1919: "The certificate of title issued by the registrar to a purchaser of land upon transfer or transmission by the proprietor thereof shall be taken by all … as conclusive evidence that the person named therein as proprietor of the land is the absolute and indefeasible owner".

326 Kanyinga, *Re-distribution from Above* (2000), p. 38.

327 Ibid., p. 41.

328 Okoth-Ogendo, *Tenants of the Crown* (1991b), p. 55.

setting up the Kenyan Land Commission in 1931. Its purpose was to hear claims by communities over lands and possibly compile some rule over the then disappearing "pre-colonial land tenure system".[329] Unfortunately, nothing came out of the claims made by the communities.[330] Instead, new ordinances and amendments were passed in 1938/39 that reinforced the rights of Europeans to exclusive occupation and ownership of land. Land sales between Europeans and Africans were prohibited, contracts between settlers and non-settlers discouraged.[331]

Pre-independence: towards the individualisation of land tenure

After World War II, its economic and imperial power severely undermined, Britain came to realize the need for integrating the African "subjects" into the colonial economy. This would serve two purposes: increase the production of export cash crops required to support the post-war reconstruction process in Britain and maintain order in the colony. The view that African farmers were not supposed to compete with the settlers[332] slowly gave way to the idea of land tenure reforms and "to devise a means of providing a better title to land in the native Land Units". This had already been recommended by the Kenyan Land Commission's Report (1934) and advocated by the colonial administration as early as in 1949.

However, the increased congestion in the reserves, the declining land-carrying capacity, several failed resettlement schemes for squatters and the disappointed hopes of the communities in general prompted in 1952 what is known as the Mau Mau uprising. A state of emergency was declared (1952-1959), but it also became apparent that the land question could no longer be ignored.

By then, as Kanyinga puts it, "the Government appeared implicitly to have abandoned the idea of community control in favour of a slow individualisation benefiting those who were considered progressive farmers".[333] This was put in evidence in 1955 by the Swynnerton Plan.[334] This plan "was devised partly in re-

---

329 Gavin Kitching, *Class and Economic Change in Kenya: The Making of an African Petite Bourgeoisie* (New Haven, Conn.: Yale University Press, 1980), p. 282.

330 The Kenyan Land Commission heard thousands of claims from communities and compiled a 1,200 page report of evidence and memorandums. See Kitching, *Class and Economic Change* (1980), p. 282.

331 Christian Graeffen, "Comments" to F.M. Ssekandi presentation on "Social, Political and Equity Aspects of Land and Property Rights", at World Bank Regional Workshop on Land Issues in Africa and the Middle East, Kampala, 2002. Available online at www.landcoalition.org/pdf/wbasekd.pdf

332 African farmers were thus gradually granted permission to grow high-value export crops, as, for instance, tea. See Donald B. Freeman, *A City of Farmers: Informal Urban Agriculture in the Open Spaces of Nairobi, Kenya* (Montreal, Quebec, Kingston, Canada: McGill-Queen's Press - MQUP, 1991).

333 Kanyinga, *Re-distribution from Above* (2000), p. 42.

334 R. J. M. Swynnerton, *A Plan to Intensify the Development of African Agriculture in Kenya* (Nairobi: Government Printer. 1955).

sponse to the Mau Mau emergency [and] was expected to create a stable class of relatively wealthy [freehold] farmers who … would help stabilize society. That desire completely overshadowed any concern for the equitable distribution of resources, as the … plan, a clear application of 1950s evolutionist 'modernization' theory in economics, made clear".[335] The Plan stated:

> In the past, the Government policy has been to maintain the tribal system of tenure so that all peoples have had bits of land and to protect the African from borrowing money against the security of his land. In the future … former Government policy will be reversed and able, energetic or rich Africans will be able to acquire more land and bad or poor farmers less, creating a landed and a landless class. This is a normal step in the evolution of a country.[336]

The strategies proposed by the Swynnerton Plan were individualization of tenure through land consolidation and registration, and improved agricultural production through extension services. The plan was supported in 1955 by the East African Royal Commission Report, which further recommended a multi-racial approach to agrarian policy,[337] and in 1956, the colonial Government declared it as its policy "to encourage the emergence of individual land tenure amongst Africans where conditions are ripe for it, and, in due course, to institute a system of registration of negotiable title."[338]

The Swynnerton Plan also promoted extensive communal grazing in pastoral districts. It identified five conditions for sound and productive use of rangelands, namely limiting the numbers of resident stock to the carrying capacity of the land; assuring an adequate system of permanent water supplies; controlling and managing grazing at a productive level. These conditions presaged in many ways some of the assumptions on which group ranches were eventually to be formed.[339]

335　Francis M. Ssekandi, "Social Political and Equity Aspects of Land and Property Rights" (2002), p. 11. Paper presented at World Bank Regional Workshop on Land Issues in Africa and the Middle East, Kampala, 2002. Available online at www.landcoalition.org/pdf/wbasekd.pdf. For an elaboration on the "modernization" theory, see, e.g., Freeman, *A City of Farmers* (1991), p. 77.

336　Swynnerton, *A Plan* (1955), p. 10, quoted in Francis M. Ssekandi, "Social Political and Equity Aspects" (2002), p. 12.

337　See Paul Maurice Syagga, "Land Ownership and Use in Kenya: Policy Prescriptions from an Inequality Perspective" in *Readings on Inequality in Kenya: Sectoral Dynamics and Perspectives* (Nairobi, Kenya: Society for International Development, Eastern Africa Regional Office, 2006), p. 297. Available online at http://www.sidint.org/files/focus/Chapter8.pdf

338　Lillian W. Njenga "Towards Individual Statutory Proprietorship from Communal Ownership" (2004). Available at http://www.fig.net/commission7/nairobi_2004/papers/ts_01_3_njenga.pdf

339　See B.E. Grandin "The Maasai: Socio-Historical Context and Group Ranches" in *Maasai Herding: An analysis of the Livestock Production System of Maasai Pastoralists in Eastern Kajiado District, Kenya,* ILCA Systems Study 4, edited by Solomon Bekure et al. (Addis Ababa, Ethiopia: ILCA - Interna-

The Swynnerton Plan resulted in several pieces of legislation, most importantly the Land Consolidation Act of 1959 (Cap 283), and the Land Registration (Special areas) Act of 1959, which introduced a registration system for individually held plots of land within the reserves or special areas, with the immediate effect that "once lands become registered under any of the systems discussed, it becomes subject to English law and no longer to customary law".[340]

One of the last laws, to be passed before independence was the Registered Land Act of 1963.[341] This Act—which is still in force—makes provision for the registration of land as well as for the registration of lease of agricultural tenancies and its legal consequences. According to Okoth-Ogendo, it "was carefully drafted to make it clear, inter alia, that the rights of an individual proprietor were not liable to be defeated by anything not shown in the register. Indeed, the act went so far as to convert all "customary rights of occupation" into tenancies from year to year, thus giving the registered owner the power, upon giving one year's notice, to terminate such occupation."[342]

Post Independence: the Africanization of land policies

All these measures, however, did not extinguish the communities' call for land restitution, and before independence, the new Kenyan political elite[343] had al-

---

tional Livestock Centre for Africa, 1991), chapter 3. Many grazing schemes, each with a livestock officer-in-charge, were started in various districts throughout the country but turned out to have little success. Most schemes ended in the 1960s by being divided in individual ranches of varying sizes.

340 Wanjala, *Land Law* (1990), pp. 9-10. Other legislation included, the Native Land Tenure Rules of 1956 regarding machinery for the adjudication and consolidation of native lands; the Native Lands Registration Ordinance of 1959 and, the Land Control (Native Lands) Ordinance of 1960 to control land transactions within the adjudicated areas. These two pieces of legislation are the forerunners of the Registered Land Act of 1963 and the Land Control Act of 1967 that operate in Kenya to the present day. See Syagga, "Land Ownership and Use in Kenya" (2006).

341 Registered Lands Act of 1963 CAP 300 (September 1963). Its introduction resulted in the repeal of all the provisions of the Land Registration (Special areas) Act of 1959. This excluded the adjudication and consolidation provisions whereby the Land Registration Act was changed to the Land Consolidation Act of 1959.

342 CAP 300 - Sections 27, 28, 30. See H.W.O. Okoth-Ogendo "The Perils of Land Tenure Reform: the Case of Kenya" in *Land Policy and Agriculture in Eastern and Southern Africa*, edited by J.W. Arntzen, L.D. Ngcongco, and S.D. Turner. Selected Papers Presented at a Workshop organised by the United Nations University in Gaborone, Botswana, 14-19 February 1982 (Tokyo: United Nations University Press, 1982).

343 On the eve of the Kenyan independence, two major political groups emerged. On the one hand, there was the KANU (Kenyan African National Union) made up essentially of Kikuyu and Luo, the two biggest ethnic groups of Kenya. On the other hand, there was the KADU (Kenya African Democratic Union) made up essentially of small pastoralist communities, such as the Maasai, Luhya, etc. In all the pre-independence negotiations, the latter wanted to have their land rights constitutionally protected, as individuals and as communities. In this sense, the passing of the Land (Group Representatives) Act of 1968 could be considered as a compromise reached by both parties. See also Kanyinga, *Re-distribution from Above* (2000), pp. 47-52.

ready come under enormous pressure from various communities denouncing the unfairness of the colonial land policies, and reclaiming their lost lands. This was coupled with a growing feeling of insecurity among the European settlers, who had become more willing to sell up and leave Kenya.

As a consequence and following independence in 1963, the Kenyan Government endeavoured Africanizing its land policy. One of the measures taken was to open up high-potential areas, such as the former White Highlands of Kenya,[344] and implement "settlement schemes, through which Africans were given access to land bought from departing European farmers".[345] Another measure was the creation of "group ranches".

According to Grandin, "by 1970, about 1.2 million ha of land had been transferred and adjudicated African farmers in the high-potential areas. This figure should be seen in contrast to only 0.21 million in the range areas, including individual farms, ranches and group ranches. However, land was given to the landless, unemployed and 'progressive' African farmers, and was not returned to the groups which occupied them traditionally".[346]

The Maasai colonial land losses, for instance, were never recouped. Yet, the situation in Maasailand was critical. From occupying prior colonization an area of 155,000 sq. km, stretching from Mt Elgon and the Loriyu Plateau in the north to Kibaya in the south (today in Tanzania), this area of land had by 1913 been reduced to 40,000 sq. km. This remaining "reserve" is roughly congruent with present-day Narok and Kajiado districts. In the following decades and right up to the 1950s, more land, including important dry-season grazing areas, was lost to farmers, in particular Kikuyus, who themselves had been chased away from their homelands by European settlers. Under the National Parks Ordinance of 1945, the Kajiado Maasai furthermore lost access to two areas bordering the District: Nairobi National Park and Tsavo National Park. This Ordinance also established a game reserve in Amboseli (3,248 sq. km), and game conservation areas at Kitengela (583 sq. km) and West Chyulu (368 sq. km), restricting the use of these areas by the Maasai. Maasai complaints about the encroachment of cultivation into dry-season grazing were common between 1940 and 1955. A drought in

---

344 Just before Independence, the departing colonisers negotiated a scheme by which white settlers were bought out of their farms by the in-coming Kenya Government. The money for this purchase was made available as a loan by the British Government. This agreement was heavily criticized by certain KANU members who found that it was not justifiable "to buy that which had been forcefully wrenched from them". See Horace Njuguna Gisemba, "A Short History of Land Settlements in the Rift Valley" (2008). Available online at http://allafrica.com/stories/200805150607.html

345 Kitching, *Class and Economic Change* (1980), p. 316. Under a number of government settlement schemes (the most notable being the Million Acre scheme), some half a million people were resettled on land purchased from the settlers. See Alexandrino Njuki, "Cadastral Systems and Their Impact on Land Administration in Kenya". Paper presented at International Conference on Spatial Information for Sustainable Development, Nairobi, Kenya, October 2001. Available online at http://www.fig.net/pub/proceedings/nairobi/njuki-TS10-2.pdf

346 Grandin, "The Maasai" (1991).

1948-50 increased conflicts between the Maasai pastoralists and non-Maasai farmers.[347]

In 1965, the Lawrence Mission on Land Consolidation and Registration was appointed to assess the problem of landlessness that several communities were facing, as a result of the pre-existing processes of consolidation and registration.[348] The Lawrence Report noted:

> We are conscious of the limitations imposed by the fact that the Kenya Government has for several years been widely committed to a policy of individual absolute ownership … In some of the semi-arid areas of the country, it would be wasteful and even harmful to register an individual ownership land which is badly eroded or denuded of grass cover, for the owners may be unable to subsist, let alone derive a cash income from holding until remedial action has been taken to restore the land to productive capacity.[349]

The Lawrence Commission made several recommendations, among others the need in range areas to provide for improved livestock husbandry among the pastoralist communities. This eventually led to the enactment of two pieces of legislation, which were to impact on Kenya's pastoralist population. One was the Land Adjudication Act of 1968,[350] which facilitated the creation of group ranches on Trust Lands, where individual ownership was not appropriate given environmental conditions and the close-knit nature of pastoralist communities, by providing for the recording of rights and interests in customary lands, and their assignment to their customary users. The other was the Land (Group Representatives) Act of 1968 which provided for the governance and administration of group ranches. [351]

These two laws symbolize the first major attempts by the Kenyan new political elite to respond to land claims of communities in legal terms. Unlike Tanzania, which enacted two major Land Acts in 1999, there had not been an important land law or related legislation passed in Kenya since the 1976 Wildlife (Conservation and Management) Act, (amended in 1989). Accordingly, as far as community

---

347 Grandin, "The Maasai" (1991).

348 Gerald Holtham and Arthur Hazlewood, *Aid and Inequality in Kenya* (London: Croom Helm and the Overseas Development Institute, 1976), p. 116; Rutten, *Selling Wealth* (1992), p. 266.

349 J.D. Lawrence et al., *Report of Mission on Land Consolidation and Registration in Kenya, 1965-66* (Nairobi 1966) pp. 34-5.

350 Land Adjudication Act, 1968, CAP 284: An Act of Parliament to provide for the ascertainment and recording of rights and interests in Trust land, and for purposes connected therewith and purposes incidental thereto (Preamble). According to Article 2, "interest", in relation to land, includes absolute ownership of the land.

351 Land (Group Representatives) Act, CAP 287: An Act of Parliament to provide for the incorporation of representatives of groups who have been recorded as owners of land under the Land Adjudication Act, and for purposes connected therewith and purposes incidental thereto (Preamble). See also Njenga "Towards Individual Statutory Proprietorship from Communal Ownership" (2004).

rights to lands are concerned, the right of "occupation" stated by the Trust Land Act of 1939[352] and the right of "ownership" recognized by the Land Adjudication Act remained, strictly speaking, the only Kenyan legal attempts to address the claims of communities for their collective right to lands.

Aimed at protecting the poor members of communities against rich and influential individuals who could easily secure titles on the reserves,[353] the Land Adjudication Act and the Land (Group Representatives) Act used, for the first time in the legal history of Kenya,[354] the expression "group's rights" of ownership over land. To some extent, these Acts applied to communal lands, even if the Land Adjudication Act included provisions for the dissolution of group ranches and thus the individualisation of these lands.

Group ranches: creation and subdivision

A group ranch has been defined as a livestock production system or enterprise where a group of people jointly own freehold title to land, maintain agreed stocking levels and herd their individually owned livestock collectively.[355] The selection of members to a particular group ranch is based on kinship and traditional land rights.[356] Group members elect group representatives to constitute a management committee that oversees pasture management and water development.[357]

Group ranching was seen by the Government as a way of modernizing the Maasai through the commoditization of their herds, while at the same time providing an evolutionary mode of transformation based on the traditional ways of the Maasai.[358]

Although there were Maasai who were consulted about the desirability of group ranches and were involved in their formation, they were primarily edu-

---

352 Trust Land Act of 1939, CAP 288, Articles 13 and 69.
353 Rutten shows that in the Maasai section of Kaputiei alone, by 1965, 22,000 ha (out of 322,000 ha) had been allocated to 28 families out of a total of approximately 8,400. See Rutten, *Selling Wealth* (1992), p. 268. Once individual titles were secured, land could then be alienated to outsiders or non-members (ibid., pp. 265-6).
354 As already shown, one of the colonial strategies for accessing native lands was to destroy any sort of collective holding of lands. This was done through a range of measures, such as the abolition of the traditional institutions on which the system was built, the individualisation of land holding and similar measures.
355 Ministry of Agriculture, 1968, quoted by J. C. Ng'ethe in "Group Ranch Concept" (1992).
356 According to Article 2 of Land Adjudication Act, "group" means a tribe, clan, section, family or other group of persons, whose land under recognized customary law belongs communally to the persons who are for the time being the members of the group, together with any person of whose land the group is determined to be the owner. See also J. C. Ng'ethe, "Group Ranch Concept" (1992).
357 Ester Mwangi, "The Transformation of Property Rights in Kenya's Maasailand: Triggers and Motivations" CAPRi Working Paper (Washington D.C.: International Food Policy Research Institute 2005), n. 2. Available at http://www.capri.cgiar.org
358 Ibid., p. 8.

cated Maasai tied into the national political system. Most researchers, however, agree that the majority of the Maasai did not accept or even understand some features of the group ranch (such as grazing quotas, boundary maintenance and the management committee). Their reasons for eventually accepting the idea of group ranches were therefore at odds with those of the Government. They primarily saw group ranching as a way to secure their land against further incursions by Government, by non-Maasai cultivators and by the elite Maasai. Another reason was the perceived possibility of increasing their traditional wealth base (livestock numbers) through the provision of water facilities, disease control and dips funded by supporting projects.[359]

Group ranching soon proved to be a failure. The objectives envisioned by the Government were not met. Livestock numbers were increasing beyond the carrying capacity of the land with ensuing environmental degradation, and the Maasai were not particularly market-oriented.[360] By the early 1980s, mounting pressure from several stakeholders to subdivide the group ranches was spearheaded by Kenya's president, Daniel Arap Moi, who, on several occasions between 1983 and 1989, voiced his support for the process of subdivision.[361] Financial institutions, such as the World Bank, too, "openly condemned [the system of] preventing other Kenyans, [not belonging to a given ranch]" from acquiring or using ranch lands.[362] A sudden demand for wheat and barley by Kenya's new middle class, furthermore, inspired investment in Green Revolution technologies, converting to agriculture land that had forever been considered too dry for agriculture, and making Narok District Kenya's leading producer of both wheat and barley by the mid-1980s.[363]

These developments coincided with an increasing disenchantment among the Maasai, who found that group ranching had deeply altered their indigenous system of land administration and land use patterns. As pointed out by Okoth-Ogendo, authority of land was now excercised by "a completely new medium ... namely the group representatives. Although the Land (Group Representatives) Act is fairly general about who may hold office as a group representative, the emerging practice appeared to be that those elected to office were people who were at least able to read and write". This meant that in areas with low levels of

359 Mwangi, "The Transformation of Property Rights" (2005), p. 10. Kenya Livestock Development Policy (KLDP) I and II with support from, among others, the World Bank, was to be the main tool through which the group ranch concept was to be implemented. See Ng'ethe, "Group Ranch Concept" (1992).

360 Instead of commercializing their production, the Maasai followed their traditional livelihood strategies, keeping a high percentage of female livestock to ensure sufficient milk as well as to guard against draught periods (in order to be able to rebuild their herd), and only selling a minimum number of animals to meet their financial commitment to the ranch.

361 As opposed to the President, Government officials from the Departments of Lands Adjudication and Range Planners from the Ministry of Livestock Development were cautious and indeed stopped short of openly discouraging group ranches against subdivision.

362 Rutten, *Selling Wealth* (1992), p. 476.

363 Cheeseman, *"Conservation and the Maasai"* (n.d.), p. 4.

literacy as for instance in the Maasai areas, "those assuming office as representatives tended … to be the younger, less influential members of indigenous society. This tended to slow down decision-making … since most decisions taken by the representatives still carried very little weight unless they were also channelled through indigenous levels of authority." As for the pattern of land use, "it was altered by severely restricting the nomadic character of pastoral communities without first improving their ability to adapt to semi-sedentary living. In particular, adequate steps were not taken to reduce the people's dependence on seasonal availability of water and stock feed. One consequence of this was that in order to minimize drought risks, clans and families often found it necessary to split herds and join different ranching schemes, a course of action that was apt to put great strain on the social institutions of pastoral society."[364]

But there were other concerns besides mismanagement and lack of access to dry-season rangelands. Increasing group ranch populations, discord between age-sets concerning registration of new members, unsanctioned allocations to unauthorized individuals, difficulties in enforcing livestock quotas, etc., were problems that created insecurity among group members and eventually pushed them to support subdivision.[365] At the same time, "the individual title was viewed as the gateway to development. A title to land represented complete and secure ownership, but more. It could be used as collateral to acquire loans for farm and livestock improvement; it could be used as security against which unforeseen circumstances such as illness could be confronted".[366]

By the early 1980s, many group ranches therefore began opting for the possibility provided by the law of sub-dividing into individual plots. As reported by Rutten, within the Kajiado District alone, by "1990 almost 80 per cent of the ranches had decided to get rid of the group ranch structure and become individual land owners instead".[367] By 2000, and out of a total of 321 group ranches in Kenya—the large majority to be found in the two most densely Maasai populated districts (Kajiado and Narok)—104 had been subdivided and 109 were in the process of being subdivided. Only 39 were in operation, the others were either dormant or to be subdivided.[368]

---

364 Okoth-Ogendo "The Perils of Land Tenure Reform (1982).
365 Shauna BurnSilver and Esther Mwangi "Beyond Group Ranch Subdivision: Collective Action for Livestock Mobility, Ecological Viability and Livelihoods" (Washington, D.C.: International Food Policy Research Institute, 2007), p. 5. Available online at http://www.capri.cgiar.org/pdf/capri-wp66.pdf
366 Mwangi, "The Transformation of Property Rights" (2005), p. 24.
367 Rutten, *Selling Wealth* (1992), p. 303.
368 Figures from the Range Management Division of the Ministry of Agricultural and Rural Development (MoARD) quoted in Yacob Aklilu et al., "An Audit of the Livestock Marketing Status in Kenya, Ethiopia and Sudan" (Nairobi:Organization of African Unity/Interafrican Bureau for Animal Resources, 2002), pp. 18-19. Available online at
    http;//www.eldis.org/fulltext/cape_new/Akliliu_Marketing_vol._1.pdf
    Shuana BurnSilver and Esther Mwangi "Beyond Group Ranch Subdivision: Collective Action for Livestock Mobility, Ecological Viability and Livelihoods" (Washington D.C.: International Food

As the Land (Group Representatives) Act did not provide detailed rules regarding dissolution of "group ranches", the Land Adjudication and Range Department[369] designed mechanisms and rules to preside over the subdivision of "group ranches" into individually held parcels of lands.[370] Although these rules continue to preside over an increasing number of group ranch subdivisions, they have never been sent to Parliament to be passed into law.

The consequences of the dissolution of group ranches have been wide ranging. Once lands were individually owned, poverty has motivated some households (that is, the male household heads) to sell in their effort to survive. In other cases, individual lands have been fraudulently appropriated by rich and influential people through various corrupt arrangements. In the opinion of M.M.E.M. Rutten, "none of those who allowed this process [of dissolution of group ranches] to start fully realised the possible negative side effects it could have for a large number of Maasai people, their children, the district's ecology, the livestock economy ...".[371] Mostly because, once divided into plots of individually owned pieces of land, former group ranches could be alienated to outsiders. As shown by several reports, once a subdivision of a group ranch is completed, the majority of those who gain access to these lands are non-Maasai, including private companies, rich politicians, civil servants, and businessmen.[372]

Furthermore, individually owned plots appear, in most cases, to be too small to accommodate the lifestyle of pastoralists. They have had to adapt to "dramatic changes in pastoral land use, [going] from a system predicated on extensive seasonal movement and intensive, short-duration grazing of successive areas of the pastoral landscape, towards one based on intensive, long-term grazing of private parcels where households have ostensibly fewer options for mobility",[373] particularly since individualisation has introduced practices such as fencing, which clearly goes against the pre-existing customary-based norm of "non-exclusive use" of lands.[374]

Policy Research Institute, 2007), p. 2. Available online at http://www.capri.cgiar.org/pdf/capri-wp66.pdf

369 The Land Adjudication and Range Department of the Kenyan Government was in charge of overseeing the running of group ranches, and therefore should have been the one to design measures and rules for the abolition of the scheme.

370 These rules stipulate that the decision has to be taken by at least 60 per cent of the concerned ranch members. Then an authorisation to subdivide has to be applied for at the "Divisional Land Control Board". After the required consent of the Registrar of Group Representatives—a body in charge of registering all group ranches—a demarcation process takes place, after which each group member can apply for an individual plot. For more details on the steps leading to the dissolution of a group ranch, see Rutten, *Selling Wealth* (1992), pp. 301-3.

371 Ibid., p. 484.

372 Ibid., p. 300.

373 BurnSilver and Mwangi "Beyond Group Ranch Subdivision (2007), p. 2.

374 Rutten, *Selling Wealth* (1992), pp. 480 and 483. There are obvious changes in Maasai lifestyles. Wage labour is said to be playing an increasingly important role. There are also changes in pas-

Thus, the last vestige of any sort of communal land holding in Kenya has begun to disappear. Group ranches still exist in Kenya, but they are under threat of subdivision as pressure for individualisation continues to build up, particularly from the young generation of the few communities that still hold on to the group ranch system. However, considering that "the official policy of the Kenyan Government is the extinguishment of customary tenure through systematic adjudication of rights and registration of title, and its replacement with a system akin to the English freehold",[375] it is difficult to see how the scheme of "group ranches" will be able to survive in the long run.[376]

Current land related policy processes

In 2003, the Ministry of Lands in consultation with other stakeholders spearheaded a National Land Policy formulation process. In May 2007, after a wide-ranging consultative process that included the participation of indigenous organizations, a final Draft National Land Policy was made public. In June 2009, this Draft was aproved by Government and eventually adopted in December by Parliament. With the vision "to guide the country towards efficient, sustainable and equitable use of land for prosperity and posterity",[377] it has raised hopes by stating that,

> Land issues requiring special intervention, such as historical injustices, land rights of minority communities (such as hunter-gatherers, forest-dwellers and pastoralists) and vulnerable groups will be addressed. The rights of these groups will be recognised and protected. Measures will be initiated to identify such groups and ensure their access to land and participation in decision making over land and land based resources.[378]

It should be noted that the Policy also addresses women's land rights.

Besides including the "restitution of land rights to those that have unjustly been deprived of such rights",[379] it also "recognizes and protects customary rights to land",[380] stating that the Government skall lay out, in the Land Act" a clear

---

turing techniques and they now have, for example, livestock of camels and other previously unknown types of animals.

375 H.W.O. Okoth-Ogendo, "Land Policy Development in East Africa: A survey of Recent Trends". Paper for the DFID Workshop on "Land Rights and Sustainable Development in sub-Sahara Africa, Berkshire, 16-19 February 1999, p. 5. Available online at
      http://www.oxfam.org.uk/resources/learning/landrights/downloads/eafover.rtf
376 Wanjala, *Land Law* (1990), p. 11.
377 Republic of Kenya, Sessional Paper No. 3 of 2009 on National Land Policy, (Nairobi: Ministry of Lands, 2007a), p. ix.
378 Ibid., p. x.
379 Ibid., para. 174.
380 Ibid., p. ix.

framework and procedures for the recognition, protection and registration of community rights to land and land based resources, taking into account multiple interests of all land users, including women",[381] and for "resolving the problem of illegally acquired trust land".[382] It also provides for the creation of a National Land Commission mandated, among other things, to "set up a Land Titles Tribunal, which will determine the *bona fide* ownership of land that was previously public or trust land".[383] Furthermore, the new policy document pays particular attention to "pastoral land issues", deriving the conclusion that:

> Pastoralism has survived as a livelihood and land use system despite changes in life styles and technological advancements. This tenacity of pastoralism testifies to its appropriateness as a production system.
>
> Colonial and post-colonial land administration in the pastoralist areas led to the deprivation of land management rights from the traditional institutions thereby creating uncertainty on the access, control, and exploitation of land based resources including grazing lands, water, and salt licks among others.[384]

The Government shall therefore "recognise pastoralism as a legitimate land use and production system"[385] and "provide for flexible and negotiated cross boundary access to protected areas, water, pastures and salt licks among different stakeholders for mutual benefit to facilitate the nomadic nature of pastoralism".[386] The role of women in pastoral systems and their special problems such as lack of access to land use rights are recognized and their rights in pastoral areas should be protected.[387]

Regarding so-called vulnerable groups such as pastoralists, hunter-gatherers, etc., the Government shall develop mechanisms for redistribution of land and resettlement in order to secure access to land and land based resources. It should also "facilitate their participation in decision making over land and land based resources" and "protect their land rights from unjust and illegal expropriation".[388]

Potentially, this new National Policy could redefine the relationship between the country's marginalized indigenous peoples and the State.

Conservation areas and wildlife have not been a matter of contention in any major legislation since the 1976 Wildlife (Conservation and Management) Act. An amendment to this Act was passed in 1989, but left untouched the abolition of the land rights of communities, whose place of ordinary residence is within the

---

381 Ibid., para. 66 (d)i.
382 Ibid., para. 66 (d)ii.
383 Ibid., paras. 41 and 62 (b).
384 Ibid., paras. 180 and 181.
385 Ibid., para. 183 (a).
386 Ibid., para. 183 (f).
387 Ibid., paras 182 and 183 (e).
388 Ibid., para 197 (b), (c) and (d).

conservation areas. In 2007, Kenya finalized a Draft Wildlife Management Policy.[389] This policy did not deal with indigenous land rights but specified that "wildlife will be utilized in a manner that does not impinge on cultural values, compromise the quality and value of the resource, or degrade the carrying capacity of supporting ecosystems, in accordance with the principle of sustainable use."[390] It also provided that "benefits accruing from wildlife will be shared equitably among stakeholders, especially paying due regard to communities living within wildlife areas".[391] In order to remedy what it called "increasing human-wildlife conflict (HWC)", the Draft Policy saw the need for ensuring "that local communities and landowners are involved in putting in place measures that mitigate HWC"[392] and proposed among other things to "erect and maintain game barriers and other approved deterrent measures to minimize HWCs."[393]

This 2007 Draft Policy was immediately criticized for its entrenched conservationist attitudes and its views on the rights of indigenous communities living in or near protected areas. In March 2007, indigenous communities living adjacent wildlife ecological zones thus issued a press release against the policy, noting with consternation that the "policy document is contrary to their views" and that they were especially concerned about issues related to communitiy participation and wildlife trust funds and to the reintroduction of sport hunting.[394] In 2009, a new Draft Wildlife Policy was presented. Whether it addresses some of the above mentioned problems is uncertain at the time of writing (late 2009), since the Bill has not yet been presented to the cabinet for debate.

A new Forests Act was passed in 2005 and a Forest Policy adopted in 2007.[395] They provide for broad-based collaboration with forest communities, recognizing their traditional cultures and values but do not mention the rights of communities in forested lands, which are considered to be public lands.

Conclusion

This chapter has shown that Kenyan indigenous peoples' right to land enjoys no protection by the judiciary. However, it is noticeable that obstacles are far from

---

389 Republic of Kenya, Final Draft Wildlife Management Policy, (Nairobi: Ministry of Tourism and Wildlife, 2007b). Available online at
http://www.tourism.go.ke/ministry.nsf/doc/DRAFT_WILDLIFE_POLICY.pdf/$file/DRAFT_WILDLIFE_POLICY.pdf
390 Ibid., Section 3.3.1. (d).
391 Ibid., Section 3.3.1 (e)
392 Ibid., Section 9.3.
393 Ibid., p. 25.
394 See Web site of IWGIA at http://www.iwgia.org/sw24404.asp
395 Republic of Kenya, The Forests Act (2005) and Sessional Paper No.1 on Forest Policy (Nairobi: Ministry of Environment and Natural Resources, 2007c). Both documents can be accessed online at http://www.kfs.go.ke/html/forest%20act.html

deterring these peoples; instead, they devise new strategies and are, for instance, increasingly using historians, researchers and historical archival material to substantiate their cases.

Contrary to Tanzania, where—as will be shown in chapter VI—there have at least been a few High Court judges who have ruled in favour of customary land rights, there has never been such a trend in Kenya, where historical unfair land dispossessions seem to never have been questioned by the judiciary. One explanation of this could be found in the different history of these two countries. This does not preclude, however, the persistent need in both countries, for sensitizing judges on the rights of indigenous peoples.

Right from the early 1900s, when the Maasai went first to court, until now, with the Endorois people and others seeking redress, Kenyan judges have been unsympathetic to the land rights of indigenous peoples. Kenyan judges tend to take a very traditional approach in almost all land court cases lodged by indigenous peoples. Generally, these judges hold on to national written legislations and consider customary law as a source of rights only if it is in accordance with written laws. This reflects a failure to understand that land dispossession of indigenous peoples and their claims to ancestral lands are a consequence of unfair and unjust laws passed without their consent. Efforts by indigenous peoples to bring in international jurisprudence on "aboriginal title" and other Kenyan international obligations have been systematically resisted by the judiciary, which remains unwilling to challenge government policies and sometimes uses delays as tactics.

When it comes to indigenous peoples, Kenyan land policies have remained fairly unchanged for decades. However, the past few years have seen the development of new policies and legislation on wildlife and land, culminating in 2009 with a new Draft Wildlife Policy and the adoption of the new National Land Policy (December 2009). The new National Land Policy represents potentially a big step forward in the recognition of indigenous peoples' rights. An open question is therefore how these two new policies eventually will play together. It should not be forgotten that Kenyan Government policies and practices are, to a large extent, motivated by the interests of the political and economic dominant sectors. A case in point is the practice that consists of "degazetting" protected areas so that non-indigenous outsiders can be settled or granted individual rights on these lands. The Ogiek community[396] has been fighting for the past twenty years against this practice, which is clearly motivated by political (electoral) interests. Another example is the influence of the Kenyan conservation/tourist sector. Up through the 1980s, this sector emerged as having the potential of becoming one of "Kenya's largest earners of foreign exchange", and it has proved to be just that.[397] At the same time, it also demonstrated its potential of attracting exter-

396 See Web site of Ogiek Welfare Council at http://www.ogiek.org
397 Tourism accounts for 10 per cent of the Gross Domestic Product (GDP), making it the third largest contributor to Kenya's GDP after agriculture and manufacturing, and Kenya's third largest

nal funding mostly from large environmental and wildlife funds but also from institutions such as the World Bank, which is said to have provided tens of millions of US dollars to the Kenyan conservation sector.[398] The benefits drawn by the Kenyan Government and the local county councils have similarly been substantive, prompting commentators as Ted Cheeseman to talk about "a 'mining attitude' toward park resources" and to note that "wildlife is now singularly utilized through the tourist trade, exacerbating the gap between who pays for wildlife and who benefits from it."[399]

Those who have hitherto paid for wildlife have in most cases been the indigenous communities living in the vicinity of national parks and reserves. In the case of Amboseli, for example, "the National Park is only a tiny part of the 6,000 sq.km Amboseli ecosystem. … Without these surrounding areas, wildlife populations are unsustainable".[400] Yet, not only have these communities not seen any benefits in form of investments and projects, they have often, as in the case of national parks, lost access to areas which they used traditionally and on which they are highly dependent. In the case of Amboseli National Park, this has several times generated violent and bloody conflicts between the Maasai and the park management. If Kenyan wildlife and its ecosystem are to be preserved, conservation interests will therefore have to be balanced with the rights of communities living within as well as outside the concerned areas,[401] and the need to solve the environmental degradation caused by failed pastoral policies.

---

foreign exchange earner after tea and horticulture. See Update on Tourism Statistics (Kenya National Bureau of Statistics 2007). Available online at http://*www.tourism.go.ke/ministry.nsf.* See *also* Cheeseman, "Conservation" (n.d), p. 10.

398 Norman N. Miller, "Land Use and Wildlife in Modern Kenya", in *Wildlife, Wild Death: Land Use and Survival in Eastern Africa,* edited by R. Yeager and N.N. Miller (New York: State University of New York Press, and the African –Caribbean Institute, 1986), p. 78; Cheeseman, "Conservation" (n.d.), p. 10.

399 Cheeseman, "Conservation" (n.d.), pp. 5 and 9.

400 Ibid., p. 11.

401 See, e.g., Rutten, *Selling Wealth,* 1992, p. 323.

CHAPTER VI
INDIGENOUS PEOPLES' LAND CLAIMS IN TANZANIA

This chapter presents and examines some of the court cases that have involved the Barabaig and the Maasai of Tanzania. It concludes with an overview of the historical and socio-political context as well as of the current legal landscape in which indigenous peoples' land rights have developed in Tanzania.

The Barabaig and their land cases

The Barabaig are indigenous pastoral people living in Hanang District, in the newly created Manyara region, in Northern Tanzania.[402] They are estimated to be more than 70,000 people. In the late 1960s, the Government of Tanzania decided to increase the production of wheat in order to reduce the country's dependency on foreign imports, and in 1968, with support from Canada, the Tanzanian Ministry of Agriculture initiated the Bassotu Wheat Complex in Hanang District. Ten thousand acres of land were put under wheat cultivation. In 1970, the project was handed over to the National Agricultural and Food Corporation (NAFCO), which was to develop large-scale commercial wheat farming. For that purpose, NAFCO targeted to acquire an additional 72,000 acres of arable land, which was to be used for wheat growing under what is generally known as the Tanzania-Canada Wheat Programme (TCWP). By the late 1970s, seven farms—the Sechet, Gawal, Gaidagamoud, Waret, Murjanda, Mulbadaw, and Bassotu farms—of about 10,000 acres each, had been developed, covering about 12 per cent of the Hanang District. These seven farms encircled and/or covered more than 72,000 acres of pastureland which included the Barabaig's residential areas, their holy shrines, their graveyards, as well as water and salt sources for both human and animal consumption. The Barabaig protested and went to court to sue both NAFCO and

---

402 African Commission, *Report of Working Group of Experts* (2005), p. 31.

the Government in 1981 and 1988. A third case filed in 1989 was dismissed by the court.[403]

Mulbadaw Village Council and 67 Others v. National Agricultural and Food Corporation (NAFCO). HC – Arusha, CV# 10/1981

Background facts and claimants' arguments

The members of the Barabaig community of Mulbadaw Village consider the land they live on as their ancestral home. In the 1970s, the Government of Tanzania handed these lands to the National Agricultural and Food Corporation (NAFCO) for wheat farming. The company subsequently moved into the area with tractors, destroying the pasture lands, graves, houses and crops of the Barabaig community.

Sixty seven village members and the Village Council sued NAFCO before the High Court for trespassing on village lands, interfering with customary land rights and damaging properties. The Barabaig plaintiffs claimed that the disputed lands were their ancestral home since time immemorial. One witness, who had worked as supervisor for the "Operation *Vijiji*", one of the policies implemented during the *Ujamaa* period (see further on in this chapter), stated that well before the establishment of Mulbadaw village by the Government and the starting of commercial activities on the lands in question, the communities, to which the 67 plaintiffs belonged, had lived in the Mulbadaw area for as long as one could remember.

The plaintiffs asked the court to declare NAFCO's activities on the disputed lands as amounting to trespassing; to recognize the disputed land as legally and customarily belonging to them; and to be granted damages for trespass and other related sufferings.

Defendant's core legal points

The defendant (NAFCO) contended that it had entered the land lawfully with the blessings of the Government and the party leaders in Hanang District and Ar-

---

403   In 1989, the *Ako Gembul and 100 Others v. Gidagamowd and Waret Farms Ltd and NAFCO* case (HC – Arusha, CV#12/1989) whereby 101 Barabaig pastoralists in Hanang District presented the claim over 20,000 acres of pasture lands appropriated by NAFCO as Waret and Gidagamowd farms, was dismissed on the grounds that (i) the Government has priority in Food Security and the acquisition of the Barabaig land is proper, as national interest overrides all other interests; (ii) the suit is bad in law as it should have been consolidated with the *Yoke Gwaku* Case (HC – Arusha, CV#52/1988). See Sengondo E. Mvungi, "Experiences in the Defence of Pastoralist Rights in Tanzania: Lessons and Prospects" in *A Study on Options for Pastoralists to Secure their Livelihoods in Tanzania*, edited by Ringo Tenga et al. (Arusha: Tanzania Natural Resource Forum, 2008), p. 3.

usha Region. It also argued that the land it occupied was land for which it held a valid right of occupancy. Three documents of right of occupancy were presented in court for that purpose. One defense witness presented an application by NAF-CO for 22,793 acres of land at Bassotu that was approved by a letter of the Regional Land Advisory Committee in 1973.

Ruling and reasoning of the court

The High Court had to deal basically with the following three main questions:

1. Whether the plaintiffs were the lawful owners of the said farming land and pastureland;
2. Whether the defendants destroyed the plaintiffs' houses, their stored crops and acres of land with maize and beans;
3. Whether the defendants' actions were lawful.

The High Court judge ruled in favour of the Village Council as holder of rights over the disputed lands:

Although the first issue was framed based on ownership, I find that once the village council, the first plaintiff, establishes lawful possession, it has established the preliminary requirement for a suit in trespass to land. In view of this, I do not consider the defendants' argument that Mulbadaw Village Council had no formal rights of occupancy over the land within the Boundaries.

Furthermore, the High Court ruled on two accounts in favour of the 67 Barabaig individual plaintiffs.

Firstly, the court found that these Barabaig individuals held customary land rights over the disputed lands for having lived there as long as one could remember. The 1923 Land Ordinance, as later amended in 1928,[404] made indeed a distinction between a "granted right of occupancy",[405] which individuals could be

---

404 The 1928 amending Ordinance to the Land Ordinance of 1923 was meant to bring into consideration the right of occupancy flowing out of customary use and occupation. The scope of the Ordinance was thus widened to accommodate occupier of land under customary law (Act. No. 7 of 1928). See also Fimbo, *Essays in Land Laws* (1992), p. 3. Since then, the ordinance has been repealed and replaced in 1999 by the Village Land Act, (Cap 113 R.E 2002), and the Land Act, (Cap 114 R.E 2002).

405 Sections 6 and 7 of the Ordinance provided for the "granted right of occupancy". This right could only be enjoyed for 99 years and was conceived as an individualistic understanding of land ownership, which favours individual titling, exclusive use, and similar characteristics. Even though groups of people could apply for a "granted right of occupancy", this did not make the scheme less individualistic as a group registration was only one step before a division of such

granted by the Government, and a "deemed right of occupancy", considered as arising out of customary use and occupation of lands.[406] A further legal point was made that such customary land rights were not extinguished under the Land Acquisition Act (No. 47 of 1967).[407] One of the first legal assaults of the *Ujamaa* policy on pre-existing rights of communities to land, was the 1967 Land Acquisition Act. This Act mandated the Tanzanian president to: "acquire any land for any estate or term where such land is required for any public purposes"[408] and defined a vacant land as land not "efficiently used or occupied".[409]

Secondly, the High Court found that it was *"proved to the extent required in civil cases or even more that the plaintiffs' growing crops, stored crops and houses were destroyed by the defendants"*. Thus the case was won by the plaintiffs and the court ruled that compensation be paid to them.

National Agricultural and Food Corporation (NAFCO) v. Mulbadaw Village Council & 66 Others. CA – Dar-es-Salaam, CA# 3/1986

Dissatisfied with the High Court's decision, the defendants decided to appeal. In appeal, the court ruled on technicalities and argued that a village council could not own land on the basis of customary law. The judge went on saying that an administrative unity does not necessarily imply that the land within its jurisdiction belongs to it. He referred to the rule that a village council could acquire land only by allocation to it by the District Development Council, as specified by the Village and *Ujamaa* Villages (Registration, Designation and Administration) Act, 1975.

Furthermore, the Justice of Appeal ruled that the few plaintiffs who testified could not represent all the others. In fact, the few plaintiffs who testified before the court had also been given mandate by the High Court to represent numerous other village members. This was pursuant to Order 1, Rule 8 of the Civil Procedure Code Act of 1966,[410] which permits a suit to be filed by one or several persons on behalf of numerous others provided that they all have the same interest in the same subject matter. The Court of Appeal ruled that, in any event, each villager had to prove his own case and that each claim was different from the other in terms of date of possession, of acreage, of the method of acquisition and so on.[411]

---

land into individually owned plots of land. This right was designed mainly for Europeans and Asians. See also Fimbo, *Essays in Land Laws* (1992), p. 2.

406 Maini, *Land Law in Eastern Africa* (1967), pp. 85-6; Chachage, "Land Issues" (1999), p. 61; Ringo Tenga, *Pastoral Land Rights in Tanzania: A Review* (London: IIED Drylands Programme: Pastoral Land Tenures Series, 1992), p. 3.

407 Land Acquisition Act (No. 47 of 1967). Cap 118 R.E 2002.

408 Ibid., Section 3.

409 Ibid., Section 12(a).

410 Cap 33 R.E 2002.

411 *National Agricultural and Food Corporation (NAFCO) v. Mulbadaw Vill age Council and 66 Others*, CA - Dar es Salaam, CA#3/1986. In the initial case of 1981, the 67 Barabaig villagers claimed to rep-

More remarkably, the Court of Appeal held that none of the villagers who had testified could be said to have held land on customary tenure, as none of them had established, or even averred that he was a native of the Hanang district. They were thus not "occupiers" in terms of the Land Ordinance.

> *If the villagers who had testified could have established that, as natives, they had right of occupancy by virtue of customary tenancies then the view of the Judge is that such villagers in this case could only be evicted or dispossessed under provisions of the Land Acquisition Act No.47 of 1967.*

Indeed, the Court of Appeal ruled that

1. *None of the villagers who had testified could be said to have held land on customary tenure, as none had established, or even averred that he was a native;*
2. *The Mulbadaw Village Council did not own any land because there was no evidence of any allocation of land to it by the District Development Council;*
3. *The fact that the village council succeeded the previous unincorporated village in its administrative function over a specified area confers no title of any type over such land on the village council;*
4. *Since the villagers were cultivating and planting with permission of the appellant ... as licensees, they can claim damages in trespass for the destruction of their property by the appellant.*[412]

Concluding observations or results/impact of the court cases

1. These two cases illustrate a situation where courts in the same country can make two fundamentally different rulings because of departing from different perspectives in their reasoning. On the one hand, the High Court ruled in favor of the indigenous plaintiffs by going beyond written laws to look into customary unwritten rules of land management and ownership in Tanzania. It thus underlined the immemorial occupation and use of the disputed land by the plaintiffs as an important factor that any subsequent written law cannot just write off in the African context, where customs and traditions are still much alive. On the other hand, the Court of Appeal based its reasoning on Tanzanian written laws, on which depends the validity of customary laws.
2. The issue of representation rose in this case when a number of villagers alleged to act in the name of many others. This was not accepted by the

---

resent their entire community. But the Court of Appeal denied them *locus standi* (i.e., the right of the litigant to act or be heard).

412 Ibid.

Court of Appeal and one lesson to be drawn could be ensuring that the claims of each claimant are the same as that of the others. Note that the law in Tanzania provides for certain requirements to be met in order for aggrieved persons to be able to file a representative suit. These are: (i) there must be numerous persons; (ii) these numerous persons must have the same interest; (iii) the intended representative must obtain permission of the court; and (iv) notice must be given to all parties to a suit.

3. The plaintiffs and their lawyers did not make use of international law and standards. This was understandable at the time, since indigenous peoples-related universal standards and jurisprudence were not yet known on the continent. However, it continued to be the case in many other lawsuits long after these standards and jurisprudence had finally become known in Africa.

4. Delaying tactics were obviously used in this case and it was clear that the Judge of Appeal avoided addressing the core issues of the case by hiding behind technicalities.

Yoke Gwaku and 5 Others v. National Agricultural and Food Corporation (NAFCO) and Gawal Farms Limited. HC – Arusha, CV# 52/1988

Background facts and claimants' arguments

Hundreds of families pertaining to the Barabaig pastoralist indigenous community lived in the Gawal area, one of the land areas attributed by the Tanzanian Government to NAFCO and Gawal Wheat Farm Limited, two farming companies. As soon as they were attributed the disputed lands, the two companies moved in with tractors and agricultural machinery, destroying a number of properties belonging to this Barabaig community.

This lawsuit was initiated in 1988 by six Barabaig individuals, who, at the same time, also applied for an authorization to represent in court more than 700 other community members. Due to a preliminary objection raised by the defendants' council on the fact that the public notice of the case did not list all the plaintiffs, the High Court of Arusha ruled that public notice must be directed to identifiable interested persons. Therefore the court found that the suit couldn't be said to have been filed for and on behalf of 788 persons, apart from the six plaintiffs who were listed in the public notice.

The plaintiffs claimed that the land, which was occupied and used by the defendants, constituted their ancestral lands and that of other members of their tribe. They claimed also that both NAFCO and Gawal Wheat Farm Limited forcefully and unlawfully evicted them from their lands. So they asked the court: (1) to declare the defendants' acquisition of that land null and void and (2) to order that the defendants be evicted from it and be permanently barred from ever-entering it.

Considering that the defendants were thought to have set fire, destroyed homesteads, crops, livestock, household goods, gravesites and sacred shrines of the Barabaig, these plaintiffs also asked the court to order the defendants to pay damages to all the persons affected by the evictions and the destructions.

The plaintiffs called in several witnesses, including international researchers such as Charles Robert Lane, then a senior Research Associate of the International Institute for Environment and Development in London, United Kingdom, who gave evidence as an expert witness. He explained to the court how, for example, the Barabaig had migrated south to the Serengeti plains, and then to the Ngorongoro highlands, finally settling, within the last 150 years, in various places along the Rift Valley, including the Hanang District.

Defendants' core legal points

The defendants alleged that the land now occupied by one of them had been lawfully acquired and that all normal procedures leading to its acquisition had been followed. They argued that, after identifying suitable land for wheat growing, they made a formal application for it to the regional authorities through the District authorities in 1979. A response to the application was received in 1981 by way of a letter from the District Development Director. The letter authorized NAFCO to start a farm in Gawal under certain conditions, some of which were to provide for cattle routes and residential land for people living south of the farm, in Gawidu. The defendants underlined also that a list of persons to be compensated had been made and payment made to each and everyone. They also showed that they occupied the disputed lands following a District Council's decision and an approval of this decision by the office of the Tanzanian Prime Minister.

Ruling and reasoning of the court

The three main questions to be dealt with by the court were:

1. Whether the plaintiffs had title in the land in dispute;
2. Whether the defendants lawfully acquired title to the land under dispute;
3. Whether the plaintiffs had suffered damages and loss as a result of the defendants trespass.

On the issue of whether the plaintiffs had title in the land in dispute, the High Court ruled that only three of the plaintiffs had founded claims of customary rights over the disputed lands and that:

> *A person can prove that he owns land under customary tenure by showing that such land was allocated to him by an authority which is competent to do so or by showing that he inherited it from a past parent. Thus, although the first plaintiff did not give the acreage of land which he inherited from his father, I have no doubt from the evidence that he, in fact, owned land in Ghama.*

Only three of the plaintiffs, who testified before the judge, could, according to him, prove they were native occupiers of the disputed lands. For instance, the first plaintiff, Yoke Gwaku, said he owned land in Ghama, now part of Gawal Wheat Farm. He argued that he inherited the land from his father and grandfather; and that he used it partly for pasture and cultivation. NAFCO (one of the defendants) ploughed up the area around his *boma*,[413] thus forcing him to move out. He acknowledged that the Village Council allocated him other land in Mulbadaw, but this new land was inadequate for his needs. He also accepted that he was paid some compensation but argued that it was not a fair and full compensation. He said that when he was evicted he owned about 1000 head of cattle, 100 goats and 40 sheep. At the time of giving evidence, he owned only 60 head of cattle, 10 goats and 20 sheep. He blamed the decimation of his livestock on the defendants who took from him the pastureland on which his livestock depended. He wanted the court to restore to him the land he lost to the defendants.

Given that each and every plaintiff was to prove he or she was a native of the area and held customary rights in the land in dispute, the claims of the plaintiffs who did not testify were dismissed. The court argued that these plaintiffs did not succeed to prove they traditionally owned the lands.

On the issue of whether the defendants lawfully acquired title to the land under dispute, the court ruled that the first defendant (NAFCO) did not hold a valid title with regard to the three plaintiffs' areas of land and that NAFCO had therefore all along been trespassing on those pieces of land.

On the issue of whether the plaintiffs had suffered damages and loss as a result of the defendants' trespass, the court ruled that the three plaintiffs suffered damages and therefore awarded to the first plaintiff general damages amounting to Tanzanian shillings (Tshs) 500,000 and another Tshs 10,000 as compensation for the grave of his grandfather; the second plaintiff was awarded 100,000 and the sixth plaintiff 50,000.

Although the court found that NAFCO had trespassed over the lands of the three successful plaintiffs and ordered the company to pay compensation, it did

---

413 Traditional house of the Barabaig (as well as of the Maasai).

not nullify NAFCO's land title or order the return of the lands in dispute to the plaintiffs. As Sengondo E. Mvungi notes, "since only a few individuals gave evidence, the court felt constrained to nullify the whole title over extensive lands to benefit a few pastoralists! Therefore, although the trespass was proved, the remedies could not be granted as prayed."[414]

The plaintiffs were not in agreement with the verdict of the High Court and launched an appeal, which is still pending. But according to Mvungi "several years later, the Court of Appeal was moved by an advocate who claimed to have no instructions from the claimants to strike down the appeal."[415] The parties to this case, including the appellants, seem no longer to believe in a judicial outcome. The situation on the ground remains unchanged.

Concluding observations and results/impact of the court case

Six members of an indigenous community tried to represent in court 788 other members. But because the public notice in a newspaper did not have the names of all the 788 plaintiffs, the court found that the suit was not filed for and on behalf of all. It is difficult to understand why the community's lawyers did not restart the whole procedure instead of proceeding with only six plaintiffs.

A number of plaintiffs accepted before the initiation of the court case some sort of compensation, which they later declared unfair. This is a practice that can compromise successes of court cases and it is not recommendable. Indigenous peoples or individuals should rather refuse a compensation they consider to be unfair than accepting it and then later declare it to be unfair.

It is interesting to note that the plaintiffs brought in researchers as witnesses, who presented the court with a wide range of historical facts on the Barabaig and their ancestral relationship to lands. Even if this testimony did not seem to make a major impact, identifying potential researchers who could testify before court is a practice that indigenous communities about to start a legal battle for their lands should consider.

The lack of detailed evaluation of damages suffered by the plaintiffs is noticeable in the presentations of different witnesses as well as in the plaintiffs' statements before the judge. This did surely have a negative impact on the amounts of compensation awarded by the court to the three successful plaintiffs. It is therefore recommendable that indigenous peoples do all they can to estimate exactly the damages suffered and that they do this as early in the process as possible, since, as years pass on, it becomes more difficult to reconstruct facts.

It is striking that the court declared NAFCO's occupation of the disputed land unlawful but failed to declare it null and return it to the plaintiffs. This is an il-

---

414 Mvungi, "Experiences" (2008), p. 5.
415 Ibid.

lustration of courts' unwillingness to challenge Governments' position and avoiding by all means making landmark decisions. This can be deduced from the following words of a former Chief Justice: "I do not agree with the jurists who say to the effect that the courts are bound to administer the law even if heaven fall. Obviously any law, the administration of which causes heaven to fall can not be law in the proper sense. Such so called law which causes instability must be a law of the jungle."[416]

This is also a court case that shows how delays are used as a tactic aiming at exhausting indigenous peoples' patience and funds. Today, international mechanisms such as communications to the African Commission on Human and Peoples' Rights should be considered in cases like this one, given that the appeal seems unlikely to proceed.

The Maasai and their land cases

The following two cases—later consolidated into one—involve the indigenous Maasai people of Mkomazi in Tanzania. The Maasai are pastoralists with a semi-nomadic lifestyle and they are estimated to number some 330,000 people in Tanzania.

Mkomazi is located in the northern part of Tanzania. Most of it was gazetted as a Game Reserve in 1951. This Game Reserve is known for its diverse fauna and a controversial 17.5 km long solar-powered electric fence prevents local communities from entering and using it clandestinely. The creation of this game reserve was expected not to affect the land rights of the Maasai communities. The Wildlife Conservation Act of 1974,[417] which repealed and replaced the Fauna Conservation Ordinance that created Mkomazi Game Reserve, indeed exempts a "person whose place of ordinary residence is within the reserve" from the general rule relating to the requirement for permits.[418]

In 1988, Government officials ordered a forcible remove of all Maasai out of the Game Reserve, (by now upgraded into a National Park), so as to provide more security to wildlife. An estimated 4,000 to 10,000 community members—who consider the reserve their ancestral lands to which they are entitled—were evicted without due compensation or any provisions for relocation.[419]

After attempts to get the Tanzanian Government to change its mind had failed, a number of Maasai decided to lodge two cases challenging the eviction. By then, six years had elapsed since the eviction happened.

---

416 Francis L. Nyalali, "The Social Context of Judicial Decisions Making". Paper presented at a workshop on The State of Human Rights in Tanzania, held at the British Council Hall, Dar es Salaam, 3 July 1998.
417 Cap 283 R.E 2002.
418 Section 7(a) of Act No. 12 of 1974.
419 The International Work Group for Indigenous Affairs (IWGIA), *The Indigenous World* 1997/98, (Copenhagen: IWGIA, 1998), p. 299. Available at: http://www.iwgia.org.

Lekengere Faru Parutu Kamunyu and 16 Others v. the Minister for Tourism, Natural Resources and Environment and 3 Others. HC – Moshi, CV#33/1994

And

Kopera Keiya Kamunyu and 44 Others v. the Minister for Tourism, Natural Resources and Environment and 3 Others. HC – Moshi, CV# 33/1995

Background facts and claimants' arguments

In court, the Maasai argued, among other things, breach of their customary land rights, destruction of their properties, killing of their livestock, and negative impact on their way of life. As detailed by Ringo Tenga, the plaintiffs claimed that:

1. Their constitutional right to live and enjoy their respective lives has been infringed;
2. They have, without due process been denied their basic right to reside in their traditional and ancestral lands;
3. Unlawful eviction constitutes a serious infringement of the claimants' customary land rights of natives of Tanganyika as recognised by land laws of Tanzania as well as the constitutional right to property;
4. They now find themselves in drought conditions, with their dwindling livestock lacking grazing and water and surround[ed] by settled villages;
5. No plans to relocate the claimants have been made;
6. Shortage of grazing for their livestock has attracted exorbitant fines of up to Tshs 400,000 for livestock straying into the Mkomazi Game Reserve (MGR);
7. They have suffered frequent beating and general harassment by employees of MGR;
8. They have lost cattle, goats, sheep and donkeys estimated at 10 billion shillings due to diseases and starvation;
9. They have lost access to customary holy places and sacred shrines;
10. Loss of grazing lands has led to vicious deprivation of the plaintiffs' employment, livelihood and ultimately, their right to life;
11. Evictions without compensation and alternative grazing land have reduced the Maasai pastoralists into squatters surrounded by hostile agricultural communities;
12. The claimants' pastoral activities have been criminalized.

The plaintiffs' lawyers submitted that the Land Ordinance of 1923 only required proof of occupation and use of land to establish a customary title to land. The Maasai plaintiffs established that they had been in MGR for generations, using the vast plains of Alilalai Lamwasuni as the community's common property for grazing and community life. Further, the authorities had listed or registered them and allowed them to keep their pre-existing rights as required by the Fauna Conservation Ordinance and the Wildlife Conservation Act of 1974.

The lawyers argued also that according to principles protecting the constitutional right to property, a land owned by a community can only be acquired by the Government in accordance with the Land Acquisition Act of 1967, whose procedures require establishing a public purpose that justifies the acquisition. This is followed by a consultative process where, upon agreement, the rights-holders are compensated and/or given alternative land. In case of disagreement, the parties have recourse in the courts. These procedures were not followed in this particular case, and therefore all actions taken should be declared null, void, and unconstitutional.[420]

Defendants' core legal points

The defendants, represented by the Attorney General, argued that the disputed lands were lawfully gazetted as a protected area since 1951, that the residents were given notice with enough time to leave the Game Reserve and that the Government had no other choice than the use of force after the plaintiffs had refused to leave the area voluntarily. The Attorney General argued also that alternative lands were provided to the plaintiffs in Handeni, Kiteto, and Ruvu. He contended furthermore that the plaintiffs were mere licensees residing on the disputed lands and had no longer the right to remain in the Game Reserve after the Government had revoked their licenses. The Attorney General argued also that the plaintiffs should have lodged a Constitutional Petition rather than a suit, given that they claim a violation of Constitutional rights. Finally the defendants' representative argued that the plaintiffs' claim for compensation should be thrown out because of being overdue or not presented within the three years required by the Tanzanian Statute of Limitations of 1971, given that the eviction occurred in 1988 and the case was filed in 1994.[421]

---

420 Ringo Tenga, "Legitimizing Dispossession: The Tanzanian High Court's Decision on the Eviction of Maasai Pastoralists from Mkomazi Game Reserve", *Cultural Survival Quarterly*, Issue 22.4 (31 January 1999).

421 Tanzanian Statute of Limitations of 1971, Cap 89, R. E 2002.

Ruling and reasoning of the court

The High Court made several points:

1. Regarding the issue of representation, the High Court ruled against the idea that a number of Maasai could represent others in court: *"The judgment shall not canvas the pastoral Maasai community en masse for the reason that this is not a representative suit"*. Accordingly, the High Court dealt only with 38 plaintiffs out of 53, who appeared in court.

2. Regarding the claim of customary rights by the plaintiffs, the High Court ruled that *"the plaintiffs held customary land rights at Umba Game Reserve, a portion of the Mkomazi Game Reserve"*. The court also ruled that the eviction of the Maasai plaintiffs from Umba Game Reserve was unlawful because it did not comply with procedures specified by the Land Acquisition Act of 1967. But the judge went on arguing that since the eviction occurred in 1988 and the case was filed more than five years later, the case had been overtaken by events and therefore a return of the plaintiffs' traditional lands was no longer possible: *"the unlawful eviction took place in May 1988, over more than five years ago. In that regards the suit has been overtaken by events"*.

3. The High Court ruled also in favour of a violation of the plaintiffs' right to property protected under article 24 of the Constitution and awarded each of them a compensation of Tshs 300,000, (more or less US$450). The judge found that game scouts and militiamen effecting the eviction assaulted pastoralists, harassed their families, mothers with newly born babies had to be carried and dumped into the bush in the rush of the eviction, cattle, donkeys and calves strayed into the wilderness where they were lost or devoured by beasts; *bomas*, huts, kraals, cattle, domestic articles, food stuffs, veterinary medicines, cash and ornaments got lost or razed down by the fires the game scouts started. Families were dislocated and broken up. In short the plaintiffs were seriously inconvenienced, put through a great crisis and thrown out of the reserve without assistance for resettlement in terms of alternative land.

4. Finally the High Court ruled that alternative lands should be provided to the plaintiffs *"so that the pastoral plaintiffs can resettle on a self-help basis."*

Lekengere Faru Parutu Kamunyu & Others v. Minister of Tourism, Natural Resources and Environment & Others. CA-CVA#53/1998, unreported, (1999)

The plaintiffs were not happy with the decision of the High Court, against which they appealed immediately. In 1998, the Court of Appeal made the following decisions in its ruling:

1. It agreed with the High Court on the issue of representation and ruled that the case concerned only the plaintiffs that had testified;
2. The Court of Appeal overturned the High Court's decision that the plaintiffs enjoyed customary right in the disputed land:

> We now come to substantive points, and we begin by considering whether the Maasai community of which the appellants are members, had an ancestral customary land title over the whole of the Mkomazi Game Reserve. We have carefully considered the indisputable surrounding circumstances which gave rise to this case, and it is apparent that the Maasai community or tribe in question was not the first tribe to arrive in the geographical area which is the subject of this case. It is apparent that the Maasai were new arrivals in the area, preceded by other tribes, such as the Pare, Shambaa and even the Kamba. It would seem that the Maasai, as a nomadic tribe, began to reach the area in the second half of the 1940s and their presence was still scanty at the time the Mkomazi Game Reserve was established in 1951. That explains why they were not involved in the consultations which preceded the creation of the Game Reserve. That being the position; we are bound to hold that the Maasai Community in question did not have ancestral customary land title over the whole of the Mkomazi Game Reserve. We are aware that the learned trial Judge found that such title existed in a portion of the Game Reserve, that is, Umba Game Reserve. The Respondents have not cross-appealed against the finding, but since that finding of the learned trial Judge is inconsistent with our overall finding, we have to invoke our revisional jurisdiction provided under Section 4(2) of the Appellate Jurisdiction Act, 1979 as amended by Act No. 17 of 1993 so as to set aside such finding which is inconsistent with ours. We do so accordingly, and find that no such title existed in the Umba Game Reserve.[422]

---

422 Mvungi, "Experiences" (2007), p.11, quoting the Certified Unreported Judgment (n.d.), p. 16-17.

Concluding observations and results/impact of the court cases

1. Sengondo E. Mvungi makes an interesting critical reading and analysis of this decision by the Court of Appeal,[423] underlining a number of wrong assumptions upon on which the Court of Appeal seemed to ground its reasoning. Firstly, the court assumed that the plaintiffs were not the first inhabitants of the disputed land and therefore could not claim customary rights over it. This court's reasoning was not correct because "the first people may have abandoned the land, or just disappeared. The groups that follow and subsequently establish long usage would not be held ransom to the fact that there existed some people in the areas some time in the past. What is required is proof of long use over time that is not contradicted by a superior title."[424] It is not necessary to be first to claim indigenous rights over a land. This has been widely proven including in the Australian *Mabo* case, where the claimant indigenous peoples were recognized as having arrived from elsewhere. Furthermore, it is almost impossible to tell which community lived where first in Africa. The Court of Appeal seemed even to distance itself from the Tanzanian legislation. This was indeed a justice badly rendered that could have prompted further national or international legal challenges.

2. The time that had lapsed between the dispossession and the filing of the case appears as an excuse by the first judge to deny justice to the plaintiffs. In numerous cases, indigenous peoples were expelled from their lands for tens or hundreds of years before taking legal actions. One could mention for example the restitution of tens of thousands of hectares to the South African ǂKhomani San on the basis of the Land Restitution Act. Had the High Court of Tanzania aimed at redressing historical injustices, it would have not only declared the eviction unlawful but also ordered a return of the plaintiffs to their ancestral lands in addition to compensation. This makes it imperative for communities' lawyers acting in this kind of cases to make as much as possible reference to any existing relevant international jurisprudence in an attempt to try and move judges away from traditional ways of thinking. Taking the case to higher courts or international bodies such as the African Commission on Human and Peoples' Rights could have been further options, which seem to never have been considered by the plaintiffs.

3. This case demonstrates also that indigenous communities should file land-related lawsuits as soon as they are dispossessed or evicted from their lands in order not to give judges cheap excuses.

---

423 Ibid., pp. 11-14.
424 Ibid., p. 14.

4. The importance of properly filing a representative suit must be under-
    lined once more as something to deal with carefully in similar cases.

Legal and policy landscape in Tanzania relating to indigenous peoples' land rights

During colonial times

In 1919, following the end of the First World War, German East Africa came under
the control of the League of Nations. The territory was later divided into three
mandated countries, of which two were given to Belgium (Rwanda and Burundi)
and one—under the name of Tanganyika Territory—to Britain.[425] In 1946, after
the collapse of the League of Nations and World War II, Tanganyika became a
British Trust Territory, since, according to the UN Charter, all territories formerly
under the League of Nations' mandate were to be covered by the trusteeship regime.[426]

   As a territory under mandate, Tanganyika, as the country was called until
1964, was not like other colonies. The League of Nations set a string of rules, including the protection of the rights of local populations.[427] This was later reinforced by the Charter of the United Nations, which also made it clear that under
the Trusteeship system, the wishes, values and customs of the inhabitants of a
trust territory must be given priority.[428]

   It emerges, however, that during the period up to World War II large areas of
land were taken away from traditional communities. Between 1923 and 1926, an
average of 24,000 acres per year, or approximately a total of 120,000 acres of lands,
were alienated on behalf of foreigners.[429] In its 1926 Report, the Permanent Mandates Commission of the League of Nations set up to oversee the British administration of Tanganyika heavily criticized the provisions of the 1923 Land Ordi-

---

425 The United Republic of Tanzania consists of the mainland, formerly known as Tanganyika, and
     the island of Zanzibar. From 1890 to 1918, Tanganyika was part of German East Africa while
     Zanzibar was a British protectorate from 1890 to 1963. Tanganyika gained independence in 1961,
     Zanzibar in 1963. The two territories were united in 1964. For more details see Rosemary E.
     Galli (ed.), *The Political Economy of Rural Development: Peasants, International Capital and the State*
     (Albany, N.Y.: State University of New York Press, 1981), p. 113.
426 Article 77 of the United Nations Charter. The Charter's chapter XII deals with the Trusteeship
     system.
427 Article 6 of the Mandate Agreement between the League of Nations and Britain (1922) relating to
     the administration of Tanganyika.
428 Article 76 of the U.N. Charter: "The Trusteeship system shall ... promote the political, economic,
     social ... advancement of the inhabitants of the trust territories".
429 Peter G. Forster and Sam Maghimbi (eds.) *Agrarian Economy, State and Society in Contemporary
     Tanzania* (Aldershot: Ashgate Publishing Co., 1999), p. 43.

nance, which stated that "the whole of the lands of Tanganyika, whether occupied or unoccupied on the date of the commencement of this Ordinance, are hereby declared to be public lands".[430] The Commission's central issue was whether, by stripping the communities of their pre-colonial full ownership of their lands,[431] the Ordinance was in breach of the terms of the Mandate regarding the need to "respect the rights and safeguard the interests of the local population".[432]

Following up on this report, the colonial Government passed another more pro-indigenous communities law in 1928,[433] which provided for the deemed right of occupancy deriving out of customary use and occupation of land and said to be "as [protective and] good as a written document or right of occupancy under the Land Ordinance".[434] Thus, indigenous peoples maintained some sort of control over their homelands. James Woodburn confirms that, "the British administrators who replaced the Germans during the First World War were content to leave the Hadzabe area, occupied by a hunter-gatherer community of northern Tanzania, much as it was".[435] Indeed, several scholars believe that most of the "customary land laws of Tanzania [remained] untouched" by the colonial system.[436]

One strong indication of the survival of the notion of collective holding of land by local communities during this era of colonial-type land laws was the recognition by the colonial ruler of a number of customary mechanisms such as the semi-feudal Nyarubanja tenure system. The beneficiaries of this mechanism were usually traditional chiefs favorable to colonial rule, whose duties and rights were later regulated by the Bukoba Chiefs Act in 1930, amended later in 1938 as the "Nyarubanja Rules" under the Native Authority Ordinance.[437]

In an attempt to keep within the margins of the international mandate, the colonial master of Tanganyika furthermore opted for a colonial system that would

430 Section 3 of the 1923 Land Ordinance, CAP 113.

431 The 1926 Report by the Permanent Mandates Commission of the League of the Nations showed some doubts about the Land Ordinance in the following terms: A "Land Ordinance was drafted in 1923 and has since been enacted … doubt had arisen whether native occupiers of communal land, to whom no certificate of occupancy had been issued, would be recognised as occupiers under the principal ordinance and be entitled to protection against arbitrary disturbances which that Ordinance gives". See also in Fimbo, *Essays* (1992), p. 66. Many scholars have indeed shown that land was collectively owned amongst most pre-colonial Tanzanian indigenous peoples. Also individuals could use and occupy land to its full extent although the proprietorship was vested in communities. See, e.g., Sally Falk Moore, *Social Facts and Fabrications: "Customary Law" in the Kilimanjaro 1880-1980* (Cambridge, UK: Cambridge University Press, 1986), p. 62; Tenga, *Pastoral Land Rights* (1992), p. 10; Eugene Cotran, "Customary Land Law in Kenya, Uganda and Tanzania", in UNESCO, *Le droit de la terre en Afrique,* (Paris: G.P. Maisonneuve et Larose, 1971), pp. 91-100.

432 Article 6 of the British League of Nations Mandate over Tanganyika.

433 Ordinance No. 7 of 1928.

434 Fimbo, *Essays* (1992), p. 66.

435 Woodburn, "Minimal Politics" (1979), p. 247.

436 Maini, *Land Law* (1967), p. 89.

437 Cotran, "Customary Land Law" (1971), p. 108.

consist of incorporating the communities, and some of their ways of life, within the overall program of the Government.[438] This could explain why in some cases, when the colonial Government needed to resettle a number of communities in new areas, it resorted to "agreements", as was the case in 1958 regarding a Maasai community of the Western Serengeti.[439] However, by the end of the 1950s, 40 per cent of Tanzania's arable lands were owned by foreign farmers.[440] A number of communities, nevertheless, had kept their lands, which they continued to use and occupy collectively according to their customs and traditions.

The Ujamaa era

After independence, in 1967, Tanzania introduced *Ujamaa* in an attempt to Africanise its land laws through a policy that considered the agricultural sector "as capable of generating growth from the [country's] own resources, while at the same time benefiting the majority of the people".[441] This policy was called by the Swahili words of *Ujamaa Vijijini*, meaning "socialism within villages" (also known as "villagization"). It consisted of "translocating" people in groups to what was called *"Ujamaa* villages", where individuals, sometimes of different cultural backgrounds, lineages and clans, were expected to work on communal farms with which they had no cultural tie or bond. By 1977, 90 per cent or more of the Tanzanians lived in some 7,300 villages.[442] This African adaptation of socialism was construed around the principle that Tanzania was to regain its economic independence by providing for itself. The principle of "self-reliance" (*kujitegemea* in Swahili) was always attached to the term *Ujamaa*, as stated in the 1967 Arusha Declaration.[443]

---

438 See Chachage, "Land Issues" (1999), p. 62, and Kiondo, "Structural Adjustment" (1999), p. 43.

439 The Agreement between the Maasai and the colonial authority stated as follows: "We, the Laigwanak (elders) of the Ngorongoro and Loliondo division of the Maasai district, agree on behalf of all the Maasai living in these areas to renounce our claim to all those parts of the Serengeti plains lying within the Northern and Lake provinces, which lie to the west of the line shown to us by the District Commissioner, on the 13th and 14th March and the 20th of April 1958. ...We understand that, as a result of this renunciation, we shall not be entitled henceforth in the years to come to cross this line which will become the boundary of the new Serengeti National Park and which will be demarcated. We also understand that we shall not be entitled to reside in or use in future the land lying to the west of this line, which we have habitually used in the past. ... We agree to move ourselves, our possessions, our cattle and all other animals out of this land by the advent of the next short rains, that is before the 31st December 1958. ...Witnessed by us at Ngorongoro this 21st day of April 1958." See Shivji and Kapinga, *Maasai Rights* (1998), p. 74.

440 Chachage, "Land Issues" (1999), p. 63.

441 Ringo Tenga, "Processing a Land Policy: The Case of Mainland Tanzania", available online at http://www.whoseland.com/paper7.html, (1998b), p. 3; Kiondo, "Structural Adjustment" (1999), p. 44.

442 Yeager and Miller, *Wildlife, Wild Death* (1986), p. 25.

443 The Arusha Declaration was made public by the Tanzanian president, Mr. Nyerere, in 1967. It consisted in nationalizing private enterprises, business and farmlands with the intent of boost-

This policy, which attempted to transform all Tanzanian communities into farmers by designing and imposing the way lands should be used and occupied,[444] emerged as a radical political change in Tanzania.[445]

The policy was also intended to be a reaction to the then surviving colonial economic system, accused of plundering national resources for the sake of individual interests.[446] Numerous private companies, which had existed since colonial time, continued to hold large parts of the most fertile lands in Tanzania.

The policy was crafted on the idea that land together with people, good policies and good leadership were "the four prerequisites of development".[447] Accordingly, private land ownership was prohibited and the "State retained the sole right to allocate land for cultivation and housing through allotment".[448] "The State was supposed to bring social services, industries, and infrastructure to the people who, in return, were expected to accept a high degree of economic control".[449] In one way or another, people were moved into *Ujamaa* villages, where they were deemed to work on communal lands.

The *Ujamaa* policy could be regarded as having had two major effects on communities' land rights based on customary tenure. On the one hand, it implicitly abolished the communal aspect of the "deemed right of occupancy" on agricultural lands. On the other hand, it could be argued that it somehow preserved the customary right of communities found within conservation areas and on other reserved lands. There had never been a law explicitly abolishing the "deemed right of occupancy". Instead, the *Ujamaa* decision makers firstly opted for the destruction of the institutional framework or the sociological pillars on which the customary land tenure was based so that everything would fall apart, once the foundation had been destroyed. Secondly, the legislator designed a strategy that consisted of uprooting local communities from lands with which they had cultural ties.

Towards a new agricultural policy

By 1980, the Tanzanian economy was assessed as not performing.[450] At the same time, Tanzania was also hit by the international economic turmoil caused by the

ing self-reliance built upon agriculture and farming by the State. See Issa G. Shivji, *Class Struggles in Tanzania* (London: Heinemann, 1976), p. 79.

444 Yeager and Miller, *Wildlife, Wild Death* (1986), p. 24.

445 Kiondo, "Structural Adjustment" (1999), p. 44.

446 J.K. Nyerere, *Ujamaa: Essays on Socialism* (London: Oxford University Press, 1968), p. 106.

447 Ibid., p. 29.

448 Donna O. Kerner, "Land Scarcity and Rights of Control in the Development of Commercial Farming in Northeast Tanzania", in *Land and Society in Contemporary Africa*, edited by R.E. Downs and S. P. Reyna (Hanover, NH: University Press of New England, 1988), p. 169.

449 Chachage, "Land Issues" (1999), p. 58.

450 Ibid., p. 59. The production of cotton was declared to have declined by 20.1 per cent, tobacco by 4.5 per cent and pyrethrum by 11.5 per cent. Many other products also had declining production

1970s oil crisis.[451] This combination of factors made Tanzania succumb to pressure from international financial institutions, and thus abandon its socialist system. Instead, the country embarked on the capitalist track. With the agricultural sector as a central pillar, efficient land management and a reinforced private sector were expected to play a key role in the ultimate goal of good food supplies and sufficient foreign exchange.[452]

Accordingly, in 1983, the Tanzanian Government adopted a *National Agricultural Policy*, aimed at increasing rural productivity. This Policy proposed the establishment of individually owned plots of land within the *Ujamaa* villages. For a village as a whole, the Policy proposed a "right of occupancy" that would not last more than 99 years.[453] The State would, however, continue to be the sole absolute owner of all Tanzanian lands and the District Councils, as organised by the Local Government Act of 1982, were given the role of management and allocation of lands in most rural areas.

The new policy did little, if anything at all, to restore to communities their lands, which in addition to being a major source of income were also the symbol of their cultural existence. On the contrary, following the suggestions made by the World Bank and the donor community in support of land titling,[454] the policy "encouraged the development of a class of big farmers" at the expense of the poor peasant masses.

The trend of ignoring customary claims to lands went on until 1987, when the "Prime Minister issued an Extinction of Customary Land Rights Order, ... which extinguished customary land rights in Arumeru, Babati, Hanang, and Mbulu Districts. In July 1989, the Prime Minister issued another order ... which covered areas in Hanang District, which Barabaig pastoralists of Hanang were claiming in court".[455]

The Shivji Report

However, the continuing burning desire for, and claims of communities to, their customary land rights—demands which had to be reconciled with the need for Tanzanian economic growth—prompted, among other things, the establishment of what is known as the Presidential Commission of Inquiry into Land Matters.[456]

---

rates. See also Fimbo, *Essays* (1992), p. 10.

451 Kiondo, "Structural Adjustment" (1999), p. 45.

452 Ibid., p. 47; Chachage, "Land Issues" (1999), pp. 58 and 68; Wøien and Lama, *Market Commerce as Wildlife Protector?* (1999), p. 8; Bourn and Blench, *Can Livestock and Wildlife Co-Exist* (1999), p. 44; Yeager and Miller, *Wildlife, Wild Death* (1986), p. 128.

453 Kiondo, "Structural Adjustment" (1999), p. 48; Chachage, "Land Issues" (1999), p. 66.

454 Tenga, "Legislating" (1998a), p. 3.

455 Tenga, *Pastoral Land Rights* (1992), p. 23.

456 Tenga, "Legislating" (1998a), pp. 4-5.

In late 1992, this Commission submitted its report, commonly referred to by the name of its author as "the Shivji Report".[457] This Report underlined the "dichotomy ... between the peasant/pastoral sector governed by customary land tenure under the deemed right of occupancy and the plantation/urban sector governed by statutory ... system under the granted right of occupancy".[458]

Giving particular attention to the pre-existing collective holding of lands by communities, the Shivji Report concluded that the 1980s Tanzanian understanding of customary land tenure was similar to the one in pre-colonial time, when traditional authorities held effective powers over lands.[459] Furthermore, the Shivji Report criticised the Government's introduction of the "process of original adjudication and issuance of titles", which it argued "became, to some extent, a process of dispossessing original rights-holders while improving the land holding of others".[460]

Accordingly, the Shivji Report proposed that there should be two types of lands: on the one hand, "national lands" that would be administered by a National Lands Commission, and on the other hand, "village lands" that would be managed by village assemblies composed of all the adult village members. In relation to village lands, the Shivji Report recommended also a formalisation of customary titles through a process of local adjudication by the elders, which could result in the issuance of customary titles. The councils of elders would compile a village lands register. Land transactions between village members would be allowed, but land dealings between members of a village with outsiders would not be possible without the consent of the elders.

The mechanisms of "village land" management, as recommended by the Shivji Report, were not the exact match of the pre-colonial mechanisms for collective land holdings. However, they could be regarded as the closest-ever alternative to the pre-colonial customary land tenure in Tanzania, where "rights in lands [were never] vested in any individual but in ... groups such as a tribe or the political authorities or the clan or family groups, and ... although an individual could have the right of use of the land, the ultimate reversion [was] in the community".[461]

Despite the important remarks made by the Shivji Report in support of customary land rights of communities, the National Environment Management Council,[462] which is the architect of the 1995 Tanzania National Conservation

---

457 The Report was published in 1994. See United Republic of Tanzania, *Report of the Presidential Commission*, Vol.1 (1994).
458 Ibid., p. 140.
459 Ibid., pp. 146-7.
460 Ibid., p. 116 and 118.
461 Cotran, "Customary Land Law" (1971), p. 90.
462 Following the adoption by Tanzania of the objectives and resolutions of the 1972 Stockholm Conference on the interdependency between, on the one hand, the natural environment and, on the other hand, human habitation, the Act No. 19 of 1983 established a National Environment Management Council with the task to advise the Government on environmental issues. Given

Strategy for Sustainable Development (NCSSD), re-focused the debate on laying the ground for a market-oriented resources management:

> The existing land legislation, land bill and institutional set-up for land tenure are inadequate to deal with dynamic changes such as the changeover to a market-oriented economy, privatisation, increased urbanisation, population increase, etc. They fail to provide incentives for more efficient use of resources, including investments for land improvements and development.[463]

Furthermore, in addition to the political willingness to make agricultural lands the power-engine of the new free market economic orientation in Tanzania, a new conservation policy was adopted aiming at increasing the contribution of this sector to the country's economy from 2 to 5 per cent of GDP by 2017.[464] The tourist industry was also identified as an important sector for Tanzania.[465] In order to achieve this, the new conservation policy was designed to incite the private sector "to invest in the wildlife industry, [in order to take]... advantage of the prevailing political stability and sound investment policies".[466]

As already mentioned in chapter IV, these efforts paid off quickly. In the 1990s, the figures were beyond projections. "Between July 1990 and August 1993, the number of investment projects approved in the country was 80 in tourism, 58 in agriculture, and 41 in natural resources".[467] In 1994, tourism contributed up to 7.5 per cent of GDP and provided up to 25 per cent of total foreign exchange earnings.[468] The Tanzanian National Park Authority (TANAPA) was making an annual amount of about US$1.3 million on entry fees and concessions in the Serengeti alone.[469]

This new shift towards an increased role of conservation and wildlife protection was to impact on the land rights of traditional communities because wildlife in Tanzania as well as in Kenya depends significantly on grazing lands outside the boundaries of protected areas, where the communities' cattle herds and the wildlife compete for the same resources.[470]

---

that conservation areas at the time covered about 26 per cent of Tanzania's land area, the collaboration between this Council and any land law-related work was regarded as essential. See in *Report of the Presidential Commission* (1994), p. 273.

463 United Republic of Tanzania, *Tanzania National Conservation Strategy for Sustainable Development (NCSSD)*, (Dar es Salaam: National Environment Management Council & Republic of Tanzania, May 1995).

464 Bourn and Blench, *Can Livestock and Wildlife Co-Exist* (1999), p. 10.

465 Yeager and Miller, *Wildlife, Wild Death* (1986), pp. 32-3.

466 Bourn and Blench, *Can Livestock and Wildlife Co-Exist* (1999), p. 10.

467 Chachage, "Land Issues" (1999), p. 67.

468 Wøien and Lama, *Market Commerce* (1999), p. 9.

469 Emerton and Mfunda, "Making Wildlife Economically Viable" (1999), p. 17.

470 Wøien and Lama, *Market Commerce* (1999), p. 9.

It is on this socio-economic and legal background that the new Tanzanian land laws were drafted.

Tanzanian twin Land Acts and traditional communities' right to lands

The need for a reformed agricultural sector compatible with the principles of the free-market economy and the increasingly undeniable role that the conservation sector was playing in the Tanzanian economy were the two driving forces behind the crafting of the twin Land Acts, namely the Land Act and the Village Land Act, both adopted in 1999.[471] These two Acts cover three types of lands: "general land", "reserved land" and "village land". The general land is understood as "all public land, which is not reserved or village land", including unoccupied and unused village land;[472] and "the reserved land" as those set apart for national parks, game reserves, forest reserves, marine parks and public recreation parks. Both the general and reserved lands are regulated by the Land Act, whereas "village lands" are regulated by the Village Land Act.

"Right of occupancy" and claims of traditional communities living on agricultural land, as regulated by the Village Land Act

Like its principal predecessor, namely the 1923 Land Ordinance, the new Tanzanian Land Act of 1999 declares that all lands shall continue to be "public land vested in the President as trustee for and on behalf of all citizens of Tanzania".[473] Accordingly, communities, individuals, as well as any other right holder can only enjoy and exercise the right of occupancy and use of lands.[474]

According to the Village Land Act, the holders of the "right of occupancy" are the villagers. The Act defines the term "village" as an entity registered as such under the Local Government (District Authority) Act 1982,[475] the Land Tenure (Village settlement) Act 1965, and "any law or administrative procedure in force

---

471 During their drafting process, these two Acts were merged into one single Act and referred to as the Land Bill. At the end, they were presented before Parliament as two separate, but related Acts, the Tanzanian Land Act (Act No. 4 of 1999) and Village Land Act (No. 5 of 1999), that both were passed on May 21, 1999. See also Tenga, "Legislating" (1998a), p. 6.

472 Village Land Act 1999, Section 2.

473 Land Act 1999, Section 4, and Village Land Act 1999, Part II (1).

474 Village Land Act 1999, Section 2. A village's "right of occupancy" of land is defined as "a title to the use and occupation of land and includes the title of a Tanzanian citizen of African descent or a community of Tanzanian citizens of African descent using or occupying land in accordance with customary law".

475 Local Government (District Authorities) Act 1982, Section 22.

at the time before [the Village Land Act 1999] comes into operation".[476] The Act defines also the term "villager" as "any person ordinarily resident in a village or who is recognised as such by the village council of the village concerned".[477] The Act goes further by stating that any aggregate of individuals can apply for a village status, provided that its members "have been in peaceful, open and uninterrupted occupation of, or have similarly used for pastoral purposes, village land for not less than twelve years". A "village", (*vijiji* in Swahili), could also result from "settlement and resettlement of people in villages commenced or carried out during and at the time between the first day of January 1970 and the thirty-first day of December 1977 for or in connection with the purpose of implementing the policy of villagisation".[478]

Most of the estimated 9,000 "villages" in Tanzania[479] are relics of the *Ujamaa* policy. By legitimising the artificial groupings created during the *Ujamaa* period, the Village Land Act clearly shows that it does not comprehend the term villagers as members of communities with cultural ties to a given land, or people sharing common values that they wish to protect and preserve through a collective ownership and control of their customary lands. In other words, the Village Land Act does not consider "villagers" as amounting to communities understood as "groups based upon unifying and spontaneous (as opposed to artificial or planned) factors essentially beyond the control of members of the group".[480] Instead, "villages" are understood by the Act as mere groupings established by deliberate and voluntary actions of their members.

This may have serious implications for indigenous peoples. The village of Mongo Wa Mono, for example, which was allegedly established in recognition of the right of its original inhabitants, the Hadzabe, has 1,700 members, including only approximately 500 Hadzabe.[481] Village land is established by a "certificate of village land".[482] According to the Village Land Act 1999, village land, such as that of Mongo Wa Mono, should be under the management of a Village Council, a body elected by all the members of the village.[483] This electoral mechanism means that the original inhabitants of the village of Mongo Wa Mono, the Hadzabe, have no control over their lands because of being a numerical minority and therefore without a chance of winning the electoral majority of the Village Council. Moreover, the Government can transform a village land into a general public land, without consulting the concerned villagers. In other circumstances, a vil-

---

476 Village Land Act 1999, Section 7(1).
477 Ibid., Part I (2).
478 Ibid., Part I (2). See also Section 15.
479 Madsen, *The Hadzabe of Tanzania* (2000), p. 66.
480 Lerner, *Group Rights* (1991), p. 29.
481 Madsen, *The Hadzabe of Tanzania* (2000), p. 29.
482 Village Land Act 1999, Section 7(5). The Certificate of Village Land is established in the name of the President of the Village Council.
483 Ibid., Section 8 (1).

lage council can be stripped of its management role of village land.[484] Despite the weaknesses of this mechanism, it is still an option that is being pursued by pastoralist organizations active on titling village lands in several districts in northern Tanzania as a way of trying to safeguard pastoral lands on a collective basis.

More indicative is the fact that the Village Land Act recognizes the possibility for a villager to apply for an individual title on village lands.[485] The immediate consequence of this alternative is that a villager, who has secured an individual title on an area of a village land, may then at will dispose of this land and sell it to outsiders.

In conclusion, it appears that the broad understanding of the concept "villager", the mechanism of election of members of Village Councils, and the possibility of individual titling on village lands, all put together, indicate that the "right of occupancy" and "certificate of village land" do bring in risks of land individualization.[486] This is also the opinion of Shivji, who argues that "individualisation has never meant individual ownership in freehold. It really means the defining of heritable, negotiable, and transferable land rights exclusively owned by a defined legal entity, be it an individual or a group of individuals".[487] In a technical analysis of the practical implications of the Acts, Geir Sundet concludes that:

> The relative ease with which the executive can appropriate village land is the aspect of the Village Land Act that has been criticised most. … There would also be a considerable risk in further proliferation of the violent conflicts over land. The impact on smallholder security of tenure will probably be negative. It follows that it does not seem likely that the Village Land Act will be conducive to economic growth and/or improved food security.[488]

"Reserved land" and the right of communities living within conservation areas regulated by the Land Act

Section 14 of the afore mentioned Village Land Act of 1999 stipulates that the rights of people, whose ordinary place of residence is within conservation areas,

---

484 Ibid., Section 8.
485 In fact, the Village Land Act provides for the "customary right of occupancy", which is an individual right granted on village lands. See Section 25 on Procedure for application for right of occupancy.
486 Issa G. Shivji, "Protection of Peasants and Pastoral Rights in Land: A Brief Review of the Bills for the Land Act 1998 and the Village Land Act 1998". Paper presented to the Parliamentary Committee for Finance and Economic Affairs' Workshop on the Bills for the Land Act and the Village Land Act, Dodoma, 26th-28th January 1999, (1999a), p. 5; and Issa G. Shivji, "Lift the Whip. Palaver: The Land Bills", *The African*, Tanzania, 1999, (1999b), p. 2.
487 Issa G. Shivji, *Not Yet Democracy: Reforming Land Tenure in Tanzania* (Dar es Salaam: IIED/Hakiardhi, Faculty of Law University of Dar es Salaam, 1998), p. 101.
488 Geir Sundet, "The 1999 Land Act and Village Land Act: A Technical Analysis of the Practical Implications of the Acts". Working Draft (February 2005), available online at http://www.oxfam.org.uk/resources/learning/landrights/east.html#Tanzania.

should continue to enjoy their rights in accordance with previous legislation, such as the 1974 Wildlife and Conservation Act, which provides for a special right to enter and reside within conservation areas for the benefit of communities whose place of ordinary residence is within these areas.[489] There is also the Game Park Laws (Miscellaneous Amendments) Act No. 14 of 1975[490] that, for example, states that the Authority in charge of management of a game park:

> [S]hall ... safeguard and promote the interest of Maasai citizens of the United Republic engaged in cattle ranching and dairy industry within the Conservation Area.[491]

It appears indeed that the Village Land Act allows for the right of people who ordinarily live or reside within conservation areas to be automatically transformed into "customary right of occupancy". The Land Act 1999 provides furthermore for the leasing of a granted right of occupancy to any person. These provisions could for example provide a legal basis for allowing the Maasai to lease ward or village land within the NCA (Ngorongoro Conservation Area) to tour operators should they so desire, as it is happening in villages outside the NCA. This could also enable the Maasai to use the land rights conferred upon them through customary rights of occupancy to leverage tourism benefits in the absence of village land titles.

However, the land rights recognized to communities and villages seems limited in weight and far from constituting land ownership rights. For instance, the president of the Republic of Tanzania could, at will, grant a right of occupancy on reserved lands to anybody, including a foreigner, provided that such a beneficiary has an investment certificate from the Investment Promotion Centre. Furthermore, the Ngorongoro Conservation Area Authority (NCAA) has statutory power to regulate land and its uses within the NCA, which reduces the ability of the Maasai to enjoy the land rights they hold.[492] Indeed, it seems unlikely that the Maasai residing in the NCA will ever obtain full land ownership (land titles) within the NCA given the powers of the Government over these lands.

In 2007, the Government of Tanzania presented a Draft Grazinglands Management and Utilisation Bill, which provides for the creation of Village Grazingland

---

489 Section 7.1(a) of the Wildlife (Conservation and Management) Act No. 12 of 1974 states that "No person other than ... a person whose place of ordinary residence is within the reserve" shall be allowed to enter in such area without an authorisation. Similar provisions are found in the 1951 Fauna Conservation Ordinance (Section 6 of CAP. 302 Supp. 64) and the Forest Ordinance of 1959 (Section 9 (3) of CAP. 389 Supp.65).

490 The Game Parks Law (Miscellaneous Amendments) Act No. 14 of 1975 includes the Ngorongoro Conservation Area Ordinance.

491 Ibid., Section 5A.

492 Shivji and Kapinga, *Maasai Rights* (1998), pp. 29-30.

Development Areas (VGDAs) and Village Grazingland Development Committee (VGDC). As Ringo Tenga writes, the Draft "Bill [yet to be adopted as law] does not directly refer to pastoralists' participation in the VGDC" And he adds "Pastoral communities are not directly recognised in the Bill as having customary titles, written or unwritten, over grazing land."[493]

Noticeably, the current Tanzanian Land Laws do not offer a better protection to communities living in conservation areas than pre-existing standards, despite being passed after the conclusion of the 1994 Presidential Commission of Inquiry into Land Matters, which stated that, "there is a need for the resolution of conflict of interests in the conservation areas sector. Ultimately, the survival of all the conservation areas will depend on the contiguous communities". The Commission went on adding that "the sooner the interests reconcile, and the contiguous villages internalize the values of conservation, the more assured will be the future of [conservation areas]".[494] These recommendations called for redress so that cases such as the electric fencing of the Mkomazi Game Reserve (MRG) by the George Adamson Wildlife Conservation Trust[495] and the evictions of ordinary residents of these areas would no longer occur.[496]

It thus appears that in relation to the protection of collective rights to communal lands, the Tanzanian Land Acts could be seen as in line with a free market-oriented system of land management. In this perspective, Ringo Tenga argues that, according to current Tanzanian land laws,

[L]and, which may be fully allocated and managed by the Village Council, appears to be land that is not traditionally owned. The customary institutions do not appear to have been significantly affected by the reforms. Actually the VLA (Village Land Act) reserves space for customary land law in the regulation of land tenure. In doing so a potential conflict or grey area exists in terms of land management—is it the responsibility of the Village authorities or of traditional land allocation authorities?

Second, common lands, which in many cases include grazing land, appear to be "no man's land" [and], as such, subject to the exclusive management of Village authorities by virtue of the VLA. For pastoralists, this

---

493 Ringo Tenga, A. Mattee, N. Mdoe, R. Mnenwa, S. Mwungi and M. Walsh, "Current Policy, Legal and Economic Issues". Main report of *A Study on Options for Pastoralists to Secure their Livelihoods*, (2008), pp. 40 and 43. Available online on the Web site of Tanzania Natural Resource Forum http://www.tnrf.org

494 United Republic of Tanzania, "Report of the Presidential Commission" (1994), p. 275.

495 The electrified fence is now reported to be 41 km long and capable of harming animals as well as human beings. See Tenga, "Legislating" (1998b), p. 7.

496 See for instance the already mentioned *Lekengere Faru Parutu Kamunyu and 16 Others v. Minister for Tourism, Natural Resources and Environment and 3 others*, HC-Moshi CV# 33/1994. In this case, the applicants claimed that they had been forcibly evicted from their homelands in violation of several domestic laws including the Wildlife Conservation Act 1974. See, for more details, Tenga, "Legislating" (1998b).

raises a critical concern in that without pro-active response to this ambiguity the VLA virtually dispossesses the pastoralists from their grazing lands.[497]

In recent years, the Government of Tanzania has taken a number of initiatives related to the Land Acts. These initiatives include, among others, the Land Bank Scheme that identifies land suitable for investment and is supported by the Investment Act of 1997, which allows non-citizens to own land for the purpose of investment; the Land Amendment Act of 2004, which creates a legislative framework that allows the sale of "bare" lands and promotes the use of land as collateral; and the "Programme to formalize the Assets of the Poor of Tanzania and strengthen the Rule of Law" (also known as MKURABITA), which promotes land registration.[498] Many of these initiatives have, with the words of William Ole Nasha, turned land into "a pure commodity, devoid of its cultural and spiritual values".[499] They have also paved the way for many of the private investments that have led to the eviction of pastoralists from areas in for example Mbeya, Iringa and Morogoro Regions,[500] and have threatened the land rights of the Hadzabe of Yaeda Chini and Mongo wa Mono.[501] A number of pastoralist organizations have also expressed fear that pastures may be looked at as "bare" or "idle" land and then be identified for investment purposes.[502] The Strategic Plan for the Implementation of the Land Laws, SPILL (2005), whose aim is to make the land laws operational, also clearly reflects that the commitment of the Government is to modernize the agricultural sector in Tanzania and, in that relation, make land an important commercial asset. The Plan has two essential strategies—to sedentarize pastoralists and

---

497 Tenga et al., "Current Policy, Legal and Economic issues" (2008), p. 44.
498 See, for instance, Celestine Nyamu-Musembi, *Breathing Life into Dead Theories about Property Rights: de Soto and Land Relations in Rural Africa*. IDS Working Paper 272. (Brighton, UK: Institute of Development Studies, IDS, University of Sussex, 2006). As pointed out by Chris Maina Peter in "Human Rights of Indigenous Minorities in Tanzania and the Courts of Law", *International Journal on Minority and Group Rights* 14 (2007), p. 470, "There is now intense pressure on the Government from both donors and international financial institutions such as the IBRD and the International Monetary Fund to commoditise land itself and make it available as collateral for loans from commercial banks."
499 William Ole Nasha, "Reforming Land Tenure In Tanzania: For Whose Benefit?" An Haki Ardhi Paper accessible at http://www.hakiardhi.org/HA-Docs/WILLIAM%20FINAL%20SUBMIS-SION.pdf
500 Rie Odgaard, "Assessment Report from Tanzania" submitted to IWGIA, August 2009 (unpublished).
501 In this particular case, the Tanzanian Government had granted a hunting concession to a private company, the UAE Safaris Limited. The Hadzabe community had not been consulted and, by all accounts, did not consent to this grant. The case was taken up by Tanzania's Legal and Human Right Center (LHRC) and other local human rights organizations and due to their pressure, the UAE Safaris Limited eventually desisted from its project. See LHRC's "Tanzania Human Rights Report 2007", p. 61, and "Tanzania Human Rights Report 2008", p. 75, accessible at http://www.humanrights.or.tz
502 Odgaard, "Assessment Report" (2009).

change their production system into a ranching system, and to introduce a system of minimum acreages for farmers through a resettlement scheme.[503] The rights of hunters and gatherers are not mentioned at all by the Plan.[504]

Other land-related policy processes have also an important bearing on indigenous peoples' land rights. A case in point is the revised Draft of the Wildlife Conservation Act No. 9 of 2008. This draft introduces several restrictions in terms of access to grazing areas for pastoralists as well as to other restrictions on various types of uses. It also includes provisions of heavy punishment in cases of non-compliance with the conditions set up by the Act.[505] The Act will thus affect not only pastoralists but also hunter-gatherers and poor farming communities who depend on access to such areas for their livelihood.[506]

The situation for pastoralists and indigenous peoples in general in Tanzania has thus worsened over the past 5-10 years. Policies and legislation have continued to undermine their land rights, and areas, on which these people use to sustain their livelihood, have been further reduced since 2006.[507] Most disturbing are the recent evictions of pastoralists and their livestock from Ihefu in Usangu Plains, Mbarali District in 2006 and 2008,[508] and the evictions from Kilosa district in Morogoro Region[509] and Loliondo division in Ngorongoro District[510] in 2009, just to mention a few that have reached the headlines in the press. That some of these incidents are in fact part of an official policy towards pastoralists, and not just isolated cases, cannot be dismissed seen in the light of the Strategic Plan for the Implementation of the Land Laws, among others.

Conclusion

It has been shown in this chapter that, in general terms, the Tanzanian judiciary has not provided the protection it should to indigenous peoples' land rights.

---

503 United Republic of Tanzania, *Strategic Plan*, (2005), pp. 9 and 14.
504 Odgaard, "Assessment Report" (2009).
505 United Republic of Tanzania, *Draft Wildlife Act of 2008* (Dar es Salaam: Ministry of Natural Resources), Part IV, V and VIII, available at http://www.tnrf.org. See also F.P. Maganga, "Tanzania's New Wildlife Law and its Implications for Rural Livelihoods". Power point presentation. Mimeo. (Dar es Salaam: Institute of Resource Assessment, University of Dar es Salaam, 2009).
506 See, e.g., Debate on the Wildlife Act of 2008 on the homepage of Tanzania Natural Resource Forum at: http://www.tnrf.org
507 See, e.g., Tenga et al., "Current Policy, Legal and Economic issues" (2008); LHRC "Tanzania Human Rights Report 2007.
508 Martin T. Walsh, "Study on Options for Pastoralists to secure their Livelihoods: Pastoralism and Policy Processes in Tanzania. Mbarali Case Study." In *A Study on Options for Pastoralists to Secure their Livelihoods in Tanzania*, Vol.2 - Case studies (Arusha, Tanzania: CORDS, PWC, IIED, MMM Ngaramtoni Centre, TNRF and UCRT, 2008). Available online on the Web site of Tanzania Natural Resource Forum http://www.tnrf.org/node/7487?group=57
509 See IWGIA Alert, March 2009. Accessible at http://www.iwgia.org/sw33422.asp Mwarabu.
510 See IWGIA Alert, August 2009. Accessible at http://www.iwgia.org/sw153.asp#516_30073

There have been a few attempts of positive decisions by a very limited number of Tanzanian judges, whose decisions have been systematically overturned in Appeal. Delays and governmental policy-oriented rulings have equally characterized the court cases initiated by indigenous peoples in quest for justice on their ancestral lands. This trend has almost everything to do with the national legal and policy landscape shaped since colonial time and up to now. It transpires indeed that, even if relatively strong communal land rights survived during colonial time because of Tanzania's international status under the League of Nations/ the United Nations, the *Ujamaa* era had a strong negative impact on indigenous peoples' land rights, as people were moved around into artificial villages managed by institutions set up by the State. The current legal and socioeconomic setting, too, is increasingly unsupportive of indigenous peoples' claims to lands. The will for a free market oriented agricultural sector and a strong and lucrative tourist sector appears as having been the main driving force behind the crafting in 1999 of the twin Land Acts, namely the Land Act and the Village Land Act, as well as subsequent policy developments and legislation, all of which have further exacerbated the situation of indigenous land rights in Tanzania.

CHAPTER VII
INDIGENOUS PEOPLES' LAND CLAIMS IN SOUTHERN AFRICA

This chapter deals with the *South African Richtersveld* case and the Botswana *Central Kalahari Game Reserve* case. These two cases are used as illustrations of a new trend that raises some hopes for a better protection of African indigenous peoples' land rights by the judiciary.

The Richtersveld community in South Africa and their land claim

Richtersveld is a territory of almost half a million hectares situated in the northwestern corner of the Northern Cape Province known as Namaqualand. It is sparsely populated and the four villages, namely Kuboes, Sanddrift, Lekkersing and Eksteenfontein, have a total population of only about 15,000, some of whom belong to the Nama people—a larger indigenous group also found in Namibia. The Nama have lived on these lands since time immemorial and share the same culture, including the same language, religion, social and political structures, customs and lifestyle derived from their Khoe-Khoe and San forefathers. The Nama self identify as indigenous to this land, as underlined by the *Report of the Working Group of Experts of the African Commission on Indigenous Populations/Communities* as well as other researchers.[511]

Following the discovery in the 1920s of diamonds in the area, the South African Government seized the disputed land from its inhabitants. At that time, the Union of South Africa was part of the British Empire and the land was claimed as "Crown land". In 1957, a fence was erected around the land, permanently denying its access to the Richtersveld community. In 1994, the ownership of the land

---

511 See, e.g., Roger Chennells and Aymone du Toit, "The Rights of Indigenous Peoples in South Africa", in *Indigenous Peoples' Rights in Southern Africa,* edited by Robert K. Hitchcock and Diana Vinding, IWGIA Document No. 110 (Copenhagen: IWGIA, 2004), p. 98.

passed to a diamond mining company called Alexkor Ltd, whose only share-holder was the South African State.

Richtersveld Community and Others v. Alexkor Ltd and Another 2001 (3) SA 1293 (LCC)

Background facts and claimants' arguments

In 2001, the Richtersveld community lodged a claim for restitution of land on the basis of section 2(1) of the Restitution of Land Rights Act 22 of 1994.[512]

The post-apartheid, interim Constitution of South Africa (1993) provides that

> *A person or a community shall be entitled to claim restitution of a right in land from the State if*
> a. *such person or community was dispossessed of such right at any time after a date to be fixed by the Act referred to in subsection (1); and*
> b. *such dispossession was effected under or for the purpose of furthering the object of a law which would have been inconsistent with the prohibition of racial discrimination contained in section 8(2), had that section been in operation at the time of such dispossession.*[513]

On the basis of this provision, the South African Parliament passed what is known as the "Restitution of Land Rights Act", which, amongst other things, states that *"a person shall be entitled to ... restitution of a right in land if (a) he or she is a person or community dispossessed of rights in land after 19 June 1913 as a result of past racially discriminatory laws or practices"*.[514]

The Richtersveld community argued that the land in dispute was its ancestral home since time immemorial, that it had been taken away as a result of past ra-cially discriminatory laws or practices and that its aboriginal title survived the arrival of colonization and the establishment of the South African State. The peo-ple of Richtersveld claimed that they had the right to exclusive beneficial occupa-tion and use of the subject land including the exploitation of its natural resources. They contended:

---

512 *Richtersveld Community and Others v. Alexkor Ltd and Another* 2001 (3) SA 1293 (LCC).

513 Constitution of South Africa, 1993 (Interim Constitution, 1994-1996), Chapter 8, section 121 (2). This provision is repeated in a slightly amended version in the 1996 Constitution of South Africa, Chapter 2, article 25 (7): *"A person or community dispossessed of property after 19 June 1913, as a result of past racially discriminatory laws or practices, is entitled, to the extent provided by an Act of Parliament, either to restitution of that property or to equitable redress."* The full text of the two constitutions can be accessed at http://www.confinder.richmond.edu

514 Restitution of Land Rights Act 22 of 1994, Article 2 (1) (a). Available online at http://www.info. gov.za/acts/1994/a22-94.pdf

The Richtersveld people held title to the subject land and that such title was not at any time prior to 19 June 1913 lawfully extinguished or diminished. They submit that this title falls within the definition of "right in land", as contained in the Restitution of Land Rights Act. In terms of the definition, "right in land" includes:

> *"any right in land whether registered or unregistered, and may include the interest of a labour tenant and sharecropper, a customary law interest, the interest of a beneficiary under a trust arrangement and beneficial occupation for a continuous period of not less than 10 years prior to the dispossession in question"…*

Their right in land is alleged to be:

> a. *ownership; alternatively*
> b. *a right based on aboriginal title allowing them the exclusive beneficial occupation and use of the subject land, or the right to use the subject land for certain specified purposes (i.e., habitation, cultural and religious practices, grazing, cultivation, hunting, fishing, water trekking and the harvesting and exploitation of natural resources); alternatively*
> c. *"a right in land" over the subject land acquired through their beneficial occupation thereof for a period longer than 10 years prior to their eventual dispossession.*

The plaintiffs alleged that they were dispossessed of their rights in land by legislative and executive state action after 19 June 1913 as a result of racially discriminatory laws and practices. They aver that they did not receive any compensation at all in respect of the dispossession, alternatively, that they did not receive just and equitable compensation….[515]

Consequently, the plaintiffs asked the Land Claims Court (LCC) to order a restitution of their rights in land under the Restitution Act.

According to the Supreme Court of Appeal, the Richtersveld Community had further contended that it possessed the above mentioned rights

> … *[U]nder indigenous law and, after annexation, under the common law of the Cape Colony or international law which protected the rights acquired under indigenous law. In the alternative, it was contended that the rights which the Community held in the subject land under its own indigenous law constituted a "customary law interest", a right in land within the meaning of the Act, even if these rights were not recognised or protected. These rights were also asserted in relation to the right of beneficial occupation for a continuous period of not less than 10 years that had been found by the LCC.* [516]

---

515 *Richtersveld Community and Others v. Alexkor Ltd and Another* 2001 (3) SA 1293 (LCC), at para. 6.
516 As ref erred in *Alexkor Ltd and Government of the Republic of South Africa v. Richtersveld Community and Others* 2003 (12) BCLR 1301 (CC), at para. 47.

Defendants/appellants' core legal points

Before all three courts (Land Claims Court, Supreme Appeal Court and the Constitutional Court), Alexkor Ltd and the Government of the Republic of South Africa—first as defendants, later as appellants—kept two major core arguments, namely that "whatever rights the Richtersveld people might have had in the Richtersveld, were extinguished before 19 June 1913", as a result of the annexation of that land by the British Crown in 1847 and that their own mining rights had been granted in compliance with the Precious Stones Act 1927. Accordingly, they argued that the dispossession was not a "result of past racially discriminatory laws or practices" provided for under section 2(1) of the Land Restitution Act 1994.

The respondents also argued that the Crown Lands Acts of 1860 and 1887 (the Acts) had extinguished the rights of the Richtersveld Community.

Ruling and reasoning of the Land Claims Court

The first judgment in this case was that of the Land Claims Court (LCC), which acknowledged that the Richtersveld community had rights over the disputed lands on the basis of "beneficial occupation for a continuous period of not less than 10 years". This very same court, however, also ruled that the claimants' rights were extinguished following the annexation of Richtersveld by the British Crown on 23 December 1847 to become part of the Cape Colony.[517] The court argued further that the land dispossession suffered by the claimants was not a result of "past racially discriminatory laws or practices", and therefore could not be restituted under section 2(1) of the Land Restitution Act.[518] On 22 March 2001, Judge Gildenhuys rejected the plaintiffs' argument based on the doctrine of aboriginal title, ruling that:

> To the extent that any of the rights claimed by the plaintiffs is dependent on the realisation or [sic] aboriginal title, such rights are dubious, because it is uncertain whether the doctrine of indigenous title forms part of our law, and if it does, what its scope and content are. It has, to my knowledge, never been recognised in any reported court decision. Even if it does form part of our law, it is uncertain whether such title would have survived the actions of the Government in making the subject land over to others.[519]

---

517 *Richtersveld Community and Others v. Alexkor Ltd and Another,* 2001 (3) SA 1293 (LCC), at paras. 37-43.
518 Ibid., at paras. 76-96.
519 Ibid., at para. 46.

Richtersveld Community and Others v. Alexkor Ltd and Another 2003 (6) BCLR 583 (SCA)

The second ruling in what is now known as the Richtersveld case was that of the Supreme Court of Appeal of South Africa, before which the community lodged an appeal against the judgment made in 2001 by the Land Claims Court.

Ruling and reasoning of the Supreme Court of Appeal

The Supreme Court of Appeal (SCA) made a favorable judgment on 24 March 2003, asserting that:

1. The Richtersveld community was in exclusive possession of the whole of the Richtersveld, including the subject land, prior to annexation by the British Crown in 1847.
2. The Richtersveld community's rights to the land (including precious stones and minerals) were akin to those held under common law owner-ship. These rights constituted a "customary law interest" and conse-quently a "right in land" as defined in the Act.
3. These rights survived the annexation and the LCC erred in finding that the community had lost its rights because it was insufficiently civilized to be recognised.
4. When diamonds were discovered on the subject land during the 1920s the State ignored the Richtersveld community's rights and, acting on the premise that the land was Crown land, dispossessed the Richtersveld community of its rights in the land in a series of steps amounting to "practices" as defined in the Act and culminating in the grant of full own-ership of the land to Alexkor.
5. These practices were racially discriminatory because they were based upon the false, albeit unexpressed premise that, because of the Richters-veld community's race and lack of civilization, they had lost all rights in the land upon annexation.

In other words, the SCA held that the manner in which the Richtersveld Com-munity was dispossessed of the subject land amounted to racially discriminatory practices as defined in the Act, and that the plaintiff was *"entitled … to restitution of the right to exclusive beneficial occupation and use, akin to that held under common-law ownership, of the subject land (including its minerals and precious stones)"* …[520]

---

520 Ibid., at para. 111.

Contrary to the conclusion arrived at by the Land Claims Court, the court also ruled that the disputed land was not a *terra nullius* at the time of annexation.

Alexkor Ltd and Government of South Africa v. Richtersveld Community and Others, 2003 (12) BCLR 1301 (CC)

The third and last judgment in this case was that of the Constitutional Court of South Africa, before which Alexkor and the South African Government lodged an appeal against the decision by the Supreme Court of Appeal (SCA).

Ruling and reasoning of the Constitutional Court

The Constitutional Court ruled in favor of the Richtersveld Community, thereby confirming the decision made by the SCA. Its ruling was based on a number of arguments related to the nature of the rights in land of the Richtersveld Community prior to annexation in 1847 and up to 1913, the characteristics of indigenous law and whether the rights of the Community had been extinguished after 1913 and on what grounds.

The Constitutional Court asserted that

> *The nature and the content of the rights that the Richtersveld Community held in the subject land prior to annexation must be determined by reference to indigenous law. That is the law which governed its land rights* [n.: compare *Oyekan & Others v. Adele* [1957] 2 All ER 785 at 788G-H]. *Those rights cannot be determined by reference to common law. ...*
>
> ...
>
> *While in the past indigenous law was seen through the common law lens, it must now be seen as an integral part of our law. Like all law it depends for its ultimate force and validity on the Constitution* [n.: see, for example, *Pharmaceutical Manufacturers Association of South Africa and Another in re Ex Parte the President of the Republic of South Africa and Others 2000 (2) SA 674 (CC); 2000 (3) BCLR 241 (CC)* at para 29]. *Its validity must now be determined by reference not to common law, but to the Constitution. The courts are obliged by section 211(3) of the Constitution to apply customary law when it is applicable, subject to the Constitution and any legislation that deals with customary law. In doing so the courts must have regard to the spirit, purport and objects of the Bill of Rights* [n.: Section 39(2) of the Constitution]. *...*
>
> ...

It is clear, therefore that the Constitution acknowledges the originality and distinctiveness of indigenous law as an independent source of norms within the legal system.[521]

Dealing with the characteristics of indigenous law, the court pointed out that,

… [I]ndigenous law is not a fixed body of formally classified and easily ascertainable rules. By its very nature it evolves as the people who live by its norms change their patterns of life … [n.: See Ex Parte Chairperson of the Constitutional Assembly : In re Certification of the Constitution of the Republic of South Africa, 1996 (4) SA 744; 1996 (10) BCLR 1253 (CC)]

In applying indigenous law, it is important to bear in mind that, unlike common law, indigenous law is not written. It is a system of law that was known to the community, practised and passed on from generation to generation. …
…
… [W]e would add that indigenous law may be established by reference to writers on indigenous law and other authorities and sources, and may include the evidence of witnesses if necessary. However, caution must be exercised when dealing with textbooks and old authorities because of the tendency to view indigenous law through the prism of legal conceptions that are foreign to it. In the course of establishing indigenous law, courts may also be confronted with conflicting views on what indigenous law on a subject provides.[522]

The court also remarked that

[T]he dangers of looking at indigenous law through a common law prism are obvious. The two systems of law developed in different situations, under different cultures and in response to different conditions.
…
The determination of the real character of indigenous title to land therefore "involves the study of the history of a particular community and its usages".[523]

As for the rights of the Richtersveld Community prior to annexation in 1847 by the British Crown, the court concluded:

In the light of the evidence and of the findings by the SCA and the LCC, we are of the view that the real character of the title that the Richtersveld Community pos-

---

521 *Alexkor Ltd and Government of the Republic of South Africa v. Richtersveld Community and Others*, 2003 (12) BCLR 1301 (CC), paras. 50 and 51.

522 Ibid., at paras. 52, 53 and 54.

523 Ibid., at paras. 56 and 57. The quote is from *Amodu Tijani v. Secretary,* Southern Provinces, Nigeria [1921] 2 AC 399 (PC).

*sessed in the subject land was a right of communal ownership under indigenous
law. The content of that right included the right to exclusive occupation and use of
the subject land by members of the Community. The Community had the right to
use its water, to use its land for grazing and hunting and to exploit its natural
resources, above and beneath the surface. It follows therefore that prior to annexation the Richtersveld Community had a right of ownership in the subject land
under indigenous law.*

....

*We are satisfied that under the indigenous law of the Richtersveld Community
communal ownership of the land included communal ownership of the minerals
and precious stones. ... Accordingly, we conclude that the history and usages of
the Richtersveld Community establish that ownership of the minerals and precious stones vested in the Community under indigenous law.*[524]

Regarding the legal consequences of the annexation of the subject land in 1847,
pursuant to the Annexation Proclamation, the court ruled that,

*In our view there is nothing either in the events preceding the annexation of Rich-
tersveld or in the language of the Proclamation which suggests that annexation
extinguished the land rights of the Richtersveld Community.*

...

*The SCA adopted the rule that indigenous rights to private property in a con-
quered territory were recognised and protected after the acquisition of sovereignty
and [we endorse the SCA's conclusion] that the rights of the Richtersveld Community survived annexation.*[525]

...

*... [T]he applicable law in the Cape Colony at the time of annexation respected and
protected land rights of the indigenous people. No act of State or legislation extinguished the land rights of the Richtersveld Community subsequent to annexation
but before 19 June 1913. The Crown Lands Acts [of 1860 and 1887] relied upon
by Alexkor did not have that effect.*[526]

After having reached the conclusion that *"the annexation of Richtersveld did not
extinguish the right of ownership which the Richtersveld Community possessed in the
subject land and that such right was not extinguished prior to 19 June 1913"*,[527] the
court looked at the steps taken by the State after 19 June 1913:

---

524 *Alexkor Ltd and Government of the Republic of South Africa v. Richtersveld Community and Others*,2003
     (12) BCLR 1301 (CC), at paras. 62 and 64.
525 Ibid., at paras. 68 and 69.
526 Ibid., at para. 76.
527 Ibid., at para. 82.

The position of the Richtersveld Community began to change from 1926 onwards with the discovery of diamonds on the subject land. It was common cause that, if the Richtersveld Community's rights survived beyond 1913, it was ultimately dispossessed of the land by the end of 1993.

...

The Precious Stones Act did not recognise the rights of those, like the Richtersveld Community, who were at the time the owners of land under indigenous law. This was because their rights had not been registered. ... The effect of this Act was that all occupants of the land except those who were registered surface owners, or those who occupied at the instance of the surface owners, lost their right to occupy and exploit the land.

This law in effect rendered the occupation of the subject land by the Richtersveld Community unlawful and dispossessed it of the rights it had as owner of the land. ...

The evidence shows that the State subsequently treated the subject land as its own, required the Community to leave it, exploited it for its own account and later transferred it to Alexkor. All this happened after 1913 and effectively dispossessed the Community of all its rights in the subject land. These rights included the right to occupy and exploit the subject land, including its minerals.[528]

The court finally resumed its arguments by declaring that it *"found that the Richtersveld Community held ownership of the subject land under indigenous law, which included the rights to minerals and precious stones"*[529] and making the following order that,

... [S]ubject to the issues that stand over for later determination, the first plaintiff [the Richtersveld Community] is entitled in terms of section 2(1) of the Restitution of Land Rights Act 22 of 1994 to restitution of the right to ownership of the subject land (including its minerals and precious stones) and to the exclusive beneficial use and occupation thereof.[530]

Concluding observations and results/impact of the court cases

1. Like many other African courts, the Land Claims Court grounded its whole reasoning on national laws and paid no consideration to customs and traditions that tend to govern land tenure systems in most African rural areas. It consequently concluded that since the disputed lands were formally annexed by the Government, communities lost all rights in it.

---

528 Ibid., at paras. 83, 89, 90, and 91.
529 Ibid., at para. 102.
530 Ibid., at para. 103 (a).

2. The Supreme Court of Appeal (SCA) took a rather different reasoning approach by going beyond national laws to find references in contemporary international jurisprudence. Citing cases such as *Mabo v. The State of Queensland* and *Delgamuukw v. British Columbia,* the court argued that *"a nomadic lifestyle is not inconsistent with the exclusive and effective right of occupation of land by indigenous people."*[531] The court noted further the importance of witnesses' accounts and presentations by multi-disciplinary researchers:

   > *Evidence was given by three anthropologists and an archeologist for the appellant concerning the history of the appellant communities, the land they and their forebears occupied and their traditional laws, customs and practices forming part of their distinctive aboriginal culture".*[532]

3. The Constitutional Court of South Africa made in fact a landmark decision that will, for a long time to come, have a major impact on the legal protection of indigenous peoples' right to lands.[533] By itself, this judgment contains most of what one could advise a lawyer of an indigenous community to take as legal arguments.

4. In its first lines of argument, the Constitutional Court states for the primacy of indigenous law over written common law and indicates that the validity of the former should not be dependant of its compliance with the latter.[534] Once this was done, the rest of the argument followed logically. The *"Constitution acknowledges the originality and distinctiveness of indigenous law as an independent source of norms within the legal system"*, the court argued. The court underlined further major particularities of indigenous law, including its dynamism and its links with culture, stressing that indigenous law may be established by reference to writers on indigenous law and other authorities and sources, and may include the evidence of witnesses, if necessary.[535]

5. The Constitutional Court did not distinguish lands rights from mineral rights, like several African legislations and judges have done. According to the court, *"under the indigenous law of the Richtersveld Community, communal ownership of the land included communal ownership of the minerals and precious stones".*[536] This is an extremely important statement that could have a major positive impact on indigenous peoples' right to lands throughout Africa.

---

531 *Richtersveld Community and Others v. Alexkor and Another,* 2003 (6) BCLR 583 (SCA), para. 23.

532 Ibid., at para. 12.

533 T. M. Chan, "The Richtersveld Challenge: South Africa Finally Adopts Aboriginal Title", in *Indigenous Peoples' Rights in Southern Africa,* edited by Robert K. Hitchcock and Diana Vinding, IWGIA Document No.110 (Copenhagen: IWGIA, 2004), p. 129.

534 See *Alexkor Ltd and Government of the Republic of South Africa v. Richtersveld Community and Others,* 2003 (12) BCLR 1301 (CC), para. 50.

535 See ibid., at para. 54.

536 Ibid., at para. 64.

6. The court meets also one of this book's points, namely that change in sovereignty does not *per se* extinguish pre existing property rights. As stated by the Constitutional Court,

> *[The SCA] found that the majority of colonial decisions favoured an approach that a mere change in sovereignty is not meant to disturb the rights of private owners ... The SCA adopted the rule that indigenous rights to private property in a conquered territory were recognised and protected after the acquisition of sovereignty and concluded that the rights of the Richtersveld Community survived annexation. [The Constitutional Court] endorses that conclusion.*[537]

7. Finally, the Constitutional Court, like the Supreme Court of Appeal, did refer widely to relevant foreign cases, which helped to bring into its reasoning a number of contemporary principles, such as the notion of "aboriginal title". This case could indeed be considered as the first one on the African continent to uphold explicitly the notion of "aboriginal title", which can no longer be considered as alien to Africa. What impact this ruling will have on other African judges is what remains to be seen.

The San of Botswana and the Central Kalahari Game Reserve case

The San (formerly known as Bushmen) are indigenous to Southern Africa and live in several countries in the region. The African Commission on Human and Peoples' Rights estimates their number at approximately 107,000 people with a majority of about 50 per cent living in Botswana.[538] San in Botswana are commonly called Basarwa or Remote Area Dwellers. [539]

The central Kalahari Desert is known to be part of the ancestral lands of the San of Botswana. In 1961, the British colonial regime set up the Central Kalahari Game Reserve (CKGR) "with the aim of not only nature conservation but also of protecting the rights of the 5,000 or so people (mostly San) living within its 52,347 sq. km who wanted to maintain hunting and gathering as part of their lifestyle".[540] This is one of Africa's most remote, unspoiled wilderness areas, well known for its lions and a variety of wildlife. It is also known to have diamond deposits.

In 1997, the Government of Botswana started moving the San out of the CKGR to new settlements such as New !Xade and Kaudwane. But until 2002, some few

---

537 Ibid., at para. 69.

538 African Commission, *Report of Working Group of Experts* (2005), p.16.

539 The terms Bushmen and Basarwa are generally considered to be derogatory and will therefore in this section only be used when reference is made to official documents.

540 Michael Taylor, "The Past and Future of San Land Rights in Botswana", in *Indigenous Peoples' Rights in Southern Africa,* edited by Robert K. Hitchcock and Diana Vinding, IWGIA Document No. 110 (Copenhagen: IWGIA, 2004), p. 152.

hundred San continued to live inside the Reserve, seen as their ancestral residential place and recognized as such by section 14(3)c of the 1966 Constitution of Botswana, which stated that restriction may be imposed *"on the entry into or residence within defined areas of Botswana of persons who are not Bushmen to the extent that such restrictions are reasonably required for the protection or well-being of Bushmen"*.[541]

Sesana and Others v. The Attorney General (52/2002) [2006] BWHC 1 (13 December 2006). Also known as the Central Kalahari Game Reserve (CKGR) case

Background facts and claimants' arguments

On 31 January 2002, the Botswana Government ceased the basic and essential services that it used to provide to the CKGR residents (San and Bakghaladi)[542] still living inside the CKGR. These services were: (i) the provision of drinking water on a weekly basis; (ii) the maintenance of the supply of borehole water;[543] (iii) the provision of rations for registered destitutes; (iv) the provision of rations for registered orphans; (v) the provision of transport for the residents' children to and from boarding school;[544] (vi) the provision of healthcare through mobile clinics and ambulance services.

This decision was taken by the Government despite previous and ongoing negotiations between the Government's Department of Wildlife and National Parks (DWNP) and the San regarding sustainable and fair management of the resources in the area on the basis of their continued residence in the CKGR.

In February 2002, 243 San and Bakgalagadi applicants brought a court case before the High Court, claiming that,

1. The termination by the Government with effect from 31 January 2002 of the following basic and essential services to the Applicants in Central Kalahari Game Reserve (CKGR) is unlawful and unconstitutional [follows a list of the services, see above];
2. The Government is obliged to

---

541 This subsection (3)c was deleted from Section 14 by the Constitutional (Amendment) Act of 2005 which also amended the sections 77, 78 and 79 of the Constitution in order to render the Constitution "tribally neutral".

542 These Bakgalagadi belong to another ethnic group but have been living in the CKGR for several generations and their livestyle is today very similar to that of the San.

543 There was only one borehole with potable water in the CKGR. The San were not allowed to make their own boreholes but had to store the water delivered by the Department of Wildlife and National Parks in large tanks. In 2002, the authorities destroyed the tanks and sealed off the borehole with cement.

544 Transport was provided at the beginning of the school term and at the end, respectively.

a. Restore ... the basic and essential services that it terminated with effect from 31 January 2002;

b. Continue to provide to the Applicants the basic and essential services that it had been providing to them immediately prior to the termination of the provision of these services; and

c. Restore land to the possession of those Applicants, whom the Government forcibly removed from the Central Kalahari Game Reserve (CKGR) after the termination of the provision to them of the basic and essential services referred to above, and who have been unlawfully despoiled of their possession of the land which they lawfully occupied in their settlements in the CKGR.[545]

At first, the application was dismissed on technical grounds. This decision was appealed and, in July 2002, the Court of Appeal took the view that the parties should first formulate and agree on the issues to be dealt with. In early 2003, the Court of Appeal observed that there were material disputes of facts and that such disputes could only be resolved by the hearing of oral evidence. The Court of Appeal made a Consent Order, which essentially turned the relief sought by the Applicants into questions for consideration and answering by the High Court.[546]

Defendants' core legal points

The defendant or respondent (the Government of Botswana) maintained that it had been justified in terminating the services as they were too expensive to maintain on a long term basis; that they never were meant to be permanent; and that the residents of the settlements in the CKGR had repeatedly been consulted before the services were terminated. The respondent also denied that the applicants were forcibly or wrongly deprived of the land they occupied in the CKGR on the grounds that the CKGR is state land and the settlements were situated on state lands. Consequently, argued the defendants, the applicants had neither ownership nor right of tenancy to the CKGR. To the question of whether the applicants lawfully occupied the land in their settlements in the CKGR before the 2002 relocations, the Government argued that the occupation by the applicants of the land in the settlements in the CKGR was unlawful because the CKGR is owned by the Government. Finally, the respondents also maintained that human residence within the reserve posed disturbance to the wildlife there and was contradictory to the policy of total preservation of wildlife.

---

545 *Sesana and Others v. the Attorney General* (52/2002) [2006] BWHC 1, per Dibotelo, para. 1. Roy Sesana has, for many years, been the chairperson of the San organisation, First People of the Kalahari (FPK).

546 Ibid., at para. 3.

Ruling and reasoning of the court

The trial commenced in July 2004. Prior to the first hearings, the judges had conducted an inspection *in loco* of the new settlements of Kaudwane and New !Xade outside the CKGR, and of the settlements of Gugamma, Kikao, Mothomelo, Metsiamanong, Molapo and Old !Xade inside the CKGR. The final judgment was given on 13 December 2006, after 130 days of trial spread over a period of just over two years.

The questions for consideration and answering by the High Court were the following.

1. whether the termination with effect from 31 January 2002 by the Government of the provision of basic and essential services to the Appellants in the Central Kalahari Game Reserve was unlawful and unconstitutional.
2. whether the Government is obliged to restore the provision of such services to the Appellants in the Central Kalahari Game Reserve;
3. whether subsequent to 31 January 2002 the Appellants were:
   a. in possession of the land which they lawfully occupied in their settlements in the Central Kalahari Game Reserve;
   b. deprived of such possession by the Government forcibly or wrongly and without their consent
4. whether the Government's refusal to:
   a. issue special game licences to the Appellants;
   b. allow the Appellants to enter into the Central Kalahari Game Reserve unless they are issued with a permit is unlawful and unconstitutional.

The case was presided over by a panel of three judges—Chief Justice Maruping Dibotelo, Justice Unity Dow and Justice M. P. Phumaphi. In a non unanimous judgment, the court ruled that:

1. *The termination in 2002 by the Government of the provision of basic and essential services to the Applicants in the CKGR was neither unlawful nor unconstitutional.* (Dow J dissenting).
2. *The Government is not obliged to restore the provision of such services to the Applicants in the CKGR.* (Dow J dissenting).
3. *Prior to 31 January 2002, the Applicants were in possession of the land, which they lawfully occupied in their settlements in the CKGR.* (Unanimous decision).
4. *The Applicants were deprived of such possession by the Government forcibly or wrongly and without their consent.* (Dibotelo J dissenting).

5. *The Government's refusal to issue special game licenses to the Applicants is unlawful.* (Unanimous decision).

6. *The Government's refusal to issue special game licenses to the Applicants is unconstitutional.* (Dibotelo dissenting).

7. *The Government's refusal to allow the Applicants to enter the CKGR unless they are issued with permits is unlawful and unconstitutional.* (Dibotelo dissenting).[547]

As mentioned by Justice Dow, it was a judgment one to three and each Justice therefore delivered in open court a full stand-alone judgment in order to substantiate their positions.

Chief Justice Maruping Dibotelo's line of reasoning was "traditional" and based on Botswana jurisprudence; he concluded in favour of the respondents in five (5) out of seven (7) rulings. The two other judges—Justice Dow and Justice Phumaphi—on the other hand, took a more "modern" stance.

This was especially the case of Justice Unity Dow whose approach differed significantly from that of her two colleagues. She began thus by stating that she held the position *"that while each of the various questions could very well be answered as stand-alone questions, there is significant inter-play and inter-connectedness between the questions, making such an approach too narrow and too simplistic."* She said, for instance, that,

> While the termination of services may, by itself, not raise constitutional questions, the consequence of such termination may well do. If, for example, it is found that the termination of services had the consequence of forcing the Applicants out of the Reserve, then the termination would necessarily raise such constitutional questions, as for example, the right to movement. And in view of the acceptance by the parties that the services were basic and essential, their termination, if that is found to have been unlawful, will necessarily raise the constitutional question of whether the right to life has been abridged"[548].

For Dow, the question of relocation was therefore the core issue and the first to be dealt with. Having once ruled the relocation to be unlawful and unconstitutional, the logical consequence was that the other actions taken by the Botswana Government were unlawful and unconstitutional. Accordingly, her ruling was in favour of the applicants on all seven questions.

Justice Dow also found *"that the fact the Applicants belong to a class of peoples that have now come to be recognised as 'indigenous peoples' is of relevance"* and referred to the Convention on the Elimination of all Forms of Racial Discrimination (ICERD), which Botswana has ratified, and to its Committee's Recommendation XXIII on

---

547 Ibid., per Dibotelo, at para. 55.
548 Ibid., per Dow, at para. H.1. b.

indigenous peoples' equal rights.[549] She also pointed out that "*the current wisdom, which should inform all policy and direction in dealing with indigenous peoples, is the recognition of their special relationship to their land*",[550] and referred to Martínez Cobo's statement regarding indigenous peoples' special relationship to their land.

As for Justice Phumaphi, his overall approach was similar to that of Chief Justice Dibotelo, with whom he sided on the two issues related to service delivery. On the other issues, however—including issue 4 on whether the applicants were deprived of their land by the Government forcibly or wrongly and without their consent—he ruled in favour of the applicants, and just like Justice Dow, used the term "indigenous" when referring to the San. He also based his arguments on international jurisprudence, making substantial quotes from the Australian Mabo case to sustain his view that the San had had "native titles" that had been extinguished neither by the Proclamation on Crown Lands (1910) nor by the creation of the Game Reserve, nor by the 1966 Constitution of Botswana.[551]

On the question of whether the applicants were consulted before the termination of basic services by the Government, both Chief Justice Dibotelo and Justice Phumaphi found that the legal concept of "legitimate expectation" (of continued service delivery) was not applicable and that witness evidence showed that the applicants had been duly consulted.[552] For these same reasons, both Justices ruled "*that the Government is not obliged to restore the provision of services*". Justice Dow, who gave a dissenting ruling, held that since "*the termination of basic and essential services was intended to force relocation*"[553] her assessment of that relocation being "*forced, wrongful and without consent applies to this issue as well.*" Regarding whether the termination was constitutional or not, she concluded that "*the right to life is a constitutional right and the termination of essential services was in essence, a breaching of that right*", since it endangered life.[554]

To the question of whether the applicants were in legal possession of the disputed land before the settlements of 2002, the response was affirmative and unanimous.[555] The same was the case with the answer to the question "whether the Applicants lawfully occupied the land in their settlements in the CKGR before the 2002 relocations". Chief Justice Dibotelo answered:

---

549 CERD (Committee on the Elimination of All Forms of Racial Discrimination), General Comment XXIII, U.N. Doc A/52/18, Annex V, at para. 4 (d). The General Comment requires of States Parties to: "ensure that members of indigenous peoples have equal rights in respect of effective participation in public life and that no decisions directly relating to their rights and interests are taken without their informed consent".

550 *Sesana and Others v. the Attorney General*, per Dow, at para.H.1.f.

551 Ibid., per Phumaphi, at para. 92.

552 Ibid., per Dibotelo, at paras 28-29 and 31-33; per Phumaphi, at paras. 41-42 and 48-49.

553 Ibid., per Dow, at paras H.12 and H.13.

554 Ibid., per Dow, at para. H.12.4.

555 Ibid., per Dibotelo, at para. 38.

I do not agree that the occupation of land in the settlements in the CKGR by the Applicants was unlawful even though the CKGR is state land and is owned by the Government, the fact of it being state land having been conceded by the Applicants as I stated earlier. I take the view that the occupation of this state land by the Applicants was lawful for the simple reason that their occupation had not been lawfully terminated by the Government; and until such occupation was lawfully terminated by the owner of the CKGR, it could not be successfully contended in my view that the Applicants occupied the land in their settlements unlawfully. As this was state land, the Applicants occupied it at the sufferance or passive consent of the Government but that did not and could not mean in my judgment that their occupation of that land was unlawful, especially when regard is had to the fact that both the British Government and its successor in title, i.e., the Botswana Government, allowed or permitted the Applicants to remain on and use that land over many years. For the avoidance of doubt, therefore, I find as a fact that the occupation of the land in the settlements by the Applicants in the CKGR was lawful.[556]

Although the ruling on this issue was unanimous, Dow and Phumaphi based their reasoning on slightly different premises, namely the fact that the Applicants were indigenous to the area and had lived in the CKGR prior to it becoming Crown Land, and had remained on the land when it became a game reserve and then state land upon Botswana attaining independence. In a line of argumentation very similar to that used in the Richtersveld case, Justice Phumaphi concluded *"that their 'native rights' had not been extinguished neither by the Proclamation in 1910 on Crown Lands, nor the creation of the game reserve"* and quoted the *Mabo* case as relevant to the case.[557]

Regarding the relocation process, however, Chief Justice Dibotelo was alone in finding that the applicants had not been deprived of their land by the Government forcibly or wrongly and without their content, and stated: *"the termination of the provision of services was never a reason or ground for their relocation, otherwise their witnesses would have said so in their evidence"*.[558] He further contended that

I have already found … ample evidence from both the Applicants and Respondent which proves that the Applicants were consulted and even told that the provision of services to them in their settlements was temporary before the decision to terminate the provision of those services was made by the Government, and that as a result, the termination of the provision of those services by the Government was lawful. Arising from those findings it cannot, in my view, be successfully con-

---

556 Ibid., per Dibotelo, at para. 40.
557 Ibid., per Phumaphi, at para. 69-82.
558 Ibid., per Dibotelo, at para. 45.

tended that the Applicants were forcibly or wrongly deprived of possession of the land they occupied in their settlements in the CKGR by the Government".[559]

Both Justice Dow and Justice Phumaphi based their affirmative ruling on whether relocation had been wrong and without the consent of the relocatees on a critical review of the circumstances and processes of the 2002 relocation and on the evidence given by witnesses to the applicants. Justice Dow saw a crucial factor in the fact that the Government had been ambiguous and unclear in its policy prior to January 2002, thereby adding to the confusion among the CKGR residents as to the Government's intentions. She also held that the respondent had failed to take into consideration how relocation might disrupt the culture of the applicants and threatened their very survival as a people. Once the respondent executed its decision,

> [I]t failed to appreciate the importance of the fact that the Applicants lived in families, compounds and small settlements ... [were] linked together by blood, marriage, mutual-cooperation and general inter-dependence. And true consent by any one to relocate could hardly be obtained unless the family, the compound and in some instances the whole settlement was taken as a unit.

Justice Dow also considered that the respondent should also have taken into consideration the relative powerlessness of the applicants and provided culturally appropriate consultations:

> The average non-politicised Applicant, illiterate, dependant upon Government services, without political representation at the high political level, was hardly in a position to give genuine consent. It was the Respondent's obligation to put in place mechanisms that promoted and facilitated true and genuine consent by individuals, families and communities.[560]

In relation to hunting rights, Chief Justice Dibotelo and his two colleagues agreed that the refusal to issue special game licenses was unlawful: the Director (of the DWNP) had acted outside the powers granted to him by law and the applicants had not had an opportunity to be heard before his decision. However, the Chief Justice did not find that the Government's refusal to issue such licenses was unconstitutional,[561] nor did he find the refusal to allow the Applicants to enter the CKGR unless they have been issued with a permit unlawful and unconstitutional since he considered that *"the receipt of compensation in the form of money as well as new plots in the settlements outside the CKGR was in replacement of the rights of the*

---

559 Ibid., per Dibotelo, at para. 47.
560 Ibid., per Dow, at para. H.9.
561 Ibid., per Dibotelo, at para. 51.

Applicants to occupy and possess land in the settlements inside the Reserve".[562] Dow's standpoint, on the other hand, was that

[A]ny rights that were lost as a result [of the relocation] were lost wrongfully and unlawfully. Any attempt to regulate the enjoyment of those rights by permits, when such permits were not, prior to the 2002 relocations, a feature of the enjoyment of such rights, is an unlawful curtailment of the right of movement of the Applicants. It is unlawful and unconstitutional.[563]

Concluding observations and results/impact of the court case

1. This case reveals the importance of constitutional recognition or protection of indigenous peoples' rights. The fact that the Botswana Constitution of 1966 provided for a special treatment on behalf of the San emerged as critical to the case. This is also believed to be the reason for the amendment of the Constitution in 2005 and the repeal of its section 14 (3)c.

2. A similarity this case has with others in this volume is the use of delay-tactics. In this instance, it took almost four years before a decision was reached. The court recessed several times, at times because money had run out for the San, but also because technicalities were invoked, expert witnesses gave lengthy and technical evidence that was *"by and large, a waste of time"*,[564] or because the witnesses of the applicants were "cross-examined" at exaggerated length by the respondent's representative.

3. This is a case where international campaigning actions were combined with legal action and the former seemed to accelerate the latter. International and national NGOs such as Survival International and the Botswana Centre for Human Rights, DITSHWANELO, undertook a number of campaigning activities on this case while the court hearings were being held.

4. Conducting an inspection *in loco* proved also highly recommendable since it brought the judges closer to the realities and conditions of life of the concerned indigenous people, both in the CKGR settlements from where people had been relocated and in the new settlements outside the CKGR where they now live.

5. The use of a large number of witnesses for the applicants, who were themselves victims of relocation, seemed also to help and is recommendable. The four hundred pages judgment reveals the extent to which witnesses' accounts were used by the three judges.

---

562 Ibid., per Dibotelo, at para. 53.
563 Ibid., per Dow, at para. H.21(17-18).
564 Ibid., per Dow, at para. F. 2.

6. This case is also a good illustration of a successful collective representative suit, which is the ideal option when the capacities are there and the concerned indigenous community is fully aware of the implications. The Government of Botswana, however, has subsequently taken the position that only the listed applicants have the right to return to the CKGR, thus disregarding the rights of former CKGR residents in general.

7. It is interesting to note that the applicants made clear that *"their legal claim is not to ownership, but to a right to use and occupy the land they have long occupied, unless and until that right is taken from them by constitutionally permissible means"*. It is difficult to understand why the San decided not to claim ownership. Was it because such right could have been difficult to prove? Or was it because the right of use and occupation is broad enough to accommodate their livelihood? The judgment and the case's proceedings do not provide us with a clear answer to these questions, which could inspire strategic legal choices by other indigenous communities.

8. The fact that a State is declared sole owner of all lands should not prevent indigenous communities from initiating legal actions for protection of their right to use and occupation of what they believe are their ancestral lands. This case reveals that a court can declare a State sole owner of a land and at the same time rule in favor of the right to use and occupation by an indigenous community. This case demonstrates also that being owner of a land does not automatically give a State the right to expel at will indigenous communities from it.

9. The San's lawyers referred widely to international law and jurisprudence such as the Australian *Mabo* case, and this seemed to pay off.

10. Like the South African Constitutional Court judge did, Judge Phumaphi relied on the principle that pre-existing rights were not extinguished following the change in sovereignty. He contended that the immemorial occupation of the disputed land by the San, as confirmed by many historical accounts, amounted to ownership under customary law. Quoting substantially the ruling in the *Mabo* case, he concluded that *"the Bushmen are indigenous to the CKGR which means that they were in the CKGR prior to it becoming Crown Land"*[565] and that:

    > The reasoning of the Australian Court is quite persuasive, but this Court would not readily endorse any action taken by the State to extinguish the "native rights" of citizens, unless it is done in accordance with the Constitution of the Republic of Botswana. I have earlier said the evidence indicates that the Bushmen were in the area now known as the CKGR prior to 1910, when the Ghanzi Crown land which included the CKGR was proclaimed. It therefore follows that they must have claimed "native rights" to land, which has since become the CKGR, as they keep referring to it in their evidence as "their land",

---

565 Ibid., per Phumaphi, at para. 67.

> *like many other inhabitants of the then Bechuanaland, who claimed rights to the land they occupied ...*
>
> *...*
>
> *The rights of the Bushmen in the CKGR were not affected by the proclamation of the land they occupied to be Crown land, as they continued to live on it, and exploit it without interference from the British Government.*[566]

11. This case reveals the positive input that each judge's separate legal opinion supporting or dissenting from the majority decision can have. Lawyers of indigenous communities could consider persuading judges to express dissenting opinions depending on the circumstances.

12. This case also highlights the problem of the implementation of judgments. The High Court made its decision on 13 December 2006, but three years later not much has been done in terms of implementing the court's ruling.[567] San continue nevertheless to move back into the CKGR although they risk being stopped and harassed by guards from the Department of Wildlife and National Parks.

Conclusion

Both the Richtersveld and the CKGR cases seem to indicate a new trend that consists of a pro-active judiciary with a better understanding of the internationally developed standards of protection of indigenous peoples' rights. An African court making a bold reference to landmark international rulings such as the *Mabo* case of Australia is something of a milestone as far as indigenous rights are concerned in Africa. One could hope that this new development grows in strength, and inspires judges, lawyers, and indigenous communities in other parts of Africa.

---

566 Ibid., per Phumaphi, at paras. 79-81.
567 See Survival International: http://www.survival-international.org/tribes/bushmen for updates.

PART III INDIGENOUS PEOPLES' LAND RIGHTS IN AN INTERNATIONAL AND AFRICAN PERSPECTIVE

CHAPTER VIII
CHARACTERISTICS AND FOUNDATION OF INDIGENOUS PEOPLES' LAND RIGHTS

This chapter deals with some of the different points of discussion that are crucial and ever emerging in most debates relating to indigenous peoples and their right to lands. These are the issue of groups' rights and collective rights, including looking at the scope and the holders of these rights; the concept of parallel use of lands by indigenous peoples; the notion of *terra nullius*; and the issue of coexistence between indigenous peoples' claims to ancestral lands and modern states. A final section looks at the African jurisprudence when it comes to the notion of indigenous peoples' land rights.

Characteristics of indigenous land rights

Group rights

The rights of indigenous peoples to lands are group rights,[568] a concept that draws on the practice adopted by European States from as early as the seventeenth century.[569]

On the basis of what is known as a "triple value scheme", it is argued by Ronald Garet that a human being consists of an unbroken grouping of three indispensable components, namely "personhood, communality, and sociality ... [which] schematizes our fundamental rights".[570] Personhood is the ground for the individual rights of each one of us towards self-accomplishment. "Communality is the ground of the right of groups to maintain themselves and to pursue their distinctive course, whereas sociality is the ground of the right of the existence of States and other artificial groupings created by men ... To rob the existence of communality, of the communal celebratory process, which forms the substance of much of our experience, would be to deny one ethical constituent of our humanity".[571] Garet thus concludes that "groups have a fundamental right to their communality, just as persons have a fundamental right to their personhood".[572] This is to say that "our most urgent interests lie not merely in individuated goods such as personal liberty and exclusive property but also in collective goods".[573]

The protection of groups' rights does not automatically flow out of the protection of individual rights and vice-versa, as demonstrated by the North American *Wisconsin v. Yoder* case from 1972.[574] This case involved members of a religious

---

568 See Ingram, *Group Rights* (2000), p. 103. A similar argument is found in Lyndel V. Prott, "Cultural Rights as Peoples' Rights in International Law", in *The Rights of Peoples,* edited by James Crawford, (Oxford: Clarendon/Oxford University Press, 1992), p. 97.

569 Lerner, *Group Rights* (1991), pp. 7-12. As early as the seventeenth century treaties, such as the 1648 Treaty of Westphalia, the 1660 Treaty of Oliva and the 1678 Treaty of Nimeguen, "incorporated clauses ensuring certain rights to individuals or groups" based on various factors, such as religion. This practice of treaties continued during the eighteenth century, with, for example, the Treaty of Paris between France and Great Britain in 1763, which included a clause on the protection of Roman Catholics, who constituted a minority within the part of Canada ceded by France. Broader and more comprehensive treaties, based on the principle of protection of minority groups, were signed in the nineteenth century. In 1878, for example, the Berlin Treaty contained protective dispositions on behalf of groups such as the Turks, the Greeks and the Romanians, who found themselves under the rule of the newly constituted autonomous Bulgarian Principality. The International Convention of Constantinople of 1881 did the same with regard to Muslim populations that were living in Greek-controlled territories.

570 Ronald Garet, "Communality and Existence: The Rights of Groups", 56 *Southern Californian Law Review,* 1983, p. 1016.

571 Ibid., p. 1002.

572 Ibid., p. 1017.

573 Green, "Internal minorities" (1994), p. 103.

574 *Wisconsin v. Yoder,* 406 U.S. at 219 (1972).

community known as the "Old Order Amish". Alleging that high school attendance would have a negative impact on the religious beliefs of their children, the Amish refused to send their children to school after completing eighth grade. Taken to court, they were found guilty by the Wisconsin Circuit Court of violating the state law on compulsory schooling for children under the age of sixteen. This decision was later overturned by both the Wisconsin Supreme Court and the US Supreme Court, on the grounds that "the respondents' conviction for violating the State's compulsory school-attendance law violated some of their rights as a group". What is interesting in this case, is that it involved three different types of legal claims: first, individual rights of the Amish children to complete their education; secondly, the State's claim for law enforcement; and thirdly, the claim of a religious group for the protection of its way of life. Could it be argued that a ruling in favour of the individual claims involved in this case could automatically result in the protection of the Amish Community's claim? One answer to this question is that "the confinement of [this case] to individual rights is troubled by the fact that the model of individual free exercise does not accommodate the control over individuals" by a community.[575]

It is also possible that a need for protection of "group rights" violates individual rights; and this is likely to happen in indigenous communities. One can consider for example practices such as forced marriages and several other customary practices that indigenous women suffer from for the sake of preserving the culture and traditions of their communities. This is indeed a question of balance between individual human rights and the right of a group to exist and maintain its identity. An interesting case in this respect is that of Sandra Lovelace, a Canadian indigenous woman who, in 1977, after having been married to a non Indian person and lived for several years outside her community—*in casu* a reserve—was not allowed to return to her reserve after her marriage had broken down. This was consistent with the Indian Act passed by the Government of Canada in 1876 and according to which indigenous persons who had spent a certain time outside their reserve would lose their Indian status and no longer be able to return to their reserve. The Government alleged to thus protect the Indian culture and territories. Unhappy with this decision, Sandra Lovelace submitted a complaint against the Canadian Government to the United Nations' Human Rights Committee alleging a breach, among others, of Article 27 (Right to enjoy a culture) of the ICCPR.[576] In 1980, the Human Rights Committee found that:

> *Whatever may be the merits of the Indian Act in other respects, it does not seem to the Committee that to deny Sandra Lovelace the right to reside on the reserve is reasonable, or necessary to preserve the identity of the tribe. The Committee there-*

---

575 Garet, "Communality and Existence" (1983), p. 1031.
576 Article 27 of the ICCPR guarantees the right to persons belonging to minorities to "enjoy their own culture, to profess and practise their own religion, or to use their own language".

fore concludes that to prevent her recognition as belonging to the band is an un-justifiable denial of her rights under article 27 of the Covenant, read in the context of the other provisions referred to.[577]

Subsequent to this conclusion by the HRC, Sandra Lovelace was allowed back into the Tobique Reserve and the Canadian Government amended the Indian Act accordingly.

The major contribution of this debate on the rights of indigenous individuals versus the rights of their communities is what the Human Rights Committee called "reasonable and objective justification" or fair balance struck between the protection of the rights and freedoms of the individual and the interests of the community or society as a whole, as required by the human rights principle of "proportionality". This is an extremely relevant point for indigenous women who are denied a number of rights and freedoms—including that of access to land and resources—on the grounds that it goes against the "group's" interests. Indeed, a number of negative cultural practices such as female genital mutilation, forced and under age marriages affect numerous African indigenous women in the name of communities' culture.

Collective rights

International documents dealing with indigenous peoples such as ILO Convention No. 169 (Article 13.1) and the U.N. Declaration on the Rights of Indigenous Peoples (Preamble) not only emphasize the special relationship indigenous peoples have with the lands or territories which they occupy or otherwise use but also stress the collective aspects of this relationship. The U.N. Declaration, for instance, recognizes and reaffirms that "indigenous peoples possess collective rights which are indispensable for their existence, well-being and integral development as peoples."

What are collective lands?

Collective lands are lands possessed under the traditional laws and customs observed by their indigenous inhabitants,[578] without option of division into individual plots. Terms like "aboriginal title", "native title" or "indigenous title" are often used indistinctively to refer to the right to such lands and to denote the

---

577 United Nations Human Rights Committee, Communication No. 24/1977, *Sandra Lovelace v. Canada*, U.N. Doc. CCPR/C/OP/1 at 83 (1984), para. 17. Available online at http://hrlibrary.ngo.ru/undocs/session13-index.html

578 See, e.g., *Mabo v. Queensland* (No.2) (1992), per Brennan, at para. 61.

"pre-sovereignty occupation" of these lands.[579] In the *Mabo* case,[580] for instance, the Australian High Court decided that indigenous people have rights that existed before colonisation and which still exist. This right is, among other names, called "native title". Generally speaking, indigenous peoples' collective lands are of a wide scope, vested in the community as a whole and used in a non-exclusive way.

Collective lands in Africa

In Africa, collective lands range from hunting and gathering areas to grazing areas, grasslands, forests, mixed savannah, wetlands, mountain sides, lakes, rivers, costal areas, fishing grounds, etc.,[581] all vested in the indigenous communities without option of individualization, as stated by the doctrine of native title. These communities also claim to have a collective right to the natural resources pertaining to these lands.[582]

The following few illustrative examples reveal that different words are used by indigenous communities in Central, Eastern, and Southern Africa with reference to their collective lands. The Mbendjele ("Pygmies") of the Republic of Congo call their forest *ndima angosu* (our forest). However, within the forest, different areas are called by different names according to their use. The *mooko* is the firm ground where it is good to camp, dig yams and a place popular with duikers. *Djamba* is the marsh, where trees are shorter, making the honey easier to collect. Mbendjele's collective lands include also the *pbai* (salt licks around a small stream that has been cleared of forest trees by elephants), *esobe* (small encapsulated savannahs), and *eyanga* (openings in the forest with still water in the centre) where visibility is good and therefore makes it perfect for hunting.[583] In this community, the "notions of exclusive individual ownership are only applied to ritual and mystic knowledge" and the Mbendjele refer to their lands as "our forest", an illustration of "a collective claim, not an individual one".[584]

The Hadzabe of Tanzania, whose land tenure system is similar to that of the "Pygmies", distinguish the *tangoto* (open land) from the *chikiko* which refers to lands with thick forest where big game such as buffalo can be found. The Hadzabe also consider all the hills (*han!a*) around the Lake Eyasi as part of their ancestral lands. For them "rights are not asserted by individuals or by groups over

---

579 Andie D. Plamer, "Evidence 'Not in a Form Familiar to Common Law Courts': Assessing Oral Histories in Land Claims Testimony after *Delgamuukw v. B.C.*", 38 *Alberta Law Review* 1040 (February 2001), p. 1046.
580 *Mabo v. Queensland* (1992), Decision.
581 Cousins, "Tenure and Property" (2000), p. 160.
582 Juviler, "Are Collective Rights Anti-Human?" (1993), p. 269.
583 Jerome Lewis, "Whose Forest is it anyway?" Draft paper presented at the Property and Equality Workshop, MPI, Halle, March 2001, (2001b), p. 7.
584 Ibid.

[collective] areas ... and other resources they contain. Anyone can and does live, hunt, and gather anywhere he or she wishes without restriction".[585]

The Maasai of both Kenya and Tanzania categorize land according to climate, topography and usage. Climatically, the land is divided in three categories: the wet highlands (*osupuko*), the dry low lands (*orpukel*) and the land between the two (*oloirishrisha*). Topographically, they divide it in mountains (*il doinyo*) and plains (*angata*). When it comes to usage, the land can be that which is immediately behind the homesteads (*auluo*), that which is reserved for calves (*olokeri*) or that which is available for cattle (*ngujit o ngishu*).

The San of Botswana, call their homelands, including lands in the Central Kalahari Game Reserve (CKGR), the *n!oresi* (traditional territories, *n!ore* in singular).

Who holds the right to collective land?

> *The land belongs to the Maasai by virtue of right. It belongs to the young and to the old, the born and those yet to be born....*[586]

Unlike many other rights, indigenous peoples' right to lands is "vested not in an individual or a number of identified individuals but in a community"[587] and not even in the chiefs or political leaders.

Although members of several hunter-gatherer communities pay respect to the elder of each band or *Kombati*, as he is called amongst the Mbendjele of the Republic of Congo, the elder does not actually play any role whatsoever as far as land use and occupation are concerned. "No one should claim exclusive ownership ... the notion that an individual, apart from *Komba* (God), could own land, rivers and forest ... evokes suspicion, incomprehension and mockery".[588] One of James Woodburn's conclusions, following his extensive observation of the Hadzabe of Northern Tanzania, is that the decision of moving a camp, for example, is not even taken by the elder of a band: "Movement of a whole camp depends on a series of *ad hoc* individual decisions, not on the decision of a leader or on consensus reached in discussion".[589]

However, most States and other actors in Central, Eastern, and Southern Africa, have, in recent times, been trying to introduce or force the notion of representation on indigenous communities. In Namibia, the Traditional Authorities Acts of 1995 and 2000 prompted the various San groups to constitute themselves as communities under the central jurisdiction of a Chief. While it has somewhat

---

585 Woodburn, "Minimal Politics" (1979), p. 245.
586 Statement by a Maasai from Iloodoariak in Kenya, quoted in Oleku Ole Roore, "The Iloodoariak Land Scandal" (1998), p. 6.
587 *Mabo v. Queensland* (1992), per Brennan, at para. 52.
588 Lewis, "Forest People or Village People" (2001a), p. 64.
589 Woodburn, "Minimal Politics" (1979), p. 253.

strengthened their political position, the results are mixed and the Government's disregard for the traditional leaders when it comes to land issues "can be seen as a continuation of the legacy of disrespect and discrimination afforded to San people".[590] In Namibia, too, for the Himba community to use the services of lawyers and other support groups in their case against the construction of the Epupa Dam on their lands by the Namibian and Angolan Governments, a body of local leaders was constituted to represent the views of the community.[591] So did the ‡Khomani San of South Africa during their struggle that has resulted so far in 40,000 hectares of their land being given back to them.[592] The Ogiek of Kenya also found themselves almost forced to bring all their elders together in order to try to enter into negotiations with their national authorities.[593]

The notion of representation seems alien to many hunter-gatherer communities in Central, Eastern, and Southern Africa. This is not to be confused with the existence of individuals with a strong influence on other community members, due to their knowledge or experience. Among the San of the Kalahari, for example, each family or band had an *!Ari=aub*, which means "hero" or someone who does valuable work for the community. In most cases, such a person would have a strong knowledge of the characteristics, boundaries, and natural resources of the *koros* or communal lands, as well as, for example, the ability to identify the footprints of any trespasser and to share information with his entire community.[594] Joram Useb, a San from Namibia who has done research on the notion of leadership amongst his community, asserts that "during an extensive survey conducted in most [San] … villages … it was established that all community groups interviewed had a similar idea of the meaning of leadership: the communities' definition of a leader refers to his/her social attitudes and skills of informed decision-making, as well as the capacity to give advice. The

---

590 Richard Pakleppa, "Civil Rights in Legislation and Practice – A Case Study from Tsumkwe District West, Namibia" in *Indigenous Peoples' Rights in Southern Africa*, edited by Robert K. Hitchcock and Diana Vinding, IWGIA Document 110 (Copenhagen: IWGIA, 2004), p. 90; *The Indigenous World 2007* (IWGIA, 2007), p. 504.
591 Corbett, "A Case Study" (1999), pp. 87-8.
592 The ‡Khomani San of South Africa launched in 1994 a claim to their aboriginal lands under the new South African (Interim) Constitution. Several ‡Khomani San groups were put together and represented by lawyers, as well as by a number of their leaders. Amongst other tactics and materials put together for strengthening their land claims was the mapping of their lands, the first exercise of this kind in Central, Eastern, and Southern Africa, at least so far as indigenous communities are concerned. For more details regarding this land claim, see chapter IV, this volume. Such mapping has also been done in Botswana, in the CKGR, for instance, as part of the San's efforts to assert their traditional land and resource rights.
593 Following the institution in 1930 in Kenya of the Carter Land Commission with the mission to look into local communities' land claims, the Ogiek sent a group of their elders who presented the case of their community on October 17, 1932. See in Sang, "Kenya: The Ogiek in Mau Forest" (2003), p. 7.
594 Joram Useb, "'One Chief is Enough!' Understanding San Traditional Authorities in the Namibian Context", in *Africa's Indigenous Peoples: 'First Peoples' or 'Marginalized Minorities'*, edited by A. Barnard and J. Kenrick (Edinburgh: Centre of African Studies, 2001), p. 19.

common definition is that a leader has to serve the people, but is not allowed to represent them unless he/she is requested to talk on their behalf".[595]

This is equally true among the Batwa of the Kahuzi-Biega in the Democratic Republic of Congo, where any individual, who tends to make himself look more important than the others, is generally subjected to much criticism and gossip. The Mbendjele and Yaka (Republic of Congo), as well as the Bagyeli (Cameroon), also recognize the important role of guidance that the elders play in the celebration of various cultural ritual ceremonies. However, none of these communities recognizes any role for elders in relation to land use, occupation or ownership. The *Poisionik* or the traditional council of elders among the Ogiek assists the community in solving disputes and carrying out a number of rituals but never issues rules on land use and occupation.

James Woodburn understands this absence of the notion of chief or representative among most hunter-gatherer communities as something that has to do with the "egalitarian immediate-return social organization ... in which internal social differentiation of power, wealth, and status is minimized and social relationships are based on sharing and mutuality".[596]

Among the Maasai, a *loibon* (or lybon),[597] although he serves "as a kind of trustee in matters concerning the land",[598] does not actually allocate lands or set rules for land use or occupation; nor can he prevent a Maasai from grazing his herds on a specific part of the Maasai land. The Maasai rely also on a Council of Elders, which is a rather informal institution that is called upon when a common serious problem arises amongst the members of a community. However, this institution does not have the power to allocate land or to set regulation for its use.

The Maasai's tradition of not recognising that their traditional political institution has the prerogative to determine rules concerning land occupation and use, could explain why the 1904 treaty between the British colonial authorities and a number of Maasai leaders that resulted in moving Maasai communities from more arable land to Laikipia and the southern part of the country, was denounced almost immediately by the people themselves, on the grounds that "the agreement was obtained by duress, and is further not binding as it [had] not received the approval of the tribe".[599]

---

595 Ibid., p. 3.
596 Woodburn, "Indigenous Discrimination" (1997), p. 352.
597 See supra footnote 282.
598 Glazier, *Land and the Uses of Tradition* (1985), p. 195.
599 *Ol le Njogo and 7 Others v. The Attorney General and 20 Others*, 5 E.A.L.R. 70, Vols. V-VII [1913-1918], pp. 79 and 94. During the appeal of this case, Justice Morris Carter also touched upon the issue of whether those who signed the two treaties in the name of the Maasai community could possibly do so: "I am of the opinion that the Court cannot go into the question of whether the Government has selected the right persons with whom to make such treaties ... the Village Headmen Ordinance, which deals with the appointment of headmen for villages, has not the effect, which the Appellants (Maasai) attach to it, of precluding the Government from recognising persons as chiefs of a tribe. ...". See also Rutten, *Selling Wealth* (1992), p. 177.

M.M.E.M Rutten illustrates this disconnection between the institution of *loiboni* and the people, as far as land use and occupation are concerned. With reference to the removal of the Maasai from Laikipia towards the south in 1911, this author shows that Lenana, the *loibon* at the time, acted in complicity with the colonial authorities, and misled his community by alleging that the move southwards was to take place for cultural purposes. Many Maasai resisted their leader's plan to move, and eventually went to court in an attempt to nullify the agreed move.[600]

This same tradition could also explain why the Maasai of the Ngorongoro area of Tanzania consider that the *Ilaigwanak* (term which refers to traditional institutions that play a role in cultural activities as well as in a number of social issues) have become manipulated and controlled by the Government and conservation authorities. In a similar vein, the "Pastoralist Council" in Tanzania, which was meant to advance Maasai's interest in the Ngorongoro Conservation Area, was considered by many ordinary Maasai as nothing more than a recent creation pushed through by Government to try to insert the idea of representation amongst the Maasai for land use, ownership, and occupation.[601]

Non-exclusive land use of collective lands

Indigenous peoples' landholding systems are also characterized by the principle of parallel use of lands by various and even different communities; and the exercise of indigenous peoples' right to lands is often not exclusive. In Leslie Green's expression, "this is an inexcludable and non-rival use of lands according to which the part used by one person or community does not perceptibly limit the space used by others because the collective enjoyment of such lands is what constitutes their values".[602]

Smokin Wanjala, a Kenyan scholar, understands this parallel use of lands by different communities as a demonstration of different rights enjoyed by different communities over the same land. Such rights are, for example, the right to graze domestic animals, the right to till, the right to pick firewood, the right to hunt, and the right to place honey barrels.[603]

Indeed, in most pre-colonial Central, Eastern, and Southern African countries, land use was regulated by the customary principle of "non-exclusive use", which made it possible for the same land to be used by different communities. It helped to accommodate different life styles and the simultaneous or consecutive exploitation of the same land. The claims made by the Dorobo

---

600 Rutten, *Selling Wealth* (1992), pp. 179-181: "The Maasai lost the case on the grounds that they were not British subjects".
601 Kaisoe and Ole Seki, "The Conflict" (2001), pp. 23-4.
602 Green, "Internal Minorities" (1993), p. 103.
603 Wanjala, *Land Law* (1990), p. 2.

(Ogiek) to consider all the forests in which they hung honey barrels as theirs were thus just as acceptable as the claims of other communities who used the very same forests for hunting, religious ceremonies, grazing or other activities: "most East African peoples did not look on land use in an exclusive way".[604] Part of the Mau Forest of Kenya, for instance, is regarded as Maasai land but was simultaneously used by the Ogiek and the forest was until Government intervention one undivided piece of land.

Anthropologists also attest that amongst the Hadzabe of Tanzania, "no effort is made even to limit the use of the land to members of their own tribe".[605] So is the Central Kalahari Game Reserve, which is claimed by the San peoples, but also used by the Bakgalagadi who have lived there for many generations.

In addition to easing various communities' access to needed resources, the practice of parallel or non-exclusive use of lands also facilitates and maintains interaction and exchange between various indigenous communities.[606] The non-exclusive use of lands and its resources appears to go beyond the usual inter-communal rivalries and denigration. For example, despite the fact that the Maasai consider the Ogiek as "backward", the latter perform the circumcision of the Maasai boys, a ritual highly respected and essential for the passage from youth to warriors and elders.[607]

Despite some Governments' attempts to abolish the rule of non-exclusive use and occupation of land through various mechanisms of gradual individualisation, such as the group ranches in Kenya and village lands in Tanzania, the practice of parallel use of lands continues to exist amongst several indigenous communities in Central, Eastern, and Southern Africa, albeit to a limited extent. Lands around the Lake Eyasi in northern Tanzania continue to be used by Maasai, Hadzabe, and Barabaig people,[608] despite mounting inter-communal tensions due to increasing land scarcity. The same is observed among the Ogiek of Kenya, who do not object to other communities' use of the Mau Forests, so long as their indigenous rights are recognized. The Serengeti ecosystem[609] continues in the same way to be used simultaneously by the

---

604 Kitching, *Class and Economic Change* (1980), pp. 282-3.
605 Woodburn, "Minimal Politics" (1979), p. 245.
606 Bahuchet, "Les Pygmées" (1991), p. 5. Commenting on the relationship between the "Pygmies" and their agriculturalist neighbours, Bahuchet notes that the two communities lived in complementarity, both culturally and economically. He cites, for example, the case of the *jengi* ritual of a "Pygmy" group in Cameroon, which consisted of circumcising "Pygmies" and non-Pygmies boys in one ceremony.
607 Woodburn, "Indigenous Discrimination" (1997), p. 357.
608 Madsen, *The Hadzabe* (2000), pp. 41-2.
609 What is known as the "Serengeti ecosystem" is an area of lands covering 25,000 square km of north western Tanzania and south western Kenya. It contains three important protected areas, namely the Maasai Mara National Reserve of Kenya, the Ngorongoro Conservation Area and the Serengeti National Park of Tanzania. It also includes less strict government-controlled conservation areas, where some consumptive utilisation and hunting are allowed under strict regula-

Hadzabe and the Wandorobo[610] of Tanzania, and the Maasai of both Kenya and Tanzania.[611]

In Central Africa, parallel use of land is also practiced. Despite considering themselves as the first inhabitants of the forests in which they live, the Mbendjele of Congo-Brazzaville do not prevent other communities from using them.[612] This is also the case in the Democratic Republic of Congo, where neighbouring communities to the Batwa, (Batembo, Bashi and others), tend to use Batwa lands for sporadic hunting, without conflict arising because parallel use of indigenous communities' lands by others has never been seen by the former as impeding their culture. Mbororo pastoralists in Cameroon, Central African Republic, and Chad do also pasture on lands that are used for other purposes by other communities.

Parallel use of lands by different communities is thus an important principle in most African indigenous communities' sustainable management of their resources, as it prevents each community from overusing its own lands and resources. Within the African environment characterized by lack of clear cut boundaries between various communities' lands, the norm of non-exclusive use of lands also helps various communities to interact culturally.

The foundation of indigenous land rights

Terra nullius versus indigenous title

The doctrine of native title questions the concept of *terra nullius*. This concept has been used to describe different situations where land was considered as "belonging to no one". Originally defined as land that was unclaimed by a sovereign State recognized by European powers, *terra nullius* has also been used in relation to land that was uncultivated or land characterized by the absence of "civilized society",[613] thereby giving legal force to the claiming and settlement of lands occupied by "backward" people, where no system of laws or ownership of property was held to exist. It was in particular used in the Australian context when Governor Bourke, in 1835, proclaimed that indigenous Australians could not sell or assign land, nor could an individual person acquire it, other than through dis-

---

tions. This is the case of the Grumeti, Ikorongo, Kijereshi and Maswa Game Reserves in Tanzania. See also in Emerton and Mfunda, *Making Wildlife Economically Viable* (1999), p. 5.

610   A hunter-gatherer community, also sometimes called "Akie".

611   Emerton and Mfunda, *Making Wildlife Economically Viable* (1999), p. 4.

612   Lewis, "Forest People or Village People" (2001a), p. 64.

613   Michael Connor, "The Invention of Territorium Nullius". Available online at:
        http://www.michaelconnor.com.au/USERIMAGES/usedinventionterritorium.pdf

tribution by the Crown.[614] In 1971, in the controversial *Gove Land Rights* case, Justice Blackburn ruled that Australia had been *terra nullius* before European settlement, and that there was no such thing as native title in Australian law.[615]

In 1975, the International Court of Justice (I.C.J.) in its Advisory Opinion on Western Sahara asserted that the land, on which Spain, Morocco, and Mauritania all claimed to have sovereignty, had not been *terra nullius* prior to Spanish colonization: "at the time of colonization, Western Sahara was inhabited by peoples which, if nomadic, were socially and politically organized in tribes and under chiefs competent to represent them".[616]

In Australia, court cases in 1977, 1979, and 1982 brought by or on behalf of Aboriginal activists tried to challenge the notion of *terra nullius* with reference to this I.C.J. ruling. These cases were rejected by the courts, but the Australian High Court eventually left the door open for a reassessment of whether the continent should be considered "settled" or "conquered". It was first in 1992, with the *Mabo* case, that the court demonstrated that the concerned lands were not *terra nullius* before the arrival of the colonial power and finally ruled, by a majority of six to one, that native title to land is recognized by the common law of Australia, throwing out forever the legal fiction that when Australia was "discovered" by Captain Cook in 1788 it had been *terra nullius*, an empty or uncivilized land. As evidence of a general rejection of the applicability of the *terra nullius* doctrine, the Australian High Court cited the Advisory Opinion of the International Court of Justice on Western Sahara.

Scholars have built upon this to underline that the notion of aboriginal title is based on immemorial occupation and use and that "for the purpose of native title, occupation is not the same as common-law possession. Rather, it is any acknowledged connection with land arising out of traditional rights to use it".[617] In other words, the means of proof of indigenous peoples' right to lands are often different from those of modern property rights, which generally are based on land titles.

Indigenous peoples' right to lands and the existence of States

In 1923, Cayuga Chief Deskaheh from the Haudenosaunee Nation in Canada, travelled to Geneva as the representative of the Six Nations of the Iroquois to present

614 Governor Bourke's Proclamation 1835 (UK). See in National Archives of Australia accessed at http://www.foundingdocs.gov.au/item.asp?dID=42

615 The *Gove Land Rights* case is also known as *Milirrpum v Nabalco Pty Ltd* (1971) 17 FLR 141. For summary, see http://www.atns.net.au/agreement.asp?EntityID=1611

616 International Court of Justice (I.C.J.) Western Sahara: Advisory Opinion I.C.J. Reports 1975, p. 12. Available online at: http://www.icj-cij.org/docket/files/61/6195.pdf

617 T.W. Bennett and C.H. Powell, "Aboriginal Title in South Africa Revisited", 15 *South African Journal of Human Rights* 4, 1999, p. 465.

the concerns of his people to the League of Nations—the predecessor of the United Nations. Unfortunately, he was not granted an audience by the League and was thus not able to express the suffering of his people in the hands of the Canadian colonial Government. A similar attempt was made in 1925 by a Maori religious leader, W.T. Ratana, who wanted to protest the breaking of the 1840 Treaty of Waitangi that recognized Maori ownership of their lands. He, too, was denied access.

These apparently failed attempts, nevertheless, became a landmark for the indigenous movement, even though more than three decades had to elapse before the international community began paying attention to indigenous issues.

The emergence of the indigenous movement has been traced back to the 1960s and linked with the decolonisation process and the civil rights movements, which, it is argued, "contained many elements for consciousness-raising that have become a major aspect of the indigenous movement".[618] The 1960s also witnessed the development of the human rights movement that took off in the aftermath of the Second World War, and its coronation with the adoption of the two Covenants (the International Covenant on Civil and Political Rights, ICCPR, and the International Covenant on Economic, Social and Cultural Rights, ICESCR), which both recognize the right to self-determination, including among others the right of peoples to control their destiny and resources.[619]

Following the extermination policies perpetrated against indigenous peoples such as the Maori of New Zealand, the Aborigines of Australia, the native Indians of the Americas and many others, it had also become morally compelling to redress the historical injustices these communities had suffered since the establishment of modern states on their ancestral lands. It appears indeed that as the States established on indigenous peoples' lands got older, the issue of justice for the first occupants became more and more morally compelling.[620]

---

618 Gray, "The Indigenous Movement", (1995), p. 43: "The late 1960s saw indigenous mobilization springing up throughout the Americas."

619 The ICCPR and the ICESCR were adopted in 1966. Article 1 is common for both Covenants and states that "All peoples have the right of self-determination. By virtue of that right they freely determine their political status and freely pursue their economic, social, and cultural development. ..."

620 By the time the civil rights movement was taking place, most American states had had at least hundred years of independence. The United States got its independence in 1776, Mexico; Colombia and Chile in 1810; Guatemala, Honduras, El Salvador and Costa Rica in 1821; Ecuador and Brazil in 1822; Bolivia in 1825; and Canada in 1867. Independence came later to Australia (1900), and much later to Indonesia (1945), the Philippines (1946), India and Pakistan (1947), Sri Lanka (1948) and Malaysia (1957). In Africa, Libya was the first country to become independent in 1951, while Ghana was the first among the sub-Sahel countries (1957).

Theories of justice and succession of sovereignty

On which grounds could one argue for indigenous peoples' rights to lands? Did the creation of current African States extinguish pre-existing indigenous peoples' right to land?

The Berlin Act of 1885, that carved up Africa and defined the current borders of African States,[621] underlined, in its Article 35, the obligation for colonial powers "*to insure the establishment of authority ... sufficient to protect existing rights*",[622] and to "*watch over the preservation of the native tribes*".[623] The importance of these provisions has been recognized in several cases. In the 1912 Maasai case, it was argued by the Court of Appeal that "*the declaration of a protectorate over an uncivilized region is deemed ... to carry with it the obligation of establishing the authority mentioned in Article 35 of the Berlin Act*".[624] In more explicit terms, the judge was of the opinion that "*whatever the interior economy of the Maasai was, they ... were sovereign over all the tracts of land included in the documents of this case*".[625]

A member of the International Court of Justice (I.C.J.) in the Western Sahara case, M. Bayona-Ba-Meya also referred to the Berlin Conference's principle of respect for pre-existing rights. He argued that before the Berlin Conference, African entities enjoyed sovereignty over their lands given "the ancestral tie between the land, or 'mother nature', and the man who was born therefrom, remains attached thereto, and must one day return thither to be united with his ancestors. This link is the basis of the ownership of the soil, or better, of sovereignty".[626]

Justice Brennan in his ruling on the *Mabo* case[627] refers to the I.C.J. and in particular to Mr. Bayona-Ba-Meya and what he calls his "spiritual notion" of land as opposed to the materialistic concept of "terra nullius". This notion "*amounts to a denial of the very concept of* terra nullius *in the sense of a land which is capable of being appropriated by someone who is not born therefrom.*"[628] Justice Brennan then goes on to conclude that "*a mere change in sovereignty does not extinguish native title to*

---

621 See Christopher Weeramantry and Nathaniel Berman, "The Grotius Lecture Series", in 14 *American University International Law Review* 1515 (1999).

622 Article 35 of the Final Act of Berlin Conference, 1885. The Berlin Conference of 1885 was a gathering of most of the European colonial powers that resulted in the division of Africa into the states that exist today.

623 Article 6 of the Final Act of Berlin, 1885.

624 *Ol le Njogo and Others v. The Attorney General and Others*, [1912], p. 92. See chapter V, this volume, for more details on this case.

625 Ibid., p. 99.

626 M. Bayona-Ba-Meya is quoted by Julie Cassidy in "Sovereignty of Aboriginal peoples", 9 *Indiana International and Comparative Law Review*, 65 (1998), p. 168. See also in Separate Opinion of Vice President Ammoun available on I.C.J.'s website at http://www.icj-cij.org/docket/files/61/6205.pdf, pp. 77-78.

627 *Mabo and Others v. Queensland* (No.2) [1992], per Brennan J., at para. 40.

628 Ibid. (quoting I.C.J.'s Vice President Ammoun), at para. 40.

land".[629] He further argues that "... *that a right or interest possessed as a native title cannot be acquired from an indigenous people by one who, not being a member of the indigenous people, does not acknowledge their laws and observe their customs. ...*".[630] He also states that "*native title is not extinguished unless there be a clear and plain intention to do so*"[631] and that such an intention "*is not revealed by a law which merely regulates the enjoyment of native title*".[632]

Showing that the proposition of absolute Crown ownership has a feudal basis, and that "*it is only the fallacy of equating sovereignty and beneficial ownership of land that gives rise to the notion that native title is extinguished by the acquisition of sovereignty*",[633] Justice Brennan made it clear in his ruling that "*there is a distinction between the Crown's title to a colony and the Crown's ownership of land in the colony*". Or—quoting Roberts-Wray—that,

> *If a country is part of Her Majesty's dominions, the sovereignty vested in her is of two kinds. The first is the power of Government. The second is title to the country*
> ...
> *This ownership of the country is radically different from ownership of the land: the former can belong only to a sovereign, the latter to anyone. Title to land is not, per se, relevant to the constitutional status of a country; land may have become vested in the Queen, equally in a Protectorate or in a Colony, by conveyance or under statute.*[634]

In reaching all the above conclusions, Justice Brennan based his reasoning on what he called "contemporary notions of justice and human rights",[635] and more specifically on what is known today as the principle to respect indigenous communities' prior and informed consent:

> *... [I]t may be assumed that, on 1 August 1879, the Meriam people knew nothing of the events in Westminster and in Brisbane that effected the annexation of the Murray Islands and their incorporation into Queensland and that, had the Meriam people been told of the Proclamation made in Brisbane on 21 July 1879, they would not have appreciated its significance. The legal consequences of these events are in issue in this case. Oversimplified, the chief question in this case is whether these transactions had the effect on 1 August 1879 of vesting in the Crown absolute ownership of, legal possession of, and exclusive power to confer title to all land in the Murray Is-*

---

629   Ibid., at para. 61.
630   Ibid., at para. 67.
631   Ibid., at para. 75.
632   Ibid., at para. 76.
633   Ibid., at paras. 47 and 52.
634   Ibid., at para. 45. The quote is from K. Robert-Wray, *Commonwealth and Colonial Law* (London: Stevens and Sons, 1966), p. 625.
635   Ibid., at para. 29. Brennan also states (at para. 42): "a common law doctrine founded on unjust discrimination in the enjoyment of civil and political rights demands reconsideration".

*lands. The defendants submit that that was the legal consequence of the Letters Pat-
ent and of the events which brought them into effect. If that admission be right, the
Queen took the land occupied by the Meriam people on 1 August 1879 without their
knowing of the expropriation; they were no longer entitled without the consent of the
Crown to continue to occupy the land they had occupied for centuries past.[636]*

The judicial reasoning in the *Mabo* case could also be regarded as grounded on
the "equality argument" in a context of "multicultural citizenship",[637] where
"group-differentiated rights" for "national minorities", including indigenous
communities, should be recognized. Liberal egalitarian theory emphasizes indeed the importance of rectifying un-chosen inequalities",[638] i.e., inequalities that
have been un-deservedly imposed on someone or, in this case, on an entire people.[639] Unlike ordinary immigrants who are considered to have made a voluntary
choice to leave their original "societal culture," most indigenous peoples have
never made the choice to abandon their "societal culture" or lands for the sake of
newly established multinational states.[640]

Given that most indigenous communities have never opted to leave their "societal culture" and because they still show a "deep bond with their own culture" [641]
"the question is not, how should the State act fairly in governing its [indigenous
communities], but what are the limits to the State's right to govern them".[642]

The argument here is that where the integration of indigenous communities
into the mainstream culture of their states was not voluntary, which appeared
to be the case for the Ogiek of Kenya, the San of the Kalahari, the Hadzabe of
Tanzania, the Batwa of the Ugandan Mugahinga and Bwindi forests, and several other African indigenous communities, then such communities are entitled
to claim their self-determination, "which can be exercised by renegotiating the
terms of [being parts of their respective states]".[643] Even with respect to communities, such as the Maasai and several Canadian natives, which are reported
to have agreed to cede their lands through treaties, it could be also argued that,
"autonomy is also justified on the historical agreement, in so far as [it is assumed that these communities] never [handed] to the … government jurisdiction over certain issues".[644] It is contended in relation to Africa that, "chiefs …
could seldom [understand] or never … understood the intentions" behind land
cession treaties signed between them and Europeans.[645] It would be otherwise

---

636 Ibid., at para 23.
637 Kymlicka, *Multicultural Citizenship* (1995), p. 108.
638 Ibid., p. 109.
639 John Rawls, *A Theory of Justice*, rev. ed. (Oxford: Oxford University Press, 1999), p. 86.
640 Kymlicka, *Multicultural Citizenship* (1995), p. 96.
641 Ibid., p. 95.
642 Ibid., p. 118.
643 Ibid., p. 117.
644 Ibid., p. 117.
645 Davidson, *Africa in History* (1992), p. 286.

difficult to understand why the Maasai went to court against the Treaty signed by a number of their leaders with the British colonial authority, as presented in chapter V of this book.[646] With regard to this case, Court Justice Morris Carter argued that "until there is annexation, formal or otherwise, a protectorate is a foreign country, and the rights held over it are still distinguished from territorial sovereignty by however thin a line."[647]

What the argument mentioned in the *Mabo* case implies, otherwise, is that property rights do "not collapse or evaporate when the sovereign is removed, but survive ... [succession of state or sovereignties]".[648] It is argued that "property ... is prior to the formation of states"[649] or better that "property rights are fundamentally independent of state sovereignty and, hence, changes in (or even the complete absence of) sovereignty or government do not affect them".[650] In theory, states are products of "social contracts", according to which all contracting parties accept to put themselves under its rule, and in return the State accepts to preserve their rights, including property rights.[651]

This is also the line of argument taken through the provisions of Article XVII(3) of the Inter-American Draft Declaration on the Rights of Indigenous Peoples, which states that "where property and user rights of indigenous peoples arise from rights existing prior to the creation of those States, the States shall recognize the titles of indigenous peoples. ... This shall [not] affect any collective community rights over them".[652]

The survival of indigenous peoples' right to lands following the arrival of colonial powers is further substantiated by the use of treaties made by several colonial powers for acquiring their territories.[653] For instance, the International Congo Society[654] concluded several treaties with "legitimate sovereigns" in the

---

646 The Maasai refused to call it a "treaty", using the term "agreement" instead. See Ndaskoi, "The Roots Causes" (n.d.), p. 8. Available online at http://www.galdu.org/govat/doc/maasai_fi.pdf.

647 *Ol le Njogo and Others v. The Attorney General and Others*, p. 92. What is now modern Kenya was a British protectorate from 1895 to 1920, after which it became a colony.

648 L. Benjamin Ederington, "Property as a Natural Institution: The Separation of Property from Sovereignty in International Law", 13 *The American University International Law Review* 263, 1997, (LexisNexis) n. 142.

649 Ibid., n. 21.

650 Ibid., n. 3.

651 Peter Laslett, *John Locke's Two Treatises of Government* (Cambridge, England: Cambridge University Press, 1964), p. 101.

652 Inter-American Commission on Human Rights, Proposed Declaration on the Rights of Indigenous Peoples, as approved by the IACHR on February 26, 1997, at its 1333rd session, 95th Regular Session, O.A.S. Doc. OEA/Ser/L/V/II.108.Doc. 62 (2000). Available online at http://www.cidh.org/indigenas/chap.2g.htm

653 M. F. Lindley, *The Acquisition and Government of Backward Territory in International Law* (London: Longmans, Green and Co., 1926), p. 39.

654 The International Congo Society was founded on November 17, 1879 by King Leopold II of Belgium to further his interests in the Congo.

Congo basin.[655] In its Advisory Opinion, the International Court of Justice also refers to the use of treaties in the Western Sahara case.[656]

Several African communities have contested, right from the start, the allegation that their pre-existing land rights were extinguished as a result of occupation or conquest of their territories. All these principles and theories seem to have inspired number of African decisions.

African jurisprudence

In the 1919 *Re Southern Rhodesia* case, the Ndebele[657] community of Southern Rhodesia argued that their right to lands survived conquest. In reference to their claim, Lord Summer, a member of the Judicial Committee of the Privy Council,[658] argued that "it is to be presumed, in the absence of express confiscation or of subsequent expropriatory legislation, that the conqueror has respected them and forborne to diminish or modify them",[659] and that:

> *According to the argument, the natives before 1883 were owners of the whole of these vast regions in such a sense that, without their permission or that of their King and trustee, no traveler, still less a settler, could so much as enter without committing a trespass. If so, the maintenance of their rights was fatally inconsistent with white ... settlement ... pioneered by the Company.*[660]

In a similar case, following a notice that certain lands in Apapa, in the Southern Provinces (Nigeria), were acquired by the Nigerian colonial Government, Chief Oluwa went to court in 1921 claiming compensation in the name of his commu-

---

655 Lindley, *The Acquisition and Government* (1926), p. 42.

656 See International Court of Justice (I.C.J.), *Western Sahara, Advisory Opinion,* (1975), p. 16.

657 The Ndebele are Bantu-speaking people who live primarily around the city of Bulawayo, Zimbabwe. They originated early in the nineteenth century as an offshoot of the Nguni of Natal, moving first to Basutoland (now Lesotho) and ultimately to Matabeleland in Southern Rhodesia (now Zimbabwe). They are a farming and herding people numbering 1.5 million.

658 The Judicial Committee of the Privy Council was the supreme appellate tribunal for the British Empire, and had the duty of determining appeals from some 150 jurisdictions in overseas possessions and dominions of the Crown as well as from certain domestic jurisdictions. Today, the Judicial Committee is still the court of final appeal for a few Commonwealth countries that have retained the appeal to Her Majesty in Council or, in the case of Republics, to the Judicial Committee. Only very few countries—most of them in the Caribbean and in the Pacific—use the JC, Jamaica being by far the largest. New Zealand opted out in 2003. See http://www.privy-council.org.uk

659 *Re Southern Rhodesia* [1919] AC 211, at paras. 233-4.

660 Ibid., at para. 234. The legal contest was a result of a resolution in April 17, 1914 by the Legislative Council of Southern Rhodesia, which stated that lands in Southern Rhodesia had not been alienated by the British South Africa Company (a corporate that was said to conquer land on behalf of the Crown).

nity, which he argued was the owner of the lands in question. Acting on appeal, the Privy Council argued that:

> *No doubt there was a cession to the British Crown, along with the sovereignty, of the radical title or ultimate title to the land, in the new colony, but this cession appears to have been made on the footing that the rights of property of the inhabitants were to be fully respected ... It is not admissible to conclude that the Crown is, generally speaking, entitled to the beneficial ownership of the land as having so passed to the Crown as to displace any presumptive title of the natives.*[661]

The Council went further arguing that *"a mere change in sovereignty is not to be presumed to disturb rights of private owners; and the general terms of a cession are prima facie to be construed accordingly".*[662]

There are several other cases supporting this argument. The Privy Council took the same line of reasoning in *Sobhuza II v. Muller and Others*, in 1926 when a Swaziland chief went to court in the name of his community to claim that "the Crown had no rights to dispossess the natives of their lands".[663] In relation to indigenous rights in Nigeria, Lord Denning argued in 1957 that, in dealing with the claims, the court *"will assume that the British Crown intends that the rights of property of the inhabitants are to be fully respected".*[664]

Similar land claims based on the notion of "indigenous title" have been made recently by various African communities. The *Mabo* case (1992) was referred to by members of the Ogiek indigenous community of Kenya, acting as plaintiffs in a legal case against their Government's action on the Mau Forest (see chapter V of this book), which this community considers as its land. The judge, unfortunately, did not respond to the plaintiffs' claim based on the Mabo jurisprudence.[665]

Similarly, the Kxoe community of Western Caprivi, Namibia, went to court in 1997 claiming aboriginal title over lands that the Government of Namibia was considering itself to be the sole owner of. The case never proceeded further because of political impediments.[666]

As also shown earlier (chapter VI) in the Tanzanian case *National Agricultural and Food Corporation (NAFCO) v. Mulbadaw Village Council and Others*, members of

---

661 *Amodu Tijani v. Secretary, Southern Provinces, Nigeria*, 2 A.C. [1921], 399 (PC), per Viscount Haldane, at 407.

662 Ibid.

663 *Sobhuza II v. Muller and Others* [1926] AC 518-19.The case was not won by the appellant, but the ruling stated a number of interesting principles relating to control of land by indigenous communities.

664 *Adeyinka Oyekan v. Mussendiku Adele* [1957], 1 WLR 876, per Lord Denning, at 880.

665 See the history of the Ogiek's legal battle on their Web site: http://www.ogiek.org/report/ogiek-ch7.htm

666 Norman Tjombe, "The Applicability of the Doctrine of Aboriginal Doctrine in Namibia: A Case for the Kxoe Community in Western Caprivi, Namibia". Paper presented at the Southern African Land Reform Lawyers Workshop, 21 February 2001, Robben Island, South Africa.

the Mulbadaw village (mostly Barabaig indigenous people) in Hanang District, North Tanzania, failed in their appeal when the judge rejected their aboriginal claim to lands on the grounds that they were not the natives of the area.[667] In the similar case filed by the Barabaig against NAFCO and Gawal Farms Ltd case (see chapter VI),[668] the court rejected the collective claim by the plaintiffs based on immemorial occupation and held that it could only deal with the case on an individual basis. The Tanzanian Court of Appeal of Arusha also denied *locus standi* to a group of Maasai who claimed, in the name of their community, aboriginal-type land rights over the Mkomazi Game Reserve.[669] Both cases indeed raised the question of "[on] who are the [collective] rights bestowed, is it individual members of the group or is it the collectivity itself";[670] and more importantly the judges refused to give authority to the notion of aboriginal title still very much alive within countries of Common Law traditions, such as Tanzania.

In some British Commonwealth countries, the decisions taken by the Judicial Committee of the Privy Council are considered persuasive. In Jamaica, for example, it is still the final court of appeal.[671] So it continues to be in Mauritius. In other countries, such as Kenya, the decisions of this colonial legal relic are given certain persuasive authority.[672] In the Zambian case *Chetankumar Shantkal Parekh v. The People* (1995), the judge clearly referred to decisions by the Privy Council as persuasive reference.[673] As shown in the *Mabo* case, it is indeed believed that "ab-

---

667   *National Agricultural and Food Corporation (NAFCO) v. Mulbadaw Village Council and 66 Others* (CA – Dar es Salaam, CA#3/1986). The villagers who were involved in this case were not all native to the land they were claiming, because during the *Ujamaa* policy in Tanzania, people were grouped into artificial or government-created villages.

668   *Yoke Gwaku and 5 others v. NAFCO and Gawal Farms Limited* (HC – Nakuru, CV#52/1998). For more cases of indigenous communities claiming aboriginal titles on land in Tanzania, see, for example, Tenga, "Legislating" (1998a) and Peter, "Human Rights of Indigenous Minorities" (2007).

669   See *Lekengere Faru Parutu Kamunyu & 16 Others v. Minister of Tourism, Natural Resources and Environment & Others* (HC – Moshi, CV#33/1994) in chapter VI, this volume.

670   Gilbert, "Minority Groups" (1992), p. 79.

671   Keith Highet and George Kahale III, "International Decisions", 88 *American Journal of International Law* 775 (October 1994). In the case *Pratt and Morgan v. Attorney-General for Jamaica* ([1993] 4 All E.R. 769, the appellants were asking for the Judicial Committee of the Privy Council to decide on whether the death row to which they had been subjected did not amount to an act of torture, inhuman and degrading treatment.

672   Highet and Kahale III "International Decisions" (1994). The opinion that decisions by the Privy Council continue to enjoy persuasive authority in Kenya is that of many Kenyan lawyers met by the author during fieldwork trips. This view is also shared by the Kenyan Legal Aid Project. One member of this Project is quoted saying that decisions by the Privy Council have helped them in several cases. The Weekly Law Reports CD-ROM "has literally transformed our practice enabling us to provide authorities for several constitutional cases, such as an application to release prisoners who had been awaiting trial for four years, based on Privy Council cases drawn from the Justis database. Given the lack of legal materials in Kenya it would not be too much an exaggeration to say that such CDs can make the difference between life and death for those on death row". See Justis Web site at: http://www.context.co.uk/

673   *Chetankumar Shantkal Parekh v. The People [1995]* SCZ/11a (unreported). The case involved individuals who were refused bail and appealed against the refusal. The judge ruled: *"We propose to*

original title" is mostly relevant in countries that inherited the common law system, because the fact of possessing significantly contributes to a claim of ownership.

In countries with "civil law" systems, some scholars argue that the notion of aboriginal title could be applicable as "an equitable principle of constitutional common law". In two Canadian cases, the defendants unsuccessfully argued that, because Quebec had always been under the tradition of French law, and because this system of law had never recognized the principle of "aboriginal title", natives of Quebec could not claim aboriginal title.[674] However, René Calinaud has argued that *la possession prolongée* or unchallenged, prolonged possession is a means of proof of land ownership, in addition to the norm in most civil law countries that the right to property in land is to be established by statute and written titles following acts of donation, sale, etc.[675] He shows indeed that, despite the fact that the French "Code Civil" was introduced in the Polynesian region of Tahiti in 1866, customary land laws of the original inhabitants of this region continued to be applied until the late 1980s.[676]

It emerges from the above sections that the notion of "aboriginal title" or indigenous peoples' land rights is relevant and arguable in most of Africa. The Richtersveld case seems to be a case in point: in this case, aboriginal title was claimed by the Richtersveld community (see presentation of case in chapter VII, this volume), but rejected by the first court, which ruled

> To the extent that any of the rights claimed by the plaintiffs is dependent on their aboriginal title, such rights are dubious, because it is uncertain whether the doctrine of indigenous title forms part of our law, and if it does, what its scope and content are. It has, to my knowledge, never been recognised in any reported court decision. Even if it does form part of our law, it is uncertain whether such title

---

dwell on these cases in a short while but the clear position we have come to is that we agree with the Privy Council and the Appellate Division in Zimbabwe and will dispose of this appeal as they did theirs and we will reject the Kenyan approach, which coincided with Mr. Mwanawasa's. Our conclusion based on these cases, which are of very high persuasive value and which dealt with provisions very similar, if not identical to ours, is that there is nothing unconstitutional in a provision which prohibits or restricts the grant of bail pending trial."

674 The two cases *(R. v. Côté* [1996] 3 SCR 139 and *R. v. Adams* [1996] 3 SCR. 101) are referred to by Bennett and Powell, "Aboriginal Title" (1999), p. 14. The cases are found in [1996] 138 DLR (4th) 385, paras 42ff and [1996] 138 DLR (4th) 657, paras 32-3. Judge Lamer ruled against the defendants and upheld that the doctrine of aboriginal title is also applicable under the civil system.

675 René Calinaud, "Les principes directeurs du droit foncier polynésien", in *Revue Juridique Polynésienne*, no. 7 (2001), p. 746: « Ailleurs, dans les quelques îles qui ont échappé à ce système, la preuve de la propriété ne peut se faire que suivant les règles du code civil, règles qui sont donc ici supplétives, c'est-à-dire au moyen d'un acte écrit s'il en existe (vente, donation, partage, etc.) et s'il n'est pas contredit par un autre, au moyen de la possession prolongée ou encore de ce que la jurisprudence dénomme 'les présomptions les meilleures et les mieux caractérisées'.»

676 Ibid., p. 746.

would have survived the actions of the Government in making the subject land over to others.[677]

Fortunately for the Richtersveld community, on appeal the Constitutional Court of South Africa held, among others, that *"the determination of the real character of indigenous title to land ... 'involves the study of the history of a particular community and its usages'. So does its determination of content"*.[678] It consequently concluded that *"the real character of the title that the Richtersveld community possessed in the subject land was a right of communal ownership under indigenous law"*.[679] Commenting on this very same case, T.M. Chan argues that the Constitutional Court's finding of "indigenous law ownership" was equivalent to ownership under the doctrine of aboriginal title.[680]

This ruling is an unprecedented landmark in recent jurisprudence that corroborates the relevance of the notion of "aboriginal title" in Africa. From this ruling and others referred to in this chapter, it also emerges that there exists an African jurisprudence dating back from colonial times and up to now, which confirms that indigenous communities pre-existing land rights were not extinguished with the arrival of colonial powers and later of modern states, even if it resulted in indigenous communities losing, and continuing to lose, their lands.

---

677 *Richtersveld Community and Others v. Alexkor Ltd and Another* 2001 (3) SA 1293 (LCC), at 46.
678 *Alexkor Ltd and Government* v. *Richtersveld Community and Others* 2003 (12) BCLR 1301 (CC), at 57, quoting *Amodu Tijani v. The Secretary.* at 404.
679 Ibid., at 62.
680 Chan, "The Richtersveld Challenge" (2004), pp. 126-127.

CHAPTER IX
CONSTITUTIONAL RECOGNITION AND STATES' PRACTICE REGARDING INDIGENOUS PEOPLES' RIGHTS

North America

Canada

In the Americas, Canada was one of the first countries to devote an entire section of its 1982 Constitution Act[681] to the "Rights of Aboriginal Peoples in Canada". Article 35 provides that

1. *The existing Aboriginal and treaty rights of the Aboriginal peoples of Canada are hereby recognized and affirmed;*
2. *In this Act, "Aboriginal peoples of Canada" includes the Indian, Inuit, and Metis peoples of Canada;*
3. *For greater certainty, in subsection (1) "treaty rights" includes rights that now exist by way of land claims agreements or may be so acquired.*

The existence of aboriginal title had, however, already been recognized in 1973 by the Canadian Supreme Court in its ruling on *Calder v. The Attorney General of British Columbia*.[682] Although the Nishga's appeal was dismissed, the fact that the Canadian Supreme Court had held that Aboriginal title is part of Canadian law, and that the Nishga had once held such title, provided the impetus for the overhauling of the land claims negotiation process in Canada.[683]

---

681 Canada's constitution is not a single written document, but is made up of acts of the British and Canadian Parliaments, as well as legislation, judicial decisions and agreements between the federal and provincial governments. The Constitution Act of 1982 is divided into seven parts. Part I is the Charter of Rights and Freedoms, Part II is on the Rights of Aboriginal Peoples in Canada.
682 *Calder v. The Attorney General of British Columbia* [1973] S.C.R. 313, (1973). The case was initiated in 1968 by the Nishga Tribal Council against the Government of British Columbia. Available online at http://www.canlii.org
683 The case failed both at trial and in the Court of Appeal. The Supreme Court overturned the Court of Appeal's finding in recognising the possible existence of Aboriginal rights to land and re-

The basis for aboriginal title was later expanded on in *Guerin v. The Queen*, (1984),[684] and, most importantly, in *Delgamuukw v. British Columbia* (1997).[685] The latter was a groundbreaking ruling since it contains the first definitive statement on the content of Aboriginal title in Canada. It also describes the scope of protection afforded by this title under subsection 35(1) of the Constitution Act 1982; defines how the title may be proved; and outlines the justification test for infringements of the title.

The Supreme Court's decision also confirmed that, pursuant to section 91(24) of the Constitution Act 1876, the Federal Government has exclusive jurisdiction with respect to Indians and their lands, and that provincial legislatures are thus unable to effect extinguishment of title.[686] It was largely in response to this holding that the Canadian Federal Government established, in 1973, a coherent federal and national policy for the negotiation and settlement of Aboriginal land claims. This policy also reconciled most of the historical differences between individual provinces in Canada.

Claims were from now on divided into two broad categories—specific and comprehensive claims. Specific claims are claims that arise from the breach or non-fulfillment of Government obligations found in treaties, agreements, or statutes, while comprehensive claims are based on the assertion of unextinguished aboriginal title to land and resources. Subsequent to extensive consultations with Aboriginal and other groups, the Comprehensive Land Claims Policy was amended in 1986 to provide greater flexibility in land tenure and better definition of subjects for negotiation. In 1991, the Indian Specific Claims Commission was created as an appeal mechanism for First Nations. Its mandate is to address disputes arising out of the specific claims process.

The Federal Government has subsequently introduced the Inherent Right Policy 1995, whereby self-government arrangements may be negotiated as a

---

sources, but was equally divided on the issue of whether the Nishga retained title. The appeal was ultimately dismissed on a technicality. See http://www.atns.net.au/agreement. asp?EntityID=2359. In 2002, the Nishga'a signed a self-government agreement with the Government of British Columbia.

684 *Guerin v. The Queen* [1984] 2 S.C.R. 335. (1984). The Supreme Court refers specifically to Section 18 (1) of the Canadian Indian Act in force at the time. Available online at http://www.canlii.org

685 *Delgamuukw v. British Columbia* [1997] 3 S.C.R. 1010. In this case, the appellants, 35 Gitksan and 13 Wet'suwet'en hereditary chiefs, claimed "ownership" of and jurisdiction over 58,000 square kilometers in British Columbia based on historical facts asserted by oral traditions. Thus, one of the questions addressed by the Court was whether oral tradition could be considered as a means of proof of title over lands. The judge dismissed the appellants' claim and ordered a new trial. He explicitly advised the parties to settle their dispute through negotiations instead of litigations. Available online at http://www.canlii.org/en/ca/scc/doc/1997/1997canlii302/1997canl ii302.html

686 Mary C. Hurley, "Aboriginal Title: The Supreme Court of Canada Decision in *Delgamuukw v. British Colombia*". Law and Government Division, January 1998, revised February 2000. Available online at http://www.parl.gc.ca/information/library/PRBpubs/bp459-e.htm

part of comprehensive claims agreements. In 1998, the Canadian Government affirmed that treaties will continue to be the basis for the ongoing relationship between Aboriginal people and the Crown. In 2003, the Specific Claims Resolution Act was enacted in response to the push for a revised specific claims process that provides effective dispute resolution, with litigation as a final resort.[687]

But the land claim process has been slow. In 2004, the Special Rapporteur on the situation of human rights and fundamental freedoms of indigenous people, Rodolfo Stavenhagen, noted that out of about 1,300 specific claims filed, 115 were being negotiated and 444 had been resolved, while 38 were being reviewed by the Indian Specific Claims Commission.[688] Since 1973, 20 comprehensive land claim agreements covering about 40 per cent of Canada's territory have been signed. Most of these agreements have been made with Inuit peoples in the northern part of the country, where the largest comprehensive claim was settled in 1993, leading in 1999 to the creation of the Nunavut Territory. The first modern treaty in British Columbia was the Nishga Final Agreement in 1996. It is also the first treaty in Canada to incorporate both land claims and constitutionally protected self-government provisions.[689]

The situation in British Columbia (BC) is somewhat different from that of the rest of Canada since most First Nations in BC have not signed or adhered to treaties. In order to facilitate the process of comprehensive land claims/ treaty negotiations between BC and its First Nations, the British Columbia Treaty Commission (BCTC) was established in 1992 as a tri-partite body of which Canada, BC and the First Nations are full parties.

The treaty process started in 1997 and by the end of 2009, 60 First Nations, representing about 2/3 of BC's aboriginal people, were participating. They have to go through five difficult and lengthy stages of negotiations that lead up to a final agreement that has to be approved by vote by the First Nation in question and by the provincial legislature before being ratified in the Federal parliament. There are currently 43 nations negotiating an Agreement-in-Principle (stage 4) and 7 negotiating a final agreement. One of these, the Maa-nulth First Nations of Vancouver Island—some 2,000 people— signed the final agreement in 2009. Once ratified, this agreement will mean that they will own in fee simple an area of approximately 24,498 hectares, including 22,342 hectares of former provincial Crown land, 2,064 hectares of former Indian reserve land and 92 hectares of private land purchased from willing sellers.[690]

---

687 For more information, visit http://www.atns.net.au/agreement.asp?EntityID=2257
688 Rodolfo Stavenhagen, Mission to Canada. U.N. Doc. E/CN.4/2005/88/Add.3, 12 December 2004, para. 44. Available at http://www2.ohchr.org/english/issues/indigenous/rapporteur/visits.htm
689 Indian Affairs and Northern Development, "General Briefing Note on the Comprehensive Land Claims Policy of Canada and the Status of Claims" (Montreal: Comprehensive Claims Branch Claims and Indian Government Sector, March 2007). Available on line at http://www.ainc-inac.gc.ca/al/ldc/ccl/pubs/gbn/gbn-eng.asp
690 See Web site of the BCTC at http://www.bctreaty.net/files/updates.php

United States

The 1787 Constitution of the United States reflects "the belief that Indian tribes constituted separate nations within the sovereign borders of the United States, and that therefore tribal members were not taxed, or given any of the rights of citizens of the U.S.".[691] The Constitution granted Congress the power to regulate commerce with the Indian tribes,[692] and empowered the President to make treaties with them subject to the consent of the Senate.[693] To this day, most American Indian affairs are dealt with administratively by the Federal Government[694] and at the policy level by several congressional committees.

Most American Indian legislation also continues to be regulated at the federal level[695] and is recorded in Statutes at Large which is codified in Title 25—Indians—of the United States Code.[696] Title 25 includes laws regarding land issues and land claim settlements, but treaties or similar agreements signed by the U.S. Federal Government with Indian tribes and judicial decisions (usually Supreme Court rulings) are equal important sources of American Indian Law, which therefore presents a complex combination of statutes, rules, regulations, tribal laws, treaties, and agency and judicial decisions.[697]

In order to claim land, a tribe must be federally recognized. There are today 550 such tribes, including 223 village groups in Alaska, and some 275 reservations in the U.S.A. The Federal Government holds some 225,000 sq. km in trust for tribes and individuals. Individual Native Americans in the U.S. who own trust land can sell this land or turn it into a normal fee simple title, subject to the Government's authorization.[698]

Indian Law distinguishes between "aboriginal title" (based on possession and use since time immemorial) and "recognized title" (based on a treaty or agreement whereby the U.S. has confirmed the Indians' right to the land).[699]

---

691 Tim Vollmann, "Recognition of Traditional Forms of Ownership of Land and Natural Resources by Indigenous Peoples in the Jurisprudence and Legislation of the U.S.A." Presentation for the Panel on Traditional forms of ownership in the legislation and practices of the Region, Organization of American States Washington, D.C., November 7, 2002. Available online at http://www.oas.org/consejo/CAJP/docs/cp10445e04.doc
692 U.S. Constitution, Article I, Section 8, Clause 3.
693 Ibid., Article II, Section 2. The Constitution has since been amended twenty-seven times, the first ten amendments being known as the Bill of Rights.
694 The Bureau of Indian Affairs (BIA) is an agency of the Federal Government within the Department of the Interior charged with the administration and management of the land held in trust by the United States for Native Americans in the U.S., Native American Tribes and Alaska Natives.
695 Congress may allow state jurisdiction to prevail if no federal statutes apply to a given situation.
696 The U.S. Code is available online at http://www.gpoaccess.gov/uscode/
697 For more information, see Researching American Indian Law at http://www.law.umkc.edu/faculty/profiles/stancel/indian.htm
698 See Bureau of Indians Affairs, "Answers to Frequently Asked Questions". Available online at http://usa.usembassy.de/etexts/soc/bia.pdf
699 See Keith H. Raker, "Reservation of Rights: A look at Indian Land Claims in Ohio for Gaming Purposes" (2005). Available online at http://www.tuckerellis.com/news/Reservation%20of%20Rights.pdf

"Aboriginal title" has since early nineteenth century been considered as a "right of occupancy". This means that the fee simple to Indian title land is held by the Government rather than by the Indians, but that grants of Indian lands take effect *subject* to the Indian right of occupancy.[700] This interpretation of Aboriginal title has never been questioned and a string of Supreme Court decisions has continued to protect Indian title from Government grants, whether issued before or after the independence of the United States, by either making the grant subject to that title or interpreting the grant to exclude the Indian lands.[701] Subsequent rulings[702] have also established that the "right of occupancy" entitles Native Americans to the complete beneficial interest, including timber and mineral rights, regardless of the uses they traditionally made of the land.

This, however, does not preclude that the Government may extinguish aboriginal title through a taking of the subject lands "either by purchase or by conquest",[703] and Indians do not have a constitutional right to compensation for congressionally authorized taking of their lands unless their title has been recognized. This was, for instance, the case in the *Tee-Hit-Ton Indians v. United States* (1955),[704] where the US Supreme Court argued that an original Indian title

[I]s not a property right but amounts to a right of occupancy which the sovereign grants and protects against intrusion by third parties but which right of occupancy may be terminated and such lands fully disposed of by the sovereign itself without any legally enforceable obligation to compensate the Indians.[705]

---

700 *Fletcher v. Peck* [1810] 6 Cranch 87 ruled that the fee simple to Indian title land is held by the Government rather than by the Indians who nonetheless have a right of occupancy entitling them, as per *Johnson v. M'Intosh* [1823] 8 Wheat. 543, to "a legal as well as just claim to retain possession of it, and use it according to their own discretion". Both cases can be found online at: http://www.findlaw.com/casecode/

701 Kent Mc Neil, "Extinguishment of Native Title: The High Court and American Law", *Australian Indigenous Law Reporter* [1997] AILR 41. Available online at http://www.austlii.edu.au/cgi-bin/sinodisp/au/journals/AILR/1997/41.html?query=%20Extinguishment

702 See *United States v. Shoshone Tribe of Indians*, [1938] 304 US 111 (1938), at 115-18; *Otoe and Missouria Tribe of Indians v. United States*, [1955] 131 F. Supp. 265, 272 (Ct. Cl. 1955). Available online at http://www.findlaw.com/casecode/

703 The Court in *Johnson v. M'Intosh* (1823) also ruled that right of occupancy was protected while the Indians were "in peace", but could be extinguished "either by purchase or by conquest" by the European powers or the United States after it became an independent nation.

704 *Tee-Hit-Ton Indians v. United States*, [1955] 348 U.S. 272, February 7, 1955. The United States had taken certain timber from Alaskan lands, which the Indians said belonged to them. They asked for compensation. Available online at http://laws.findlaw.com/us/348/272.html

705 Ibid., at II (a). The Court foreheld that the Indians, whose claims to ownership of land had not been recognized by Congress and who had used "land in a manner similar to nomadic States Indians", were not entitled to compensation for United States' taking of timber from occupied land. Ibid., at paras. 4. and 5.

The *Tee-Hit-Ton* decision continues to be upheld and applied by United States courts.[706]

"Recognized title" stands in stark contrast to "aboriginal title" since it is title to Indian property that has been created, or *recognized*, by action of the Federal Government, typically by federal treaty or statute.[707] The primary goal of treaties was to obtain Indian lands via purchase. Indian property with recognized title may or may not have been part of the aboriginal territory of the tribe. In fact, the Federal Government has in the past designated certain lands as Indian property even though a tribe has no aboriginal claim to these lands whatsoever. [708]

The primary advantage of recognized title is its relative permanence. It is more difficult for the Federal Government to extinguish claims to lands to which Indians have recognized title. In contrast to aboriginal title, a taking of lands to which an Indian tribe has recognized title is compensable under the Fifth Amendment.[709]

Although the unfairness of the treaty negotiation process was long recognized, it was not until 1946 that Congress created the Indian Claims Commission (ICC) to allow tribes to make claims against the United States based on unconscionable transactions.[710]

The Claims Commission was an attempt to recognize, settle, and extinguish American Indians' legal claims to land and resources in exchange for financial compensation.[711] By the time the commission expired thirty-three years later (1979), more than a half billion dollars had been awarded. But many tribes wanted property rights, not money, and, in a few cases, tribes refused to accept a financial settlement, continuing instead to assert claims for land transfer or resource use.[712]

A case in point is that of the Sioux Indians of South Dakota, who, in 1979, were awarded the largest Indian land settlement in American history—US$105 million dollars—for the illegal seizure of the Black Hills in 1880, but refused to accept the money. They wanted the land instead, for it represented more than just an eco-

---

706 As in the case of *Karuk Tribe of California, et al. v. United States*, [2000] (Court of Appeals for Federal Circuit 2000) 209 F.3d 1366. Available at http://www.laws.findlaw.com/fed/995002r.html

707 The United States first treaty with an Indian tribe was concluded in 1778 and until 1871some 370 Indian Treaties were signed. Since then, relations are established by Congressional Acts, Executive Orders or Executive Agreements. See http://usa.usembassy.de/etexts/soc/bia.pdf

708 Raker, "Reservation of Rights" (2005).

709 The Fifth Amendment is part of the Bill of Rights adopted in 1791. It states, among other things, that "No person shall … be deprived of life, liberty, or property, without due process of law; nor shall private property be taken for public use, without just compensation.

710 The commission heard claims that had been filed prior to 1951 until its expiration in September, 1978. Claims not adjudicated before the commission expired were transferred to the U.S. Court of Claims.

711 Anne Flaherty, "This Land is My Land: The Politics of American Indian Land Claims Settlements". Draft Paper prepared for the American Political Science Association Annual Conference; Chicago, Illinois (August 2007), p. 1, quoting Rosenthal (1990).

712 Ibid., p.7.

nomic opportunity—they saw it as a chance once again to be reunited as one nation in their traditional homeland. Since then, no solution has been found and the money in the interest bearing accounts of the tribes is today close to $1 billion dollars.[713]

Another example is the struggle of the Western Shoshone Nation for the recognition of their land and treaty rights, which started back in the 1940s and has not yet been settled. This struggle has taken on a variety of forms, including the use of political, legal and international mechanisms.[714] After having exhausted their domestic legal remedies, the Western Shoshone thus sought international recognition of their land rights before two international forums: the Inter-American Commission on Human Rights (IACHR) of the Organization of American States in 1993, and the Committee for the Elimination of Racial Discrimination (CERD) of the United States in 1999 in relation with the U.S. periodic report. Both forums expressed their concerns and made recommendations to the U.S. Government.[715]

In 2005 and 2006, Western Shoshone groups submitted several petitions for Urgent Action to CERD. In its decision under the special "Early Warning and Urgent Action" procedure, CERD urged the U.S. Government to halt any plans to appropriate Western Shoshone territory for private development or environmentally destructive Government projects.[716]

---

713 Tim Giago, "A Story Dying to be Told" *Lakota Country Times,* September 25, 2008, available at http://www.lakotacountrytimes.com/news/2008/0925/tim_giago/
714 In 1985, the Supreme Court held in the *United States v. Dann* case [1985] 470 US 39, that the Western Shoshone had been paid because the Government had placed funds into a trust account in the name of the Western Shoshone, and that such payment barred the Dann sisters from raising Western Shoshone title as a defense against the federal Government's trespass charges. The underlying basis of the Court's decision was that American Indians are classified under the U.S. Indian law system to be "wards" of the United States Government. Thus, the Court deemed that the U.S. federal Government could pay itself as the Indians' "guardian" and say that therefore the Indians had been paid. The Dann's response was that they were grazing their cattle on Western Shoshone land as recognized in the Treaty of Ruby Valley, in 1863. For more information, see: http://www.law.uidaho.edu/default.aspx?pid=88508
715 The IACHR recommended in 2002 the United States to "review its laws, procedures and practices to ensure that the property rights of indigenous persons are determined in accordance with the rights established in the American Declaration, including Articles II, XVIII and XXIII of the Declaration". It further writes that "The State (i.e., the U.S.) has not provided the Commission with updated information regarding compliance with the recommendations in this case", and that it has received information from the Petitioners that the United States has done nothing to comply with the Commission's recommendations and that their rights have been further violated. See IACHR Annual Report 2007, at paras. 585 and 586. Available online at http://www.iachr.org/annualrep/2007eng/Chap.3q.htm. The Committee on Elimination of Racial Discrimination (CERD), in its Conclusions and Recommendations in 2001, expressed concerns over the fact that "treaties signed by the [U.S.] Government and Indian tribes, described as 'domestic dependent nations' under national law, can be abrogated unilaterally by Congress and that the land they possess or use can be taken without compensation by a decision of the Government". See para. 400 in CERD, Conclusions and Recommendations, United States of America, 14/08/2001. A/56/18, at 380-407. For text, see http://hrlibrary.ngo.ru/country/usa2001.html
716 CERD also criticized the U.S. Government for levying fees and restrictions on Western Shoshone people for using their own land, and urged the Government to negotiate formally with tribal leaders on unresolved land-ownership issues.

While the Indian Land Claims Commission dealt with most treaty litigation, the Congress has resolved previously unsettled cases. An example is the Alaska Native Claims Settlement Act, (ANCSA), the largest land claims settlement in United States history signed into law in 1971. ANCSA was intended to resolve the long-standing issues surrounding aboriginal land claims in Alaska, as well as to stimulate economic development throughout Alaska. The settlement extinguished Alaska Native claims to the land by transferring titles and compensation to twelve Alaska Native regional corporations and over 200 local village corporations. A thirteenth regional corporation was later created for Alaska Natives who no longer reside in Alaska.

The existence of the Claims Commission created the impression among many people in the U.S. that the debt owed indigenous people for the conquest and taking of their aboriginal lands was now being paid in full. This, however, overlooked two important facts: (1) a significant amount of land in the West was never the subject of a treaty of cession; and (2) many other lands, particularly in the East, were the subject of transactions never approved by Congress, as required by the Nonintercourse Act of 1790.[717]

Several eastern Indian tribes have during the past years brought lawsuits seeking the recovery of lands based upon claims that the 1790 Nonintercourse Act had been violated.[718] Legislative settlements have been successfully negotiated with tribes in Rhode Island (Narragansett), Connecticut (Mashantucket Pequot, who now own the largest casino in the U.S.), South Carolina (Catawba), and Florida (Seminole and Miccosukee).[719]

While a fair amount of American Indian land claims have been settled in the past decades, many others have been dismissed or are still pending.[720] Litigation tends to be lengthy, complex and expensive.

Neither Canada nor the United States have adopted ILO Convention No. 169, and both countries voted against the U.N. Declaration on the Rights of Indigenous Peoples in 2007.

---

717 Vollmann, "Recognition of Traditional Forms of Ownership" (2002), p. 7. Congress adopted the first Indian Nonintercourse Act in 1790. This act reserved the right to acquire Indian lands to the United States to the exclusion of individuals and states, and that a sale of Indian lands was not valid unless "made and duly executed at some public treaty, held under the authority of the United States".

718 Ibid., pp. 7-8.

719 See, e.g., *South Carolina v. Catawba Indian Tribe, Inc.* 476 U.S. 498 (1986) at htpp://www.find-law/com/casecode; *Mashpee Tribe v. New Seabury Corp.* 592 F.2d 575 (1st Cir. 1979); *Narragansett Tribe v. Southern R.I. Land Dev. Corp.*, 418 F.Supp. 798 (D.R.I. 1976)—both at htpp://www.alt-law.org.

720 See, e.g., the Web page of Native American Rights Fund at http://www.narf.org/cases/index.html#older

Latin America

Before the 1980s, few, if any, Latin American constitutions referred to the rights of indigenous peoples, although some of the countries had passed laws dealing with indigenous issues, as for instance in **Brazil** where the *Estatuto do Indio* (Statute of the Indians or Law 6.001/73) was introduced in 1973. This law stated, among other provisions, that "the lands occupied by [Indians] in accordance with their tribal usage, customs and tradition, including territories where they carry on activities essential for their subsistence or that are of economic usefulness, constitute territory of the Indians".[721]

Brazil was also the first country in Latin America to give a constitutional status to the concept of indigenous lands when the undemocratic Constitution of 1967 was replaced by the 1988 Federal Constitution. In its Article 231, paragraph 2, the new Constitution defines indigenous lands as:

> *Lands traditionally occupied by the Indians are those that they have inhabited permanently, used for their productive activity, their welfare and necessary for their cultural and physical reproduction, according to their uses, customs and traditions.*

The 1988 Constitution also granted greater rights to indigenous peoples and several of its provisions are in contradiction with the *Estatuto do Indio*, which is very much grounded in the antiquated view that Indians have to be protected and eventually integrated into mainstream society.[722]

The Brazilian Federal Constitution of 1988 is therefore considered by many as a watershed, a benchmark,[723] and it was soon followed by other constitutions in the region that recognized the social-diversity of their countries. The 1992 Constitution of **Paraguay** contains an entire Chapter V that deals with "Indian peoples", and in which the State *"recognizes the existence of Indian peoples, defined as ethnic groups whose culture existed before the formation and constitution of the State of Paraguay"*.[724] Article 64 provides that:

---

721 See Inter-American Commission on Human Rights, Resolution 12/85, case 7615 (Brazil), March 5, 1985. OAS/Ser.L/V/II.66 Doc.10 rev.1 October, 1985. Available at http://www.cidh.oas.org/casos/84.85.eng.htm

722 The 1988 Constitution (see at http://www.confinder.richmond.edu) does not call for the integration of indigenous peoples into Brazilian society, but ensures them, on the contrary, the right for them to be different from the rest of the country. In 1994, a new statute of the Indians was proposed and approved by a special commission of the Chamber of Deputies, but the passage of the bill has been blocked up until now. See http://www.socioambiental.org/

723 See Instituto Socioambiental, "ISA 10 Years", p. 5. Available at:
     http://www.socioambiental.org/e/inst/mm/melh_2004_ing.pdf

724 Constitution of Paraguay (1992), Article 62 (see at http://www.confinder.richmond.edu).

1. *Indian peoples have the right, as communities, to a shared ownership of a piece of land, which will be sufficient both in terms of size and quality for them to preserve and to develop their own lifestyles. The State will provide them with the respective land, free of charge. This land, which will be exempt from attachments, cannot be divided, transferred, or affected by the statute of limitations, nor can it be used as collateral for contractual obligations or to be leased. It will also be exempt from taxes;*

2. *The removal or transfer of Indian groups from their habitat, without their express consent, is hereby prohibited".[725]*

In 2008, **Ecuador** adopted a new Constitution.[726] While the former 1998 Constitution also had provisions specifically addressing "indigenous peoples", the new Constitution, already in its Article 2, recognizes indigenous languages as part of the national heritage and the right of indigenous peoples to use these languages as official languages. Chapter 4 on the "Rights of communities, peoples and nationalities" includes in its Article 58, twenty-two paragraphs on their collective rights, including their right to their communal lands and the right to participate in the use, enjoyment and administration of the renewable natural resources in their lands. While the old Constitution spoke about their right to be consulted, Article 58 (7) introduces the concept of prior, free and informed consent when it comes to development plans on their lands. As in the old Constitution, indigenous peoples have the right to not be displaced from their ancestral lands.

The 1999 Constitution of **Venezuela**[727] states in chapter VIII – Rights of Native, Article 119:

The State recognizes the existence of indigenous peoples and communities, their social, political and economic organization, their cultures, practices and customs, languages and religions, as well as their habitat and original rights to the lands they ancestrally and traditionally occupy, and which are necessary to develop and guarantee their way of life. It shall be the responsibility of the National Executive, with the participation of the indigenous peoples, to demarcate and guarantee the right to collective ownership of their lands, which shall be inalienable, not subject to the law of limitations or distrait, and nontransferable, in accordance with this Constitution and the law.

The Constitution (Article 120) furthermore stipulates that:

Exploitation by the State of the natural resources in indigenous habitats shall be carried out without harming the ... integrity of such habitats, and likewise subject

---

725 Ibid., Article 64.
726 The Constitution is available at http://www.confinder.richmond.edu
727 The Venezuelan Constitution is available at http://www.confinder.richmond.edu

to prior information and consultation with the indigenous communities con-
cerned. Profits from such exploitation by the native peoples are subject to the Con-
stitution and the law.

In **Mexico**, the Constitution, which goes back to 1917 (and has been amended
numerous times), was amended in 2001 to recognize and guarantee the legal,
social and economic rights of indigenous peoples. Article 2 thus states that,

> *The nation is pluricultural based originally on its indigenous tribes which are*
> *those that are descendants of the people that lived in the actual territory of the*
> *country at the beginning of the colonization and that preserve their own social,*
> *economic, cultural, political institutions. … They are integral communities of an*
> *indigenous tribe those that form a social, economic and cultural organization.*[728]

In **Bolivia**, a constitutional revision process was initiated by the newly elected Evo
Morales government in 2005. The process has been marked by deep political divisions but, in October 2008, the Congress approved a draft constitution that in January 2009 was passed with a comfortable majority by national referendum. Strengthening the rights and power of Bolivia's indigenous majority, the Constitution incor-
porates the principles of the United Nations Declaration on the Rights of Indigenous Peoples; it recognizes the pluri-national character of the State, indigenous
languages as official languages, and indigenous autonomy. This autonomy

> *[C]onsists of self-government and the exercise of self-determination for rural indig-*
> *enous nations and native peoples who share territory, culture, history, language,*
> *and unique forms of juridical, political, social, and economic organization.*[729]

Local indigenous governments will also be allowed to levy some taxes and appropriate the funds as well as to carry out community justice according to their
traditional practices—as long as government laws are not violated.

Many other Latin American countries recognize in their constitutions their
ethnic and cultural diversity, define themselves as pluricultural nations and
guarantee the social, economic and cultural rights of indigenous peoples. Most
Latin American countries have ratified ILO Convention No. 169 and all, with the
exception of Colombia who abstained, voted in favour of the UN Declaration on
the Rights of Indigenous Peoples in 2007. Many have engaged in land reform
processes, including land demarcation and titling, in favour of indigenous peoples. Land issues, however, continue to affect indigenous peoples, especially in
relation to mining, oil exploration and conservation policies.

---

728 Text available online at http://www.juridicas.unam.mx/infjur/leg/legmexfe.htm
729 Article 289 of the new Bolivian Constitution 2009. See http://www.confinder.richmond.edu

The Pacific and Asia

Australia

The legal claims of the Aboriginal peoples and Torres Strait Islanders on their lands are guaranteed by the 1993 Australian Native Title Act, which *"recognises and protects native title"* and *"provides that native title cannot be extinguished contrary to the Act"*.[730]
   According to Section 223 (1)

[T]he expression native title or native title rights and interests means the communal, group or individual rights and interests of Aboriginal peoples or Torres Strait Islanders in relation to land or waters, where:
   a. *the rights and interests are possessed under the traditional laws acknowledged, and the traditional customs observed, by the Aboriginal peoples or Torres Strait Islanders; and*
   b. *the Aboriginal peoples or Torres Strait Islanders, by those laws and customs, have a connection with the land or waters; and*
   c. *the rights and interests are recognised by the common law of Australia.*

Section 223 (2) furthermore stipulates that *"rights and interests includes hunting, gathering or fishing rights and interests"*.[731]
   The Act was part of the Federal Government's response to the High Court's decision in the *Mabo v. Queensland* case,[732] which held that *"that the Meriam people are entitled as against the whole world to possession, occupation, use and enjoyment of the island of Mer"*,[733] and found that Australian common law can recognize the rights and interests over land and water possessed by indigenous peoples in Australia under their traditional laws and customs—i.e., their "native title". The Act also established a national machinery—the National Native Title Tribunal—that assists people to resolve native title issues over land and waters and acts as a mediator.[734] The Tribunal likewise administers the so-called future act processes

---

730 Australian Native Title, Section 10. The 1993 Native Act contains essentially laws that help to determine whether a native title exists on a given part of lands or waters. See http://www.com-law.gov.au/
731 Ibid., Section 225.
732 *Mabo and Others v. Queensland* (No.2) [1992]. The case involved indigenous peoples from the Murray Islands in the Torres Strait. The communities living on these islands since before the arrival of European settlers and known as the Meriam people, claimed to have maintained their native rights on these lands despite the arrival of Europeans. Available online at http:// www.aiatsis.gov.au
733 Ibid., at para. 97.
734 However, applications made under the Native Title Act for a determination of native title or for compensations for the loss of native title, etc., are under the responsibility of the Federal Court of Australia.

which are proposed activities or developments generally related to mining that attract the right to negotiate (but not to veto).

The Native Title Act has been amended several times. In 1998, it was done against the express wishes of Aboriginal and environmental groups, who saw it as a deliberate act from the Government's side—very much prompted by the 1996 *Wik Peoples v. Queensland* case—to largely extinguish native title. The High Court in the *Wik* case had ruled that native title rights could only be extinguished by deliberate act; they could co-exist with pastoral leases, but where there was inconsistency, the pastoral lease would prevail.[735] The 1998 amendments redefined the nature of pastoral leases, increased the powers of the mining and pastoral industries and State governments at the expense of native title claimants, imposed new and unrealistic requirements on native title claimants, and largely replaced the right to negotiate about future developments with a right to be consulted.[736]

Recent initiatives relevant for indigenous land rights include the Indigenous Protected Area Programme launched in 1997[737] and the creation of the Indigenous Land Corporation (ILC) in 2005.[738]

New Zealand

New Zealand's constitutional arrangements can be found in a number of key documents, which, together with New Zealand's constitutional conventions, form the nation's Constitution. Key written sources include the Constitution Act 1986, the New Zealand Bill Of Rights Act 1990, the Electoral Act 1993, the Standing Orders of the House of Representatives and the Treaty of Waitangi.[739] This Treaty, which dates back to 1840, is today widely accepted to be a constitutional

---

735 *The Wik Peoples v. The State of Queensland & Ors*; *The Thayorre People v. The State of Queensland & Ors* [1996] HCA 40 (23 December 1996). Can be accessed at http://www.austlii.edu.au/databases.html - High Court cases. See also Web site of Australian Institute of Aboriginal and Torres Strait Islanders Studies at http://ntru.aiatsis.gov.au – Native Title Research Unit.

736 See, for example, http://www.nlc.org.au/html/land_native_amend.html

737 An Indigenous Protected Area (IPA) is an area of indigenous-owned land or sea where Traditional Owners have entered into an agreement with the Australian Government to promote biodiversity and cultural resource conservation. The IPA programme is part of the Australian Government's national reserve system. See, e.g., http://www.facsia.gov.au/indigenous/specific_evaluations07/page6.htm, accessed January 2009.

738 The ILC was established by the *Aboriginal and Torres Strait Islander Act 2005* as an indigenous controlled "statutory authority to assist indigenous people to acquire and manage land to achieve economic, environmental, social and cultural benefits". See Web site at http://www.ilc.gov.au

739 Aspects of the Constitution are also found in United Kingdom and other New Zealand legislation, judgments of the courts, and broad constitutional principles and conventions. See at http://www.confinder.richmond.edu

document, which establishes and guides relationships between the Crown in New Zealand (as embodied by the New Zealand Government) and Maori.[740]

Native title was recognized under the common law of New Zealand as early as 1847 in the case of *R v. Symonds*.[741] Apart from confirming the existence of common law native title in New Zealand, this decision also noted its recognition in accordance with the country's founding document—namely, the Treaty of Waitangi (1840).[742] The Native Rights Act 1865 also supported Maori native title rights, but already in 1877, the *Wi Parata v. Bishop of Wellington* case[743] reversed these earlier interpretations, concluding that the Treaty of Waitangi had no effect and denying the existence of customary law.[744]

In the 1970s, growing Maori protests about unresolved Treaty grievances led to the establishment of the Waitangi Tribunal (1975).[745] This permanent commission of inquiry hears reports and makes recommendations on claims by Maori that have been or may be "prejudicially affected" by laws, actions and policies of the Crown that are contrary to the principles of the Treaty of Waitangi of 1840.[746] In 1985, the Tribunal was given retrospective jurisdiction to examine Crown actions affecting Maori since 1840.

In cases of justified claims, and since it is not a court but rather a commission of inquiry, the Tribunal can only make recommendations relating to land restitution, regardless of the size and current use of such land. Settlements continue therefore to be negotiated through the Maori Land Court,[747] which, together with the Maori

---

740 New Zealand Ministry of Justice, The New Zealand Legal System accessed at http://www.justice.govt.nz/pubs/other/pamphlets/2001/legal_system.html

741 *R. v. Symonds* (1847) N.Z.P.C.C. 387. For summary, see
http://www.atns.net.au/agreement.asp?EntityID=1744

742 The Treaty of Waitangi was signed in 1840 between the British Crown and the Maori chiefs of what is now known as New Zealand. See, e.g., http://www.waitangi-tribunal.govt.nz/treaty/

743 *Wi Parata v. Bishop of Wellington* [1877] 3 NZLR 72. For summary see
http://www.atns.net.au/agreement.asp?EntityID=1745

744 See Australian Institute of Aboriginal and Torres Strait Islander Studies (AIATSIS), "A Comparison of Native Title Laws", 2004 (Updated 2007), available online at http://www.aiatsis.gov.au – Native Title Research Unit.

745 The Waitangi Tribunal takes its name from the 1840 Treaty and was established under the Treaty of Waitangi Act 1975. The tribunal may have up to 17 members, who sit in divisions as small as three (3), of whom one member must be Maori. Sittings are usually headed by a member with legal training or a judge of the Maori Land Court. The chairperson is the Chief Judge of the Maori Land Court. Once a claim under the Treaty of Waitangi has been lodged, there ensues a process of negotiation seeking to achieve a fair and just settlement of Crown historical breaches of the Treaty. The Treaty settlement process is intended to be reparative and to provide redress for historical misconduct. The Government does not provide full compensation for losses suffered historically by Maori, but negotiates a compromise. See Web site of Tribunal at http://www.waitangi-tribunal.govt.nz/

746 According to section 6 of the Treaty of Waitangi Amendment Act 2006, the Waitangi Tribunal is not permitted to register claims submitted on or after 2 September 2008 that are either new historical Treaty claims or historical amendments to contemporary claims. See http://www.waitangi-tribunal.govt.nz/

747 The Court was originally established as the Native Land Court under the Native Land Act 1865. It has been called the Maori Land Court since 1954.

Appellate Court, operates in a tribunal-type manner and deals with issues relating to lands held communally by Maori communities—Maori Lands. According to some estimates, Maori lands cover 4.5 per cent of New Zealand's land area or some 1,305,698 hectares. In 1993, the Maori Land Act was passed and provides for various working mechanisms applying to Maori land.[748]

The Maori land rights' struggle, however, goes on. In November 2004, the Government enacted the Foreshore and Seabed Act, thereby removing the right of the Maori to seek ownership of the foreshore and seabed.[749] This legislation was subsequently criticized by both the Committee on the Elimination of Racial Discrimination[750] and the U.N. Special Rapporteur on the situation of human rights and fundamental freedoms of indigenous people.[751] Since then, however, some *iwi* (clans) have chosen to negotiate agreement within the bounds of the act and the first agreement was ratified in October 2008.[752] In September 2008, the *Central North Island Forests Land Collective Settlement Act of 2008* was passed. It will return 176,000 hectares of forested land to seven *iwi*, who are members of the Central North Island Collective[753] and to the Trust Holding Company, CNI Iwi Holdings Limited.

Malaysia

The Constitution of Malaysia (1957)[754] does not provide any special protection to its indigenous peoples, communally called "Orang Asli", a collective term that means original or first peoples in Malay. In 1954, the country passed an "Aboriginal Peoples Act",[755] which unfortunately provides for, among others, weak

---

748 See at the following Web site: http://www.kennett.co.nz/maorilaw/index.html#contents

749 This legislation was prompted by a ruling made in 2003 by the Court of Appeal according to which Maori could seek customary title to areas of the New Zealand foreshore and seabed, and overturning assumptions that such land automatically belonged to the Crown. The Court of Appeal followed overseas precedence, and held that legislation must be explicit if it is to extinguish customary rights to land. There were massive demonstrations against the Act prior to its adoption and it became a political issue. For more information, see, e.g., http://www.converge.org.nz/pma/fsinfo.htm#ong

750 CERD, Procedural Decisions on the Elimination of Racial Discrimination, New Zealand [Foreshore and Seabed Act 2004], March 2005. U.N. Doc. CERD/C/DEC/NZL/1. Available online at http://www1.umn.edu/humanrts/cerd/decisions/newzealand2005.html

751 Rodolfo Stavenhagen, Mission to New Zealand, U.N. Doc. E/CN.4/2006/78/Add.3 13 March 2006 (2006), at paras. 43-55. Available at http://www2.ohchr.org/english/issues/indigenous/rapporteur/visits.htm

752 See Agreement between Ngati Porou and the Crown at Ngati Porou Web site: http://www.ngatiporou.com/sitemap.asp

753 The land will be vested in a trust holding company, CNI Iwi Holdings Limited, in which 86 per cent of the assets are hold by the indigenous collective. Accessed January 2009 at http://www.scoop.co.nz/stories/PA0809/S00538.htm,.

754 The Constitution of Malaysia at http://www.confinder.richmond.edu

755 For text of Aboriginal Peoples Act 1954, Act 134, see Web site of FAO: faolex.fao.org/docs/texts/mal33568.doc

land rights (usufructuary and mere use) for the Orang Asli who became thus tenants on their own traditional lands and territories. Consequently, the Government can at will affect to other uses lands occupied by indigenous communities.

This has been in fact the case of the Temuan people forcibly evicted in 1995 by Government authorities and others from their ancestral lands, needed for building a high way leading to Kuala Lumpur international airport. In 2002, a High Court ruling upheld customary land ownership rights of the Temuan people and requested state authorities and all other defendants to compensate the plaintiffs for loss of property. In September 2005, the Malaysian Court of Appeal upheld the High Court`s 2002 ruling that the Temuan tribe is the customary owner of disputed land, from which they were forcibly evicted for the purpose of building public infrastructures.[756] Unhappy with that second ruling in favour of the Temuan peoples, state authorities and all other appellants have appealed to the Federal Court seeking reversal of the previous court rulings. The case it yet to be concluded, but early 2009 there were reports that one of the main defendants, namely the Selangor Government, would withdraw its appeal to the Federal Court in recognition of the indigenous peoples' rights as proclaimed in previous judgments[757].

Philippines

The 1987 Constitution of the Philippines has several provisions of relevance to indigenous peoples, which are called "indigenous cultural communities" (ICC). The State, among other things, recognizes and promotes the rights of ICC "within the framework of national unity and development"[758] and "subject to the provisions of this Constitution and national development policies and programs" commits to protecting "the rights of ICC to their ancestral land to ensure their economic, social, and cultural well-being".[759] The Constitution also includes several provisions that, taken together, could serve as a basic framework for recognizing and promoting indigenous peoples' rights.

In 1997, the Philippine Congress adopted the Indigenous Peoples' Rights Act (IPRA), which created the National Commission on Indigenous Peoples (NCIP), a body aiming to promote and protect indigenous rights, including rights to

---

756　*Kerajaan Ngeri Selangor and 3 Others. v. Sagong bin Tasi and 6 Others* [2005] 2 MLJ 591. Can be accessed at
　　http://www.malaysianbar.org.my/selected_judgements/kerajaan_negeri_selangor_3_ors_v_sagong_bin_tasi_6_ors_2005_ca.html

757　See on the Web site: http://www.thenutgraph.com/sgor-withdraw-appeal-dispute-temuans; see also Minority Rights Group International, *World Directory of Minorities and Indigenous Peoples—Malaysia: Orang Asli*, 2008, available at:
　　http://www.unhcr.org/refworld/docid/49749ce85.html [accessed 9 September 2009]

758　Constitution of the Philippines (1987), Art. II Sec. 22. Available online at
　　http://www.chanrobles.com/philsupremelaw1.htm

759　Ibid., Art. XII Sec. 5.

lands and culture, and the mechanisms of free, prior and informed consent (FPIC). IPRA also created the so-called indigenous peoples' Consultative Bodies, which shall be convened by the NCIP and be consulted regularly to advise the NCIP on matters relating to problems, aspirations and interests of the indigenous peoples of the Philippines.

Aside from legal inconsistencies and ambiguities in IPRA itself, there are political factors that weaken the law and hamper its full implementation.[760] In his mission report from the Philippines, the former U.N. Special Rapporteur on the situation of human rights and fundamental freedoms of indigenous peoples, Rodolfo Stavenhagen, therefore recommended that

> [T]he National Commission on Human Rights (NCHR) expand its activities in the area of indigenous rights and incorporate and train an increasing number of indigenous legal defenders to be active in taking up the human rights grievances of indigenous peoples. NCHR could, for example, spearhead a movement to create a broader structure to determine and certify prior, free and informed consent by indigenous peoples, whenever necessary."[761]

In the Pacific and in Asia, only Fiji (1998) and Nepal (2007) have ratified ILO Convention No. 169. When it comes to the UN Declaration on the Rights of Indigenous Peoples, both Australia and New Zealand voted against, while Samoa, Bhutan and Bangladesh abstained. After a change of government in 2008, New Zealand and Australia revised their position in April 2009 and have now endorsed the UN Declaration.

Western Europe

In Western Europe, one of the indigenous communities most frequently referred to is the Saami,[762] found in Finland, Sweden, Norway and Russia. In some of these countries, the Saami have enjoyed good standards of protection of their rights, including the right to lands, and the Saami language is taught in schools and even in some universities. In 1956, the Nordic Sámi Council was established to promote cooperation amongst the Saami in Finland, Norway, and Sweden. This council has

---

760 For more information, see, e.g., the Web site of IWGIA at http://www.iwgia.org – Country Profile: The Philippines.

761 Rodolfo Stavenhagen, Mission to the Philippines. Report of the Special Rapporteur on the situation of human rights and fundamental freedoms of indigenous people. U.N. Doc. E/CN.4/2003/90/ Add.3, 5 March 2003 (2003b). Available from
http://www2.ohchr.org/english/issues/indigenous/rapporteur/visits.htm

762 The Saami are thought to be descended from the people who settled in the Scandinavian Peninsula after the last Ice Age, about 7,500 years BC.

twelve members, four from each country. Currently, a draft Nordic Saami Convention is being discussed by the respective Nordic Governments.

In 1988, the Parliament of **Norway** passed a new Act inspired by the UN Covenant on Civil and Political Rights of 1966. This Constitutional Act §110a provides recognition and protection of the Saami language, culture and society. The following year, Norway recognized the Saami's political rights by establishing the Saami Parliament, and in 1990, Norway ratified LO Convention No. 169 as the first European country to do so. However, it was to take more than a decade before the first broad effort of implementing the Convention took place through the adoption, in 2006, of the Finnmark Act. This was also the first time substantial consultations as recommended by Article 6 of the ILO Convention were carried out between the Norwegian Parliament and the Saami Parliament. The Finnmark Act and the legislative adoption of the recent (2007) Agreement on Consultation Procedures between the Government and the Executive Council of the Saami Parliament have been seen as the first progressive steps towards indigenous self-governance in Norway.[763]

Sweden also has a Saami Parliament (1993) and particular measures aiming at protecting the way of life of the Saami have been taken as, for instance, the 1971 Reindeer Husbandry Act which, as argued by the Swedish Government in the *Ivan Kitok v. Sweden* case[764] before the Human Rights Committee, aims to "secure the preservation and well-being of the Saami". However, it should be said that the Saami consider that the Swedish Government has yet to make more efforts towards full enjoyment of their rights. In **Finland**, which also has a Saami Parliament (1996), Section 121 of the 1999 Constitution states that *"in their native region, the Saami have linguistic and cultural self-government, as provided by an Act"*.

In **Russia**, the 1,600 Saami living on the Kola Peninsula are included in the so-called "numerically small indigenous peoples of the North, Siberia and the Far East". These indigenous peoples are recognized and protected by the Constitution and three framework laws. However, these are declarative and their provisions have remained largely theoretical. This is true first and foremost for land

---

763 The Finnmark Act establishes a new autonomous organisation for the administration of land, water and resources in Finnmark called the Finnmark Estate (Finnmarkseiendommen). An area the size of Denmark is being transferred from the state to this autonomous organization. See Johan Mikkel Sara, "Indigenous Governance of Self-Determination. The Saami model and the Saami Parliament in Norway". Paper presented at the Symposium on "The Right to Self-Determination in International Law", The Hague, Netherlands, 29 September-1 October 2006. Available at http://www.unpo.org/downloads/JohanMikkelSara.pdf

764 U.N. Human Rights Committee, Thirty-third session (1988), Communication No. 197/1985 (1988). U.N. Doc. CCPR/C/33/D/197/1985 (1988). Available at http://hrlibrary.ngo.ru/undocs/session33-index.html. The communication before the Human Rights Committee was made by Mr. Kitok against the Swedish Government on the grounds that the Swedish Reindeer Husbandry Act of 1971 violated the provisions of articles 1 and 27 of the ICCPR. The Human Rights Committee ruled in favour of the Swedish Government by arguing that in the interest of preservation of a community's welfare, individual rights could be limited under certain circumstances.

rights. The Saami have thus been gradually forced off their traditional grazing land by a steady expansion of industry, forestry, mining, etc.[765]

Greenland became a Danish colony in the early eighteenth century. Its indigenous inhabitants belong to the Inuit people who live in the North American Arctic. In 1953, the Danish Constitution changed the status of Greenland and this Arctic island became an overseas county of Denmark. In 1978, the Danish Government passed the Greenland Home Rule Act[766] that granted Greenlanders a wide range of powers through their local government and parliament. As stated by Erica A. Daes, the 1978 Greenland Home Rule Act was "one of the best examples of constructive framework legislation to accommodate the rights and aspirations of indigenous peoples". The Act provided for strong ownership of land on behalf of the Greenlander Inuit who, not only had the power of decision over the use of their lands, but more importantly, enjoyed the power of veto over development activities.[767]

A few years ago, Greenland negotiated an agreement with Denmark regarding greater self-governance, and in late 2008, a referendum on self-rule was held. It passed with 75 per cent voting for greater autonomy. The new arrangement came into force in June 2009. Apart from securing more self-governance, it will also allow Greenland to take over the control of revenues from potential oil, gas and mineral finds.

Besides Norway, the only European countries to have ratified ILO Convention No. 169 are Denmark (in 1996), the Netherlands (1998) and Spain (2007). All the European countries voted for the UN Declaration on the Rights of Indigenous Peoples, with the exception of the Russian Federation, which abstained.

Constitutional provisions regarding indigenous peoples in Africa

An overview of the constitutions of most Central, Eastern, and Southern African States corroborates the view that these States do not provide any sort of special protection to their indigenous communities. Only a few of them recognize the multi-cultural and -ethnical diversity of their inhabitants. A recent joint publication by the ILO and the ACHPR documents constitutional, legal and administrative measures relevant to indigenous peoples in twenty four (24) African countries. This publication is highly recommended to anyone interested in the enforcement, the protection and the promotion of the rights of indigenous peoples on the continent.[768]

---

765 For more information, see, e.g., IWGIA Web page: http://www.iwgia.org
766 The Greenland Home Rule Act (Act No.56) of 21 February 1978 came into force on 1 May 1979 following a referendum in Greenland.
767 Daes, "Indigenous Peoples and Their Relationship to Land" (2001), para. 109.
768 ILO and ACHPR, *Constitutional and Legislative Protection of Indigenous Populations in Africa, ILO and ACHPR* (Geneva and Banjul, The Gambia: ILO and ACHPR, 2009).

Central Africa

The 2004 Constitution of the **Central African Republic**[769] does not use the term "indigenous" nor does it contain special provisions for such communities. However, it is based on the principle of equality by what is known as the principle *Zo Kwe Zo* (all human beings are equal), enshrined in the Constitution. The Constitution also recognizes "cultural and ethnic diversity" and states that the "*Central African people … is resolved to build a State based on the rule of law and a pluralist democracy that guarantees security of persons and their belongings, protection of the weakest, including vulnerable persons, minorities*" and "*the full enjoyment of rights and fundamental freedoms*".[770] In early 2010, the Central African Republic became the first African country to ratify ILO Convention No. 169.

The 1972 Constitution of **Cameroon,** amended in 1996 and in 2008, mentions human rights in its Preamble. The Preamble, which is to be considered as an integral part of the Constitution,[771] states "*The Republic of Cameroon … shall recognize and protect traditional values that conform to democratic principles, human rights and the law*";it also states that no discrimination on the grounds of race, religion, etc. shall be tolerated, and more specifically that: "*the State shall ensure the protection of minorities and shall preserve the rights of indigenous populations in accordance with the law*".

Although the Cameroonian Constitution, by using the term "indigenous population", puts itself in a class of its own, Cameroon, like many other African countries, has never passed a law dealing specifically with the protection of indigenous peoples' rights.

The 1991 Constitution of the **Republic of Gabon,** as amended in 1997 and 2000, does not contain an explicit recognition of indigenous communities or minorities' rights. However, it states—but without any further details—that the right to property can be enjoyed and exercised individually or collectively.[772] One of its most important land-related laws, the 2001 Forest Code, provides for mere usage rights of any communities over forests (community forests), without making any specific reference to its indigenous peoples, the "Pygmies", albeit recog-

---

769 Constitution of Central African Republic is available online at http://confinder.richmond.edu/

770 Preamble of the Constitution of the Central African Republic. In French, it reads "*Le Peuple Centrafricain … est résolu de construire l'Etat de droit fondé sur une démocratie pluraliste, garantissant la sécurité des personnes et des biens, la protection des plus faibles, notamment les personnes vulnérables, les minorités et le plein exercice des libertés et droits fondamentaux*". Available online at http://confinder. richmond.edu/

771 Constitution of Cameroon, Article 65 states: "*the preamble shall be part and parcel of this Constitution*". Full text available online at http://confinder.richmond.edu/

772 Constitution of Gabon, Article 1(10). Full text of Constitution as per 2000 is available online at http://www.droitsdelhomme-france.org/IMG/Constitution_du_Gabon.pdf

nized as the oldest inhabitant of African tropical forests.[773] The country's land tenure system is mainly regulated by the Law 14/63 of 8 May 1963, which states that all lands belong to the Government and that communities hold no right over lands unless explicitly granted by the State. In other words, occupation and use, be it immemorial, does not grant legal rights over lands.[774]

The 2002 Constitution of the **Republic of Congo** does not *expressis verbis* provide for indigenous communities. There is only a provision on the right to culture.[775] The new Forest Code from 2000 does not either provide for a special protection of the "Pygmies". It uses instead the terms "local populations" and "local communities" entitled to usage rights, which include hunting, collecting and pasture.[776] Unfortunately, non timber products from usage rights such as hunting products cannot be commercialised.[777] However, the adoption in December 2009 of a law regarding the promotion and protection of indigenous peoples (*Loi portant promotion et protection des peuples autochtones en République du Congo*) has raised great expectations. This legal instrument is also the first of its kind in Central Africa and elsewhere in Africa and could set a good precedent for a better protection of indigenous peoples in Africa.

The 2006 Constitution of the **Democratic Republic of Congo**[778] does not use the term "indigenous" but its Article 13 does prohibit, among others things, racial and ethnic discrimination, stating that:

> *No Congolese shall be discriminated against in relation with access to education and to public services nor should a Congolese be discriminated against, whether by a law or an act of the executive, on the basis of his/her religion, family origin, social condition, residence, opinions, political beliefs, race, ethnicity, culture, or language.*[779]

---

773 Law No. 016/01 Portant Code forestier en République Gabonaise. See, e.g., Volker Kohler & Franz Schmithüsen, "Comparative Analysis of Forest Laws in Twelve Sub-Saharan African Countries". FAO Legal Papers Online #37 (Rome: FAO, July 2004). Available online at http://www.fao.org/legal/pub-e.htm,

774 Joseph Comby, "Quel cadastre, pourquoi faire ? Exemple du Gabon". An online article: http://perso.orange.fr/joseph.comby/cadastre_Gabon.html

775 Constitution of the Republic of Congo, Article 22 states that everybody should enjoy his or her right to a culture. For full text of Constitution, see http://confinder.richmond.edu

776 The new Forest Code, Article 40 states (in French): "*Les populations locales jouissent de droits d'usage leur permettant de: (1) récolter les perches, gaulettes et autres produits ligneux nécessaires à la construction et à l'entretien de leurs habitations, meubles, ustensiles domestiques et outils, ainsi que les bois morts et les plantes d'intérêt culturel, alimentaire ou médicinal; (2) chasser, pêcher et récolter les produits dans les limites prévues par la loi; et (3) établir des cultures ou des ruches et faire paître leur bétail ou récolter du fourrage.*"

777 Ibid., Article 42 .

778 The Constitution of DRC (2006) is available in French online at http://www.confinder.richmond.edu/

779 Author's translation. The original text in French reads: "*Aucun Congolais ne peut, en matière d'éducation et d'accès aux fonctions publiques ni en aucune autre matière, faire l'objet d'une mesure discriminatoire, qu'elle résulte de la loi ou d'un acte de l'exécutif, en raison de sa religion, de son origine familiale,*

The Constitution devotes furthermore the entire chapter 3 of its second part to "collective rights" and states in its article 51 that:

> *The State shall ensure and promote peaceful and harmonious coexistence of all national ethnic groups. It shall also ensure the protection and promotion of vulnerable groups and minorities. It shall guarantee their development.*[780]

More interestingly, the Constitution protects both private and collective ownership: "The State guarantees the right to individual or collective property acquired according to the law or to customs."[781] One could read this recognition of collective ownership on the basis of customary law as an important entry point for strong claims of indigenous peoples' right to land.

In 2002, the DR Congo passed a new forest code,[782] which also does not use the term indigenous peoples or communities, but nevertheless contains provisions on community forests and benefit sharing that could be valuable for the promotion and protection of indigenous peoples. Article 22 of this Code provides for instance that a community could transform part of or all its customarily occupied forests into a community-controlled and managed concession. However, a number of implementing measures of the Congolese Forest Code do use the word "indigenous communities", including a 2008 prime ministerial decree on the commission for conversion of logging titles[783] and a legal text on a national consultative council on forest (Conseil Consultatif National des Forêts),[784] which provides that one member of the council must be an indigenous person.

Eastern and Horn of Africa

In 2005, **Burundi** ratified a new Constitution, which does not use the term indigenous but talks about ethnic diversity.[785] However, this national legal framework provides for a power sharing mechanism between the three ethnic groups that

---

de sa condition sociale, de sa résidence, de ses opinions ou de ses convictions politiques, de son appartenance à une race, à une ethnie, à une tribu, à une minorité culturelle ou linguistique."

780 Author's translation. The original text in French reads: "L'Etat a le devoir d'assurer et de promouvoir la coexistence pacifique et harmonieuse de tous les groupes ethniques du pays. Il assure également la protection et la promotion des groupes vulnérables et de toutes les minorités. Il veille à leur épanouissement."

781 Author's translation. The original text in French reads: "L'Etat garantit le droit à la propriété individuelle ou collective, acquis conformément à la loi ou à la coutume."

782 Loi No.011/2002 du 29 août 2002 portant Code Forestier de la République Démocratique du Congo

783 *Décret No. 08/02 of 21 January 2008*

784 Décret No.08/03 of 26 January 2008

785 Constitution of Burundi, Article 2. Full text available at http://confinder.richmond.edu

live in the country, namely the Hutu, the Tutsi and the indigenous "Pygmy" community known as the Batwa. Article 164 of the Constitution specifies indeed that three Members of Parliament should come from the Batwa indigenous community[786] and Article 180 stipulates the same level of Batwa representation in the Senate.

The post-genocide Government of **Rwanda** has been very hesitant to amend its June 2003 Constitution[787] or pass minority or community-friendly legislation, given the fact that the 1994 genocide was rooted, amongst other things, in bitter inter-ethnic rivalries. Trying to heal the country from such divisions, the 2003 Constitution does not mention any sort of special regime on behalf of a given social group but states in its Preamble that *"We have the privilege to have a same country, a same language, a same culture..."* and in Article 9 (2) that a fundamental principle is *"the eradication of ethnic, regional and other divisions and the promotion of national unity"*.

Regarding land rights, the Constitution recognizes the right to private propriety, individual or collective.[788] The land question has been and remains a major issue. Faced with the resettlement of more than 1.5 million returning refugees.[789] Rwanda opted for the so-called "villagization" policy. This policy became highly controversial since it grouped people into villages without consideration of their culture, former residence, etc. In 2004, after several years of debates, a new land policy was launched, followed in 2005 by a new national land law. This law promotes land consolidation and may, according to international observers, make it more difficult for the Batwa to keep the little land they still own, as it will give the Government complete authority over land use, potentially subjecting owners to loss of land without compensation.[790]

The **Ethiopian** Constitution (1994) provides for the "rights of peoples". This constitution uses particularly unusual wording given the context of the aspiration of African States to promote national unity. It states that *"human rights and democratic rights of citizens and peoples shall be respected"*;[791] Article 39 provides specifically for the *"rights of Nations, Nationalities and Peoples"*; and paragraph 5 of this Article defines the term "people" (without an "s") as a synonym of the terms "nation" and "nationality":

---

786   Ibid., Article 164 states that Parliament is constituted by at least 100 members—60 per cent Hutu, 40 per cent Tutsi, including a minimum of 30 per cent women, elected by universal vote; and three members from the Twa ethnic group coopted in accordance with the electoral code.

787   The Rwanda Constitution is available online at http://www.cjcr.gov.rw/eng/**constitution**_eng. doc

788   Article 29: *"Toute personne a droit à la propriété privée, individuelle ou collective."*

789   Following the 1994 genocide, more than 2 million people fled Rwanda to neighboring countries.

790   See http://www.irinnews.org/InDepthMain.aspx?InDepthId=9&ReportId=58606 and *The Indigenous World 2007* (IWGIA, 2007), p. 495,

791   Constitution of Ethiopia (1994), Article 10. Full text available online at http://www.findlaw.com /01topics/06constitutional/03forconst/index.html

A "Nation, Nationality or People" for the purpose of this Constitution, is a group of people who have or share a large measure of a common culture or similar customs, mutual intelligibility of language, belief in a common or related identities, a common psychological make-up, and who inhabit an identifiable, predominantly contiguous territory.

The right to self-determination for these groups, including the right to secession,[792] is also enshrined in the Constitution. With regard to land, it also demarcates itself from the general African trend. Firstly, it states that the right to ownership of rural and urban land, as well as of all natural resources, is exclusively vested in the State and the "peoples of Ethiopia";[793] secondly, and more remarkably, it provides pastoralists with a special protective regime:

Ethiopian pastoralists have the right to free land for grazing and cultivation as well as the right not to be displaced from their own lands. The implementation shall be specified by law.[794]

Kenya's current Constitution dates from 1963 but has since been amended over thirty times, last in 2000.[795] The Constitution uses neither the terms "indigenous" nor "minorities". Nor does it recognize the "aboriginal titles" of its indigenous communities over their lands. Instead, it devotes an entire Chapter IX to "Trust Lands",[796] a term used to refer to lands managed by County Councils, a government-made institution, which allegedly acts in the name and interests of the local communities but, in reality, is a government controlled body.

---

792 Ibid., Article 39 (1). Article 39 (2) stipulates that *"Every Nation, Nationality and People in Ethiopia has the right to speak, to write and to develop its own language; to express, to develop and to promote its culture; and to preserve its history"*.

793 Ibid., Article 40 (3).

794 Ibid., Article 40 (5).

795 The Kenyan Constitution is available online at
     http://www.kenyalawreport.co.ke/kenyalaw/klr_app/frames.php

796 Ibid., Article 114 defines Trust Lands as: *(a) land which is in the Special Areas (meaning the areas of land the boundaries of which were specified in the First Schedule to the Trust Land Act as in force on 31st May, 1963), and which was on 31st May, 1963 vested in the Trust Land Board by virtue of any law or registered in the name of the Trust Land Board; (b) the areas of land that were known before 1st June, 1963 as Special Reserves, Temporary Special Reserves, Special Leasehold Areas and Special Settlement Areas and the boundaries of which were described respectively in the Fourth, Fifth, Sixth and Seventh Schedules to the Crown Lands Ordinance as in force on 31st May, 1963 communal reserves by virtue of a declaration under section 58 of that Ordinance, the areas of land referred to in section 59 of that Ordinance as in force on 31st May, 1963 and the areas of land in respect of which a permit to occupy was in force on 31st May, 1963 under section 62 of that Ordinance; and (c) land situated outside the Nairobi Areas (as it was on 12th December, 1964) the freehold title to which is registered in the name of a county council or the freehold title to which is vested in a county council by virtue of an escheat: Provided that Trust land does not include any estates, interests or rights in or over land situated in the Nairobi Area (as it was 12th December, 1964) that on 31st May, 1963 were registered in the name of the Trust Land Board under the former Land Registration (Special Areas) Ordinance.*

While the Constitution under the same chapter, Article 115 (2), states that

The Councils shall give effect to such rights, interests or other benefits in respect of the land as may, under the African customary law for the time being [sic] in force and applicable thereto, be vested in any tribe, group, family or individual.

it also adds that:

No right, interest or other benefit under African customary law shall have effect for the purposes of this subsection so far as it is repugnant to any written law.

thus making it unequivocally clear that it does not give much consideration to the land rights of indigenous communities, which are by principle based on customary law.

The Constitution of Kenya contains also a general provision on the norm of non-discrimination. Its Article 82 (1) states that *"no law shall make any provision that is discriminatory either of itself or in its effect"*, defining the expression *"discriminatory"* as *"affording different treatment to different persons attributable wholly or mainly to their respective descriptions by race, tribe, place of origin …"*.[797]

For many Kenyans, "Kenya's current constitution is a symbol of both British colonialism and domestic political oppression."[798] In the early 1990s, calls for a multi-party system and constitutional reforms eventually led to some constitutional amendments and, in 1997, to the Constitution of Kenya Review Act. This Act was amended in 2001 to provide a comprehensive and participatory review of the constitution and the option to draft a new document that would open up the country to wide-ranging political and institutional reforms ensuring socioeconomic development and the protection of human rights. The review process was delayed several times and produced three draft constitutions before a referendum to approve or reject the third proposed draft constitution was held in November 2005. Sixty-seven per cent of the voters rejected the draft and the process was thereafter stalled due to, among other things, the elections and the post-elections political crisis. In March 2008, a new agreement on the constitutional reform was reached, and a Constitution of Kenya (Amendment) Act passed.[799] In November 2009, the appointed Committee of Experts (CoE) published a Harmo-

---

797 Ibid., Article 82(3).
798 The Constitution was negotiated with the British prior to independence and the many amendments have been made by Kenya's ruling party for purposes that included centralizing power, strengthening executive authority, and, for a significant portion of Kenya's history, banning opposition parties. See Alicia L. Bannon, "Designing a Constitution-Drafting Process: Lessons from Kenya", *Yale Law Journal*, June 2007.
799 Civil society, religious groups and other interest groups will form part of the process. The Committee of Experts has 11 members. There are three foreigners on the team and three women. For further information, see Web page of the Committee on http://www.coekenya.go.ke

nized Draft Constitution. This draft will be discussed for 30 days so that the public can reconsider the proposals in the draft and submit comments to the CoE. The CoE will then have 21 days to incorporate views of the public and submit the draft to the Parliamentary Select Committee on the Constitution (PSC). The road map further includes tabling the draft in Parliament, and a referendum after approval by Parliament, a process which is expected to last 200 more days.

The 1995 Constitution of **Uganda** (amended in 2005), in its statement regarding "National objectives and directive principles of state policy" stipulates that

> *Every effort shall be made to integrate all the peoples of Uganda while at the same time recognising the existence of their ethnic, religious, ideological, political and cultural diversity.*

and that

> *Everything shall be done to promote a culture of cooperation, understanding, appreciation, tolerance and respect for each other's customs, traditions and beliefs.*[800]

Even though the Constitution does not use the term "indigenous peoples" in its current meaning, Article 10 on citizenship nevertheless specifies that:

> *The following persons shall be citizens of Uganda by birth—*
> > *(a) every person born in Uganda one of whose parents or grandparents is or was a member of any of the indigenous communities existing and residing within the borders of Uganda as at the first day of February, 1926, and set out in the Third Schedule to this Constitution. ...*

The Third Schedule lists the 56 "Ugandan Indigenous Communities as at 1st February 1926" and includes, among others, the Batwa.

The Ugandan Constitution also provides "Protection of rights of minorities" and "Right to culture and similar rights"[801] and institutes an independent Human Rights Commission, which among other things, is tasked "*to monitor the Government's compliance with international treaty and convention obligations on human rights*" [802]

Regarding land, the Ugandan Constitution makes the following provisions in Article 237:

---

800 Constitution of Uganda (1995), Section III (ii) and (iii) on National unity and stability. Available online at http://www.confinder.richmond.edu

801 Ibid., Articles 36 and 37.

802 Ibid., Articles 51, 54 and 52.1 (h).

1. *Land in Uganda belongs to the citizens of Uganda and shall vest in them. ...*
2. *Land in Uganda shall be owned in accordance with the following land tenure systems*
    a) customary; b) freehold; c) mailo;[803] *and d) leasehold.*
4. *On the coming into force of this Constitution—*
    a. *all Uganda citizens owning land under customary tenure may acquire certificates of ownership in a manner prescribed by Parliament; and*
    b. *land under customary tenure may be converted to freehold land ownership by registration.*

The 1977 Constitution of **Tanzania**, (last amended in 2005), does not specifically provide for indigenous peoples. Nor does it use the words "indigenous" and "minorities". It only recognizes the general principle of non-discrimination.[804] Because of this lacuna, a number of early attempts by lawyers to make a case for indigenous communities' right to lands were built upon the constitutional right to property.[805]

Southern Africa

Like Rwanda, the Constitution of **South Africa** (1996) is based upon the desire to heal the State from its history of racial discrimination. This is stated in the Preamble as well as in Section 1 (b).[806] However, despite articulating the principle of equality of all before the law, the Constitution of South Africa also provides that in order *"to promote the achievement of equality, legislative and other measures designed to protect or advance persons, or categories of persons, disadvantaged by unfair discrimination, may be taken".*[807]

The cultural, linguistic, and identity rights of the very diverse groups and communities that live in South Africa are also protected. Section 31, states:

1. *Persons belonging to a cultural, religious or linguistic community may not be denied the right, with other members of their community, to:*
    a. *enjoy their culture, practice their religion and use their language; and*

---

803 Ibid., Article 237 (3). *Mailo*—a kind of feudal tenure—was introduced by the British in 1900 and gave land to some individuals to own in perpetuity. The owner of Mailo land was and is entitled to a certificate of title.
804 Constitution of Tanzania, Chapter 3, Sections 12 and 13, which deals with human rights. Full text of Constitution available online from http://confinder.richmond.edu
805 Ibid., Section 24 states the right to property. See also Shivji and Kapinga, *Maasai Rights* (1998), pp. 31-5, and Tenga, *Pastoral Land Rights* (1992), p. 24.
806 The full text of the 1996 Constitution of South Africa is available online at http://confinder.richmond.edu
807 Constitution of South Africa (1966), Section 9 (2).

> b. *form, join and maintain cultural, religious and linguistic associations and other organs of civil society.*
>
> 2. *This right in subsection (1) may not be exercised in a manner inconsistent with any provision of the Bill of Rights*

The Constitution of South Africa also recognizes the status, functions, and role of traditional chiefs,[808] and section 235 recognizes the right to self-determination of communities:

> *The right of the South African people as a whole to self-determination, as manifested in this Constitution, does not preclude, within the framework of this right, recognition of the notion of the right of self-determination of any community sharing a common cultural and language heritage, within a territorial entity in the Republic or in any other way, determined by national legislation.*

Although not referring to the term "indigenous", the Constitution of South Africa appears, nevertheless, to have taken a very progressive approach and set a good legal framework for communities to reclaim back indigenous lands. Regarding property rights, the Constitution of South Africa thus provides that:

> *A person or community dispossessed of property after 19 June 1913, as a result of past racially discriminatory laws or practices, is entitled, to the extent provided by an Act of Parliament, either to restitution of that property or to equitable redress.*[809]

This provision was already included in the 1993 Interim Constitution[810] and in 1994, The Restitution of Land Rights Act, No. 2 of 1994 established a Commission on Restitution of Land Rights and a Land Claims Court. Restitution became also part of the national Land Reform programme launched in 1994. As described in chapter VII of this book, these various legal and institutional provisions were instrumental in both the Richtersveld court case and in the ‡Khomani land claim.

Like the Constitution of South Africa, the Constitutions of almost all other Southern African countries with a political history of racial discrimination, refrain from using the term "minorities" and "indigenous", arguably because there has always been this fear that this would resuscitate the old evil of racial discrimination. Perhaps with the same fear in mind, they all contain recognition of the principle of non-discrimination.

---

808 Ibid., Sections 211 and 212.
809 Ibid., Section 25 (7).
810 Interim Constitution of South Africa (1993), Article 8 (3),b and Articles 121-123. Available online at http://confinder.richmond.edu

This is the case of the Constitutions of **Malawi**, (1994, latest amended in 2001), **Zambia** (1991, latest amended in 1996), **Zimbabwe** (1979, amended several times, latest in 2005), **Mozambique** (2004) and **Lesotho** (1993).[811]

Botswana's Constitution (1965) in its Chapter II provides for the *"protection of fundamental rights and freedoms of individuals"*. However, in relation to the protection of freedom of movement articulated in section 14, the Constitution allows in subsection (3)(c),

> [T]he imposition of restrictions on the entry into or residence within defined areas of Botswana of persons who are not Bushmen to the extent that such restrictions are reasonably required for the protection or well-being of Bushmen".[812]

This provision has specifically been of importance to the residents of the CKGR since it protected their way of life and culture by preventing non-San to settle in the Reserve; the provision was also invoked in the court case as an argument for the residents' rights to remain in the Reserve. In 2005, however, a Constitutional (amendment) Act was passed with the stated purpose of making the Constitution tribally neutral. Besides revising Sections 77, 78 and 79 that hitherto had regulated the selection of members to the House of Chiefs and gave special rights to the eight main tribes in the country thereby clearly discriminating the so-called minor tribes, the Act also abrogated Section 14 (3)(c) under pretence that it was discriminatory to non-San by limiting their freedom of movement. Human Rights organizations in Botswana saw this as a political expedient, given the pending decision at the time of the CKGR case. Although the Act has been passed by parliament and assented to by the president, it has not yet commenced and consequently, the current status of Section 14 (3)(c) is not clear.[813]

The 1990 Constitution of **Namibia** does not specifically recognize the rights of indigenous peoples, but provides in Article 10 (2), that *"No persons may be discriminated against on the grounds of sex, race, colour, ethnic origin, religion, creed or social or economic status"*; and in Article 19, that *"Every person shall be entitled to enjoy, practice, profess, maintain and promote any culture, language, tradition or religion subject to the terms of this Constitution"*.[814] Customary law is also recognized,[815] and Article 102(5) states that a Council of Traditional Leaders shall be established in order to advise the President on the control and utilization of communal land and on all such other matters as may be referred to it by the President for advice.

---

811 The full text of these constitutions is available online at http://confinder.richmond.edu

812 See http://www.idasa.org.za/gbGovDocs.asp?RID=1

813 See the website of DITSHWANELO – the Botswana Human Rights Center at http://www.ditsh-wanelo.org.bw

814 The full text of the Namibian Constitution is available online at http://confinder.richmond.edu

815 Article 66 (1) reads: "Both the customary law and the common law of Namibia in force on the date of Independence shall remain valid to the extent to which such customary or common law does not conflict with this Constitution or any other statutory law …"

This has prompted several San groups to elect a chief that could represent them in the Council. So far, only a few of the established San traditional authorities have been formally recognized by Government. [816]

When it comes to land, neither indigenous land rights nor native titles are legally recognized.[817] The Constitution has instead perpetuated the situation created before independence where a vast number of people were dispossessed of their land and restricted to certain parts of the county, the so-called communal areas (reserves). By explicitly stating that,

[L]and, water and natural resources below and above the surface of the land and in the continental shelf and within the territorial waters and the exclusive economic zone of Namibia shall belong to the State if they are not otherwise lawfully owned,[818]

the Constitution has further dispossessed the majority of Namibians from ownership of land and has limited their capacity to participate in the national economy.[819] Most indigenous peoples in Namibia, like the San and the Khoesan, live on communal lands but only an infinite per centage of them have rights of occupancy in these communal areas.[820] A governmental resettlement programme for the San has not had the expected results on the ground.[821]

Although few African Constitutions make any reference to the rights of their indigenous communities, it deserves mentioning that a number of African States have taken steps that denote an emerging sensibility towards indigenous peoples. These steps are, for instance, the restitution of several tens of thousands of hectares of lands to the ‡Khomani San by the South African Government; the adoption of a law on indigenous peoples by the Government of the Republic of Congo; the organization by that same country of the first African Government hosted international seminar on indigenous peoples' rights entitled "International Forum for Indigenous People of Central Africa" and held in April 2007 in Brazzaville; the adoption by the Cameroonian Government of an Indigenous Peoples Development Plan and the elaboration of similar plans in Gabon and the Democratic Republic of Congo; the inclusion of a Batwa representative in a national land commission by the Burundian Government; the new Kenyan National Land

---

816   The Traditional Authorities Act (1995) provides, among other things for the official recognition of Chiefs and Traditional Authorities (Councillors).

817   Sidney L. Harring, "Indigenous Land Rights and Land Reform in Namibia" in *Indigenous Peoples' Rights in Southern Africa*, edited by Robert K. Hitchcock and Diana Vinding. IWGIA Document 110 (Copenhagen: IWGIA, 2004), p. 66.

818   Article 100 of the Constitution of Namibia.

819   Clement Daniels, "Indigenous Rights in Namibia" in *Indigenous Peoples' Rights in Southern Africa*, edited by Robert K. Hitchcock and Diana Vinding. IWGIA Document No. 110 (Copenhagen: IWGIA, 2004), p. 44.

820   Harring, "Indigenous Land Rights" (2004), pp. 64-68.

821   Daniels, "Indigenous Rights" (2004), p. 57.

Policy that addresses many issues related to indigenous peoples' land issues; and, not least, the recent ratification by the Central African Republic of ILO Convention No. 169.

This ratification was a major breakthrough and so far, no other African country has ratified ILO Convention No. 169 regardless of the many recommendations made by the international community and the efforts by national Civil Society and Human Rights organizations. With respect to the U.N. Declaration of Indigenous Peoples' Rights, the vast majority of African States ended by voting in favour, including countries such as Botswana that had been openly opposed to it at the beginning.[822] None voted against and only three—Burundi, Kenya and Nigeria—abstained.[823]

Conclusion

This chapter shows that a large number of countries, including a few African ones, provide either constitutional or legal protection to indigenous peoples' right to lands. In relation to Africa, it emerges also that a country can provide constitutional protection for its indigenous communities without using the term indigenous, as shown by the Burundian, South African and Ethiopian Constitutions. It also comes out of this chapter that a country might use the term indigenous in its constitution without any further legislative action, as seems to be the case of Cameroon. So, one should be careful about the mere use of the term indigenous in constitutions without attaching explicit rights to it. Similarly, countries with constitutions containing measures of positive discrimination on behalf of certain categories of their populations should be explicit on who are the holders of such rights in order to avoid confusion. These are remarks valid also for North and South America, Asia and South Pacific where there are often gaps between the legal provisions and the conditions of life of indigenous communities.

It is also noticeable that numerous African constitutions—if not all—refer to international human rights instruments as references and sources of standards. An example is the Preamble of the Constitution of the Republic of Congo that declares that

> *The fundamental principles proclaimed and guaranteed by the 1945 Charter of the United Nations, the 1948 Universal Declaration of Human Rights, the 1981 African Charter on the Human and Peoples' Rights and all duly ratified pertinent international texts ... are an integral part of the present Constitution.*

---

822 See Albert Kwoko Barume, "Responding to the Concerns of the African States" in *Making the Declaration Work*, edited by Claire Charters and Rodolfo Stavenhagen. IWGIA Document No. 127 (Copenhagen: IWGIA, 2009), p. 180.

823 Ibid.: "It should be noted, however, that 15 African countries were absent from the room."

This is an entry point that African judges, lawyers, civil society organizations and indigenous communities should eventually use to safeguard and protect the rights of indigenous peoples.

It emerges also from the chapter that there is indeed an increasingly widespread practice by States and numerous other international actors for recognising and accepting, in different ways, indigenous peoples' rights and in particular their right to lands. One way has been through constitutional amendments or, sometimes, the adoption of new constitutions that include—to varying extent—the notion of ethnic pluralism and indigenous peoples' specific rights, including their collective land rights. This practice is most visible in the Americas and Western Europe but examples can also be found in the Pacific region and Asia. However, this practice is yet to find its way in Africa, where few countries have constitutions that specifically recognize indigenous peoples, let alone their right to lands.

There are also countries such as South Africa, which have taken indirect actions to restore rights to communities, including indigenous communities who before had been unfairly denied these rights.

It seems, on the whole, that States and other international actors increasingly feel that the recognition of indigenous peoples' land rights responds to compelling values and principles of "humanity", fairness, and justice. This trend was recently confirmed by the adoption by a large number of States (144 out of 159), including African States, of the United Nations Declaration of the Rights of Indigenous Peoples.

It can therefore be argued that the protection of indigenous peoples' right to land can be considered an obligation deriving from duties vis-à-vis "the international community as a whole",[824] or, in other words, a "norm of customary international law".[825]

On this basis, the current Special Rapporteur James Anaya has argued that some aspects of indigenous land rights can be regarded as having been widely accepted as customary international law.[826] It is this book's opinion that such an argument could be used by African judges, lawyers and communities when dealing with indigenous land claims.

---

824 Alfred de Zayas, "The Right to One's Homeland, Ethnic Cleansing and the International Criminal Tribunal for the Former Yugoslavia", *Criminal Law Forum* 6 (2) (1995), pp. 257-314.

825 Ian Brownlie, *Principles of Public International Law* (Oxford: Oxford University Press, 1998), p. 5. On p. 7, this author points out that a norm of customary international law consists of an objective element and a subjective one. The objective component, which is understood as States' practice, consists of material acts, such as treaties, decisions of international and national courts, national legislation, diplomatic correspondences, opinions of national legal advisers, and practices of international organizations. Brownlie comments further that States' practice may even be revealed through policy statements, press releases and comments on drafts produced by international bodies. In addition to the objective component, an international custom must contain a subjective element known as *opinio juris*, which distinguishes a norm of customary law from a mere usage. It could be understood as a common and widely accepted belief among states that a given practice has become as binding as a conventional international obligation. The understanding is that they are compelling values and principles of 'humanity', fairness and justice.

826 Anaya, *Indigenous Peoples in International Law* (1996), pp. 50-56.

CHAPTER X
MAIN U.N. INSTRUMENTS AND MECHANISMS RELEVANT FOR INDIGENOUS LAND RIGHTS

This and the following chapter examine how indigenous peoples' rights to lands, territories and natural resources are protected by international law and what international and regional mechanisms indigenous peoples, including African indigenous peoples, can use when claiming these rights.

The present chapter looks at the United Nations system and how it has dealt with indigenous peoples' land rights.

The first section of the chapter focuses on the United Nations Declaration on the Rights of Indigenous Peoples (UNDRIP), whose adoption by the U.N. General Assembly in September 2007 constituted a milestone in the history of indigenous rights and must be considered as a major achievement for indigenous peoples, worldwide. This section also looks at some of the U.N. Declarations and U.N. conferences and summits that preceded UNDRIP but contributed to raising the general awareness of indigenous peoples and their rights. The section finally surveys some of the U.N. mechanisms specifically targeting indigenous peoples.

UNDRIP can indeed be seen as the culmination of a long process during which human rights in general but indigenous rights in particular—including their rights to lands, territories and resources—have been defined, recognized and enshrined in binding international legal instruments. The second section of this chapter looks at these international legal instruments, which include the most relevant U.N. Human Rights treaties—as, for instance, the International Covenant on Civil and Political Rights and the Convention on the Elimination of All Forms of Racial Discrimination—international instruments that have been ratified by almost every African country (for list of ratifications, see Appendix 2, Table 1). The section also deals with ILO Convention No. 169 Concerning Indigenous and Tribal Peoples in Independent Countries. Adopted in 1989, this Convention can be seen as one of the results of the momentum generated by the Martínez Cobo study and the indigenous movement in the 1970s, and it is of particular relevance for indigenous peoples since it is the only legally binding instrument that exclusively concerns itself with the rights of indigenous peoples. Although the convention has been ratified so far by a mere 22 countries,[827] including the Central African Republic—as yet, the only African country to do so—it is considered worldwide as a standard setting instrument and used as a reference whenever indigenous rights are being raised.

The United Nations Declaration on the Rights of Indigenous Peoples

The United Nations has worked consistently on the issue of indigenous peoples since 1971, when José Martínez Cobo was appointed by the U.N. Sub-Commission on Prevention of Discrimination and Protection of Minorities to carry out a study on "the problem of discrimination against indigenous populations".[828] This work by the United Nations culminated in 2007 with the adoption of the U.N. Declaration on the Rights of Indigenous Peoples (UNDRIP).[829] In other words, it took more than 20 years of intense work—first by the Working Group on Indigenous Population (see below), later by the Ad Hoc Working Group on the Draft Declaration—to draft a declaration and get it adopted, first by the Human Rights Council in 2006, later by the U.N. General Assembly in 2007.

Although a Declaration is not legally binding for the signatories, "the fact that the [UNDRIP] text is consistent with international law and its progressive development, and more importantly the purposes and principles of the U.N. Charter, ensures that it will play a dynamic and lasting role in the future of specific indigenous/state relations and international law generally".[830] It is therefore expected that it will become a standard setting document in the same way as ILO Convention No. 169.

The rights to lands, territories and resources have a prominent place throughout the Declaration. Its Preamble thus expresses concern for *"the dispossession"* of lands, territories and resources suffered by indigenous peoples, preventing them *"from exercising, in particular, their right to development in accordance with their own needs and interests."* Accordingly, it therefore recognizes the *"urgent need to respect and promote ... especially [indigenous peoples'] rights to their lands, territories and resources"*, and it is through the *"control by indigenous peoples over*

---

827 As per May 2010.
828 ECOSOC (United Nations Economic and Social Council) Resolution 1589(L), May 21 1971. Text available at http://www.un.org/ga/search/view_doc.asp?symbol=E/RES/1589(L). The Cobo study was released in 1986/7.
829 The Declaration was adopted in September 2007 by 144 votes in favour, 4 against (Canada, Australia, New Zealand, and the United States) and 11 abstentions (Azerbaijan, Bangladesh, Bhutan, Burundi, Colombia, Georgia, Kenya, Nigeria, Russian Federation, Samoa, Ukraine). U.N. Doc. A/RES/61/295. For full text, see http://www.un.org/esa/socdev/unpfii/en/declaration.html
830 Dalee Sambo Dorough, "Human Rights" in *State of the World's Indigenous Peoples*, edited by the UNPFII. (New York: United Nations, 2009), p. 198.

developments affecting them and their lands, territories and resources" that they will be able *"to maintain and strengthen their institutions, cultures and traditions, and to promote their development in accordance with their aspirations and needs."*[831]

Several UNDRIP articles address indigenous peoples' land-related concerns. Article 8.2(b) and (c) respectively deal with the prevention of and redress for dispossession of lands, territories or resources as well as the prevention of any form of forced population transfer. The issue of forced removals is reiterated in Article 10, which stipulates that

> *... No relocation shall take place without the need for free, prior and informed consent of the indigenous peoples concerned and after agreement on just and fair compensation and, where possible, with the option of return.*

Article 28.1 and 2 elaborates further on the right to redress and the modalities of a

> *... just, fair and equitable compensation, for the lands, territories and resources which they have traditionally owned or otherwise occupied or used, and which have been confiscated, taken, occupied, used or damaged without their free, prior and informed consent.*

Article 25 recognizes the special relationship that indigenous peoples have with their lands, and establishes their

> *... right to maintain and strengthen their distinctive spiritual relationship with their traditionally owned or otherwise occupied and used lands, territories, waters and coastal seas and other resources and to uphold their responsibilities to future generations in this regard.*

Article 26 confirms that this right to lands, territories and resources also includes *"their right to own, use, develop and control these lands, territories and resources"*, and urges States to *"give legal recognition and protection to these lands, territories and resources ... with due respect to the customs, traditions and land tenure systems of the indigenous peoples concerned"*. In this regard, Article 27 requires that

> *States shall establish and implement, in conjunction with indigenous peoples concerned, a fair, independent, impartial, open and transparent process, giving due recognition to indigenous peoples' laws, traditions, customs and land tenure systems, to recognize and adjudicate the rights of indigenous peoples pertaining to their lands, territories and resources, including those which were tradition-*

---

831 UNDRIP, Preamble.

ally owned or otherwise occupied or used. Indigenous peoples shall have the right to participate in this process.

Article 23 addresses indigenous peoples' right to determine their own priorities for development, and thus links lands, territories and resources with the ability to exercise human rights, including the human right to development. This right is further elaborated in Articles 29, 30 and 32 that deal respectively with indigenous peoples' right to conserve and protect the environment and productive capacity of their lands or territories and resources; their right to protect these lands and territories from military activities; and their right to determine and develop priorities and strategies for the development and use of their lands or territories and resources. Article 32 furthermore specifies that

States shall consult and cooperate in good faith with the indigenous peoples concerned through their own representative institutions in order to obtain their free and informed consent prior to the approval of any project affecting their lands or territories and other resources, particularly in connection with the development, utilization or exploitation of mineral, water or other resources.

From 29 June 2006—when the Draft Declaration[832] was adopted by the Human Rights Council with favorable votes from only three African countries, namely Cameroon, South Africa and Zambia—to its adoption by the U.N. General Assembly in September 2007, more than a year elapsed. This delay was due to concerns expressed by African States and Governments, which led to important negotiations. It should be noted that during these negotiations, African States agreed to accept the above articles on land rights in exchange of a specific provision on territorial integrity, which was inserted in Article 46.1. This article reads:

Nothing in this Declaration may be interpreted as implying for any State, people, group or person any right to engage in any activity or to perform any act contrary to the Charter of the United Nations or construed as authorizing or encouraging any action which would dismember or impair, totally or in part, the territorial integrity or political unity of sovereign and independent States.

This means that the vast majority of African States and Governments have committed themselves to recognize, protect, and promote indigenous peoples' rights to lands as long as these rights don't become a threat to territorial integrity. This deal and understanding should be kept alive and infused into domes-

---

832 For more details on the process and summary of the content of the Draft, see Web page of the U.N. Working Group on Indigenous Populations: http://www.unhchr.ch/html/racism/indileaflet5.doc

tic efforts by African States to implement the Declaration. It is therefore to be recommended that lawyers working on behalf of indigenous communities remind the judges of this context every time a land-related lawsuit involving indigenous communities is concerned. Furthermore, the Declaration will certainly strengthen the international conviction that indigenous peoples' land rights are part of international law.

Other U.N. declarations, conferences and summits

Prior to the adoption of the Declaration on the Rights of Indigenous Peoples, there had already been several U.N. declarations and conferences that were relevant for indigenous peoples and their land rights.

Among the most important declarations are the U.N. Declaration on the Rights of Persons belonging to National or Ethnic, Religious and Linguistic Minorities (1992),[833] which, in its Article 1, states that

1. *States shall protect the existence and the national or ethnic, cultural, religious and linguistic identity of minorities within their respective territories and shall encourage conditions for the promotion of that identity.*
2. *States shall adopt appropriate legislative and other measures to achieve those ends*

and the UNESCO Universal Declaration on Cultural Diversity (2001),[834] which, in its Article 4 on human rights as guarantees of cultural diversity, establishes that,

The defence of cultural diversity is an ethical imperative, inseparable from respect for human dignity. It implies a commitment to human rights and fundamental freedoms, in particular the rights of persons belonging to minorities and those of indigenous peoples. No one may invoke cultural diversity to infringe upon human rights guaranteed by international law, nor to limit their scope.

A number of U.N. conferences and summits have likewise dealt with indigenous issues, including land rights. To name a few examples: it was following the United Nations Conference on Environment and Development, held in Rio de Janeiro in June 1992, that the Convention on Biological Diversity (CBD) was adopted, providing, among other provisions, for the rights of indigenous communities (see section on CBD in this chapter). But this Conference also adopted the Rio Declaration and Agenda 21. These two instruments establish international legal standards that recognize indigenous peoples' unique relationship to their lands

833 U.N. Doc. A/47/135 at http://www2.ohchr.org/english/law/minorities.htm
834 See http://www2.ohchr.org/english/law/diversity

and go towards protecting their rights to their traditional knowledge and practices in the area of environmental management and conservation.[835]

In 1993, the Vienna World Conference on Human Rights adopted, amongst other recommendations, that the "General Assembly proclaim an international decade of the world's indigenous people, to begin from January 1994, including action-orientated programmes, to be decided upon in partnership with indigenous people". Recommendation 32 further stated, "In the framework of such a decade, the establishment of a permanent forum for indigenous people in the United Nations system should be considered".[836]

Two years later, the World Summit for Social Development (Copenhagen, 1995) in its para. 32 recognized traditional rights to land and other resources and indigenous traditional knowledge systems.[837]

The issue of indigenous peoples was also given attention and consideration at the 2001 Durban (South Africa) United Nations World Conference against Racism, Racial Discrimination, Xenophobia and Related Intolerance. This Conference's final Declaration recognized

> [T]he invaluable contributions of indigenous peoples to political, economic, social, cultural and spiritual development throughout the world to our societies, as well as the challenges faced by them, including racism and racial discrimination.

One of its recommendations was therefore that "indigenous peoples [should be consulted] on any matter that may affect their physical, spiritual or cultural integrity."[838]

That same year, the World Summit on Sustainable Development (Johannesburg, 2001) identified indigenous communities as one of the groups that deserve particular attention by States.[839] This Summit adopted the Johannesburg Plan of Action, which, in a number of paragraphs, refers to indigenous rights regarding access to land and resources as well as to their traditional knowledge. Article 7(h), for instance, states that the eradication of poverty includes actions that will "provide access to agricultural resources for people living in poverty, especially women and indigenous communities, and promote, as appropriate, land tenure

---

835 Of particular relevance is Section 3, Chapter 26 of Agenda 21 "Recognizing and strengthening the role of indigenous people and their communities". The full text is available online at http://www.un.org/esa/sustdev/documents/agenda21/english.

836 The full text of recommendations is available online at http://www.unhchr.ch/hridocda/huridoca.nsf/(Symbol)/A.CONF.157.23.En

837 For further information, see Web site of the World Summit for Social Development at http://www.un.org/esa/socdev/wssd

838 World Conference against Racism, Racial Discrimination, Xenophobia and Related Intolerance, Final Declaration, available online at http://www.unhchr.ch/pdf/Durban.pdf

839 For further information, see Web site of the World Summit on Sustainable Development at http://www.johannesburgsummit.org/)

arrangements that recognize and protect indigenous and common property resource management systems".[840]

U.N. mechanisms targeting indigenous peoples

The Martínez Cobo Report was submitted during the years 1981-1984[841] and created, together with the advocacy of the indigenous movement, a momentum that led to the establishment of the first U.N. mechanism targeting indigenous peoples, namely the U.N. Working Group on Indigenous Populations (WGIP) in 1982. More were to follow.

The U.N. Working Group (WGIP)

This Working Group was created by the U.N. Economic and Social Council (ECO-SOC) in 1982[842] with a two-fold mandate: to review developments pertaining to the promotion and protection of human rights and fundamental freedoms of indigenous peoples and to give attention to the evolution of international standards concerning indigenous rights. One of the WGIP's main achievements was to start the drafting of the U.N. Declaration on the Rights of Indigenous Peoples. It also commissioned and published a number of important standard-setting studies on crucial issues such as indigenous peoples' relationships to land, agreements between States and indigenous populations, etc. As an international platform, it served indigenous communities, encouraged organisations from different parts of the world to share their experiences, and most importantly to advocate their case together. Each year, its annual session would gather almost 1,000 indigenous representatives from around the world. The WGIP was abolished in 2006 when the new Human Rights Council was established in replacement of the Commission of Human Rights.

The two International Decades of the World's Indigenous Peoples

The international Decades have brought focus on indigenous peoples. The First Decade (1994-2004) was proclaimed by the U.N. General Assembly on 21 December 1993. At the same time, the General Assembly instructed the Commission on Human Rights to work for the establishment of a permanent forum.

---

840 For full text of Johannesburg Plan of Action, see:
     http://www.un.org/esa/sustdev/documents/docs_key_conferences.htm
841 The Martínez Cobo study can be accessed at http://www.un.org/esa/socdev/unpfii/
842 See ECOSOC Resolution 1982/34 of May 1982.

The first Decade achieved a number of important advances, the two major ones being the establishment of the U.N. Permanent Forum on Indigenous Issues in 2000 and the appointment, in 2001, of a Special Rapporteur on the situation of human rights and fundamental freedoms of indigenous people by the Commission on Human Rights. [843]

The Second Decade was adopted by the General Assembly's Resolution 59/174 (2005-2014). One of its five main objectives is to "promot[e] full and effective participation of indigenous peoples in decisions which directly or indirectly affect their lifestyles, traditional lands and territories, their cultural integrity as indigenous peoples with collective rights or any other aspect of their lives, considering the principle of free, prior and informed consent."[844]

The Permanent Forum on Indigenous Issues

The UNPFII was established in 2000 by the Economic and Social Council (ECOSOC)[845] as an advisory body to the Council. It has had its own Secretariat since 2003.

The Forum has a broad mandate, namely to discuss economic and social development, culture, the environment, education, health and human rights, and to advise the Economic and Social Council and the U.N. system on all matters pertaining to its mandate; promote the coordination and integration of indigenous issues in the U.N. system; raise awareness about indigenous issues; and produce material to inform about indigenous issues. It consists of 16 members acting in an individual capacity as independent experts on indigenous issues. Eight of these members are nominated by Governments and eight by the President of ECOSOC on the basis of a broad worldwide consultation with indigenous groups. This parity composition makes it a unique body: for the first time in their history, indigenous peoples are on an equal footing with members nominated by the States in a permanent U.N. body.

The Forum convenes once a year in New York and gathers a large number of indigenous representatives, who have the status of observers and therefore the right to make verbal interventions in order to express their views and

---

843 Other achievements of the First Decade are: the celebration of an annual day for indigenous peoples (U.N. General Assembly Resolution 49/214 of 23 December 1994, para. 8); the establishment of a fellowship programme within the office of the High Commissioner for Human Rights (U.N. General Assembly Resolution 50/157 of 21 December 1995); and the creation of a voluntary fund for indigenous peoples to fund indigenous peoples' participation in U.N. meetings and provide indigenous peoples with support for small projects. See Web site of the United Nations High Commission on Human Rights: http://www.unhchr.ch/html/menu6/2/fs9.htm

844 See UNPFII Web page at http://www.un.org/esa/socdev/unpfii for more details on the Second Decade.

845 ECOSOC Resolution 2000/22 of July 2000. Document available at http://www.un.org/esa/documents/ecosocmainres.htm

recommendations on the different issues included in the working agenda. Each session has a special theme, and in May 2007, at its sixth session, the special theme was "Territories, Lands and Natural Resources". The final report of this session indicates that "the protection of their right to lands, territories and natural resources is a key demand of the international indigenous peoples' movement and of indigenous peoples and organizations everywhere."[846]

An Inter-Agency Support Group (IASG) has been established with the mandate to support and promote the mandate of the Forum within the United Nations system. It is composed of 31 U.N. agencies such as UNDP, WHO, the World Bank and ILO.[847]

The Special Rapporteur on the situation of the human rights and fundamental freedoms of indigenous peoples

This mechanism was established in 2001 with the mandate to present annual reports on particular topics or situations of special importance regarding the promotion and protection of the rights of indigenous peoples; to undertake country visits; to exchange information with Governments concerning alleged violations of the rights of indigenous peoples; and to undertake activities to follow-up on the recommendations included in his reports. The first Special Rapporteur (Rodolfo Stavenhagen 2001-2008) attended a session of the African Commission on Human and Peoples' Rights and visited numerous countries including South Africa (2005) and Kenya (2006).[848] He also published important reports that, among other topics, deal with land rights.[849] A new Special Rapporteur (S. James Anaya) was appointed by the Human Rights Council in March 2008. His mandate is to investigate human rights violations against indigenous peoples on the basis of, among other things, complaints received from indigenous organizations or individuals and provide recommendations to the U.N. Human Rights Council and Governments around the world to improve their situations.

---

846 United Nations Permanent Forum on Indigenous Peoples Issues, Report of the Sixth Session (14-25 May 2007), U.N. Doc. E/2007/43, E/C.19/2007/12. Available online at the Web site of UN-PFII, http://www.un.org/esa/socdev/unpfii

847 Further members of this Agency can be found on the following Web site: http://www.un.org/esa/socdev/unpfii/en/iasg.html

848 The Rapporteur's Country Visit Reports can be accessed at http://www2.ohchr.org/english/issues/indigenous/rapporteur/visits.htm

849 See, e.g., Rodolfo Stavenhagen, Report of the Special Rapporteur on the situation of human rights and fundamental freedoms of indigenous people submitted in accordance with Commission resolution 2001/65, Fifty ninth Session, Item 15 of the provisional agenda (human rights and indigenous issues). U.N. Doc. E/CN.4/2003/90, 21 January 2003. (2003a) Available online at http://www.iwgia.org/sw7652.asp

The Expert Mechanism on the Rights of Indigenous Peoples

The Expert mechanism was established in 2007 as the result of the adoption, by consensus, by the Human Rights Council, of Resolution 6/36. Its mandate is to assist the Human Rights Council in the implementation of its mandate by providing thematic expertise and making proposals to the Council pertaining to the rights of indigenous peoples. The mechanism consists of five independent experts and the resolution 6/36 clearly recommends that the Council, in its selection and appointment process, gives due regard to experts of indigenous origin. The annual meeting of the Expert Mechanism is open to the participation—as observers—of States, United Nations mechanisms, U.N. bodies and specialized agencies as well as to indigenous peoples' organizations, non-governmental organizations, national human rights institutions, academics, etc. At its second session in August 2009, a "Study on lessons learned and challenges to achieve the implementation of the right of indigenous peoples to education" was presented and adopted.

U.N. Human Rights Treaties

Two Human Rights Treaties are particularly relevant: the International Covenant on Civil and Political Rights (ICCPR) and the International Convention on the Elimination of All Forms of Racial Discrimination (ICERD).

ICCPR and indigenous peoples' right to lands

This Covenant (1966) is considered as the main universal international instrument that protects the rights of indigenous peoples, and its Articles 1 and 27 as the two major provisions protecting indigenous peoples' right to lands.

Article 1 on self-determination

This article stipulates that

1. *All peoples have the right of self-determination. By virtue of that right they freely determine their political status and freely pursue their economic, social and cultural development.*
2. *All peoples may, for their own ends, freely dispose of their natural wealth and resources without prejudice to any obligations arising out of international eco-*

nomic co-operation, based upon the principle of mutual benefit, and interna-
tional law. In no case may a people be deprived of its own means of subsistence.

3. *The States Parties to the present Covenant, including those having responsibility*
    for the administration of Non-Self-Governing and Trust Territories, shall pro-
    mote the realization of the right of self-determination, and shall respect that right,
    in conformity with the provisions of the Charter of the United Nations.

The question is whether indigenous peoples' right to lands can be considered as included within the scope of the right to self-determination?

The right to self-determination is recognized by almost all international human rights instruments, including the Charter of the United Nations,[850] the two Covenants[851] and the African Charter.[852] However, none of these instruments elaborate on the meaning of this right. This question did preoccupy the drafters of the ICCPR, but no final decision was taken.[853] Nor has the Human Rights Committee—a body made of independent experts mandated to oversee the implementation of the ICCPR by States Parties—expanded on the scope of the right to self-determination.[854] One human rights researcher even argues that the Committee "has demonstrated an unwillingness to consider allegations of denial of the right to self-determination because [they consider the] area [as] politically charged".[855]

An example of this is the conclusion reached by the Human Rights Committee (HRC) on the communication submitted by the Chief of the Lubicon Lake Band against the Canadian Government. The Canadian Government had granted leases to private companies for exploitation of oil, gas, and other resources, on the lands of the Lubicon Cree of Alberta Province, Canada. As a result of the com-

---

850 Article 1, paragraph 2 of the U.N. Charter states that the United Nations aims *"to develop friendly relations among nations based on respect for the principle of equal rights and self-determination of peoples".*

851 Article 1 of the two Covenants—the ICCPR and the International Covenant on Economic and Social Rights (ICESR)— are identical.

852 The African Charter, chapter 1, Article 20. 1, states that, *"All peoples shall have the right to existence. They shall have the unquestionable and inalienable right to self-determination. They shall freely determine their political status and shall pursue their economic and social development according to the policy they have freely chosen."* The Charter can be downloaded at http://www.hrcr.org/docs/Banjul/afrhr. html. See also in Thornberry, *International Law* (1991), p. 21.

853 Marc J. Bossuyt, *Guide to the "Travaux Préparatoires" of the International Covenant on Civil and Political Rights* (Dordrecht and Boston: Martinus Nijhoff Publishers, 1987), p. 32. A number of delegates to the drafting sessions of the ICCPR proposed unsuccessfully that the right to self-determination be given a precise content and that it includes "the right of every person to participate, with all the members of a group inhabiting a compact territory, to which he belongs ethnically, culturally, historically or otherwise, in free exercise of the right to secede and to establish a politically and economically independent State, and the right to choose the form of this government".

854 All documents issued by the Human Rights Committee can be accessed at the UNHCHR Treaty Body database at http://www.unhchr.ch/tbs/doc.nsf/Documentsfrset?OpenFrameSet

855 Mary Ellen Turpel, "Indigenous People's Rights of Political Participation and Self-Determination: Recent International Legal Development and the Continuing Struggle for Recognition, *Cornell International Law Journal* 579 (1992), p. 585.

mercial exploitations carried out on their lands, the Lubicon Cree's way of life and health were adversely affected. In 1984, Chief Bernard Ominayak, claiming to represent all members of his tribe, accused the Canadian Government of violating its international obligations under the provisions of Articles 1 and 27 of the ICCPR.[856] Regarding Article 1, however, the Committee avoided addressing the self-determination claim by stating in May 1990 that,

> [T]he Covenant recognizes and protects in most resolute terms a people's right of self-determination and its right to dispose of its natural resources, as an essential condition for the effective guarantee and observance of individual human rights and for the promotion and strengthening of those rights. However, the Committee observed that the author, as an individual, could not claim under the Optional Protocol to be a victim of a violation of the right of self-determination enshrined in article I of the Covenant, which deals with rights conferred upon peoples, as such.[857]

Nevertheless, in its General Comment 12 of 1984 on "the right to self-determination of peoples" in Article 1 of the ICCPR,[858] the HRC gives a strong hint that the right to self-determination could be exercised and enjoyed without upsetting the territorial integrity of States: "With regard to paragraph 1 of Article 1, States Parties should describe the constitutional and political process which in practice allow the exercise of this right".[859] The Committee continues by stating: "Paragraph 2 [of Article 1] affirms a particular aspect of the economic content of the right of self-determination, namely the right of peoples, for their own ends, freely 'to dispose of their natural wealth and resources … In no case may a people be deprived of its own means of subsistence.'"[860]

Commenting in 1999 on a State Party report by Canada, the HRC recognized that indigenous peoples could enjoy the right to self-determination within a state:

> The right to self-determination requires, inter alia, that all peoples must be able to freely dispose of their natural wealth and resources and that they may not be deprived of their own means of subsistence. The Committee also recommended that the practice of extinguishing inherent ab-

---

856 U.N. Human Rights Committee, Communication No. 167/1984 *The Lubicon Lake Band v. Canada*, (1990).
857 Ibid.
858 U.N. Human Rights Committee, General Comments 12, Article 1 (Twenty-first session, 1984). Reprinted in Compilation of General Comments and General Recommendations Adopted by Human Rights Treaty Bodies, U.N. Doc. HRI/GEN/1/Rev. 1 at 134 (2003). Available online at http://hrlibrary.ngo.ru/gencomm/hrcomms.
859 Ibid., para. 4.
860 Ibid., para. 5.

original rights should be abandoned because it is incompatible with article 1 of the Covenant.[861]

While the HRC has not been very active in relation to the right to self-determination, other U.N. bodies and human rights experts have, in contrast, addressed this right. In his 1981 Study on the Right to Self-Determination,[862] Aureliu Cristescu, the United Nations Special Rapporteur of the Sub-Commission on Prevention of Discrimination and Protection of Minorities, elaborates on the content of this right. He indicates, amongst other issues, that "peoples", "nations", and "States" are all holders of the right to self-determination. Further, he argues that the right to self-determination should not only be understood as meant to deal with colonialism; but also as a legal means to ensure permanent sovereignty of peoples over their natural wealth and resources.[863] This is based on the understanding that "the term 'peoples' applies not only to States but also to other entities".[864]

In this same vein, several expert opinions have identified a distinction between "internal self-determination" and "external self-determination". The former is understood as including rights, such as the right to autonomy and self-governance,[865] whereas the latter is considered as referring to the claim for statehood. However, this distinction is not reflected in any universal international human rights instrument.[866] It is seen as an invention of political thinking,[867] and as not being part of the traditional legal literature on self-determination.[868] Principle VIII of the Helsinki Final Act (1975) also enunciates that

---

861 U.N. Human Rights Committee, Concluding Observations, Canada. U.N. Doc./CCPR/C/79/
      Add.105. (1999), para. 8. Available online at
      http://hrlibrary.ngo.ru/hrcommittee/canada1999.html
862 Aureliu Cristescu, "The Right to Self-Determination: Historical and Current Development on the
      Basis of the United Nations Instruments". Study prepared by the Special Rapporteur of the Sub-
      Commission on Prevention of Discrimination and Protection of Minorities. U.N. Doc. E/CN.4/
      Sub.2/404/Rev.1 (1981). This Study was requested by the Commission on Human Rights to the
      Sub-Commission through resolution 10 (XXIX) of 22 March 1973. The formulation of the man-
      date was to study "the historical and current development of the right to self-determination on
      the basis of the Charter of the United Nations and the other instruments adopted by United Na-
      tions organs, with particular reference to the promotion and protection of human rights and
      fundamental freedoms". See also U.N. Doc. E/CN.4/Sub.2/404/Rev.1, p. 1.
863 Cristescu, "The Right to Self-Determination" (1981), pp. 43-45.
864 Ibid., pp. 38-9.
865 See Allan Rosas, "Internal Self-Determination", in *Modern Law of Self-Determination*, edited by
      Christian Tomuschat, (Dordrecht: Martinus Nijhoff Publishers, 1993), p. 239. See also Antonio
      Cassese, *Self-Determination of Peoples: A Legal Reappraisal* (Cambridge, UK.: Cambridge Univer-
      sity Press, 1995), p. 101.
866 Cassese, *Self-Determination* (1995), p. 103.
867 Gudmundur Alfredsson, "Self-Determination and Indigenous Peoples", in *Modern Law of Self-De-
      termination*, edited by Christian Tomuschat, (Dordrecht: Martinus Nijhoff Publishers, 1993), p. 50.
868 Ibid., pp.53-54. Alfredsson, for instance "believes that we should call the right offered by their
      correct names and not try to advocate their image by doubtful labelling". See also Douglas Sand-

[B]y virtue of the principle of equal rights and self-determination of peoples, all peoples always have the right, in full freedom, to determine, when and as they wish, their internal and external political status, without external interference, and to pursue, as they wish, their political, economic, social, and cultural development.[869]

The right to self-determination has been linked to the right of indigenous peoples over their natural resources. Judge Weeramantry, in his dissenting opinion in the East Timor case before the International Court of Justice,[870] thus argued that the East Timorese people had the right *"to determine how their wealth and natural resources should be disposed ... [and that] any action which may in fact deprive them of this right must thus fall clearly within the category of acts which infringe on their right to self-determination".*[871]

The view that the right of indigenous peoples over their natural resources, including lands, constitutes an integral part of their right to self-determination is indeed corroborated by many authors.[872] It is argued that the right to self-determination could be satisfied "also through unitarism, multipartism, confederation, federalism or other relations that conform to the wishes of the

---

ers, "Self-Determination and Indigenous Peoples", in *Modern Law of Self-Determination,* edited by Christian Tomuschat, (Dordrecht: Martinus Nijhoff Publishers, 1993), p. 80.

869 The Helsinki Final Act closed the Conference on Security and Co-operation in Europe (CSCE) held in Helsinki, Finland July-August 1975. Principle VIII is one of the ten principles enumerated in the Act's "Declaration on Principles Guiding Relations between Participating States. The Final Act is available online at http://www.hri.org/docs/Helsinki75.html. See also in Lâm, *At the Edge of the State,* (2000), p. 130.

870 International Court of Justice, Case Concerning East Timor *(Portugal v. Australia)* Judgment June 1995. Available on line at
http://www.icj-cij.org/docket/index.php?sum=430&code=pa&p1=3&p2=3&case=84&k=66&p3=5

871 The United Nations did not recognize Indonesia's invasion of the former Portuguese colony, East Timor, in 1978. Instead, it continued recognizing Portugal as the administrating power although Portugal was *de facto* prevented from exercising its responsibilities as such. In 1989, Australia signed the Timor Gap Treaty with Indonesia regarding the joint exploration of petroleum resources within East Timor's seabed. As a result, Portugal brought Australia before the International Court of Justice, claiming that "Australia has failed to respect the rights of Portugal as the administrating Power ... and the right of the people of East Timor to self-determination and related rights" and that the Timor Gap Treaty was in violation of a *jus cogens* obligation. While stressing the importance of self-determination as *"one of the essential principles of contemporary international law"*, the I.C.J. dismissed the possibility of exercising its jurisdiction since it *"would necessarily have to rule upon the lawfulness of the conduct of a State [i.e., Indonesia, which is not a party to the case], as a prerequisite for deciding on Portugal's contention that Australia violated its obligation to respect Portugal's status as administering Power, East Timor's status as a non-self governing territory and the right of the people of the Territory to self-determination and to permanent sovereignty over its wealth and natural resources"*.

872 Cassese, *Self-Determination* (1995), pp. 188-9. See also Yoram Dinstein, "Collective Human Rights of Peoples and Minorities", 25 *International and Comparative Law Quarterly* 25, 102 (1976), p. 110. This author argues that the right over natural resources is simply a right closer to the right to self-determination.

peoples".[873] On the same note, the U.N. Declaration on the Rights of Indigenous Peoples (UNDRIP) indicates that, by the virtue of their right to self-determination, indigenous peoples *"freely determine their political status and freely
pursue their economic, social and cultural development"* (Article 3); indigenous
peoples, in exercising the right of self-determination, furthermore have *"the
right to autonomy or self-government in matters relating to their internal and local
affairs, as well as ways and means for financing their autonomous functions"* (Article 4). However, UNDRIP Articles 3 and 4 should be read in conjunction with
Article 46, which, as already mentioned, was amended at the request of the
African States and Governments, which feared that the right to self-determination could negatively impact on their territorial integrity.

These various interpretations of the right to self-determination may be
useful to the Human Rights Committee (HRC) when they address this issue.
However, it is important to recognize that the provisions of ICCPR Article 1
have not been a frequent fertile ground for the indigenous peoples' legal battle, because States remain resistant to consider indigenous communities as
"peoples".

Nevertheless, slow changes may be taking place, as evidenced in 2000 by
the HRC's decision in *Apirana Mahuika et al. v. New Zealand*, where 19 Maori
individuals, claiming to represent several Maori tribes, alleged, amongst other things, violations of ICCPR Articles 1 and 27 by New Zealand.

The plaintiffs had traditional fishing rights that were protected by the 1840
Waitangi Treaty, and later by the 1983 Fisheries Act. In 1986, a system of fishing
quota and control over Maori commercial fishing was introduced by the New
Zealand Government, prompting a number of Maori to file a court case on violation of their fishing rights, as protected by the 1983 Act. Following a number
of events, a group of Maori and the Government of New Zealand reached an
agreement, which resulted in the 1992 Treaty of Waitangi (Fisheries Claims) Settlement Act. According to this Act, the New Zealand Government would provide Maori with the financial help they needed to buy a fishing company and,
in return, the Maori would renounce all present and future fishing claims.

The authors of the Communication before the HRC alleged that this Settlement Act violated, amongst other things, their rights to self-determination and to
enjoy their culture. The HRC declared itself unable to address claims relating to
self-determination under the procedure of individual communication. However,
in an unprecedented line of argument, the Committee, in paragraph 3 of its Communication, importantly recognized that the authors' claims relating to *"issues
under Articles 14(1) and 27 [should be examined] in conjunction with Article 1"*. It

---

873 U.O. Umozurike, *The African Charter on Human and Peoples' Rights* (The Hague: Martinus Nijhoff
     Publishers, 1997), p. 53. See also Martin Scheinin, "Indigenous Peoples' Rights under the Inter-
     national Covenant on Civil and Political Rights", in *International Law and Indigenous Peoples*, ed-
     ited by Joshua Castellino and Niamh Walsh (Boston: Martinus Nijhoff Publishers, 2005), p. 9.

"noted that only the consideration of the merits of the case would enable the Committee to determine the relevance of Article 1 to the authors' claims under Article 27" and added (in paragraph 9.2) that *"The provisions of Article 1 may be relevant in the interpretation of other rights protected by the Covenant, in particular Article 27".*[874]

Article 27 on cultural rights

This article states that,

In those States in which ethnic, religious or linguistic minorities exist, persons belonging to such minorities shall not be denied the right, in community with the other members of their group, to enjoy their own culture, to profess and practise their own religion, or to use their own language.

Article 27 of the ICCPR is today seen as the most prominent protection provided by international law to land rights of indigenous peoples. This derives from a direct link established between indigenous peoples' right to lands and their cultures. In general terms, "culture" is understood as "an evolving achievement of artistic and scientific creation" of a society,[875] a "way of life", or better, a "cluster of social and economic activity, which gives a community its sense of identity".[876] A culture is understood as a "complex whole, which includes knowledge, beliefs, art, law, custom and other capabilities, and habits acquired by man as a member of society".[877]

The right to culture is one of the most debated rights in international law, in part because of the constant evolution of its scope.[878] The right to culture is

---

874 U.N. Human Rights Committee, Communication No 547/1993: *Apirana Mahuika et al. v. New Zealand.* Seventieth session (2000). U.N. Doc. CCPR/C/70/D/547/1993 (2000). Available online at http://hrlibrary.ngo.ru/undocs/session70-index.html. Para. 3 reads: *"When declaring the authors' remaining claims admissible in so far as they might raise issues under articles 14(1) and 27 in conjunction with article 1, the Committee noted that only the consideration of the merits of the case would enable the Committee to determine the relevance of article 1 to the authors' claims under article 27."* Para. 9.2 reads: *"The Committee observes that the Optional Protocol provides a procedure under which individuals can claim that their individual rights have been violated. These rights are set out in Part III of the Covenant, articles 6 to 27, inclusive. As shown by the Committee's jurisprudence, there is no objection to a group of individuals, who claim to be commonly affected, to submit a communication about alleged breaches of these rights. Furthermore, the provisions of article 1 may be relevant in the interpretation of other rights protected by the Covenant, in particular article 27."*
875 Asbjørn Eide, "Economic, Social and Cultural Rights as Human Rights", in *Economic, Social and Cultural Rights: A Textbook,* edited by A. Eide, Catarina Krause and Allan Rosas (London: Martinus Nijhoff Publishers, 1995), p. 231.
876 Rodley, "Conceptual Problems" (1995), p. 59.
877 Thornberry, *International Law* (1991), p. 188.
878 Janusz Symonides, "Cultural Rights: A Neglected Category of Rights", *International Social Science Journal,* Vol. 50, 1998, p. 560. John Packer, "On the Content of Minority Rights", in *Do We Need Minority Rights?* edited by J.Räikkä (Netherlands: Kluwer Law International, 1996), pp. 130-141.

recognized in terms similar to those of the ICCPR by several other instruments and texts,[879] including the Limburg Principles[880] and the Maastricht Guidelines.[881] Most of these instruments, however, do not, unfortunately, elaborate on its scope.[882]

---

879 See, for instance, Article 15 of the Universal Declaration of Human Rights: "*Everyone has the right to freely participate in the cultural life of the community, to enjoy the art and to share in scientific advancement and its benefits ... Everyone has the right to the protection of the ... material interests resulting from any scientific literacy or artistic products of which he is the author*"; Article 15 of the Covenant on Economic, Social and Cultural Rights: "*The States Parties ... recognize the right of everyone: a) to take part in cultural life, b) to enjoy the benefits of scientific progress and its applications, c) to benefit from the protection of the moral and material interests resulting from any scientific, literary or artistic production of which he is the author*"; Article 15 of the European Framework Convention for the Protection of National Minorities (1995): "*The Parties shall create the conditions necessary for the effective participation of persons belonging to national minorities in cultural, social and economic life and in public affairs, in particular those affecting them*". See also this Convention's Article 5 (1) on the promotion of "*the conditions necessary for persons belonging to national minorities to maintain and develop their culture*" and Articles 5(2) and 6(1) that prohibit any policy of assimilation. This Convention is seen as having been adopted in order to address the absence of a specific minorities-disposition in the European Human Rights Convention. See Council of Europe document H (95) 10, available online at http://conventions.coe.int/Treaty/Commun/ListeTraites.asp?CM=8&CL=ENG; and Gilbert, "Minority Rights in Europe" (1992), p. 94. See also the African Charter's Article 22: "*All peoples shall have the right to their economic, social, and cultural development with due regard to their freedom and identity*"; Article 17: on the right of "*every individual [to] freely take part in the cultural life of his community ... [and more specifically on] the promotion and protection of morals and traditional values recognized by the community*"; Article 16 of the American Convention on Human Rights, 1969 (at http://www.oas.org/juridico/English/treaties/b-32.html): "*Everyone has the right to associate freely for ... cultural ... and other purposes*"; and Article 1 of the UNESCO Declaration of the Principles of International Cultural Cooperation, November 4, 1966 (see http://portal.unesco.org/en/ev.php-URL_ID=13147&URL_DO=DO_PRINTPAGE&URL_SECTION=201.html).

880 The Limburg Principles were adopted by ECOSOC in 1986 and aim to provide parties to the Covenant on Economic, Social and Cultural Rights, with guidelines for their implementation. See in U.N. Doc. E/CN 4/1987/17. Appendix 1. Text available at http://www.acpp.org/RBAVer1_0/archives/Limburg%20Principles.pdf. See also in *Human Rights Quarterly* 9 (1987), pp. 122-135.

881 The Maastricht Guidelines (1997) are nothing more than an updated version of the Limburg Principles. They were adopted in the spirit of being used by those "who are concerned with understanding and determining violations of economic, social and cultural rights and in providing remedies thereto, in particular monitoring and adjudicating bodies at the national, regional, and international levels". See Urban Morgan Institute for Human Rights et al., "The Maastricht Guidelines on Violations of Economic, Social, and Cultural Rights", *Human Rights Quarterly* 20, no. 3 (1998), pp. 691-704.

882 However, several scholars have attempted to delineate the right to culture. Eide, for instance, considers the right to culture as including: (a) a right to participate in community life, (b) a right to enjoy art, (c) a right to share advantages and benefits of scientific advancement, (d) a right to the moral and material protection of interest resulting from scientific, literary or artistic products, (e) a right to use one's own language, (f) and a right to profess and practice one's own religion (Eide, "Economic, Social and Cultural Rights" (1995), p. 232); Göran Melander argues that the right to education, the right to information and the right to freedom of expression can also be considered as related to culture ("Article 27", in *Universal Declaration of Human Rights: A Commentary*, edited by A. Eide et al. (Norway: Scandinavian University Press, 1993), p. 430); while Symonides in "Cultural Rights" (1998), p. 560, argues that "the right to education is generally considered to be a cultural right".

General Comment 23 on Article 27 of the ICCPR by the Human Rights Committee explicitly links indigenous peoples' right to lands and their right to culture. It states in para. 7:

> With regard to the exercise of the cultural rights protected under article 27, the Committee observes that culture manifests itself in many forms, including a particular way of life associated with the use of land resources, especially in the case of indigenous peoples. That right may include such traditional activities as fishing or hunting and the right to live in reserves protected by law. The enjoyment of those rights may require positive legal measures of protection and measures to ensure the effective participation of members of minority communities in decisions which affect them.[883]

If it is beyond controversy that the right of indigenous peoples to their lands is an integral part of the scope of Article 27 of the ICCPR, what does this mean conceptually in terms of States' international obligations?

In relation to the Maastricht guidelines, it has been noted that, "like civil and political rights, economic, social, and cultural rights impose three different types of obligations on States: the obligation to respect, protect and fulfil".[884] The international obligation of "respect" requires States to refrain from interfering with the right to enjoy rights,[885] in other words, to provide a kind of *"laissez vivre"*.[886] The obligation of "protection" binds States to prevent violations of rights by a third party.[887] This can be considered to be a horizontal responsibility, which requires States to act against "threats posed by all sources, whether governmental or private".[888]

The fact that indigenous peoples should attain a *"laissez-vivre"* and be protected against third party's actions was upheld in the decision of the Human Rights Committee in the aforementioned *Lubicon Lake Band* case and the *Länsman* case, against Canada and Finland respectively.

Regarding the *Lubicon Lake Band* case, one of the allegations was that the Canadian Government by granting leases to private extraction corporations violated among others the Lubicon Cree's right to dispose of natural wealth and resources and the right to enjoy a culture. In 1990, the HRC concluded, in what has been described as an "expansive decision",[889] that the commercial exploitation of

---

883 U.N. Human Rights Committee, General Comment 23 (1994a). See also Raoul Wallenberg Institute, *Human Rights Committee* (2006), p. 72.
884 Urban Morgan Institute for Human Rights et al., "Maastricht Guidelines" (1998), p. 693.
885 Ibid., pp. 696-7.
886 Packer, "On the Content of Minority Rights" (1996), p. 154.
887 Urban Morgan Institute for Human Rights et al., "Maastricht Guidelines" (1998), pp. 696-7.
888 Packer, "On the Content of Minority Rights" (1996), p. 155.
889 Benedict Kingsbury, "Claims by Non-States Groups in International Law", *Cornell International Law Journal*, vol. 25 (1992), p. 490.

natural resources that was taking place on Lubicon Cree lands, threatened the "way of life and culture" of this community and amounted to a "violation of Article 27 [by Canada] so long as they [continued]".[890]

In *Länsman et al. v. Finland*, a group of Saami alleged that Finland violated the provisions of Article 27 by granting a private company authorisation to extract stones from Mt. Riutusvaara, which the Saami consider as sacred land and important for their traditional reindeer herding. Even if the Human Rights Committee found that there was no violation of Article 27, it did emphasize the plaintiffs' cultural ties with Mt. Riutusvaara.[891]

Finally, regarding the third obligation to "be fulfilled", States Parties are required to take appropriate legislative, administrative, budgetary, judicial and other measures towards the full realisation of rights.[892] As noted by Nowak,[893] this obligation implies that States put in place institutions and procedural safeguards "aimed at protecting specific rights". This obligation was elaborated upon by the HRC in its conclusions in *Kitok v. Sweden*.[894]

According to the Swedish 1971 Reindeer Husbandry Act, a Saami who leaves his community or has not been involved in the community's activities for more than three years, could lose his or her membership and be prevented from practising reindeer husbandry in addition to other cultural activities that are generally carried out on Saami lands. This legislation is considered to be a means to protect and preserve the Saami culture. When Mr. Kitok, a Swedish Saami, wanted to return home and become once more an active member of his Saami community, his application was turned down. He appealed his community's decision to a Swedish court, which ruled against him. This was the basis for Kitok's communication against Sweden before the Human Rights Committee, in which he alleged that the Swedish Government violated his right to culture by failing to overturn his community's decision.

The Human Rights Committee found that Sweden was not in violation of the provisions of Article 27 by not allowing Mr. Kitok to return to his community. It argued that Sweden was under the international obligation to protect the Saami culture and that, in doing so, Sweden could lawfully restrict rights of individual members of the Saami community. The Committee argued that a *"restriction upon the right of an individual member of a minority must be shown to have a reasonable and objective justification and be necessary for the continued viability and welfare of the minority as a whole"*.[895]

---

890   U.N. Human Rights Committee, Communication *No. 167/1984 (1990)*, para. 33.
891   U.N. Human Rights Committee Communication No. 511/1992 *Länsman et al. v. Finland*. Fifty-second session, 1994. U.N. Doc. CCPR/C/52/D/511/1992 (1994), para. 9.6 (1994b). Available online at http://hrlibrary.ngo.ru/undocs/session52-index.html
892   Urban Morgan Institute for Human Rights et al., "Maastricht Guidelines" (1998), pp. 696-7.
893   Manfred Nowak, *U.N. Covenant on Civil and Political Rights: CCPR Commentary*. (Kehl-Strassburg-Arlington: N.P. Engel Publisher, 1993), p. 37.
894   U.N. Human Rights Committee, Communication No. 197/1985 *Ivan Kitok v. Sweden*, U.N. Doc. CCPR/C/33/D/197/1985 (1988).
895   Ibid., para. 9.8.

It emerges from these cases that States are frequently required to balance the right to culture of indigenous peoples on the one hand, and other competing interests, such as investments and similar public or private interests, on the other hand. This was, for instance, the case in the *J.G.A. Diergaardt et al. v. Namibia* (2000). The HRC ruled that although the Rehoboth Baster community had lived on the disputed land for more than one hundred years, it could not establish a strong tie between the community's way of life and the land in question.[896]

It is recommendable to indigenous activists and other persons interested in land rights issues to use the mechanism of the Human Rights Committee. Under the rules of the Optional Protocol to this Covenant, an individual or a group of individuals can complain to the Human Rights Committee for violation of one or several provisions of the ICCPR by a State. The most explicit decisions on land rights of indigenous peoples have been made following claims of violation of ICCPR Article 27 to the Human Rights Committee. The HRC has so far never dealt with a complaint made by an African indigenous person or group of persons, despite the fact that many African countries with indigenous peoples are parties to both the Covenant and its Optional Protocol.

The HRC has, however, criticized reports submitted by African States Parties, for failing to report on the human rights situation of indigenous peoples under Article 27. Concluding on the third report of the Democratic Republic of Congo in April 2006, the HRC pointed out:[897]

> While noting the State Party's comments on the Government's policy of preserving the cultural identity of the various ethnic groups and minorities (paragraph 294 of the report), the Committee is concerned at the marginalization, discrimination and at times persecution of some of the country's minorities, including Pygmies (Article 27 of the Covenant).
>
> The State Party is urged to provide detailed information in its next report on measures envisaged or taken to promote the integration of minorities and the protection of their rights and to guarantee respect for their cultures and dignity.

Concluding on a report by Gabon in 2000, HRC states,

---

896 U.N. Human Rights Committee, Communication No. 760/1997 *J.G.A. Diergaardt (late Captain of the Rehoboth Baster Community) et al. v. Namibia.* Sixty-ninth session (2000). U.N. Doc. CCPR/C/69/D/760/1997 (2000a). Available online at http://hrlibrary.ngo.ru/undocs/session69-index.html The case involved the Rehoboth Baster community that accused the Namibian Government of land dispossession. The community alleged, amongst other things, that their rights protected under Article 27 of the ICCPR were violated by the Government.

897 U.N. Human Rights Committee, Concluding Observations, Democratic Republic of the Congo, U.N. Doc. CCPR/C/COD/CO/3 (2006).

The Committee is concerned to note that the State Party denies the existence of minorities in its territory. The Committee is concerned to note that the steps taken to guarantee the rights of people belonging to minorities, as set forth in Article 27 of the Covenant, are inadequate, particularly with regard to the Baka people.[898]

In 2000, when dealing with the Republic of Congo, the Committee wrote,

The Committee regrets the lack of specific information on the different ethnic groups in the Congo, particularly the Pygmies, and on measures taken to guarantee, simultaneously, the full and equal enjoyment of their civil and political rights and respect for their rights under Article 27, to enjoy their own cultural traditions [and recommends that] more detailed information on this matter and on the measures taken to protect the rights of persons belonging to minority groups ... be provided in the State Party's third periodic report.[899]

Similar concerns on indigenous peoples were unfortunately not raised by the Human Rights Committee in relation to reports by the Central African Republic and Kenya during the same session. One reason could be that there was no shadow report submitted by indigenous groups, communities or NGOs. The mechanism of "shadow or complementary reports" by third parties is indeed recognized in almost all United Nations and regional human rights machineries. It consists of a third party providing the monitoring committees of the U.N. treaty bodies (and other regional human rights machineries) with supplementary information that can be helpful in balancing official opinions on a given situation of human rights.

ICERD and indigenous peoples' rights to land

Article 1 of the International Convention on the Elimination of all Forms of Racial Discrimination (ICERD, 1965)[900] states that:

The term "racial discrimination" shall mean any distinction, exclusion, restriction or preference based on race, colour, descent, or national or ethnic origin which has the purpose or effect of nullifying or impairing the recognition, enjoyment or exercise, on an equal footing, of human rights and fundamental freedoms.

---

898 U.N. Human Rights Committee, Concluding Observations, Gabon, U.N. Doc. CCPR/CO/70/GAB, November 2000 (2000b).
899 U.N. Human Rights Committee, Concluding Observations, Republic of the Congo, U.N. Doc. CCPR/C/79/Add.118, March 2000 (2000c).
900 ICERD entered into force January 4, 1969. U.N. Doc. A/6014 (1966). The text of the Convention is available online at, e.g., http://hrlibrary.ngo.ru/instree/d1cer.d.htm

In its General Comment no. 18 (1989), the Human Rights Committee has shed more light on the scope of the concept "discrimination", which obliges States to take:

[A]ffirmative actions in order to diminish or eliminate conditions that cause or help to perpetuate discrimination prohibited by the Covenant. For example, in a State where the general conditions of a certain part of the population prevent or impair their enjoyment of human rights, the State should take specific actions to correct those conditions.[901]

However, it was not until the 1997 General Recommendation XXIII of the Committee on the Elimination of Racial Discrimination (CERD)[902] that the non-recognition of indigenous peoples' right to lands was explicitly referred to as amounting to an act of racial discrimination:

Discrimination against indigenous peoples falls under the scope of the [anti-racial] Convention. The Committee especially calls upon States Parties to recognize and protect the rights of indigenous peoples to own, develop, control, and use their communal lands, territories and resources.[903]

Since then, CERD has become very instrumental and vocal in relation to indigenous peoples' right to lands, and in 1998, CERD flagged out an indigenous land issue in relation to the periodic report of Cameroon:

Protection of the rights of minorities and indigenous peoples to enable them to live in harmony in their environment is, especially as regards the Pygmies and Boro, a subject of concern in the light of article 2, paragraph 2, of the Convention and of the Committee's General Recommendation XXIII on the rights of indigenous peoples.[904]

It went on to recommend that:

With a view to promoting and protecting the rights of minorities and indigenous peoples..., the State Party [should] take all appropriate measures, particularly as regards deforestation that may harm such population groups.

---

901 U.N. Human Rights Committee, General Comment No.18 Non discrimination. U.N. Doc. HRI/GEN/1/Rev.1 at 26 (1994), para. 10. Available online http://hrlibrary.ngo.ru/gencomm/hrcomms.htm

902 The Committee (CERD) is the monitoring body of ICERD. Documents from CERD are available from http://hrlibrary.ngo.ru/google/localsearch.html and the UNHCHR Treaty Database at http://www.unhchr.ch/tbs/doc.nsf/Documentsfrset?OpenFrameSet

903 CERD, General Recommendation XXIII Rights of indigenous peoples (Fifty-first session, 1997), U.N. Doc. A/52/18, annex V at 122 (1997), adopted on August 18, 1997.

904 CERD, Conclusions and recommendations, Cameroon, U.N. Doc. CERD/C/304/Add.53 (1998). Paras. 9 and 17.

In 2003, CERD made an interesting concluding observation on the second to tenth periodic reports by Uganda:

> The Committee is concerned by reports of the difficult human rights situation of the Batwa people, particularly in relation to the enjoyment of their rights over lands traditionally occupied by them, and requests information on their situation in accordance with General Recommendation XXIII.[905]

Similar remarks were made by CERD on the eighth to sixteenth periodic reports by Tanzania in March 2007:

> The Committee notes with concern the lack of information from the State Party regarding the expropriation of the ancestral territories of certain ethnic groups, and their forced displacement and resettlement (art. 5).

> The Committee notes with concern the lack of information on certain vulnerable ethnic groups, notably nomadic and seminomadic populations, inter alia the Barabaig, Maasai and Hadzabe, on the difficulties they allegedly face due to their specific way of life and on special measures taken to guarantee the enjoyment of their human rights (arts. 5 and 2).[906]

Recommending in the latter case that

> [T]he State Party provide detailed information on the situation of nomadic and seminomadic ethnic groups and on any special measures taken with a view to ensuring the enjoyment of their rights under the Convention, notably their freedom of movement and their right to participate in decisions which affect them.[907]

Concluding on the fifth and sixth periodic reports submitted by the Botswana Government, CERD noted with concern in 2006:

> [T]he discrepancy between the information provided by the State Party that residents of the Central Kalahari Game Reserve have been consulted and have agreed to their relocation outside the Reserve, and persistent allegations that residents were forcibly removed, through, in particular, such measures as the termination of basic and essential services inside the Re-

---

905 CERD, Conclusions and Recommendations, Uganda, U.N. Doc. CERD/C/62/CO/11 (2003), para. 14. 1
906 CERD, Conclusions and Recommendations, Tanzania, U.N. Doc. CERD/C/TZA/CO/16 (2007), paras. 14 and 16.
907 Ibid.

serve, the dismantling of existing infrastructures, the confiscation of live-stock, harassment and ill-treatment of some residents by police and wild-life officers, as well as the prohibition of hunting and restrictions on free-dom of movement inside the Reserve (Articles 2 and 5).[908]

It therefore recommended:

> [T]hat a rights-based approach be adopted during the negotiations. To that end, the State Party should, in particular, (a) pay particular attention to the close cultural ties that bind the San/Basarwa to their ancestral land; (b) protect the economic activities of the San/Basarwa that are an essential element of their culture, such as hunting and gathering practices, whether conducted by traditional or modern means; (c) study all possible alterna-tives to relocation; and (d) seek the prior free and informed consent of the persons and groups concerned.[909]

Within the framework of its efforts to prevent racial discrimination, the CERD may also decide to initiate urgent action procedures aimed at responding to prob-lems requiring immediate attention to prevent or limit the scale or number of serious violations of the Convention. An increasing number of indigenous peo-ples are using this mechanism, which can, among other things, lead to a country visit. In 2007, Batwa from the Democratic Republic of Congo used it in relation to forest reforms, which were seen as not taking into account the rights of its most ancient inhabitants.

ILO Convention No. 169 and indigenous peoples' right to lands

As already mentioned, ILO Convention No. 169 is the only legally binding in-strument that exclusively concerns itself with indigenous peoples' rights.[910] It rec-ognizes *"their rights of ownership and possession over the lands which they tradition-ally occupy"*; their right to *"use lands not exclusively occupied by them but to which they have traditionally had access for their subsistence and traditional activities"*; and their *"right to participate in the use, management and conservation of the natural re-sources pertaining to their lands."*[911]

---

908 CERD, Conclusions and Recommendations, Botswana. U.N. Doc. CERD/C/BWA/CO/16 (2006), para. 12.
909 Ibid.
910 All ILO Conventions and their status of ratification can be accessed at the ILO Database on Inter-national Labour Standards, ILOLEX, at: http://www.ilo.org/ilolex/
911 ILO Convention No. 169 (1989), Articles 14.1 and 15.

The principle in ILO Convention No. 169 that recognizes indigenous peoples' rights to their lands can be seen as building upon ILO Convention No. 82 concerning Social Policy in Non-Metropolitan Territories (1947).[912] In its article 8(c), this Convention stipulates the need for *"control, by the enforcement of adequate laws or regulations, of the ownership and use of land and resources to ensure that they are used, with due regard to customary rights, in the interest of inhabitants of the [non-metropolitan] territories"*. The same norm was also adopted by the drafting Committee of ILO Convention No. 107, which proposed a similar provision, namely that: "The property rights, either collective or individuals, as the case may be, of indigenous peoples over the lands they traditionally occupy should be recognized".[913]

Several State representatives at the International Labour Conference, which was to adopt ILO Convention No. 107,[914] objected to the use of the term "property" in the definition of the right which was to be recognized to indigenous peoples over their lands. Amongst the grounds for objection was the view that the ties of indigenous peoples to their lands would not amount to a full property right.[915] Thus, the term "property" was substituted by "ownership" in the final text of the Convention's Article 11:

> *The right of ownership, collective or individual, of the members of the populations concerned over the lands, which these populations traditionally occupy, shall be recognised.*[916]

An interesting question emerges at this point. Did ILO Convention No. 169 amend its predecessor's position not to recognize the indigenous peoples' full property rights over their lands? The *travaux préparatoires* of this convention go some way to answer this question and are the focus of this section.

A thorough reading of the records of the drafting sessions of this Convention reveals that instead of recognising strong property rights of indigenous peoples over their lands, ILO Convention No. 169 responded to indigenous peoples' land claims by recognising three separate rights, namely a "right of ownership and possession", a "right to use" and a "right to participate in the use, management and conservation of

---

912 Article 8(c) of ILO Convention No. 82 (1947) Concerning Social Policy in Non-Metropolitan Territories. See in International Labour Organisation, *International Labour conventions and recommendations 1919-1951* (1996), p. 498.

913 International Labour Conference, "Protection and Integration" (1957a), p. 31.

914 ILO Convention No. 107 has been ratified by six African countries, namely Angola, Egypt, Ghana, Guinea Bisau, Malawi and Tunesia, and is still in force.

915 The Government of the United Kingdom thus suggested that the word "property" be deleted "since it is assumed that the provisions of Article 11 are not intended to be restrictive in this sense". See also International Labour Conference, "Protection and Integration" (1957a), p. 21. The employer representative from Mexico also proposed that the term "ownership" be used instead of "property", without any fundamental reason. See International Labour Conference, "Records of Proceedings" (1958), p. 727.

916 ILO Convention No. 107, Article 11.

resources". As the following analysis shows, each one ofthese rights has a different scope and is meant to apply to a different element of indigenous peoples' land claim.

The right to "ownership and possession"

The initial text of Article 14.1, as proposed by the drafting Committee of ILO Convention No. 169, was formulated as follows: "The peoples concerned shall be accorded *exclusive* rights of ownership, possession, and *control* to the largest practicable portion of their traditional territories" (emphasis added).[917]

The use of two strong terms—namely *"exclusive"* and *"control"*—were not considered acceptable by several State representatives, and both terms were eventually deleted from the provisions of Article 14.1 that ended up looking as follows:

> *The rights of ownership and possession of the peoples concerned over the lands, which they traditionally occupy, shall be recognised.*

This limited right of "ownership and possession" is designed to apply to lands that indigenous peoples traditionally used and which they still occupy or have recently occupied, as revealed in a statement by some delegations to the drafting sessions.[918] This meaning has been acknowledged by the ILO governing body.[919] An increasingly strong opinion argues also that the wording "land they traditionally occupy" used in Article 14.1 could to some extent include also any territory ever occupied or lost lands.[920]

ILO Convention No. 169 thus guarantees indigenous peoples' right of ownership and possession over lands that they still occupy and those they recently lost unfairly or without their free and informed consent.

The "right to use"

Article 14.1 of ILO Convention No. 169 also articulates the right of indigenous peoples "to use lands not exclusively occupied".

---

917 International Labour Conference, "Partial revision" (1989), p. 34.

918 Ibid., p. 35. The United States proposed the following formulation: "The rights of ownership and possession of the [peoples/populations] concerned over the lands which have been reserved for their use or which they currently occupy and for which they have a tradition of use and possession shall be recognized ..." Although the exact wording of this U.S. proposition was not adopted, the idea that ownership and possession was recognized only to lands still occupied by indigenous peoples was adopted.

919 Ibid., p. 36.

920 Lee Swepston, "A New Step in International Law on Indigenous and Tribal Peoples: ILO Convention No. 169 of 1989", *Oklahoma City University Law Review* 15 (fall 1990), pp. 677–714.

In general, the right to use is understood as being limited and insecure. Some define it as "a right to enjoy a thing belonging to another and to take the fruits thereof".[921] It is a temporary right to use something which may be owned by another proprietor.

As stated earlier, the "right to use" was designed by the delegates to the drafting sessions of ILO Convention No. 169 to apply to "lands not exclusively occupied [but land to which indigenous peoples] traditionally had access for their subsistence and traditional activities". Alternatively, as put by the drafting Committee, "those portions of [indigenous] traditional territories which have been occupied or are used by other persons".[922]

This is indeed a very weak right and that weakness was highlighted during the drafting session. The Swedish Government thus made an important observation, indicating that such a limited and weak right to use would have a most negative impact upon nomadic indigenous peoples, whose historical rights are essentially based upon "use", and who do not tend to settle in one place but require extensive areas of land for their cattle herding, fishing, hunting and religious ceremonies.[923] The pertinence of this Swedish remark is seen as having influenced the wording of the last sentence of Article 14(1) in the adopted text, which states: *"Particular attention shall be paid to the situation of nomadic peoples and shifting cultivators in this respect"*.

ILO Convention No. 169 thus provides for indigenous peoples' usage right of lands beyond what is considered as theirs, or lands that they use in conjunction with other peoples. These territories or lands appear like a kind of buffer zone outside the lands on which indigenous peoples enjoy the right of ownership. These lands or territories might be the property of other persons or entities but indigenous peoples' usage right must be accommodated.

The "right to participate in the use, management and conservation of the resources"

A third type of right of indigenous peoples over their lands is articulated by Article 15, which gives indigenous peoples certain rights regarding natural resources such as mineral sub-surface resources, fauna, flora, sea-ice, etc., pertaining to their land.[924]

---

921 P.A. Crépeau and J.E.C. Brierley, *Code Civil* (Montréal, Canada: Société Québécoise d'Informations Juridiques, 1981), Article 487.

922 Article 14.1 of the draft text of ILO Convention 169.

923 International Labour Conference, "Partial revision" (1989), p. 35.

924 ILO Convention No. 169, Article 15 reads as follows: "1. *The rights of the peoples concerned to the natural resources pertaining to their lands shall be specially safeguarded. These rights include the right of these people to participate in the use, management, and conservation of these resources. 2. In cases in which the State retains the ownership of mineral or sub-surface resources or rights to other resources*

While the inclusion of the right to "participate in the use, management and conservation" is important because it indicates that indigenous peoples must be consulted in processes relating to the development of their traditional lands or lands that they use, the text that was eventually adopted was not as strong as anticipated.

The issue was the degree of control indigenous peoples should have in cases in which the State retains the ownership of mineral or sub-surface resources or rights to other resources pertaining to the lands. During drafting, there was some debate and the Colombian Government raised a proposal to make the consent of indigenous peoples mandatory by inserting the words "obtain consent" in order to guarantee "a direct participation of the peoples concerned in the control and management".[925] Yet this proposal was not adopted.[926]

In the view of a Workers' delegate from Denmark, the non-adoption of the obligation to obtain consent watered down the principle of free and informed consent by implicitly authorising a removal of indigenous peoples from their lands without their consent.[927] This lack of a right to meaningful participation is reinforced by a provision in Article 16.2 which explicitly states that "where their consent cannot be obtained, relocation shall take place ... following appropriate procedures".

ILO Convention No. 169 thus failed to restore indigenous peoples' full property rights over their own land. As eloquently put by Ms. Sharon Venne, an Indian Cree from Canada:

> The revised Convention proposes an unacceptably ambiguous definition of the term "lands" in a manner that could curtail our territorial rights. Only land rights based on present, and not past, occupation are explicitly recognized ... we are outraged and bitter at the prejudicial treatment of our territorial and resources rights by the tripartite Committee.[928]

Whatever weaknesses it bears, ILO Convention No. 169 remains the only binding instrument that guarantees indigenous peoples' right of ownership over their ancestral lands. Similar to initial concerns expressed by African countries towards the UN Declaration on the rights of indigenous peoples, a number of African States fear that the ratification of ILO Convention 169 could further ethnic divi-

---

pertaining to lands, governments shall establish or maintain procedures through which they shall consult these people, with a view to ascertaining whether and to what degree their interests would be prejudiced, before undertaking or permitting any programmes for the exploration or exploitation of such resources ... The peoples concerned shall wherever possible participate in the benefits of such activities, and shall receive fair compensation for any damages which they may sustain as a result of such activities."

925 International Labour Conference, "Partial revision" (1989), p. 37.

926 The Australian Government, for instance, argued that despite the requirement to consult with indigenous peoples, they should not be given the power to veto states' actions or projects.

927 International Labour Conference, "Partial revision" (1989), p. 31-35.

928 Ibid., p. 31-7.

sions of their national populations. The situation in countries that have ratified this Convention reveal that the States have nothing to fear. In several countries, the ratification of ILO Convention No. 169 has on the contrary been advantageous since it tends to improve the human rights situation and opens up a constructive and democratic dialogue with indigenous peoples. As noted earlier, there are a few African countries that have taken or are in the process to take legislative or policies measures directed at indigenous peoples. The implementation of these measures would be facilitated by a ratification of ILO Convention No. 169.

The ratification of ILO Convention No. 169 is therefore highly recommendable. Indeed, its ratification by the Central African Republic is a very positive step and it can only be hoped that other African countries will follow suit.

CHAPTER XI
OTHER RELEVANT GLOBAL AND REGIONAL INSTRUMENTS

Several other important global and regional instruments deal with indigenous peoples' land rights. The first section of this chapter looks at the Convention on Biological Diversity, the UNESCO Conventions, the Geneva Conventions and other international humanitarian and criminal laws. This book considers these as the most relevant areas of international law as far as indigenous peoples' rights to lands are concerned,[929] and most of them have been ratified by the African countries (see Appendix 2, Table 2).

Turning to Africa, a second section examines the African regional frameworks such as the African Charter and the African Commission on Human and Peoples' Rights. These are of special importance for African indigenous peoples and they, too, have been endorsed by most African countries (see Appendix 2, Table 2).

A final section makes a brief survey of multilateral banks and major donor policies targeting indigenous peoples.

The Convention on Biological Diversity and indigenous peoples' land rights

The Convention on Biological Diversity, commonly known as CBD, is a prominent international instrument that has become essential in the protection of indigenous peoples' rights regarding, among others, their traditional knowledge and practices related to land and natural resources and protected areas.[930] Its articles 8(j) and 10(c) provide respectively that States Parties should as much as they can:

> [R]espect, preserve and maintain knowledge, innovations and practices of indigenous and local communities embodying traditional lifestyles relevant for the conservation and sustainable use of biological diversity and promote their wider ap-

---

929 The chapter, therefore, does not deal with international instruments such as, for instance, the Convention on the Rights of the Child, which contains specific provisions on indigenous children, too (Article 30), but does not deal specifically with land rights.

930 The Convention can be accessed at http://www.cbd.int

plication with the approval and involvement of the holders of such knowledge, innovations and practices and encourage the equitable sharing of the benefits arising from the utilization of such knowledge, innovations, and practices.

And

Protect and encourage customary use of biological resources in accordance with traditional cultural practices that are compatible with conservation or sustainable use requirements ...

As presented by the Convention, traditional knowledge refers to the knowledge, innovations and practices of indigenous and local communities around the world.[931] The relevance of this matter led the Conference of Parties (COP) to the creation of a Working Group on Article 8(j), with the mandate to address the implementation of this article and related provisions of the Convention. This working group is open to all Parties and indigenous and local communities' representatives play a full and active role in its work. In 1996, the third Conference of the Parties (COP3) created the International Indigenous Forum on Biodiversity (IIFB),[932] which, in 2000, was officially acknowledged by COP5 as a formal advisory body to the CBD. As such, the IIFB enhances the presence and voices of indigenous peoples within all CBD processes and meetings. It promotes linkages between the work of the CBD on protected areas and the implementation of Article 8(j), and, at the same time, it promotes indigenous and cultural diversity approaches in environment and development. In 1998, an Indigenous Women's Biodiversity Network was established to draw attention to indigenous women's "full and effective participation in the conservation and sustainable use of biological diversity within their communities, as well as their rights as knowledge holders".[933]

In 2004, COP7 adopted what is known as the *Akwé: Kon guidelines.* These voluntary guidelines provide a collaborative framework ensuring the full involvement of indigenous and local communities in the assessment of cultural, environmental and social impact of proposed developments on sacred sites and on lands and waters they have traditionally occupied. Moreover, guidance is provided on how to take into account traditional knowledge, innovations and practices as part of the impact-assessment processes and promote the use of appropriate tech-

931 Traditional knowledge tends to be collectively owned and takes the form of stories, songs, folklore, proverbs, cultural values, beliefs, rituals, community laws, local language, and agricultural practices, including the development of plant species and animal breeds.
932 IIFB can be accessed at http://www.indigenousportal.com/Biological-Diversity/
933 See "Statement on behalf of the Indigenous Women's' Biodiversity Network (IWBN)", U.N. Doc. E/C.19/2004. Available at
      http://www.un.org/esa/socdev/unpfii/pfii/documents/other%20docs/Doc%20Netherlands%20Centre.htm

nologies. They also suggest a ten-step process for impact assessment of proposed development projects with regards to Article 8(j).[934]

Each State Party to the CBD appoints a focal point, mandated to liaise between the Convention's bodies and Government.[935] Indeed, a National Focal Point is a key part of implementing the CBD, as it is expected to collect and share information, raise awareness and report on progress concerning the CBD on numerous issues, including indigenous peoples' rights. In numerous countries, these focal points are in permanent contact with indigenous peoples and communities.

Each State Party to the CBD must produce regular reports on the progress or measures taken to implement the Convention, and elaborate a National Biodiversity Strategy and Action Plan (NBSAPs). There are guidelines on developing and implementing all these international obligations, which require active participation of indigenous peoples. All these CBD mechanisms are yet to be fully, meaningfully and strategically used by many African indigenous communities, which could for example maintain regular contacts with national focal points or contribute to national reports, national biodiversity strategies and plans. Indigenous organizations could do the same with the Indigenous Forum. There is for instance a recent work done by a group of NGOs reviewing Uganda's implementation of the CBD Programme of Work on Protected Areas.[936] These are important policy documents likely to interest even judges and lawyers involved in indigenous peoples-related court cases.

The UNESCO Conventions

UNESCO also pays particular attention to indigenous peoples' rights and several of its Conventions could provide protection to indigenous peoples' land rights. This is, for instance, the case of the 1972 Convention Concerning the Protection of the World Cultural and Natural Heritage.

However, it is in particular two other conventions that are relevant for indigenous land rights, namely the Convention on the Promotion and Protection of the Diversity of Cultural Expressions (2005) and the 1954 Hague Convention on the Protection of Cultural Property in the Event of Armed Conflict.

---

934 For full text of Guidelines, see http://www.cbd.int/programmes/socio-eco/traditional/akwe. aspx
935 See list of contacts of all national focal points at http://www.biodiv.org/doc/lists/nfp-cbd.pdf.
936 Forest Peoples Programme, UOBDU and Care International, "The Indigenous Batwa People and Protected Areas in Southwest Uganda: A review of Uganda's Implementation of the CBD Programme of Work on Protected Areas". Available online at Web site of Forest Peoples Programme: http://www.forestpeoples.org/documents/conservation/uganda_review_cbd_pa_jan08_eng. pdf

The UNESCO Convention on the Promotion and Protection of the Diversity of Cultural Expressions

This Convention states that,

> *The protection and promotion of the diversity of cultural expressions presuppose the recognition of equal dignity of and respect for all cultures, including the cultures of persons belonging to minorities and indigenous peoples.*[937]

Article 7 of this Convention states also that the protection of indigenous territories is part of measures to be taken by States in order to promote and protect the culture of these communities:

> *Parties shall endeavour to create in their territory an environment that encourages individuals and social groups:*
> a. *to create, produce, disseminate, distribute and have access to their own cultural expressions, paying due attention to the special circumstances and needs of women as well as various social groups, including persons belonging to minorities and indigenous peoples;*
> b. *to have access to diverse cultural expressions from within their territory as well as from other countries of the world.*

This is an instrument that more than 20 African countries have ratified.[938] Policies and laws are expected to be adopted by all parties, which are also required to create an environment encouraging individuals and groups to create and disseminate their own cultural expressions. Since indigenous peoples' culture is tied to their lands, any measures taken in that respect are likely to have a positive impact on the communities' land claims.

The 1954 Hague Convention and indigenous land rights

This UNESCO Convention on the Protection of Cultural Property in the Event of Armed Conflict including its Protocols is, together with the Geneva Conventions (see below), among the more than 100 international humanitarian laws that deal with people's rights in case of armed conflicts. The Hague Convention could be

---

937 UNESCO Convention on Cultural Expressions (2005), Article 2. For full text of Convention, see http://www.unesco.org/culture/en/diversity/convention.

938 The following African countries have ratified this Convention: Benin, Burkina Faso, Cameroon, Chad, Congo, Côte d'Ivoire, Djibouti, Egypt, Ethiopia, Gabon, Guinea, Kenya, Madagascar, Mali, Mauritius, Mozambique, Namibia, Niger, Nigeria, Senegal, Seychelles, South Africa, Sudan, Togo, Tunisia and Zimbabwe. See also Appendix 2, Table 2.

relevant for indigenous peoples as far as it looks at the protection of cultural property, defined as being "movable or immovable property of great importance".[939] It does not list, however, what should be understood as "cultural property of great importance". It can, nevertheless, be argued that lands are of great importance to all indigenous peoples and in addition to being a means of survival, they are often the pillar of these peoples' whole culture. In other words, one can argue that "lands" of indigenous peoples could be considered to be included amongst the cultural properties protected by the 1954 Hague Convention.

In line with this broad understanding of the concept "cultural property", Thomas Adlercreutz argues that "culturally valuable land" should be protected by various domestic laws.[940] This is the case in Sweden, where the Swedish Act on Cultural Monuments includes graves, burial grounds, places of cult, etc., amongst the properties to be protected because of their cultural values.[941] Similarly, the United States' Native American Graves Protection and Repatriation Act (NAGPRA),[942] defines a native cultural patrimony as any tribal property or object necessary for the tribe's culture, way of life, traditions, and maintenance of its history.[943] It has been said that this issue must be "central to the Native American culture or group".[944] This view is also held by Andrew Corbett who, examining the possible effect on communities of the proposed Epupa hydropower dam in Namibia, argues that the Himba's burial sites are an important part of this community's culture and that their destruction would dangerously affect the livelihood of this community's members.[945] Therefore by intending to protect cultural sites, such as burial sites, it is possible that international and domestic instruments have implicitly recognized that parts of, if not all, indigenous peoples' lands constitute a cultural patrimony that deserves protection.

The second Protocol to the 1954 Hague Convention, which entered into force on 9 March 2004, is expected to strengthen the protection afforded to cultural heritage during both international and non-international armed conflicts.[946] Equa-

---

939 Hague Convention for the Protection of Cultural Property in the Event of Armed Conflict (1954), Article 1. The Convention and its two Protocols are accessible online at http://www.icrc.org/ihl.nsf

940 Thomas Adlercreutz, "Property Rights and Protection of Cultural Heritage in Sweden", *International Journal of Cultural Property* 7, no. 2 (1998), p. 410.

941 Ibid., p. 418.

942 U.S. Code, Title 25, Section 3001(3) (D) (1994). Available from http://www.gpoaccess.gov/uscode/

943 Dawn Elyse Goldman, "The Native American Graves Protection and Repatriation Act: A Benefit and a Burden: Refining NAGPRA's Cultural Patrimony Definition", *International Journal of Cultural Property* 8, 1 (1999), p. 229.

944 Ibid., p. 232.

945 Corbett, "A Case Study" (1999), pp. 84-5.

946 Jan Hladik, "Diplomatic Conference on the Second Protocol to the Hague Convention for the Protection of Cultural Property in the Event of Armed Conflict (March 15-26 1999)", *International Journal of Cultural Property*. 8, no. 2 (1999), p. 527.

torial Guinea and Gabon are among the first African States that have ratified it. This instrument is also expected to provide more understanding and guiding principles for a better interpretation of the norm of "military necessity", which is often referred to in international humanitarian law.[947] However, this text seems to consider only movable cultural properties. Such an understanding could be detrimental to indigenous peoples' land rights given than land is not a movable property.

The Geneva Conventions and other international humanitarian and criminal laws

The Geneva Conventions—a whole system of legal safeguards that cover the way wars may be fought and the protection of individuals in time of war—are at the core of international humanitarian law.[948] Most relevant for indigenous peoples are the Fourth Geneva Convention relative to the Protection of Civilian Persons in Time of War (1949), and Protocols I and II to the Geneva Conventions relating to the Protection of Victims of International and Non-International Armed Conflicts, respectively (1977). International criminal laws deal with international crimes and include among other legal instruments, the charter and statutes of various international tribunals.[949]

International humanitarian and criminal laws do not provide any special protection for indigenous peoples. Yet, this section of the world's population is particularly affected by armed conflicts, be they international or internal. Research shows, for example, that the Batwa of Rwanda were particularly affected by the 1994 genocide as they were caught in the fight between the two main ethnic groups.[950] In the Democratic Republic of Congo, the alleged acts of war crimes—including crimes against humanity and acts of cannibalism—committed against Batwa in the Ituri area are thought to have a link with traditional belief that these

---

947 Françoise Hampson, "Military Necessity", in *Crimes of War: What the Public Should Know,* edited by Roy Gutman and David Rieff (New York and London: W.W. Norton, 2007). Available online at http://www.crimesofwar.org/thebook/military-necessity.html. Hampson. defines the norm of "military necessity" as "a legal concept used in international humanitarian law (IHL) as part of the legal justification for attacks on legitimate military targets that may have adverse, even terrible, consequences for civilians and civilian objects".

948 The four Geneva Conventions were adopted in 1864, 1906, 1929 and 1949 respectively. The three oldest Conventions were revised in 1949. There are three amendment protocols to the 1949 Geneva Conventions, Protocols I and II adopted in 1977 and Protocol III adopted in 2005. For more information, see International Committee of the Red Cross Web site at http://www.icrc.org/web/eng/siteeng0.nsf/html/genevaconventions

949 For full text of 1954 Hague Convention, see http://www.icrc.org/ihl.nsf/FULL/400?OpenDocument

950 Jerome Lewis and Judy Knight, *The Twa of Rwanda*, IWGIA Document No. 78 (Copenhagen and UK: IWGIA and World Rainforest Movement, 1995), pp. 62-69. These two authors estimate that up to 30 per cent of the Twa population (approx. 6-9,000) died or were killed between October 1993 and June 1995, and a similar number fled outside the country (pp. 92-93).

peoples' flesh contains magical bulletproof powers. Similarly, many fighters believe that sexual relations with "Pygmy" women have a curative effect on a number of diseases, including HIV/AIDS. Dorothy Jackson, in her report on Twa women in the Great Lakes Region, writes that, "perpetrators of the armed conflict in the region have inflicted appalling sexual violence on women of all backgrounds, contributing to an increase in HIV/AIDS infection".[951] In most cases, the ancestral lands of these indigenous peoples—usually forested areas—are turned into operational bases of armed militia, with all the type of problems that such an occupation entails. In DR Congo, for example, both sides in the conflict often used "Pygmies" as guides and on numerous occasions retaliatory actions by either side have been directed at "Pygmies", accused of siding with enemies.

Both sets of legal instruments are nevertheless relevant since it is possible to interpret several of their provisions in a way that includes indigenous peoples' rights to land.

Fourth Geneva Convention and indigenous peoples' rights to land

Article 49 of the Fourth Geneva Convention prohibits deportation of civilians, non-combatants, and other protected persons from their homes, except if their security is under threat.[952] Furthermore, *"Persons thus evacuated shall be transferred back to their homes, as soon as hostilities in the areas in question have ceased"*. Protocol I elaborates on these same provisions, and states that

> *[S]hall be regarded as grave breaches of this Protocol ... the transfer by the occupying Power of parts of its own civilian population into the territory it occupies, or the deportation or transfer of all or parts of the population of the occupied territory within or outside this territory, in violation of Article 49 of the Fourth Convention. ...* [953]

Protocol II, furthermore, states in its Article 17 on Prohibition on Forced Movement of Civilians that

---

951 Dorothy Jackson, *Twa Women, Twa Rights in the Great Lakes Region of Africa* (London: Minority Rights Group International, 2003), p. 13. Twa women are also at added risk from the cultural practices of the dominant society. In all four countries covered by this report, Twa women told about the belief that if a non-Twa man has a backache he can cure it by sleeping with a Twa woman. This belief prevails also in the Republic of Congo. See also FIMI/IIWF, "Mairin Iwanka Raya: Indigenous Women Stand against Violence". A Companion report to the United Nations Secretary General's Study on violence against women (New York: FIMI/IIWF, 2006).

952 See Web site of the International Committee of the Red Cross: http://www.icrc.org for full text of Fourth Geneva Convention and its Protocols.

953 Article 85.4(a) of Protocol I to the Geneva Conventions of 12 August 1949, and relating to the Protection of Victims of International Armed Conflicts. See Web site of the International Committee of the Red Cross: http://www.icrc.org.

1. *The displacement of the civilian population shall not be ordered for reasons related to the conflict unless the security of the civilians involved or imperative military reasons so demand. Should such displacements have to be carried out, all possible measures shall be taken in order that the civilian population may be received under satisfactory conditions of shelter, hygiene, health, safety and nutrition.*
2. *Civilians shall not be compelled to leave their own territory for reasons connected with the conflict.*[954]

In what could be considered a more specific language, the Articles 54.2 of Protocol I and 14 of Protocol II prohibit acts of destruction of "objects indispensable to the survival of civilian populations", including drinking water, livestock, and so on. This provision gives rise to two important considerations. First, the terms "objects indispensable to the survival of civilian populations" implies objects without which the civilians in question would not survive. It becomes thus important to understand the criterion that makes an object indispensable to the survival of a civilian population and whether or not the lack or destruction of such an object would lead to forced movement or starvation.

In this regard, could the lands of indigenous peoples be considered as "indispensable for their survival" within the meaning of the two Protocols? Commenting on NATO's action in Kosovo, it has been argued that "the NATO attack on the factories at Pancevo [which] may have rendered the city's water supply useless" has to be assessed on the basis of, amongst other issues, whether the action left "the civilian population with such inadequate food and water as to cause its starvation or force its movement".[955] If livestock and agricultural areas for the production of foodstuffs, which are *expressis verbis* referred to by Protocols I and II to the 1949 Geneva Conventions,[956] constitute objects indispensable to the survival of agricultural and pastoralist communities respectively, then hunting and gathering lands on which hunter-gatherer communities depend should be considered to be included in the scope of these provisions in the two Protocols. Relevantly, the provisions in both Protocols use an open-ended language—"such as"—in listing objects that should be considered as indispensable to the survival of civilian populations. This

---

954 Article 17 of Protocol II to the Geneva Conventions of 12 August 1949, and relating to the Protection of Victims of Non-International Armed Conflicts. There are numerous examples of indigenous communities that have been forced to leave their lands by the warring factions. One case is that of the Miskito in Nicaragua who were forcefully removed by the Nicaraguan Government during the Contra War from their territories along the Honduras border.

955 Aaron Schwabach, "Environmental Damage Resulting from the NATO Military Action against Yugoslavia", *Columbia Journal of Environmental Law* 25, 1 (2000), p. 127. Available at Social Science Research Network's (SSRN) Web site:http://ssrn.com/abstract=224028

956 Article 54 of Protocol I and Article 14 of Protocol II to the 1949 Geneva Conventions.

suggests that indigenous lands and other objects could be included in the scope of these provisions, depending upon the situation on the ground.

International criminal law and indigenous land rights

Deportation and transfer of populations, including the act of ethnic cleansing, has frequently occurred in recent times in various parts of the world, such as in Yugoslavia. J.M. Henckaerts quotes in his book, *Mass Expulsion in Modern International Law and Practice*, a 1994 *Human Rights Watch Report* that defines ethnic cleansing as "the forcible deportation and displacement, execution, confinement in detention camps or ghettos" of civilian populations. He also refers to the evidence submitted to the International Criminal Tribunal for the Former Yugoslavia (ICTY) by the U.S. Government on cases of mass forcible expulsions and deportation of civilians, to argue that the international crime of "ethnic cleansing" is developing in scope.[957] Is it possible that this defini-tion of crime might further develop to include acts often committed by States to force indigenous communities out of their lands for conservation and other economic interests? This possibility should be further investigated with more focused research.

Henckaerts also argues that acts of deportation, forcible expulsion or up-rooting of civilians from their homelands could amount to the crime of geno-cide. But then he indicates that this is not entirely self-evident as generally ethnic cleansing aims to remove a population from a certain area, without the intent of destroying it as a group.[958]

It must be emphasised again that this branch of international law does not provide specifically designed protection for indigenous peoples' right to lands. However, as the scope of several international crimes evolves, neces-sary changes could be consequential. Importantly, a United Nations' report already states that acts, which destroy the rainforests and threaten the exist-ence and well-being of forest-dwelling indigenous and tribal peoples, can be considered as ethnocide, whether the acts are deliberate or negligent. This report supports the view that ethnocide is a crime against humanity.[959] How-ever, the concept of ethnocide is referred to in neither the Charter of the Nu-remberg Tribunal (1945), the Nuremberg Principles (1950), the Statutes of both the International Criminal Tribunal for the Former Yugoslavia—ICTY (1993)

---

957 Jean Marie Henckaerts, *Mass Expulsion in Modern International Law and Practice* (The Hague: Mar-tinus Nijhoff, 1995), p. 163.

958 Ibid., p. 164.

959 Benjamin Whitaker, "Revised and Updated Report on the Question of the Prevention and Pun-ishment of the Crime of Genocide". Report prepared by the Special speaker, B. Whitaker, for ECOSOC. U.N. Doc. E/CN.4/Sub.2/1985/6, at 17.

and the International Criminal Tribunal for Rwanda—ICTR (1994),[960] nor in the Draft Code of Crimes against the Peace and Security of Mankind (1996).[961]

African legal instruments and institutions

There are a number of African regional instruments and institutions that are relevant to indigenous peoples, in general, and to their right to lands, in particular. They include human rights legal instruments such as the African Charter on Human and Peoples' Rights, human rights institutions like the African Commission on Human and Peoples' Rights (ACHPR) and organizations with a more economic development focus such as, among others, the New Partnership for African Development (NEFAD).

The African Charter on Human and Peoples' Rights

The African Charter on Human and Peoples' Rights came into force on 21 October 1986 after its adoption in Nairobi, Kenya, by the Assembly of Heads of States and Governments of the then Organisation of African Unity (OAU). The OAU was disbanded in July 2002 and has since been replaced by the African Union (AU).

The African Charter is credited with a number of particular features.[962] It states in its Preamble that *"virtues of … historical tradition and the values of African civilization … should inspire and characterize [African States Members']reflection on the concept of human and peoples' rights"*. It also does not distinguish civil and political rights from economic, social and cultural rights.

Its Article 17 states that:

1. *Every individual shall have the right to education;*
2. *Every individual may freely take part in the cultural life of his community;*
3. *The promotion and protection of morals and traditional values recognised by the community shall be the duty of the State.*

Furthermore, the African Charter is almost the only human rights instrument stating the rights of peoples, including communities within States. Articles 19 to 24 provide for these rights, such as the right to self-determination, which can also

---

960 The ICTY statutes were prepared and adopted by Security Council resolution 827 (1993) of 25 May 1993 and are available online at http://www2.ohchr.org/english/law/itfy.htm. Those of the ICTR were likewise prepared and adopted by Security Council resolution 955 (1994) of 8 November 1994. Available online at http://www2.ohchr.org/english/law/itr.htm.

961 Code established by the International Law Commission. For full text, see: http://untreaty.un.org/ilc/texts/instruments/english/draft%20articles/7_4_1996.pdf

962 The full text of the Charter is available at http://www.hrcr.org/docs/Banjul/afrhr.html

be enjoyed by a community within a given State. For instance, Article 19 asserts that "*All peoples shall be equal; they shall enjoy the same respect and shall have the same rights. Nothing shall justify the domination of a people by another.*"

Guidelines by the African Commission on Human and Peoples' Rights[963] on the above mentioned Article 17 indicate that States shall take "overall policy and specific measures aimed at the promotion of cultural identity as a factor of mutual appreciation amongst groups, communities".[964] In 2000, for instance, the Government of Mauritania was found to have violated Article 17 for discriminating against black sections of its population. The African Commission on Human and Peoples' Rights concluded indeed that "language is an integral part of the structure of culture; it in fact constitutes its pillar and means of expression par excellence".[965]

Article 20 of the African Charter dealing with the right to self-determination could also be considered as relevant to the protection of indigenous peoples' right to lands, since it is understood to include also the rights to self governance, autonomy and control over resources, as clearly presented by the African Commission on Human and Peoples' Rights in a legal Advisory Opinion on the United Nations Declaration on the Rights of Indigenous Peoples:

> The notion of self-determination has evolved with the development of the international visibility of the claims made by indigenous populations whose right to self-determination is exercised within the standards and according to the modalities which are compatible with the territorial integrity of the Nation States to which they belong.[966]

Article 21 of the African Charter enshrines the right of all peoples "*to freely dispose of their wealth and natural resources*". Article 22 provides for the right of all peoples "*to their economic, social, and cultural development*". These provisions have been used by the African Commission on Human and Peoples' Rights to enhance the protection of indigenous peoples' rights to lands. In 2002, for instance, the Government of Nigeria was found to have violated Article 21 by allowing oil exploi-

---

963 The African Commission on Human and Peoples' Rights is the treaty-based monitoring body of the African Charter. It is based in Banjul in The Gambia, and holds annual meetings during which states report on the implementation of the African Charter and other international instruments are examined.

964 African Commission of Human and Peoples' Rights, 1990 Activity Report, *Human Rights Law Journal* 1990: 417. See also Barume, *Heading towards Extinction* (2000), pp. 115-6.

965 Collectifs des veuves et ayants droits, Association mauritanienne des droits de l'homme C/ Mauritanie, 13ième Rapport d'activités de la Commission Africaine 1999-2000, ACHPR/RTP/13th, Annex V, Paragraph 137.

966 African Commission on Human and Peoples' Rights, Advisory Opinion on the United Nations Declaration on Rights of Indigenous Peoples (2007), para. 22, p. 6. See Appendix 1, this volume. Also available at www.achpr.org/english/Special%20Mechanisms/Indegenous/Advisory%20opinion_eng.pdf

tations that had devastating effect on the well-being of the Ogoni people. On this same occasion, the African Commission linked the right to life of individual Ogoni, protected under Article 4 of the Charter, with the effects that oil exploitation had on their lands.[967] In its 2007 Advisory Opinion on the United Nations Declaration on the Rights of Indigenous Peoples, the African Commission stated in relation to Article 21 of the Charter that:

> Similar provisions are contained in many other instruments adopted by the AU such as the African Convention on the Conservation of Nature and Natural Resources whose major objective is: "*to harness the natural and human resources of our continent for the total advancement of our peoples in spheres of human endeavour*" (Preamble) and which is intended "*to preserve the traditional rights and property of local communities and request the prior consent of the communities concerned in respect of all that concerns their access to and use of traditional knowledge*" … [968]

One could also use Articles 2 and 3 of the African Charter to advocate before courts the right of indigenous peoples to lands.[969] This is an argument to be built around the principle of equal protection by the law and that of non discrimination. Since in most African countries, customary land ownership, use and occupation is recognized for most agriculturalists, it is arguable that non recognition of land use and occupation by nomadic hunters, gatherers, and pastoralists communities amounts to a discriminatory practice and an unequal protection by the law.

The African Commission on Human and Peoples' Rights (ACHPR)

The establishment of the African Commission was provided for by the African Charter and was officially inaugurated on 2 November 1987 in Addis Ababa, Ethiopia. A few years later, a permanent Secretariat was secured for the Commission in Banjul, The Gambia.

The ACHPR is composed of 11 commissioners elected by secret ballot by the Assembly of Heads of States and Governments of the African Union (AU) for a 6-year renewable term. Its mandate is to promote and protect human and peoples' rights in Africa and to interpret the African Charter on Human and Peoples' Rights. The Commission focuses on promotional activities, which includes awareness-raising, fact-finding missions as well as documenting and collecting

---

967 Fergus MacKay, "African Commission on Human and Peoples' Rights", (Forest Peoples Programme, 2001). Available at:
http://www.forestpeoples.org/documents/africa/af_com_brf_human_rights_oct01_eng.shtml
968 African Commission on Human and Peoples' Rights, Advisory Opinion (2007), para. 35. See Appendix 1, this volume.

information relating to human and peoples' rights in Africa through various mechanisms as for instance Special Rapporteurs and Working Groups within specific areas of concern.

The ACHPR Working Group on Indigenous Populations/ Communities

It took the African Commission of Human and Peoples' Rights (ACHPR) almost fifteen years to address the issue of indigenous peoples' rights seriously. The very first steps were taken in 1999, during the 26th ACHPR session in Kigali, Rwanda, when the Commission began debating the human rights situation of indigenous populations/communities and a Committee made up of three Commissioners was constituted with the mandate to consider the issue of indigenous peoples in Africa and advise accordingly. In 2000, during the 28th Ordinary Session in Benin, the situation of indigenous peoples was for the first time included as a separate item on the agenda and a "Resolution on the Rights of Indigenous Populations/Communities in Africa" was adopted resolving to set up a working group with the mandate to:

- Examine the concept of indigenous peoples and communities in Africa
- Study the implications of the African Charter on the human rights and well-being of indigenous communities especially with regard to:
  – the right to equality (Article 2 and 3)
  – the right to dignity (Article 5)
  – the protection against domination (Article 19)
  – the right to self-determination (Article 20) and
  – the promotion of cultural development and identity (Article 22)
- Consider appropriate recommendations for the monitoring and protection of the rights of indigenous communities
- Submit a report to the African Commission.[970]

The Working Group of Experts on the Rights of Indigenous Populations/Communities in Africa was officially established by the African Commission at its 29th Ordinary Session in Libya, in 2001. It is a small task force to which a few people are nominated by the African Commission in their personal capacity as experts. It was originally composed of three Commissioners and four—three indigenous and one independent—experts. The mandate of the Working Group has been renewed a number of times, lastly in November 2009 at the 46th ACHPR

---

970 See International Work Group for Indigenous Affairs, *The Indigenous World 2001-2002*, (Copenhagen: IWGIA 2002), 452-456. See also African Commission, *Report of the Working Group of Experts* (2005), p. 69.

Session where it was renewed for another two years. In 2007, the number of experts was increased with two new members.[971]

The Working Group came up with its report in 2003.[972] In this report, which was received with unprecedented acknowledgement by the African regional human rights body, the Working Group concluded that there are indigenous peoples in Africa, that they suffer from particular discrimination, that the African Charter on Human and Peoples' Rights provides special protection to those communities, which suffer from particular discrimination. The report made also numerous recommendations to the African Commission on Human and Peoples' Rights.

Today, this Report has become a valuable document for advancing rights of indigenous peoples on the continent. In relation to lands, the Report states clearly that "the protection of rights to land and natural resources is fundamental for the survival of indigenous communities in Africa and such protection relates both to Articles 20, 21, 22, and 24 of the African Charter."[973] The Working Group has since the Report's publication undertaken numerous activities, including country visits to Botswana, Namibia and Niger, Rwanda and Burkina Faso, information and research visits to Burundi, Libya, the Republic of Congo, the Central African Republic, Uganda, Gabon and DR Congo.[974] Two sensitization seminars have been held by the Working Group for Government and AU representatives in 2006 and 2008, respectively. Publicly available reports are being produced from all these visits and seminars.[975] The Working Group has also, in collaboration with the ILO and the Human Rights Centre of the University of Pretoria in South Africa, produced a report on legal provisions relevant to indigenous peoples' rights in twenty four African countries.

The African Court on Human and Peoples' Rights

Since the creation of the Working Group on Indigenous Populations/Communities, the African Commission has remained interested in the human rights situation of in-

---

971 For more information, see IWGIA's website at http://www.iwgia.org
972 The Report was published by the ACHPR in cooperation with the International Work Group for Indigenous Affairs (IWGIA) in 2005 in English and French under the title *Report of the African Commission's Working Group of Experts on Indigenous Populations/Communities—submitted in accordance with the "Resolution on the Rights of Indigenous Populations/Communities in Africa" adopted by The African Commission on Human and Peoples' Rights at its 28ᵗʰ ordinary session*. A summary of the Report, *Indigenous Peoples in Africa: The Forgotten Peoples?* has been published in English, French, Arabic and Portuguese, and will soon also be available in Tamazight and Fulani Available in English online at http://www.iwgia.org/sw2186.asp and
      http://www.achpr.org/english/_info/wgip_others.htm
973 ACHPR, Report of the Working Group (2005), p. 21.
974 The Working Group's country visits reports can be accessed at the Web sites of the ACHPR—
      http://www.achpr.org—and IWGIA—http://www.iwgia.org/sw2186.asp
975 See Web sites of ACHPR and IWGIA.

digenous peoples via numerous other mechanisms including the examination of States Parties' periodic reports. The African Commission also receives land-related communications. This was, for example, the case of the indigenous Endorois people of Kenya claiming ancestral lands around the Lake Bogoria. As already mentioned, the Commission has recently concluded this case in favour of the Endorois people and has issued a number of strong recommendations to the Government of Kenya. Complaints can be filed by individuals, NGOs, groups of individuals and indigenous peoples, either on their own behalf or on behalf of others. The author (i.e., the person/entity submitting the complaint) need not reside in the state against which the complaint is made. Allegations must be about *"a series of serious or massive"* violations of human and peoples' rights by a State Party to the Charter. There are indeed very particular procedures and formalities to respect as detailed in a publication by Forest Peoples Programme.[976] Until recently, however, there has not been any mechanism to enforce decisions taken by the Commission. This has prompted the interest in establishing an African human rights court, and in April 2005, at the 37th session of the ACHPR, a resolution was adopted on the establishment of an African Court on Human and Peoples' Rights to sit in Arusha/Tanzania. The appointment of judges took place in January 2006. Meant to issue legal binding decisions, the court could be seized by the African Commission on Human and Peoples' Rights, States, NGO and individuals. It is also expected that efforts by the African Commission regarding indigenous peoples' land rights will be taken forward by the African Court of Human Rights.

Other African regional bodies

There are several other African sub regional organizations with rules and laws that could be helpful in ensuring a better protection and promotion of indigenous peoples' right to lands. The most relevant seems to be the **Southern African Development Community (SADC)** that comprises 14 African countries from DR Congo and southwards. Article 3.2(g) of its Forestry Protocol[977] provides for respect of communities' rights, stating that, in order

> *[t]o achieve the objectives of this Protocol, States Parties shall co-operate by*
> *...*
> *promoting respect for the rights of communities and facilitating their participation in forest policy development, planning, and management with particular attention to the need to protect traditional forest-related knowledge and to develop adequate mechanisms to ensure the equitable sharing of benefits derived from forest resources and traditional forest-related knowledge without prejudice to property rights.*

---

976 See Forest Peoples Forests Programme Web site:
http://www.forestpeoples.org/documents/africa/af_com_brf_human_rights_oct01_eng.shtml
977 The text of the Protocol on Forestry is available online at http://www.sadc.int/index.php

This Protocol insists also on occupation of lands by communities (Articles 12 and 16). Similar principles and rules are upheld in SADC's Protocol on Wildlife Conservation and Law Enforcement.[978]

The New Partnership for African Development (NEPAD) is another institution that has developed rules that could contribute to the protection of indigenous peoples' right to lands. One of its mechanisms is known as the African Peer Review Mechanism (APRM), an instrument voluntarily acceded to by Member States of the African Union (AU) and put in place to ensure that the policies and practices of participating States conform to the agreed political, economic and corporate governance values, codes and standards contained in the African Union's Declaration on Democracy, Political, Economic and Corporate Governance. In 2005, for instance, the APRM recommended an in-depth dialogue between the Government of Rwanda and the Batwa after the following finding:

> With respect to the Batwa minority, the approach adopted by the authorities was based on a policy of assimilation. There appears to be a desire to obliterate distinctive identities and to integrate all into some mainstream socio-economic fabric of the country.[979]

The Economic Community of West African States (ECOWAS) has legal instruments that provide for the rights to culture, environment and non discrimination but they do not contain anything specific regarding the protection of indigenous peoples' land rights.

Multilateral Development Banks

Development Banks provide financial support and professional advice for economic and social development activities in developing countries. The term Multilateral Development Banks (MDBs) typically refers to the World Bank Group[980] and four regional development banks: the African Development Bank (AfDB),

---

978 Available online at: http://www.sadc.int/index/browse/page/164
979 NEPAD, African Peer Review Mechanism (APRM), Country Review Report of the Republic of Rwanda, November 2005, paras. 153 and 156:
     http://www.nepad.org/2005/files/aprm/FINAL_RWANDA_REPORT_SEPT_22_2006.pdf
980 The World Bank Group is made up of five institutions: the International Bank for Reconstruction and Development and the International Development Association—IDA—(known as the World Bank), the International Finance Corporation (IFC), the Multilateral Investment Guarantee Agency (MIGA), and the International Centre for Settlement of Investment Disputes (ICSID).

the Asian Development Bank (ADB), the European Development Bank and the Inter-American Development Bank (IDB).[981]

Another important international financial mechanism is the Global Environment Facility (GEF) that has become the largest funder of projects to improve global environment.[982] Although the GEF is an independent financial entity, its projects and programmes are implemented through agencies, as for instance the UNDP, the World Bank, and the AfDB.

The World Bank as well as the Asian Development Bank,[983] the Inter-American Development Bank [984] and the GEF[985] have all developed policies or strategies that deal with indigenous peoples. Unlike its continental counterparts, the African Development Bank does not have an indigenous peoples policy, although the existence of indigenous populations/communities on the African continent has been recognized by AU and ACHPR. The World Bank is therefore the most relevant multilateral bank in an African context, with more than 525 projects across the continent,[986] including GEF funded projects.

The World Bank and indigenous peoples' land rights

Operational Directive (OD) 4.20

The World Bank's first major effort towards better protection of indigenous peoples' land rights resulted in the 1991 Operational Directive (OD) 4.20 on indigenous peoples—in force until 2005. As a positive input, the Directive provided a broad understanding of the concept "indigenous peoples", and required prior consultation with indigenous groups, whose lands were to be affected by Bank supported projects.[987]

---

981 The regional banks are characterized by a broad membership, including both borrowing developing countries and developed donor countries, and not limited to member countries from the region. Each bank has its own independent legal and operational status—but with a similar mandate and a considerable number of joint owners, the MDBs maintain a high level of cooperation.

982 The GEF has since 1991 assisted countries in meeting their obligations under the conventions that they have signed and ratified, such as the Convention on Biological Diversity (CBD), the United Nations Framework Convention on Climate Change, the U.N. Convention to Combat Desertification (UNCCD), etc. GEF provides grants for projects related to the following six focal areas: biodiversity, climate change, international waters, land degradation, the ozone layer, and persistent organic pollutants.

983 On Asian Development Bank (ADB)'s policy "Sharing Development with Indigenous Peoples" and other policy documents, see http://www.adb.org/IndigenousPeoples/default.asp

984 On Inter-American Development Bank (IDB)'s Strategy for Indigenous Development, see http://www.iadb.org/sds/IND/site_401_e.htm

985 On GEF's Focal Area Strategies and Strategic Programming for GEF-4 (2007), see http://thegef.org/interior.aspx?id=18428

986 See World Bank projects portfolio for Africa on http://web.worldbank.org

987 World Bank, OD 4.20, para. 8. Can be accessed at http://www.austlii.edu.au/au/journals/AILR/2003/14html

Following consultations, borrowers were required to present an "indigenous peoples development plan", which, among many other prerequisites, should ensure "a proper protection of the rights of indigenous peoples".[988] Regarding land, the indigenous development plan should give "[p]articular attention... to the rights of indigenous peoples to use and develop the lands that they occupy, to be protected against illegal intruders, and to have access to natural resources (such as forests, wildlife, and water) vital to their subsistence and reproduction."[989] Furthermore, "when local legislation [regarding land tenure] needs strengthening, the Bank should offer to advise and assist the borrower in establishing legal recognition of the customary or traditional land tenure systems of indigenous peoples."[990]

However, when it came to communities' right not to be removed from their homeland, OD 4.20 contained ambiguous and problematic provisions that in fact limited indigenous peoples' rights to land.[991]

In 1993, the Inspection Panel, a three-member body, was created to provide an independent mechanism, whereby groups of two or more citizens, who found that they or their interests had been—or could be—directly harmed by a project financed by the World Bank, could present their concerns through a request for inspection.

On the African continent, both OD 4.20 and the Inspection mechanism have been used. In 2000, for example, and following the World Bank's participation in the financing of the US$3.7 billion Tchad-Cameroon pipeline project that affected, amongst others, the "Pygmies" of Cameroon, the Cameroonian Government drew up, as required by OD 4.20, a US$600,000 "Indigenous Peoples Plan" covering a 28 year period. In 2002, the Panel received a Request for Inspection based on a complaint by, among others, indigenous communities who claimed that the World Bank did not live up to its own policy standards. The inspection took place in 2003, but since the Inspection Panel is not a judiciary body and its decisions are not binding for the World Bank, not much came out of this procedure in terms of benefits to the communities. The Inspection Panel has also taken up a complaint from "Pygmies" living in the Democratic Republic of Congo, and who believe that ongoing reforms of the forest sector sustained by the Bank fail to protect their rights. As a result of this action, measures are currently being considered by the Congolese Government and its international partners in order to raise the standards of protection and recognition of the rights of indigenous peoples affected by forest reforms.[992] Despite the criticism that may be leveled against the Inspection Panel, it remains a mechanism available to indigenous peoples.

Operational Directive 4.20 has been criticized for not having been "fully respected, partly because of uncertainties of interpretation and significant practical

---

988 Ibid., para. 15.
989 Ibid., para. 15(a).
990 Ibid., para. 15(c).
991 See, e.g., ibid., para. 15(c).
992 See, e.g., Roger Muchuba, "The Indigenous Voice in the REDD process in the Democratic Republic of Congo", *Indigenous Affairs* 1-2/09 on REDD and Indigenous Peoples (Copenhagen: IWGIA 2009).

difficulties of implementation … also because of the innovative character of the policy and the unfamiliarity of some task managers with indigenous peoples' issues".[993] Indigenous peoples have also been critical and consistently demanded that World Bank policies provide, among other things, for their right to free, prior and informed consent and the recognition and protection of territorial rights. They have also pointed out that the World Bank Group's own evaluations demonstrate consistent failures to adhere to its own policy prescriptions and that compliance, enforcement and grievance mechanisms must be incorporated into project instruments.[994]

Operational Policy (OP) and Bank Procedures (BP) 4.10

On May 10, 2005, the Executive Directors of the World Bank approved a revised safeguard policy on indigenous peoples—OP/BP4.10—in substitution of the Operational Directive 4.20. The result of a protracted and contentious revision process, including a number of workshops with indigenous participants, OP/BP4.10, however, does not live up to the expectations of indigenous peoples, even though certain of its elements may be considered improvements.[995]

When dealing with land and land rights, OP/BP4.10 is far more detailed than OD 4.20.[996] Indigenous peoples' close ties "to land, forests, water, wildlife, and other natural resources" are thus recognized as well as the need for "special considerations … if the project affects such ties". Paragraph 16 thus stipulates that particular attention is to be given to:

a. the customary rights of the Indigenous Peoples, both individual and collective, pertaining to lands or territories that they traditionally owned, or customarily used or occupied, and where access to natural resources is vital to the sustainability of their cultures and livelihoods;

b. the need to protect such lands and resources against illegal intrusion or encroachment;

c. the cultural and spiritual values that the Indigenous Peoples attribute to such lands and resources; and

d. Indigenous Peoples' natural resources management practices and the long-term sustainability of such practices.[997]

---

993 Kingsbury, "Indigenous Peoples in International Law" (1998), p. 443.
994 Fergus MacKay, "The Draft World Bank Operational Policy 4.10 on Indigenous Peoples: Progress or more of the same?" *The Arizona Journal of International and Comparative Law Online,* 22, 1 (2005), pp. 68-69. Available online at
     http://www.law.arizona.edu/journals/ajicl/AJICL2005/vol221/vol221.htm
995 Ibid., p. 97.
996 The text of OP/BP4.10 is available online at
     http://web.worldbank.org/WBSITE/EXTERNAL/TOPICS/EXTSOCIALDEVELOPMENT/E
     XTINDPEOPLE/0,,menuPK:407808~pagePK:149018~piPK:149093~theSitePK:407802,00.html
997 World Bank, OP/BP4.10, para. 16.

Regarding land tenure, paragraph 17 stipulates that the Indigenous Peoples Plan (IPP) sets forth an action plan for the legal recognition of land ownership, occupation, or usage. Such legal recognition may take different forms. If these options are not possible under domestic law, the IPP includes measures for legal recognition of perpetual or long-term renewable custodial or use rights."[998]

Paragraph 20 concerns physical relocation, which should be "avoided" and is an option only "in exceptional circumstances, when it is not feasible to avoid [it]". In such cases, "the borrower will not carry out such relocation without obtaining broad support for it from the affected Indigenous Peoples' communities as part of the free, prior, and informed consultation process".[999]

In his critical analysis of the final Draft World Bank Operational Policy 4.10, Fergus MacKay points out that the terminology used in the above mentioned paragraphs 16 and 17 is often confusing and undefined, and that "there is not a clear statement in the OP that prior resolution of and adequate guarantees for indigenous peoples' rights to lands, territories, and resources are required in relation to all projects that affect indigenous peoples' lands, territories and resources".[1000] He also argues that "the conversion of customary rights to individual ownership rights without the express free, prior and informed consent of the affected indigenous peoples is contrary to human rights law and indigenous peoples' cultures and customs".[1001] On the other hand, certain paragraphs, especially Paragraph 20 on physical relocation, represent a significant evolution in thinking within the Bank.[1002]

But as critiques note, the extent of the potential improvements in OP 4.10 ultimately turns on the definition of what the World Bank's Operational Policy calls "free, prior and informed consultation" resulting in "broad community support". OP/BP 4.10 states that,

> For all projects that are proposed for Bank financing and affect Indigenous Peoples, the Bank requires the borrower to engage in a process of free, prior, and informed consultation. The Bank provides project financing only where free, prior, and informed consultation results in broad community support to the project by the affected Indigenous Peoples.[1003]

Free, prior and informed consultation is understood by the World Bank as a

> [C]ulturally appropriate and collective decisionmaking process subsequent to meaningful and good faith consultation and informed participa-

---

998 Ibid., para. 17.
999 Ibid., para. 20.
1000 MacKay, "The Draft World Bank Operational Policy 4.10" (2005), p. 92.
1001 Ibid.
1002 Ibid., p. 95.
1003   World Bank, OP 4.10, para. 1.

tion regarding the preparation and implementation of the project. It does not constitute a veto right for individuals or groups.[1004]

The World Bank has been severely criticized for using the word "consultation" rather than "consent", which is enshrined by the UN Declaration on the Rights of Indigenous Peoples. This is obviously an issue to be addressed by the World Bank if it has to be consistent with international law. The Bank is also criticized for not defining what "broad community support" means and for not providing

> [A]ny prompt and simple mechanism for indigenous peoples to challenge and complain about faulty or false assessments of broad community support nor require that such support and the conditions thereof be subject to written agreements between the borrower and affected indigenous peoples. Without prompt and effective grievance, complaints and verification mechanisms, adherence to OP/BP4.10 is largely dependent on the good will of the borrower and the Bank.[1005]

In 2008, responding to a complaint by several NGOs working on indigenous peoples' rights in DR Congo, the Inspection Panel of the World Bank came up with the following conclusion:

> The Panel found, however, that there was a failure during project design to carry out the necessary initial screening to identify risks and trigger the safeguard policies so that crucial steps would be taken to address needs of the Pygmy peoples and other local people.[1006]

Major donor agencies targeting indigenous peoples

United Nations agencies and indigenous land rights

Several U.N. agencies have developed policies or guidelines on indigenous peoples, with clear statements regarding land rights. This is the case of the United Nations Development Programme in its policy statement "UNDP and Indigenous Peoples: A Practice Note on Engagement" (2007),[1007] which, among other things, states that

---

1004   Ibid., para. 1n4.

1005   MacKay, "The Draft World Bank Operational Policy 4.10" (2005), p. 98.

1006   World Bank Africa, New Release No. 2008/188/AFR, See complete report of the Inspection Panel at: http://siteresources.worldbank.org/EXTINSPECTIONPANEL/Resources/FINALINV

1007   Available online at http://www.undp.org/biodiversity/pdfs/CSODivisionPolicyofEngagement.pdf

UNDP promotes the recognition of indigenous rights to lands, territories and resources; laws protecting indigenous lands; and the inclusion of indigenous peoples in key legislative processes;

and

recognizes the rights of distinct peoples living in distinct regions to self-determined development and control of ancestral lands.[1008]

In its "Draft Guidelines: A Human Rights Approach to Poverty Reduction Strategies", the United Nations High Commissioner for Human Rights (UNHCHR) underlines that "efforts must be made to secure indigenous peoples' right to the lands (including forests, grazing lands and other common property resources) on which they depend for their food."[1009]

It should also be mentioned that through their participation in the Inter-Agency Support Group to the UNPFII, most United Nations agencies have now stepped up their involvement with indigenous peoples. To name a few: the U.N. Food and Agriculture Organization (FAO) has initiated a wide programme on conservation and adaptive management of Globally Important Agricultural Heritage Systems (GIAHS) aiming to establish the basis for the global recognition, conservation and sustainable management of such systems and their associated landscapes, biodiversity, knowledge systems and cultures. In Africa, one of the systems and sites identified are the Traditional Maasai Pastoral Rangeland Management (Kenya and Northern Tanzania).[1010] The International Fund for Agricultural Development (IFAD) has also a long tradition for working with indigenous peoples, notably with the purpose of ensuring their land rights.[1011]

The European Union and indigenous peoples' right to lands

The development of a European Union policy on indigenous peoples is relatively recent. In 1998, the Council of Ministers of the European Union adopted a Council Resolution on Indigenous Peoples within the Framework of the Development Cooperation of the Community and Members States, which provides the main guidelines for support to indigenous peoples.

1008 UNDP, *UNDP and Indigenous Peoples: A Practice Note on Engagement* (2007), paras. 29 and 30.
1009 The OHCHR Draft Guidelines are meant to help countries eligible to debt cancellation streamline human rights into their efforts and policies to fight poverty. See http://www2.ohchr.org/english/issues/poverty/guidelines.htm. The author of this book was one of the consultants who contributed to this project commissioned by the Office of the U.N. High Commissioner for Human Rights.
1010 See http://www.fao.org/sd/giahs/africa.asp
1011 See http://www.ifad.org/english/indigenous/index.htm

In this Resolution, the Council calls for "concern for indigenous peoples to be integrated into all levels of development cooperation, including policy dialogue with partner countries". It also encourages "the full participation of indigenous peoples in the democratic processes of their country" within an approach that "asserts they should participate fully and freely in the development process", recognizing "their own diverse concepts of development" and "the right to choose their own development paths", including "the right to object to projects, in particular in their traditional areas" and "compensation where projects negatively affect the livelihoods of indigenous peoples". It thereby acknowledges the importance that indigenous peoples attach to their own self-development, that is, the shaping of their own social, economic and cultural development and their own cultural identities. The Resolution states, "Indigenous cultures constitute a heritage of diverse knowledge and ideas, which is a potential resource to the entire planet".[1012]

In 2002, a Review of Progress of Working with Indigenous Peoples—as required by the 1998 Council Resolution—restated the need for recognition of indigenous peoples' right to land.[1013] Following the review, a Conference on Indigenous Peoples, was held in Brussels in June 2002 with indigenous representatives. On the basis of the conclusions reached at this conference, the Council adopted on November 18, 2002 a document entitled "Conclusions on indigenous peoples issues". In this document, the Council recalls its commitment to the 1998 Resolution and invites the Commission and the Member States to continue implementing it. It also invites the Commission to "mainstream indigenous peoples issues into the European Union's policies, practices and work methods. Where relevant, indigenous peoples should be able to fully and effectively participate at all stages of the project cycle (programming, identification, planning, implementation, and evaluation".[1014] In 2005, the Council and the representatives of the Member States issued a joint statement entitled "The European Consensus on Development" which confirmed earlier commitments, stating, among other things, that, "the key principle for safeguarding indigenous

---

1012 European Commission, Council Resolution of 30 November 1998: "Indigenous Peoples within the Framework of the Development Cooperation of the Community and the Member States". 214th Council Meeting – Development. Brussels (1998b). Available online at http://www.ec.europa.eu/external_relations/human_rights/ip/docs/council_resolution1998_en.pdf. The Resolution was grounded on the European Commission, "Working Document of the Commission on Support for Indigenous Peoples in the Development Co-operation of the Community and the Member States" (1998a). This Document is available online at http://www.ec.europa.eu/external_relations/human_rights/ip/work_doc98.pdf

1013 European Commission, "Review of progress of working with indigenous peoples", Brussels, 11.6.2002, COM (2002) 291 final (2002a). Available online at http://www.eur-lex.europa.eu/LexUriServ/LexUriServ.do?uri=COM:2002:0291:FIN:EN:PDF

1014 The Conclusions of the EU Council (2002b) are available (as a summary) online at http://www.europa.eu/legislation_summaries/development/sectoral_development_policies/r12006_en.htm

peoples' rights in development cooperation is to ensure their full participation and the free and prior informed consent of the communities concerned". [1015]

The EU has also been very instrumental in the adoption of the Convention on Biological Diversity and numerous other international processes and instruments dealing with indigenous peoples. Since 1999, the rights of indigenous peoples have been included as a thematic priority under the European Initiative for Democracy and Human Rights (EIDHR), which has become an important source of funds for research and development projects focusing on indigenous peoples. [1016] It is also understood that the EU is in the process of integrating support for promoting the rights and issues of indigenous peoples within the European Commission's cooperation with the ACP (African, Caribbean and Pacific) countries.

Donor agencies

Within Europe, and apart from countries like Sweden, Norway and Finland that have their own indigenous communities (the Saami), there are also individual European countries, without self-identified indigenous peoples, which have introduced relevant standards for the protection of indigenous peoples into their development aid policies. These countries include Denmark that issued the Danish Strategy for Support to Indigenous Peoples in 1994. This strategy proposes the integration of indigenous issues into policy-dialogue and development practices and increased financial support to projects addressing the issues of self-determination, land-rights, capacity building, bilingual education, and the sustainable use of natural resources. It also proposes that programme components and projects address territorial and environmental issues of indigenous peoples through assistance to the conservation, improvement, and sustainable use of the territories, lands, and natural resources. This may include support to national policies concerning their legal rights to their territory and its biodiversity to increase awareness of indigenous peoples and their relationship to and dependence on their territories and natural resources at national, regional, and local levels of the situation. [1017] Germany published in 2002 its Sector Strategy for Forests and Sustainable Development, whose goal is,

---

1015 European Commission, "The European Consensus on Development – Joint statement by the Council and the Representatives of the Governments of the Member States meeting within the Council, the European Parliament and the Commission" (2005). Available online at http://ec.europa.eu/development/icenter/repository/eu_consensus_en.pdf

1016 See on the Web site of the European Commission: http://ec.europa.eu/comm/external_relations/human_rights/doc/com02_291.htm

1017 Danish Ministry of Foreign Affairs (DANIDA), 2004, Strategy for Danish Support to Indigenous Peoples. Available online at http://amg.um.dk/en/menu/policiesandstrategies/indigenouspeoples

among others, to "contribute to poverty reduction and sustainable development, specifically by ensuring the livelihood of the indigenous peoples who live in the forests and from its products, by better meeting their basic needs and by improving the infrastructure of rural areas".[1018] Other European countries, like Spain, have adopted strategies for their cooperation with indigenous peoples.[1019]

1018 The Sector Strategy is available at:
http://www.bmz.de/en/service/infothek/fach/konzepte/090.pdf
1019 Spanish Strategy Paper for Cooperation with Indigenous Peoples (1997)is available online at
http://www.aeci.es

CHAPTER XII
GENERAL CONCLUSIONS AND RECOMMENDATIONS

A frica is home to a number of communities that identify themselves—and are being identified by the African Commission on Human and Peoples' Rights—as indigenous. These communities are characterized by having, for centuries, "experienced subjugation, marginalisation, dispossession, exclusion or discrimination"[1020] by colonial powers and modern nation-states. They, nevertheless, persist, as confirmed by the 2005 Report of the African Commission on Human and Peoples' Rights, in attaching a multidimensional importance to their ancestral lands. For these communities, lands are not just commodities but the base for their way of life and survival as distinct peoples. Yet, their access to these lands is constantly being threatened by the building of nation-states, industrial farming, free market-oriented land management, conservation interests, mining, logging, fishing, and other extracting activities, thereby putting their very existence in jeopardy.

This is the reason why African indigenous communities, when their land rights are being denied or threatened, resist as best as they can and why they sometimes have used judicial venues as a way of addressing their predicament.

Yet, as this book has shown, there is a long way to go in terms of protection of indigenous peoples' rights to lands by the African judiciary, and indigenous communities seeking legal redress face a number of constraints.

Like other indigenous communities, African indigenous communities base their land claims on immemorial or —for some nomadic pastoralists—centuries long occupation and use of specific land areas. For many years, the concept of *terra nullius* was used worldwide to contest indigenous peoples' land rights. In 1975, however, the International Court of Justice in its Advisory Opinion in the Western Sahara case,[1021] established that the lands of indigenous peoples were not *terra nullius* at the time of conquest and a succession of sovereigns does not affect pre-existing property rights. In other words, the rights of African indigenous communities were not extinguished by the formalization of European coloniza-

---

1020   Daes, "Working Paper on the Concept of "Indigenous People" (1996), para. 69 (d).
1021   International Court of Justice (I.C.J.) Western Sahara: Advisory Opinion (1975), p. 12.

tion in 1885 or the subsequent creation of modern African States. Furthermore, relevant principles of social justice indicate that communities that have never made the free choice to abandon their "societal culture" should be entitled to "external protection" aiming at protecting such communities' cultural identities. This line of argument was later used in Australia (the *Mabo* case), and more recently in Southern Africa (see chapter VII, this volume). However, the concept of Aboriginal title is yet to find fertile ground in African courts.

Another constraint is the issue of "indigenousness". As discussed in chapter II, the concept of "indigenous peoples" has only recently been domesticated in Africa with the adoption by the African Commission on Human and Peoples Rights of the Report of its Working Group of Experts on Indigenous Populations/ Communities, and as chapter IX shows, only a few African Constitutions make any reference to the rights of their indigenous communities. Many African Governments even do still not recognize the existence of indigenous populations within their borders.

It comes, therefore, as no surprise that national legislations, in particular laws concerning land and land-related issues, do not provide any specific recognition or protection of the livelihoods and needs of indigenous populations. Taking the example of Kenya and Tanzania, it thus appears that land laws and policies since colonial time have evolved through three mainstream types of legislation. The first category of these laws, which could be called "colonial-type land laws", includes not only the major colonial land legislation, but also a number of post-colonial laws, which were no more than a re-statement of colonial policies, and as a rule promoted sedentary agriculture rather than nomadic pastoralism. The second type of land laws are those that were enacted mainly from the late 1960s, and which were aimed at shaping an African-grown economic approach as well as addressing the situation of landlessness faced by countless former colonised people. Commercial agriculture was now seen as the adequate solution. The last and third category consists of land laws passed in reaction to the failure of the "African economic renaissance", and which tie Kenya and Tanzania to the free market economy as well as to conservation interests. In both countries, it is clear that existing land and conservations laws contain almost no explicit provisions that provide specifically for the rights of indigenous peoples. Consequently, communities in both countries have been forced out of their lands for the sake of economic and conservation interests. As this book shows, the situation is very similar in Central and Southern African countries.

African indigenous peoples' organizations should therefore, among other things, lobby for a revision of the constitutions of their respective countries so that the existence and special status of indigenous peoples are recognized. Another priority should be to promote land and land-related legislation recognizing collective property rights and protecting the specific land use and occupation by nomadic and semi-nomadic indigenous peoples. The work done by the ACHPR

Working Group in disseminating information on indigenous peoples and their human rights situation, and organizing sensitization seminars for Governments and AU representatives is important in this aspect. Another recommended initiative to be taken by indigenous organizations is lobbying for the adoption of ILO Convention No. 169.

A third constraint, which is particular clear from the cases discussed in this book, is the attitude of the African judiciary, which, in line with most African Governments, considers the concept of "indigenous rights" as, at best, controversial. The recent judgments quoted in this book show that, barring judges in South Africa and Botswana, the majority of judges neither understand nor recognize indigenous peoples' customary land rights and often dismiss the way of life of nomadic hunter-gatherers and pastoralists as being irrelevant (the allegation being that they have moved away from their traditional way of life and embraced modernity) or incompatible with property rights (see, e.g., the Ogiek cases in Chapter V). Judges also seem to tend giving primacy to written laws and governments' policies over indigenous peoples' claims and customary tenure rights. They also tend to hold on any technicality they can come across, including delaying tactics, to deny justice or to avoid challenging established interests.

Sensitising African judges on rights of indigenous peoples could be beneficial and lay grounds for a better protection of indigenous peoples' rights. A recommendation to the African Commission's Working Group of Experts on Indigenous Populations/Communities would be to include the judiciary as a new target group for their sensitization seminars.

It appears also that Kenyan and Tanzanian judges dealing with indigenous land-related lawsuits dismiss or do not refer to international standards or jurisprudence. This despite the fact that Kenya and Tanzania, as practically all other African States, have ratified or signed up most of the international instruments that protect indigenous communities, notably, the ICCPR, the Convention on Elimination of Racial Discrimination, the Convention on Biological Diversity, the African Charter, and, with the exception of Burundi, Kenya and Nigeria (who abstained), the U.N. Declaration on the Rights of Indigenous Peoples.

Since few African countries have taken domestic legislative measures that protect and promote the rights of indigenous peoples, reference to international jurisprudence and instruments would constitute an important alternative source of law in support of indigenous land claims. A good example of how this can be done is the positive trend that has emerged from South Africa and Botswana, and which consists of a new judicial approach to indigenous peoples' rights to lands. In recent rulings, judges from these two countries have gone beyond domestic standards and grounded their arguments on the concept of aboriginal title which, it is argued, was not extinguished as a result of indigenous peoples' land dispossession by sovereign modern States. These decisions have gone as far as recognizing rights of indigenous peoples on lands that had become protected areas and rich mining sites. These rulings should—and are likely to—inspire judges from other parts of the African continent. Other sources of inspiration should be the work of the African Commission on Human and Peoples' Rights on the issues of indigenous peoples (as, for instance, in the recent decision regarding the Endorois people) and the U.N. Declaration on the Rights of Indigenous Peoples.

Such a new approach, however, implies that the judiciary is informed about and subsequently trained in using international jurisprudence and instruments. It is therefore recommended that such an aspect be taken up by the ACHPR Working Group and included in their sensitization seminars.

Observations and recommendations

Throughout this book, there have been a number of recommendations made in relation to improving the protection of the rights of indigenous peoples via other channels than the judiciary. The following list of recommendations, which in no way is exhaustive, relates, however, specifically to court cases and the whole process that surrounds them. They highlight some of the lessons that can be learned by indigenous peoples and their lawyers from the examples given in this book.

Because court cases are lengthy—most cases are heard by two, sometimes three different courts—and extremely costly in terms of fees to lawyers, transport, accommodation and instruction of witnesses, it is important to make extensive and in-depth preparations, collecting, for instance, archival or other historical evidence, calling on local and foreign expertise, taking judges to sites, etc., and becoming familiar with procedures and rules in order to avoid a case being dismissed on technicalities. Other aspects that may also be useful taking into account are the use of international mechanisms and international jurisprudences, of States' periodic reports to the treaty bodies and these bodies' observations.

1. It is recommended that indigenous communities carry out legal feasibility studies prior to lodging court cases. Successful court cases require financial resources and competent lawyers. Many indigenous communities have lost court cases for lack of necessary funds. In other cases, long delays are often caused by the time it takes for a community to raise funds (see the *CKGR* case in chapter VII). It can also be difficult to find a lawyer who is willing to take on a case of an indigenous community or who understands and grasps the notion of indigenous peoples' rights to land. This is partly due to the lack of teaching on the subject of rights of indigenous peoples in many African law schools. Whatever the situation is, such a feasibility study could provide an idea on not only the costs but also the legal arguments available or intended to be used by lawyers.

2. It is recommended to take account of regional or even local differences when preparing a case. In Tanzania, for instance, there have been cases where pastoralist peoples' customary land rights have been to some extent recognized by lower judges (see the Barabaig and the Maasai cases in chapter VI) but not by higher judges. The picture is a bit different in Kenya, where customary rights seem to enjoy less protection in written laws. In South Africa, it was the higher courts that recognized the validity of indigenous law.

3. Indigenous communities should lodge their complaints in courts as soon as incidents occur or as soon as they find out that they do not agree with compensation measures. In the Maasai cases involving the Mkomazi Game Reserve (chapter VI), torts-related claims of the plaintiffs were thrown out because the suit was filed more than three years after the facts. Letting several years elapse before filing a suit could be counterproductive since it might affect the quality of witnesses' accounts as well as the chances for collecting evidences; the outside support might also lose momentum.

    On the other hand, there are numerous cases where indigenous peoples have been expelled from their lands for hundreds or tens of years before taking legal actions. One could mention for example the restitution of tens of thousands of hectares to the South African ‡Khomani San on the basis of the Land Restitution Act. In this kind of cases, it is imperative for community lawyers to make as much as possible reference to any existing relevant international jurisprudence in an attempt to try and move judges away from traditional ways of thinking. Taking the case to higher courts or international bodies such as the African Commission on Human and Peoples' Rights could be further options.

4. It is recommended that any indigenous community taking its land grievances to court should list all the plaintiffs in the lawsuit. Otherwise, the plaintiffs might have to apply first for a leave to institute a representative suit on their own and on behalf of others, as done among others in the Kenyan Tinet Ogiek case (*Francis Kemai and others v. The Attorney General*) where ten individuals were allowed to plead and represent 5,000 other members of the community. However, such permission is not always granted, and in the Tanzanian cases examined in chapter VI, the attempts to represent others in court failed. Another aspect is that non-listed plaintiffs may be excluded from benefiting from the court's ruling, as it turned out to be the case in the *CKGR* case (see chapter VII).

5. It is recommended to go beyond traditional legal means of proof as they may not always be sufficient when indigenous communities suing for

their ancestral lands have to prove that they are natives of such lands. Other means must be found, as, for instance, in the case of the ‡Khomani San, who based their land claim on a multidisciplinary research and cultural reconstruction which in turn made it possible to establish the different waterholes, ritual places, hunting areas, etc., and enabled them to map their land (see chapter VII). In the Tanzanian Gawal case (*Yoke Gwaku and 5 others v. NAFCO*, chapter VI), the concerned Barabaig indigenous community called upon an anthropologist who had done research in their community to testify for them. Historians, social scientists and other knowledgeable persons may, based on their work with a community, shed important light on indigenous peoples' claims.

6. Indigenous plaintiffs should make references to national legal documents, like, e.g., the Constitution, whenever relevant. Although most African constitutions do not mention indigenous peoples, they do have clauses on equal rights, on the prohibition of discrimination and sometimes even on the protection of minorities, which can be invoked in a court case.

7. The fact that a State is declared sole owner of all lands should not prevent indigenous communities from initiating legal actions for protection of their right to use and occupation of what they believe are their ancestral lands. The *CKGR* case (chapter VII) reveals that a court can declare a State sole owner of a land and at the same time rule in favor of the right to use and occupation by an indigenous community. This case demonstrates also that being owner of a land does not automatically give a State the right to expel at will indigenous communities from it.

8. It is recommendable to base indigenous peoples' land rights court cases on strong rights, such as the right to life, to food security, etc.; invoking several other rights that are non derogatory, could also make a good strategy. In human rights theory and principles, certain rights (right to life, etc.) are to be respected and protected at any time and cost by Governments. They also cannot be suspended, even in case of a state of emergency. The two Ogiek cases in Kenya (chapter V) and the cases regarding Mkomazi Game Reserve in Tanzania (chapter VI) show the benefits of arguing for strong rights, including the right to life of the members of a community. A similar approach was also taken by one of the judges in the *CKGR* case (chapter VII).

9. It is also recommended that indigenous communities and their lawyers ground their arguments on theories of social justice, which have emerged

as persuasive in numerous court battles for indigenous peoples' lands, such as the *Mabo* case in Australia and the *Richtersveld* case in South Africa. The judicial reasoning in the *Mabo* case, for instance, could be regarded as grounded on the liberal egalitarian theory that emphasizes the importance of rectifying un-chosen inequalities: given that most indigenous communities have never opted to leave their societal culture and because they still show a deep bond with their own culture, the question is not, how should the State act fairly in governing its [indigenous communities], but what are the limits to the State's right to govern them (see chapter VIII).

10. Indigenous peoples and their legal teams are recommended to go beyond domestic written laws and use historical, cultural and sociological evidences as well as bringing to shore unwritten customary land-related laws. In numerous cases, judges tend to focus on domestic laws, paying no considerations to customs and traditions. The Endorois case (chapter V) and that of the San of Botswana (chapter VII) are good illustrations of this situation. Judges, who have positively land-marked this area of human rights, have instead, in most cases, grounded their thinking on historical injustices and facts generally uncovered by existing domestic legal instruments. In the Tinet Ogiek case (chapter V), for example, the Kenyan court found reasons not to take into account the Australian *Mabo* case jurisprudence possibly because of the positive impact such a judgment would have had in favour of the plaintiffs. However, it is interesting to notice that the judges did not dismiss the applicability of the *Mabo* case jurisprudence in the African context. They recognized that had the plaintiffs and the defence team provided them with relevant customary law, land statutes, and consistent principles of common law as was done in the *Mabo* case, they might have taken them into account.

11. It is recommended that an indigenous community make an evaluation report or assessment of damages suffered by its members as a result of land dispossessions, forcible removals and similar acts. The Mkomazi Game Reserve case (Tanzania, chapter VI) reveals that a lack of such evaluation can lead to unjust compensation measures. International and national NGOs may help making such reports. It is therefore recommendable that indigenous peoples do all they can to estimate exactly the damages suffered and that they do this as early in the process as possible, since, as years pass on, it becomes more difficult to reconstruct facts

12. It is recommendable that indigenous peoples or individuals rather refuse a compensation they consider to be unfair than accepting it and then later

declare it to be unfair. In one of the Barabaig cases (*Yoke Gwaku and 5 others v. NAFCO*, chapter VI), a number of plaintiffs accepted before the initiation of the court case some sort of compensation, which they later declared to be unfair. Such a practice is counterproductive and can compromise the success of a court case.

13. Having the judges visit the disputed lands or the settlements where the evicted indigenous peoples live after dispossession is recommended. This can contribute to the judges' assessment of the implications the loss of land and relocation may have on the livelihood of the plaintiffs.

14. It is recommended that lawyers representing indigenous communities should be acquainted with relevant international jurisprudence that can enlighten and inspire their line of arguments. It could also be advantageous for communities in court to refer to relevant positive jurisprudence from other African countries, even if it might not be binding upon the judge. This is likely to bear more fruits now with the ruling of the Constitutional Court of South Africa in the *Richtersveld* case and to some extent the CKGR case in Botswana (chapter VII). The African Commission's recent communication on the Endorois case may also be used as an important reference.

15. Legal teams representing indigenous communities should—whenever relevant—refer to international instruments protecting indigenous peoples' rights to lands, especially when they have been ratified by the concerned country. With the exception of the *Richtersveld* case, most other cases examined in this book make no such reference. Obviously, this fact comforted the judges in their national-laws-oriented thinking. Had the plaintiffs, at least, referred to international instruments and the doctrine of aboriginal title, this would have prompted a judge's response. This disregard of international standards by the courts is probably one of the reasons why the Endorois community decided to take its case before the African Commission on Human and Peoples' Rights.

16. Now that the U.N. Declaration on the Rights of Indigenous Peoples has been adopted, it is recommendable that communities and their lawyers use some of its provisions, which could be considered as universally accepted principles of justice.

17. It is also recommendable that indigenous communities and their legal teams make extensive use in courts of state reports, expert reports, concluding observations by treaty bodies related to the ICCPR (Human

Rights Committee), the Convention against Racial Discrimination (CERD) and the CBD, as well as concluding observations of the ACHPR in order to shed more light on a number of issues. Sometimes, States argue one thing in court and say the contrary in their periodic reports to treaty bodies or in similar official documents. Other documents such as reports of the African Peer Review Mechanism could also be useful to look into.

18. It is recommended to consider using international mechanisms when Governments make obvious use of delay tactics. For example, none of the numerous court cases filed by the Ogiek indigenous community in Kenya have been dealt with in time. While endless court cases continue, orders to encroach more Ogiek land are issued; more non-indigenous families are being settled on the disputed lands and titles deeds are even processed. In the example from Botswana, (chapter VII), the case—initiated in early 2002 and closed in late 2006—was delayed first on technicalities, later because the attorney general went on a sabbatical leave and later because of lengthy witness hearings. At a certain point, funding for the San ran out, causing another delay. In the end, the court case turned out to be the most expensive ever. Such prolonged and strategic delays could justify concerned communities to think of international mechanisms. Most international mechanisms can only be used after all domestic remedies have been exhausted. However, it is arguable that long delays amount to inefficiency of domestic remedies and there is jurisprudence that backs obvious delaying as proof of inefficient domestic remedies. Communications or complaints by indigenous peoples can be brought to the African Commission on Human and Peoples' Rights, the U.N. Human Rights Committee, the Committee on the Elimination of Racial Discrimination (CERD) and the Special Rapporteur on the situation of human rights and fundamental freedoms of indigenous peoples. These are some of the international mechanisms available to indigenous peoples. There is also the mechanism of urgent action by the CERD, which could be well combined with court cases in order to prevent escalation of a given situation. These international mechanisms are relevant in Africa since most countries are parties to these instruments.

19. Court procedures are often very lengthy. It is therefore recommendable that indigenous people request the court for intermediary measures, similar to the Court Order that the Ogiek plaintiffs of East Mau asked for and obtained from the Kenyan High Court, in order to stop the situation from worsening as the court case proceeds.

20. Indigenous peoples and their lawyers should be careful when considering combining court cases with international attention and similar high level campaigning activism. At a certain level, this strategy seemed to pay off in the San case in Botswana since it did provide the San with funds and a lawyer. But it also exacerbated the Government's and to a certain extent the general public's hostile feeling towards the San. So one might think of striking the right balance.

BIBLIOGRAPHY

Adlercreutz, Thomas
　1998　"Property Rights and Protection of Cultural Heritage in Sweden". *International Journal of Cultural Property* 7, no. 2 (1998).

African Commission on Human and Peoples' Rights
　1990　"African Commission of Human and Peoples' Rights, 1990 Activity report". *Human Rights Law Journal* (1990).

　2005　*Report of the African Commission's Working Group of Experts on Indigenous Populations/Communities—submitted in accordance with the "Resolution on the Rights of Indigenous Populations/Communities in Africa" adopted by The African Commission on Human and Peoples' Rights at its 28ᵗʰ ordinary session.* Banjul, The Gambia and Copenhagen, Denmark: ACHPR and IWGIA.

　2006　*Indigenous Peoples in Africa: The Forgotten Peoples? A Summary of the Report of the African Commission's Working Group of Experts on Indigenous Populations/Communities.* Available online in English, French and Portuguese at IWGIA's Web site, http://www.iwgia.org/sw2186.asp

　2007　"Advisory Opinion on the United Nations Declaration on the Rights of Indigenous Peoples". Available online at http://www.achpr.org/english/Special%20Mechanisms/Indegenous/Advisory%20opinion_eng.pdf

Akermark, Athanasia S.
　1997　*Justification of Minority Protection in International Law.* London: Kluwer.

Aklilu, Yacob, Patrick Irungu and Alemayehu Reda
　2002　*An Audit of the Livestock Marketing Status in Kenya, Ethiopia and Sudan.* 2 vols. Nairobi: Organization of African Unity/Interafrican Bureau for Animal Resources. Available online at http://www.eldis.org/fulltext/cape_new/Akliliu_Marketing_vol_1.pdf

Alden Wily, Liz
　2003　*Community-based Land Tenure Management. Questions and Answers about Tanzania's New Village Land Act, 1999.* IIED Issue Paper no. 120. London: IIED.

Alfredsson, Gudmundur
　1993　"Self-Determination and Indigenous Peoples". In *Modern Law of Self-Determination,* edited by Christian Tomuschat. Dordrecht: Martinus Nijhoff Publishers.

Amin, Samir
　1993　"The Challenge of Globalisation: Delinking". In *Facing the Challenge: Responses to the Report of the South Commission,* edited by the South Centre. London: Zed Books.

Amnesty International et al.
　2007　"Kenya Nowhere to Go: Forced Evictions in Mau Forest". Briefing Paper, May 2007. Available online at http://www.asiapacific.amnesty.org/library/Index/ENGAFR320062007?_open&of=ENG-398

Anaya, S. James
　1996　*Indigenous Peoples in International Law.* New York and Oxford, UK: Oxford University Press.

Annandale, Charles
　1999　*Home Study Dictionary.* London: Peter Haddock Ltd.

Archer, Clive
1983   *International Organizations*. London: George Allen and Unwin.
Asian Development Bank (ADB)
2009 (1998)   "Sharing Development with Indigenous Peoples". Available on line at:
        http://www.adb.org/IndigenousPeoples/default.asp
Australian Institute of Aboriginal and Torres Strait Islander Studies (AIATSIS)
(2004) 2007   "A Comparison of Native Title Laws". Available online at:
        http://www.ntruaiatsis.gov.au.
Bahuchet, Serge
1991   "Les pygmées changent leur mode de vie". *Vivant Univers* No. 396, Novembre-Décembre
        1991.
Bannon, Alicia L.
2007   "Designing a Constitution-Drafting Process: Lessons from Kenya". *Yale Law Journal*, June
        2007.
Barsh, Russell L.
1996   "Indigenous Peoples and the UN Commission on Human Rights: A Case of the Immov-
        able Object and the Irresistible Force". *Human Rights Quarterly*, 18 (1996).
2000   "The World's Indigenous Peoples". Available online at http://www.calvert.com/pdf/
        white_paper_barsh.pdf
Barume, Albert Kwoko
2000   *Heading Toward Extinction? Indigenous Rights in Africa: The Case of the Twa of the Kahuzi-Biega
        National Park, Democratic Republic of Congo*. IWGIA Document No. 101. Copenhagen:
        IWGIA and FPP.
2003   "Le nouveau code forestier congolais et les droits des communautés forestières". Paper
        prepared for the Working Group on Forests/Rainforest Foundation and presented at the
        Workshop on the Implementation Process of the Forestry Code of the Democratic Republic
        of Congo, Kinshasa 17-19 November 2003. Available online at http://archive.niza.nl/
        docs/200501181516531833.pdf.
2005a   "Etude sur le cadre légal pour la protection des droits des peuples indigènes et tribaux au
        Cameroun". Genève: Organisation Internationale du Travail/International Labour Orga-
        nization.
2005b   "Indigenous Battling for Land Rights: The Case of the Ogiek of Kenya". In *International
        Law and Indigenous Peoples*, edited by J. Castellino and N. Walsh. Boston: Martinuus Nijhoff
        Publishers.
2009   "Responding to the Concerns of the African States". In *Making the Declaration Work*, edited
        by Claire Charters and Rodolfo Stavenhagen. IWGIA Document No. 127. Copenhagen:
        IWGIA.
Bennett, T.W. and C.H. Powell
1999   "Aboriginal Title in South Africa Revisited". 15 *South African Journal of Human Rights* 4
        (1999).
Bernan, Bruce
1990   *Control and Crisis in Colonial Kenya: The Dialectic of Domination*. London, Nairobi, and Ath-
        ens, Ohio: Currey, Heinemann Nairobi, and Ohio University Press.
Bevan, James
2007   "Armed Violence in African Pastoral Communities." Report commissioned by the Gov-
        ernment of Kenya, the Swiss Confederation and UNDP. Available online at http://www.
        genevadeclaration.org/pdfs/pastoral.pdf
Bishop, Kristyna
1998   "Squatters on Their Own Lands: San Territoriality in Western Botswana". 31 *Comparative
        and International Law Journal of Southern Africa*, 92 (1998).
Borrows, John
2000   "Landed Citizenship: Narratives of Aboriginal Political Participation". In *Citizenship in Di-
        verse Societies*, edited by W. Kymlicka and W. Norman. Oxford and New York: Oxford
        University Press.

Bossuyt, Marc J.
   1987   Guide to the "Travaux Préparatoires" of the International Covenant on Civil and Political Rights. Dordrecht and Boston: Martinus Nijhoff Publishers.
Bourn, David and Roger Blench
   1999   Can Livestock and Wildlife Co-Exist: An Inter Disciplinary Approach. London: Overseas Development Institute and the Environmental Research Group Oxford.
Boursier, Daniel
   1991   "Réflexion sur l'évangélisation des Baka". Univers Vivant No. 396, Novembre-Décembre 1991.
Brody, Hugh
   2000   The Other Side of Eden: Hunter-Gatherers, Farmers and the Shaping of the World. London: Faber and Faber.
Brownlie, Ian
   1988   "Rights of Indigenous Peoples in Modern International Law". In The Rights of Peoples, edited by J. Crawford. Oxford: Clarendon Press.
   1998   Principles of Public International Law. Oxford: Oxford University Press.
Brownlie, Ian and F.M. Brookfield
   1992   Treaties and Indigenous Peoples. Oxford: Clarendon Press.
Bruch, Carl
   2000   Constitutional Environmental Law: Giving Force to Fundamental Principles in Africa. Washington: Environmental Law Institute. Available at http://www.elistore.org/reports_detail.asp?ID=527
Búrca, Gránne de
   1982   "The Principle of Proportionality and its Application in the EC Law". In Yearbook of European Law, vol. 13 (1982), edited by A. Barav and D.A. Wyatt. London: Clarendon Press.
Burger, Julian and Paul Hunt
   1994   "Towards the International Protection of Indigenous Peoples' Rights". Netherlands Quarterly of Human Rights (NQHR) 4 (1994).
BurnSilver, Shauna and Esther Mwangi
   2007   "Beyond Group Ranch Subdivision: Collective Action for Livestock Mobility, Ecological Viability and Livelihoods". Washington, D.C.: International Food Policy Research Institute. Available online at http://www.capri.cgiar.org/pdf/capriwp66.pdf
Calinaud, René
   2001   "Les principes directeurs du droit foncier polynésien". Revue Juridique Polynésienne, no. 7 (2001).
Cassese, Antonio
   1995   Self-Determination of Peoples: A Legal Reappraisal. Cambridge, UK: Cambridge University Press.
Cassidy, Julie
   1998   "Sovereignty of Aboriginal Peoples". 9 Indiana International and Comparative Law Review, 65 (1998).
Castellino, Joshua and Niamh Walsh
   2005   International Law and Indigenous Peoples. Boston: Martinuus Nijhoff Publishers.
CERD (U.N. Committee on the Elimination of Racial Discrimination)
   1997   General Recommendation XXIII "Rights of Indigenous Peoples". Adopted at fifty-first session, August 18, 1997. U.N. Doc. A/52/18, annex V (1997). Available online at http://www1.umn.edu/humanrts/gencomm/genrexxiii.htm
   1998   Conclusions and Recommendations, Cameroon. U.N. Doc. CERD/C/304/Add.53 (1998). Available online at http://hrlibrary.ngo.ru/country/cameroon1998.html
   2001   Conclusions and Recommendations, United States of America. 14/08/2001. U.N. Doc. A/56/18, paras. 380-407. Available online at http://hrlibrary.ngo.ru/country/usa2001.html
   2003   Conclusions and Recommendations, Uganda. U.N. Doc. CERD/C/62/CO/11 (2003). Available online at http://hrlibrary.ngo.ru/country/uganda2003.html

2005 Procedural Decisions on the Elimination of Racial Discrimination, New Zealand [Foreshore and Seabed Act 2004]. U.N. Doc. CERD/C/DEC/NZL/1 (2005). Available online at http://www1.umn.edu/humanrts/cerd/decisions/newzealand2005.html

2006 Conclusions and Recommendations, Botswana. U.N. Doc. CERD/C/BWA/CO/16, (2006). Available online at http://hrlibrary.ngo.ru/country/botswana2006.html

2007 Conclusions and Recommendations, Tanzania. U.N. Doc. CERD/C/TZA/CO/16, (2007). Available online at http://hrlibrary.ngo.ru/country/tanzania2007.html

CESCR (U.N. Committee on Social, Economic and Cultural Rights)

1990 General Comment No. 2, International technical assistance measures (Article 22). U.N. Doc. E/C.12/1990/23 Annex III at 86 (1990). Available at http://hrlibrary.ngo.ru/gencomm/epcomm2.htm

Chachage, C.S.L.

1999 "Land Issues and Tanzania's Political Economy". In *Agrarian Economy, State and Society in Contemporary Tanzania,* edited by P.G. Forster, and S. Maghimbi. Aldershot, UK: Ashgate Publishing Co.

Chan, T. M.

2004 "The Richtersveld Challenge: South Africa Finally Adopts Aboriginal Title". In *Indigenous Peoples' Rights in Southern Africa,* edited by Robert K. Hitchcock and Diana Vinding. IWGIA Document No. 110. Copenhagen: IWGIA.

Charters, Claire and Rodolfo Stavenhagen (eds.)

2009 *Making the Declaration Work.* IWGIA Document No. 127. Copenhagen: IWGIA.

Cheeseman, Ted

n.d. "Conservation and the Maasai in Kenya. Tradeoff or Lost Mutualism". Available online at http://www.environmentalaction.net/aa_kenya_policy.htm

Chennells, Roger

2003 "The ‡Khomani San of South Africa". In *Indigenous Peoples and Protected Areas in Africa: From Principles to Practice,* edited by J. Nelson and L. Hossack. Moreton-in-Marsh, UK: Forest Peoples Programme.

Chennells, Roger and Aymone du Toit

2004 "The Rights of Indigenous Peoples in South Africa". In *Indigenous Peoples' Rights in Southern Africa,* edited by Robert K. Hitchcock and Diana Vinding. IWGIA Document No. 110. Copenhagen: IWGIA.

Chomsky, Noam

1993 "World Orders, Old and New". In *Facing the Challenge: Responses to the Report of the South Commission,* edited by the South Centre. London: Zed Books.

Collins

1993 *Collins School Dictionary.* UK: HarperCollins Publishers.

Comby, Joseph

1995 "Quel cadastre, pourquoi faire ? Exemple du Gabon". Online article available at http://perso.orange.fr/joseph.comby/cadastre_Gabon.html

Connor, Michael

n.d. "The Invention of Territorium Nullius". Available online at: www.michaelconnor.com.au/USERIMAGES/usedinventionterritorium.pdf

Corbett, Andrew

1999 "A Case Study on the Proposed Epupa Hydropower Dam". *Indigenous Affairs,* "Dams, Indigenous Peoples and Ethnic Minorities", no. 3-4/1999. Copenhagen: IWGIA.

Cotran, Eugene

1971 "Customary Land Law in Kenya, Uganda and Tanzania". In UNESCO, *Le droit de la terre en Afrique.* Paris: G.P. Maisonneuve et Larose.

Council of Europe

1995 Framework Convention for the Protection of National Minorities. Council of Europe document H (95) 10. Available online at http://www.conventions.coe.int/Treaty/Commun/ListeTraites.asp?CM=8&CL=ENG

Cousins, Ben
    2000   "Tenure and Common Property Resources in Africa". In *Evolving Land Rights, Policy and Tenure in Africa,* edited by C. Toulmin and J. Quan. London: Department for International Development, International Institute for Environment, and Development/Natural Resources Institute.

Crépeau, P.A. and J.E.C. Brierley
    1981   *Code Civil.* Montréal: Société Québécoise d'Informations Juridiques.

Cristescu, Aureliu
    1981   "The Right to Self-Determination: Historical and Current Development on the Basis of the United Nations Instruments". Study prepared by the Special Rapporteur of the Sub-Commission on Prevention of Discrimination and Protection of Minorities. U.N. Doc. E/CN.4/Sub.2/404/Rev.1. Available online at http://documents.un.org/mother.asp

Daes, Erica-Irene A.
    1996a   "Standard-Setting Activities: Evolution of Standards Concerning the Rights of Indigenous People—Working Paper on the Concept of 'Indigenous People'". U.N. Doc. E/CN.4/Sub.2/AC.4/1996/2, 10 June 1996. Available online at http://www.unhchr.ch/Huridocda/Huridoca.nsf/(Symbol)/E.CN.4.Sub.2.AC.4.1996.2.En?Opendocument
    1996b   Paper presented at the Pacific workshop on "The United Nations Draft Declaration on the Rights of Indigenous Peoples", Suva, Fiji, September 1996.
    2001   "Study on Indigenous Peoples and their Relationship to Land". Final Working Paper by the Special Rapporteur to the Commission on Human Rights. U.N. Doc. E/CN.4/Sub.2/2001/21, 11 June 2001. Available at http://www.unhchr.ch/Huridocda/Huridoca.nsf/(Symbol)/E.CN.4.Sub.2.2001.21.En?Opendocument

Daniels, Clement
    2004   "Indigenous Rights in Namibia". In *Indigenous Peoples' Rights in Southern Africa,* edited by Robert K. Hitchcock and Diana Vinding. IWGIA Document No. 110. Copenhagen: IWGIA.

Danish Ministry of Foreign Affairs (DANIDA)
    2004   "Strategy for Danish Support to Indigenous Peoples". Available online at http://amg.um.dk/en/menu/policiesandstrategies/indigenouspeoples

Davidson, Basil
    1992   *Africa in History.* London: Phoenix Press.

Delville, L.P.
    2000   "Harmonising Formal Law and Customary Land Rights in French-Speaking West Africa". In *Evolving Land Rights, Policy and Tenure in Africa,* edited by C. Toulmin and J. Quan. London: Department for International Development, International Institute for Environment and Development/Natural Resources Institute.

Dinstein, Yoram
    1976   "Collective Human Rights of Peoples and Minorities". *International and Comparative Law Quarterly* 25 (1976).

Djonovich, Dusan J. (ed.)
    1973   *United Nations Resolutions.* Series I. New York: Ocean Publications.

Dorough, Dalee Sambo
    2009   "Human Rights". In *State of the World's Indigenous Peoples,* edited by the United Nations Permanent Forum on Indigenous Issues. ST/ESA/328 United Nations Publication. New York: United Nations.

ECOSOC (U.N. Economic and Social Council)
    1971   Resolution 1589(L), May 21 1971. Text available at http://www.un.org/ga/search/view_doc.asp?symbol=E/RES/1589(L)
    1986   "The Limburg Principles". U.N. Doc. E/CN 4/1987/17 Appendix 1. Available at http://www.acpp.org/RBAVer1_0/archives/Limburg%20Principles.pdf

Ederington, Benjamin L.
    1997   "Property as a Natural Institution: The Separation of Property from Sovereignty in International Law". 13 *The American University International Law Review* 263 (1997).

Eide, Asbjørn
   1995   "Economic, Social and Cultural Rights as Human Rights". In *Economic, Social and Cultural Rights: A Textbook,* edited by A. Eide, Catarina Krause and Allan Rosas. London: Martinus Nijhoff Publishers.

Emerton, Lucy and Iddi Mfunda
   1999   *Making Wildlife Economically Viable for Communities Living around the Western Serengeti, Tanzania.* Evaluating Eden Series, Working Paper No.1. London: International Institute for Environment and Development (IIED). Available online at: http://www.iied.org/pubs

European Commission
   1998a   "Working Document of the Commission on Support for Indigenous Peoples in the Development Co-operation of the Community and the Member States". May 1998. Available online at http://www.ec.europa.eu/external_relations/human_rights/ip/work_doc98.pdf
   1998b   "Council Resolution of 30 November 1998: Indigenous Peoples within the Framework of the Development Cooperation of the Community and the Member States". 214th Council Meeting – Development. Brussels, 30 November 1998. Available online at http://www. ec.europa.eu/external_relations/human_rights/ip/docs/council_resolution1998_en.pdf
   2002a   "Review of Progress of Working with Indigenous Peoples". COM (2002) 291 final. Available online at http://www.eur-lex.europa.eu/LexUriServ/LexUriServ.do?uri=COM- :2002:0291:FIN:EN:PDF
   2002b   Council Conclusions: Indigenous Peoples. General Affairs Council - 18 November 2002. A resumé is available online at http://www.europa.eu/legislation_summaries/development/sectoral_development_policies/r12006_en.htm
   2005   The European Consensus on Development – Joint statement by the Council and the Representatives of the Governments of the Member States meeting within the Council, the European Parliament and the Commission. Available online at http://www.ec.europa. eu/development/icenter/repository/eu_consensus_en.pdf

Fimbo, G. M.
   1992   *Essays in Land Laws of Tanzania.* Dar es Salaam: University of Dar Es Salaam Press.

FIMI/IIWF (Foro Internacional de Mujeres Indígenas/International Indigenous Women's Forum)
   2006   "Mairin Iwanka Raya: Indigenous Women Stand against Violence". FIMI Companion Report to the United Nations Secretary General's Study on violence against women. New York: IIWF/FIMI.

Flaherty, Anne
   2007   "This Land is My Land: The Politics of American Indian Land Claims Settlements". Draft Paper Prepared for the American Political Science Association Annual Conference; August 2007, Chicago, Illinois. Available online at http://www.allacademic.com/meta/p_mla_apa_research_citation/2/1/0/6/1/ p210611_index.hhtm

Forest Peoples Programme, UOBDU and Care International
   2008   "The Indigenous Batwa People and Protected Areas in Southwest Uganda: A Review of Uganda's Implementation of the CBD Programme of Work on Protected Areas". Available online at Web site of Forest Peoples Programme: http://www.forestpeoples.org/documents/conservation/

Forster, Peter G. and Sam Maghimbi (eds.)
   1999   *Agrarian Economy, State and Society in the Contemporary Tanzania.* Aldershot, UK: Ashgate Publishing Co.

Freeman, Donald B.
   1991   *City of Farmers: Informal Urban Agriculture in the Open Spaces of Nairobi, Kenya.* Montreal, Quebec, Kingston, Canada: McGill-Queen's Press – MQUP.

Galli, Rosemary E. (ed.)
   1981   *The Political Economy of Rural Development: Peasants, International Capital and the State.* Albany, N.Y.: State University of New York Press.

Garet, Ronald
   1983   "Communality and Existence: The Rights of Groups". 56 *Southern Californian Law Review* (1983).

GEF (Global Environment Facility)
   2007   "Focal Area Strategies and Strategic Programming for GEF-4". See http://www.thegef.
           org/interior.aspx?id=18428
Giago, Tim
   2008   "A story dying to be told". *Lakota Country Times*, September 25, 2008, available at
           http://www.lakotacountrytimes.com/news/2008/0925/tim_giago/
Gilbert, Geoff
   1992   "Minority Rights in Europe". *Netherlands Yearbook of International Law*, vol. XXIII.
Gisemba, Horace Njuguna
   2008   "A Short History of Land Settlements in the Rift Valley". Available online at http://www.
           allafrica.com/stories/200805150607.html
Glazier, Jack
   1985   *Land and the Uses of Tradition among the Mbeere of Kenya.* Lanham, MD: University Press of
           America.
Goldman, Dawn Elyse
   1999   "The Native American Graves Protection and Repatriation Act: A Benefit and a Burden: Re-
          fining NAGPRA's Cultural Patrimony Definition". *International Journal of Cultural Property*,
          8, no. 1 (1999).
Graeffen, Christian
   2002   "Comments" to F.M. Ssekandi presentation on "Social, Political and Equity Aspects of
           Land and Property Rights", at Regional Workshop on "Land Issues in Africa and the Mid-
           dle East", Kampala, 2002. Available online at http://www.landcoalition.org/pdf/
           wbasekd.pdf
Grandin, B.E.
   1991   "The Maasai: Socio-Historical Context and Group Ranches". In *Maasai Herding: An Analy-
           sis of the Livestock Production System of Maasai Pastoralists in Eastern Kajiado District, Kenya,*
           edited by Solomon Bekure et al. ILCA Systems Study 4. Addis Ababa, Ethiopia: Interna-
           tional Livestock Centre for Africa (ILCA).
Gray, Andrew
   1995   "The Indigenous Movement in Asia". In *Indigenous Peoples in Asia,* edited by R.H. Barnes,
           A. Fray and B. Kingsbury. Ann Arbor, Michigan: Association for Asian Studies Inc.
   1997   *Indigenous Rights and Development: Self-determination in an Amazonian Community.* Provi-
           dence, R.I. and London: Berghahn Books.
Green, Leslie
   1994   "Internal Minorities and their Rights". In *Group Rights,* edited by J. Baker. Toronto: Univer-
           sity of Toronto Press.
Hampson, Françoise
   2007   "Military Necessity". In *Crimes of War: What the Public Should Know,* edited by Roy Gutman
           and David Rieff. New York and London: W.W. Norton. Available online at http://www.
           crimesofwar.org/thebook/military-necessity.html
Harring, Sidney L.
   2004   "Indigenous Land Rights and Land Reform in Namibia". In *Indigenous Peoples' Rights in
           Southern Africa,* edited by Robert K. Hitchcock and Diana Vinding. IWGIA Document No.
           110. Copenhagen: IWGIA.
Hazzah, Leela and Stephanie Dolrenry
   2007   "Coexisting with Predators". Paper presented at Nature, Wildlife, People – A symposium
           on wildlife protection and people's livelihoods, September 2007. Accessible online at
           http://www.india-seminar.com/2007/577.htm
Henckaerts, Jean Marie
   1995   *Mass Expulsion in Modern International Law and Practice.* The Hague: Martinus Nijhoff.
Highet, Keith and George Kahale III
   1994   "International Decisions". 88 *American Journal of International Law* 1 (October 1994).
Hitchcock, Robert K.
   n.d.   "Background Notes on the Central Kalahari Game Reserve and Ghanzi: Land and Re-
           sources". Available online at http://www.kalaharipeoples.org/documents/ghanzi.htm

Hladik, Jan
  1999   "Diplomatic Conference on the Second Protocol to the Hague Convention for the Protection of Cultural Property in the Event of Armed Conflict (March 15-26 1999)". *International Journal of Cultural Property*, 8, no. 2 (1999).

Holtham, Gerald and Arthur Hazlewood
  1976   *Aid and Inequality in Kenya*. London: Croom Helm and the Overseas Development Institute.

Hughes, Lotte
  2006   *Moving of the Maasai: A Colonial Misadventure*. London: Palgrave Macmillan.
  2007   "Rough Time in Paradise: Claims, Blames and Memory Making Around Some Protected Areas in Kenya". *Conservation and Society*, 5, no. 3 (2007). Available online at http://www.conservationandsociety.org/cs-5-3-307.pdf

Hurley, Mary C.
  2000   "Aboriginal Title: The Supreme Court of Canada Decision in *Delgamuukw v. British Colombia*". Law and Government Division, January 1998, revised February 2000. Available online at http://www.parl.gc.ca/information/library/PRBpubs/bp459-e.htm

Hutchful, Eboe
  1991   "Reconstructing Political Space: Militarism and Constitutionalism in Africa". In *State and Constitutionalism: An African Debate on Democracy*, edited by Isaac G. Shivji. Harare, Zimbabwe: Southern Africa Printing and Publishing House (APPHO).

Indian Affairs and Northern Development
  2007   "General Briefing Note on the Comprehensive Land Claims Policy of Canada and the Status of Claims". Montreal: Comprehensive Claims Branch Claims and Indian Government Sector. Available on line at http://www.ainc-inac.gc.ca/al/ldc/ccl/pubs/gbn/gbn-eng.asp

Ingram, Dave
  2000   *Group Rights*. Kansas: University Press of Kansas.

Instituto Socioambiental
  2004   "ISA 10 Years". Available at: http://www.socioambiental.org/e/inst/mm/melh_2004_ing.pdf -Ambiental

Inter-American Commission on Human Rights (IACHR)
  1984   Report on the Situation of Human Rights of a Segment of the Nicaragua Population of Miskito Origin. OEA/Ser.L/V/II.62 Doc. 26 May 1984. Available online at http://www.cidh.oas.org/countryrep/Miskitoeng/toc.htm
  1985   Resolution No.12/85, Case No. 7615 (Brazil), March 5, 1985. Annual Report 1984-1985, OEA/Ser.L/V/II.66 Doc.10 rev.1. October 1985. Available online at http://www.cidh.oas.org/casos/84.85.eng.htm
  1997   Report on the Situation of Human Rights in Ecuador. OEA/Ser.L/V/II.96 Doc. 10 rev.1. April 1997. Available online at http://www.cidh.oas.org/pais.eng.htm
  2000   Proposed Declaration on the Rights of Indigenous Peoples, as approved by the Inter-American Commission on Human Rights on February 26, 1997, at its 1333rd session, 95th Regular Session. OEA/Ser.L/V/II.108 Doc. 62 (2000). Available online at http://www.cidh.org/indigenas/chap.2g.htm
  2007   Annual Report 2007. Available online at http://www.iachr.org/annualrep/2007eng/Chap.3q.htm.

Inter-American Development Bank (IDB)
  2006   "Operational Policy on Indigenous Peoples (OP-765) Strategy for Indigenous Development". Available online at http://www.iadb.org/sds/IND/site_401_e.htm

International Alliance of Indigenous and Tribal Peoples of the Tropical Forests
  1996   *Indigenous Peoples, Forests and Biodiversity*. IWGIA Document No. 82. London and Copenhagen: International Alliance and IWGIA.

International Court of Justice (I.C.J)
  1950   Colombian-Peruvian Asylum Case, Judgment November 20th, 1950: I.C.J. Reports. Available online at http://www.icj-cij.org/docket/files/7/1849.pdf
  1975   Western Sahara: Advisory Opinion: I.C.J. Reports. Available online at: http://www.icj-cij.org/docket/files/61/6195.pdf

1995   Case Concerning East Timor *(Portugal v. Australia)*, Judgment June 1995. Available on line at http://www.icj-cij.org/docket/index.php?sum=430&code=pa&p1=3&p2=3&case=84 &k=66&p3=5

International Labour Conference
1935   "Records and Proceedings". 19th Session. Geneva: International Labour Office.
1946   "Proposed International Labour Obligations in Respect of Non-self Governing Territories". Report IV (1), 29th session (Montreal 1946). Geneva: International Labour Office.
1956a   "Information and Reports on the Application of Conventions and Recommendations". Report III (I), 39th session. Geneva: International Labour Office.
1956b   "Living and Working Conditions of Indigenous Populations in Independent Territories". Report VIII (1) and (2), 39th session. Geneva: International Labour Office.
1957a   "Protection and Integration of Indigenous and other Tribal and Semi-Tribal Populations in Independent Countries". Report VI,(1) and (2), 40th session. Geneva: International Labour Office.
1957b   "Records of Proceedings", 40th session. Geneva: International Labour Office.
1958   "Records of Proceedings", 41st session. Geneva: International Labour Office.
1988a   "Partial Revision of the Indigenous and Tribal Populations Convention, 1957 (No. 107)". Report VI (2), 75th session. Geneva: International Labour Office.
1988b   "Records of Proceedings", 75th session. Geneva: International Labour Office.
1989   "Partial revision of the Indigenous and Tribal Populations Convention, 1957 (No. 107)". Report IV (1 and 2A), 76th session, Geneva: International Labour Office.

International Labour Organization (ILO)
1946 (1919) ILO Constitution. Available from http://www.ilo.org/ilolex/english/constq.htm
1996   *International Labour Conventions and Recommendations 1919-1951*, vols. I & II. Geneva: International Labour Office.

ILO and ACHPR
2009   *Constitutional and Legislative Protection of Indigenous Populations in Africa*. Geneva and Banjul, The Gambia: ILO and ACHPR.

International Work Group for Indigenous Affairs (IWGIA)
1986–   *The Indigenous World*. Annual publication available at http://www.iwgia.org

IRIN
2000   Central and Eastern Africa – Weekly Round-up 509, 15 December 2000. Available online at http://iys.cidi.org/humanitarian/irin/ceafrica/00b/0028.html

Jackson, Dorothy
2003   *Twa Women, Twa Rights in the Great Lakes Region of Africa*. London: Minority Rights Group International.

Jochnick, Chris
1999   "Confronting the Impunity of Non-States Actors: New Field for the Promotion of Human Rights". *Human Rights Quarterly*, 21 (1999).

Johnston, Darlene M.
1999   "Native Rights as Collective Rights: A Question of Group Self-Preservation". In *The Rights of Minority Cultures*, edited by W. Kymlicka. New York: Oxford University Press.

Juviler, Peter
1993   "Are Collective Rights Anti-Human: Theories on Self-Determination and Practice in Soviet Successor States". *Netherlands Quarterly of Human Rights* 3/1993.

Kaisoe, M. and W. Ole Seki
2003   "The Conflict between Conventional Conservation Strategies and Indigenous Systems: The Case Study of Ngorongoro Conservation Area". In *Indigenous Peoples and Protected Areas*, edited by John Nelson and Lindsay Hossack. Moreton-in-Marsh, UK: Forest Peoples Programme.

Kanyinga, Karuti
2000   *Re-Distribution from Above: The Politics of the Land Rights and Squatting in Coastal Kenya.* Upssala, Sweden: Nordiska Afrikainstitutet.

Kapupu. M.
1996   "Etude du milieu des pygmées voisins du Parc National de Kahuzi-Biega, zones rurales de Kabare et Kalehe". A study commissioned by the German Agency of International Cooperation (GTZ).

Kenya National Bureau of Statistics
2007   Update on Tourism Statistics. http://www.tourism.go.ke/ministry.nsf

Kerner, Donna O.
1988   "Land Scarcity and Rights of Control in the Development of Commercial Farming in Northeast Tanzania". In *Land and Society in Contemporary Africa*, edited by R.E. Downs and S. P. Reyna. Hanover, NH: University Press of New England.

Kingsbury, Benedict
1992   "Claims by Non-States Groups in International Law". *Cornell International Law Journal*, vol. 25 (1992).

1995   "Indigenous Peoples as an International Legal Concept". In *Indigenous Peoples in Asia*, edited by R. H Barnes, A. Fray and B. Kingsbury. Ann Arbor, Michigan: Association for Asian Studies Inc.

1998   "Indigenous Peoples in International Law: A Constructivist Approach to the Asian Controversy". 92 *The American Journal International Law* (1998).

Kiondo, A.S.Z.
1999   "Structural Adjustment and Land Reform Policy in Tanzania: A Political Interpretation of the 1992 National Agricultural Policy". In *Agrarian Economy, State and Society in Contemporary Tanzania*, edited by P. G. Forster and S. Maghimbi. Aldershot: Ashgate Publishing Co.

Kipuri, Naomi
nd.   "Indigenous Peoples in Kenya : An Overview". Available online at http://www.Whoseland.com/paper6.

Kishel, Shannon, Emily Mcalpin, and Aaron Molloy
1999   "The Maasai Culture and Ecological Adaptations". Mimeo. Denison University, Ohio: Environment Studies Program.

Kitching, Gavin
1980   *Class and Economic Change in Kenya: The Making of an African Petite Bourgeoisie*. New Haven, Conn.: Yale University Press.

Kohler, Volker and Franz Schmithüsen
2004   "Comparative Analysis of Forest Laws in Twelve Sub-Saharan African Countries". FAO Legal Papers Online #37. Rome: FAO, July 2004. Available online at http://www.fao.org/legal/pub-e.htm

Kweka, J.
2004   "Tourism and the Economy of Tanzania: A CGE Analysis". Paper presented at the CSAE Conference on Growth, Poverty reduction and Human Development in Africa (21-22 March 2004), Oxford, UK. Available online at http://www.csae.ox.ac.uk/conferences/2004-GPRaHDiA/papers/1f-Kweka-CSAE2004.pdf

Kymlicka, Will
1995   *Multicultural Citizenship*. Oxford: Clarendon Press.

Kymlicka, Will and Will Norman (eds.)
2000   *Citizenship in Diverse Societies*. Oxford and New York: Oxford University Press.

Lâm, Maivân Clech
2000   *At the Edge of the State: Indigenous Peoples and Self-Determination*. Ardsley, New York: Transnational Publishers, Inc.

Laslett, Peter
1964   *John Locke's Two Treatises of Government*. Cambridge, UK: Cambridge University Press.

Lawrence, J.C.D. et al.
1966   *Report of the Mission on Land Consolidation and Registration in Kenya, 1965-66*. London: Republic of Kenya.

Legal Aid Committee
1985   *Essays in Law and Society*. Dar es Salaam: Faculty of Law.

Legal and Human Rights Centre
2007   "Tanzania Human Rights Report 2007". Dar es Salaam: LHRC. Available at http://www.humanrights.or.tz

2008   "Tanzania Human Rights Report 2008". Dar es Salaam: LHRC. Available at http://www.humanrights.or.tz

Lerner, Nathan
    1991   *Group Rights and Discrimination in International Law.* Dordrecht: Martinus Nijhoff Publishers.

Lewis, Jerome
    2000   *The Batwa Pygmies of the Great Lakes Region.* London: Minority Rights Group International.
    2001a   "Forest People or Village People: Whose Voice will be Heard?". In *Africa's Indigenous Peoples: 'First Peoples' or 'Marginalized Minorities'?*, edited by Alan Barnard and Justin Kenrick. Edinburgh: Centre of African Studies, University of Edinburgh.
    2001b   "Whose Forest is it Anyway". Draft paper presented at the Property and Equality Workshop, MPI, Halle, March 2001.

Lewis, Jerome and Judy Knight
    1995   *The Twa of Rwanda.* IWGIA Document No. 78. Copenhagen and UK: IWGIA and World Rainforest Movement.

Lindley, M.F.
    1926   *The Acquisition and Government of Backward Territory in International Law.* London: Longmans, Green and Co.

Lissu, Tundu
    2000   "Policy and Legal Issues on Wildlife Management in Tanzania's Pastoral Lands: The Case Study of the Ngorongoro Conservation Area". *Law, Social Justice and Global Development, (LGD)* 2000 (1). Available online at http://www2.warwick.ac.uk/fac/soc/law/elj/lgd/2000_1/lissu/#a8.1

Longman
    1995   *Dictionary of Contemporary English.* 3rd ed. Harlowe: Longman.

Luling, Virginia and Justin Kenrick
    1998   "Forest Foragers of Tropical Africa. A Dossier on the Present Condition of the 'Pygmy' Peoples". London: Survival International.

McAuslan, Patrick
    2000   "Only the Name of the Country Changes: Diaspora of European Land Law in Commonwealth Africa". In *Evolving Land Rights and Tenure in Africa,* edited by C. Toulmin, and J. Quan. London: DFID/IIED, Natural Resources Institute.
    2007   "Land Law and the Making of British Empire". In *Modern Studies in Property Law,* edited by Elisabeth Cooke. London: Hart Publishing.

MacKay, Fergus
    2000   "The Rights of Indigenous Peoples in International Law". A briefing paper for the Department for International Development. Unpublished. Available online at http://www.sdnp.org.gy/apa/topic3.htm
    2001   "African Commission on Human and Peoples' Rights". Forest Peoples Programme. Available at: http://www.forestpeoples.org/documents/africa/af_com_brf_human_rights_oct01_eng.shtml
    2002   *A Guide to Indigenous Peoples' Rights in the Inter-American Human Rights System.* IWGIA Document no. 106. Moreton-in-Marsh and Copenhagen: Forest Peoples Programme & IWGIA.
    2005   "The Draft World Bank Operational Policy 4.10 on Indigenous Peoples: Progress or More of the Same?" *The Arizona Journal of International and Comparative Law Online* 22, no. 1, (65-98), 2005. Available online at
        http://www.law.arizona.edu/journals/ajicl/AJICL2005/vol221/vol221.htm

Mc Neil, Kent
    1997   "Extinguishment of Native Title: The High Court and American Law". *Australian Indigenous Law Reporter* ([1997] AILR 41) Available online at http://www.austlii.edu.au/cgi-bin/sinodisp/au/journals/AILR/1997/41.html?query=%20Extinguishment

Madsen, Andrew
    2000   *The Hadzabe of Tanzania: Land and Human Rights for a Hunter-Gatherer Community.* IWGIA Document No. 98. Copenhagen: IWGIA.

Maganga, F.P.
    2009   "Tanzania's New Wildlife Law and its Implications for Rural Livelihoods". Power point presentation, mimeo. Dar es Salaam: Institute of Resource Assessment, University of Dar es Salaam.

Maini, Krishna M.
  1967   *Land Law in Eastern Africa.* Nairobi: Oxford University Press.

Martínez, Alfonso
  1991   "Study on Treaties, Agreements and Other Constructive Agreements between States and In-
          digenous Populations". U.N. Doc/E/CN 4/Sub 2/1999/20, 22 June 1999. Available online at:
          http://www.unhchr.ch/Huridocda/Huridoca.nsf/(Symbol)/E.CN.4.SUB.2.RES.1999.22.
          En?Opendocument

Martínez Cobo, José
  1987   "Study of the Problem of Discrimination against Indigenous Populations". Final Report
          submitted by the Special Rapporteur. Available online from the Web site of UNPFII:
          http://www.un.org/esa/socdev/unpfii

Maxon, Robert M.
  1993   *Struggle for Kenya: The Loss and Reassertion of Imperial Initiative 1912-1923.* Madison, N.J.:
          Fairleigh Dickinson University Press.

Melander, Göran
  1993   "Article 27". In *Universal Declaration of Human Rights: A Commentary,* edited by A. Eide et
          al. Oslo, Norway: Scandinavian University Press.

Mendelsohn, Oliver and Upendra Baxi (eds.)
  1994   *The Rights of Subordinated Peoples.* Delhi: Oxford University Press.

Miller, Norman N.
  1986   "Land Use and Wildlife in Modern Kenya". In *Wildlife, Wild Death: Land Use and Survival in
          Eastern Africa,* edited by Rodger Yeager and Norman N. Miller. New York, N.Y.: State Uni-
          versity of New York Press and the African–Caribbean Institute.

Minority Rights Group International
  2008   *State of the World's Minorities 2008 - Kenya,* 11 March 2008. Accessed online 25 December
          2008 at: http://www.unhcr.org/refworld/docid/48a7ead441.html [

Moore, Sally Falk
  1986   *Social Facts and Fabrications: "Customary Law" in the Kilimanjaro 1880-1980.* Cambridge, UK:
          Cambridge University Press.

Morel, Cynthia and Korir Singoei
  2004   "Matter: Right to Land, Case 151, Kenya 1". *Applied Human Rights Association* (AHRA),
          July 2004. Available online at http://www.ilsbu.com/cases_page/default.htm

Muchuba, Roger
  2009   "The Indigenous Voice in the REDD process in the Democratic Republic of Congo". *Indig-
          enous Affairs* 1-2/09 on REDD and Indigenous Peoples. Copenhagen: IWGIA.

Mwanjala, J.
  2005   "An Overview of Wildlife and Tourism Management in Kenya". Paper presented on be-
          half of Kenya Wildlife Service at the 3rd International Institute for Peace through Tourism
          (IIPT) African Conference on Peace through Tourism, held in Lusaka, Zambia, February
          6-11, 2005.

Mwangi, Ester
  2001   "The Transformation of Property Rights in Kenya's Maasailand: Triggers and Motiva-
          tions". CAPRi Working Paper. Washington D.C.: International Food Policy Research Insti-
          tute. Available at http://www.capri.cgiar.org

Mvungi, Sengondo E.
  2008   "Experiences in the Defence of Pastoralist Rights in Tanzania: Lessons and Prospects". In
          A Study on Options for Pastoralists to Secure their Livelihoods in Tanzania, edited by Ringo
          Tenga et al. Arusha, Tanzania: Tanzania Natural Resource Forum. Available online at
          http://www.tnrf.org/files/E-INFO-RLTF_VOL1_MAINREPORT_A_Study_on_options_
          for_pastoralism_to_secure_their_livelihoods_in_Tanzania_2008.pdf

Nasha, William Ole
  n.d.   "Reforming Land Tenure In Tanzania: For Whose Benefit?" Paper prepared for Haki Ardhi
          Organisation. Available at: http://www.hakiardhi.org/HA-Docs/WILLIAM%20FI-
          NAL%20SUBMISSION.pdf

Ndaskoi, Navaja Ole
   n.d.   "The Roots Causes of Maasai Predicament". Paper available online at http://www.galdu.
            org/govat/doc/maasai_fi.pdf
NEPAD
   2005   Country Review Report of the Republic of Rwanda, November 2005. African Peer Review
            Mechanism (APRM) Report. Available online at http://www.nepad.org/2005/files/
            aprm/FINAL_RWANDA_REPORT_SEPT_22_2006.pdf
Ng'ethe, J. C.
   1993   "Group Ranch Concept and Practice in Kenya with Special Emphasis on Kajiado District".
            In *Future of Livestock Industries in East and Southern Africa.* Proceedings of a Workshop held
            at Kadoma Ranch Hotel, Zimbabwe, 20-23 July 1992, edited by J. A. Kategile and S. Mubi.
            Addis Ababa, Ethiopia: ILCA (International Livestock Centre for Africa). Available online
            at http://www.fao.org/wairdocs/ILRI/x5485E/x5485e0t.htm.
Njenga, Lillian W.
   2004   "Towards Individual Statutory Proprietorship from Communal Ownership". Available
            online at http://www.fig.net/commission7/nairobi_2004/papers/ts_01_3_njenga.pdf
Njuki, Alexandrino
   2001   "Cadastral Systems and Their Impact on Land Administration in Kenya". Paper presented
            at the International Conference on Spatial Information for Sustainable Development, Nai-
            robi, Kenya, October 2001. Available online at http://www.fig.net/pub/proceedings/
            nairobi/njuki-TS10-2.pdf
Nowak, Manfred
   1993   *U.N. Covenant on Civil and Political Rights: CCPR Commentary.* Kehl-Strasbourg-Arlington:
            N.P. Engel Publisher.
Nyalali, Francis L.
   1998   "The Social Context of Judicial Decisions Making". Paper presented at a workshop on The
            State of Human Rights in Tanzania, held at the British Council Hall, Dar es Salaam on 3
            July 1998.
Nyamu-Musembi, Celestine
   2006   *Breathing Life into Dead Theories about Property Rights: de Soto and Land Relations in Rural Africa.* IDS
            Working Paper 272. Brighton, UK: Institute of Development Studies, University of Sussex.
Nyerere, Julius K.
   1968   *Ujamaa: Essays on Socialism.* London: Oxford University Press.
Odgaard, Rie
   2009   "Assessment Report from Tanzania". Report submitted to IWGIA, August 2009 (unpub-
            lished).
Okoth-Ogendo, H.W.O.
   1982   "The Perils of Land Tenure Reform: The Case of Kenya". In *Land Policy and Agriculture in
            Eastern and Southern Africa.* Selected Papers presented at a Workshop organised by the
            United Nations University in Gaborone, Botswana, 14-19 February 1982, edited by J.W.
            Arntzen, L.D. Ngcongco, and S.D. Turner. Tokyo: United Nations University Press.
   1991a   "Constitutions without Constitutionalism: Reflections on an African Political Paradox". In
            State and Constitutionalism, edited by I.G. Shivji. Harare, Zimbabwe: Southern Africa Print-
            ing & Publishing House.
   1991b   *Tenants of the Crown: Evolution of Agrarian Law and Institutions in Kenya.* Nairobi, Kenya:
            African Centre for Technology Studies.
   1999   "Land Policy Development in East Africa: A Survey of Recent Trends". Paper for the DFID
            Workshop on "Land Rights and Sustainable Development in Sub-Sahara Africa", Berk-
            shire, 16-19 February 1999. Available online at www.oxfam.org.uk/resources/learning/
            landrights/downloads/eafover.rtf
Oleku Ole Roore, Sammy
   1998   "The Iloodoariak Land Scandal". In *Pastoralists in the Horn of Africa,* Minority Rights Group
            Report of a Workshop on Social and Economic Marginalisation (8-10 December 1998),
            Nairobi-Kenya. London: MRG. Available online at http://www.unhcr.org/refworld/
            pdfid/469cbfd10.pdf

Ostrom, Elinor
1990 *Governing the Commons: The Evolution of Institutions for Collective Action.* Series Political Economy of Institutions and Decisions. Cambridge: Cambridge University Press.

Packer, John
1996 "On the Content of Minority Rights". In *Do We Need Minority Rights?* edited by J. Räikkä. Netherlands: Kluwer Law International.

Pakleppa, Richard
2004 "Civil Rights in Legislation and Practice – A Case Study from Tsumkwe District West, Namibia". In *Indigenous Peoples' Rights in Southern Africa*, edited by Robert K. Hitchcock and Diana Vinding. IWGIA Document no. 110. Copenhagen: IWGIA.

Peter, Chris Maina
2007 "Human Rights of Indigenous Minorities in Tanzania and the Courts of Law". *International Journal on Minority and Group Rights* 14, no. 4 (2007).

Plamer, Andie D.
2001 "Evidence 'Not in a Form Familiar to Common Law Courts': Assessing Oral Histories in Land Claims Testimony after *Delgamuukw v. B.C.*". 8 *Alberta Law Review* 1040 (February 2001).

Prott, Lyndel V.
1992 "Cultural Rights as Peoples' Rights in International Law". In *The Rights of Peoples,* edited by James Crawford. Oxford: Clarendon/Oxford University Press.

Puyana, Alicia
1993 "New Challenges for Developing Countries". In *Facing the Challenge: Responses to the Report of the South Commission,* edited by the South Centre. London: Zed Books.

Raker, Keith H.
2005 "Reservation of Rights: A Look at Indian Land Claims in Ohio for Gaming Purposes". Available online at http://www.tuckerellis.com/news/Reservation%20of%20Rights.pdf

Raoul Wallenberg Institute
2006 *Human Rights Committee.* Vol.1 of *Collection of General Comments or Recommendations adopted by U.N. Human Rights Treaty Bodies.* Lund, Sweden: Raoul Wallenberg Institute.

Rawls, John
1999 *A Theory of Justice.* Rev. ed. Oxford: Oxford University Press.

Republic of Kenya
2005 *The Forests Act.* Nairobi: Ministry of Environment and Natural Resources. Available online at http://www.kfs.go.ke/html/forest%20act.html
2007a *Final Draft Wildlife Management Policy.* Nairobi: Ministry of Tourism and Wildlife. Available online at http://www.tourism.go.ke/ministry.nsf/doc/DRAFT_WILDLIFE_POLICY.pdf/$file/DRAFT_WILDLIFE_POLICY.pdf
2007b *Sessional Paper No.1 on Forest Policy.* Nairobi: Ministry of Environment and Natural Resources. Available online at http://www.kfs.go.ke/html/forest%20act.htm
2009 *Sessional Paper No. 3 on National Land Policy.* Nairobi: Ministry of Lands.

Republic of South Africa
1993 *Constitution of South Africa* (interim Constitution). Available online at http://www. confinder.richmond.edu/country.php
1996 *Constitution of South Africa.* Available online at http://www. confinder.richmond.edu/country.php

Robert-Wray, K.
1966 *Commonwealth and Colonial Law.* London: Stevens and Sons.

Rodley, Nigel
1995 "Conceptual Problems in the Protection of Minorities: International Legal Development". *Human Rights Quarterly* 17 (1995).

Rosas, Allan
1993 "Internal Self-Determination". In *Modern Law of Self-Determination,* edited by Christian Tomuschat. Dordrecht: Martinus Nijhoff Publishers.

Rutten, M.M.E.M.
1992   *Selling Wealth to Buy Poverty: The Process of Individualization of Landownership Among the Maasai Pastoralists of Kajiado District, Kenya, 1890-1990.* Saarbrüchen and Fort Lauderdale: Verlag Breitenbach Publishers.

Sanders, Douglas
1993   "Self-Determination and Indigenous Peoples". In *Modern Law of Self-Determination,* edited by Christian Tomuschat. Dordrecht: Martinus Nijhoff Publishers.

Sang, J.K.
2003   "Kenya: the Ogiek in Mau Forest". In *Indigenous Peoples and Protected Areas in Africa: From Principles to Practice,* edited by J. Nelson and L. Hossack. Moreton-in-Marsh, UK: Forest Peoples Programme.

Sara, Johan Mikkel
2006   "Indigenous Governance of Self-Determination. The Saami Model and the Saami Parliament in Norway". Paper presented at the Symposium on "The Right to Self-Determination in International Law", The Hague, Netherlands, 29 September-1 October 2006. Available at http://www.unpo.org/downloads/JohanMikkelSara.pdf

Scheinin, Martin
2005   "Indigenous Peoples' Rights under the International Covenant on Civil and Political Rights". In *International Law and Indigenous Peoples,* edited by Joshua Castellino and Niamh Walsh. Boston: Martinus Nijhoff Publishers.

Schmidt-Soltau, Kai
2006   "Indigenous Peoples Planning Framework for the Western Kenya Community Driven Development and Flood Mitigation Project (WKCDD/FM) and the Natural Resources Management Project (NRM)". Final Report. Nairobi: Republic of Kenya.

Schwabach, Aaron
2000   "Environmental Damage Resulting from the NATO Military Action against Yugoslavia". *Columbia Journal of Environmental Law,* 25, 1 (2000). Available at Social Science Research Network (SSRN) Web site: http://www.ssrn.com/abstract=224028

Shivji, Issa G.
1976   *Class Struggles in Tanzania.* London: Heinemann.
1989a   "The Right of Peoples to Self-Determination: An African Perspective". In *Issues of Self-Determination,* edited by W. Twining. Aberdeen, Scotland: Aberdeen University Press.
1989b   *The Concept of Human Rights in Africa.* CODESRIA Book Series. London: CODESRIA.
1998   *Not Yet Democracy: Reforming Land Tenure in Tanzania.* Dar es Salaam: IIED/Hakiardhi, Faculty of Law University of Dar es Salaam.
1999a   "Protection of Peasants and Pastoral Rights in Land: A Brief Review of the Bills for Land Act 1998 and the Village Land Act 1998". Paper presented to the Parliamentary Committee for Finance and Economic Affairs' Workshop on the Bills for the Land Act and the Village Land Act, Dodoma, 26-28 January 1999.
1999b   "Lift the Whip. Palaver: The Land Bills". *The African,* Tanzania (6 February 1999).

Shivji, Issa G. (ed.)
1991   *State and Constitutionalism: An African Debate on Democracy,* Southern Africa Political Series. Harare, Zimbabwe: Southern Africa Printing & Publishing House.

Shivji, Issa G. and Wilbert B. L. Kapinga
1998   *Maasai Rights in Ngorongoro, Tanzania.* Dar es Salaam: Hakiardhi, The Land Rights and Resources Institute.

Simat, Mary
1999   "The Situation of the Maasai Women". *Indigenous Affairs* 2/1999. Copenhagen: IWGIA.

Simpson, Tony
1997   *Indigenous Heritage and Self-determination.* IWGIA Document No. 86. Copenhagen: IWGIA.

Ssekandi, Francis M.
2002   "Social, Political and Equity Aspects of Land and Property Rights". Paper presented at a World Bank Regional Workshop on Land Issues in 2002. Available online from Web site of International Land Coalition: http://www.landcoalition.org/docs/t6la.htm,

Stavenhagen, Rodolfo

2003a   Report of the Special Rapporteur on the situation of human rights and fundamental free-doms of indigenous people, submitted in accordance with Commission resolution 2001/65, 59th Session, Item 15 of the provisional agenda (Human Rights and Indigenous Issues). U.N. Doc. E/CN.4/2003/90, 21 January 2003.

2003b   Mission to the Philippines. Report of the Special Rapporteur on the situation of human rights and fundamental freedoms of indigenous people. U.N. Doc., E/CN.4/2003/90/Add.3, 5 March 2003. See http://www2.ohchr.org/english/issues/indigenous/rapporteur/

2004   Mission to Canada. Report of the Special Rapporteur on the situation of human rights and fundamental freedoms of indigenous people. U.N. Doc. E/CN.4/2005/88/Add.3, 12 December 2004. See http://www2.ohchr.org/english/issues/indigenous/rapporteur/

2006   Mission to New Zealand. Report of the Special Rapporteur on the situation of human rights and fundamental freedoms of indigenous people. U.N. Doc. E/CN.4/2006/78/Add.3, 13 March 2006. See http://www2.ohchr.org/english/issues/indigenous/rapporteur/

Steiner, Henry J. and Philip Alston

1996   *International Human Rights in Context*. New York: Oxford University Press.

Sundet, Geir

2005   "The 1999 Land Act and Village Land Act: A Technical Analysis of the Practical Implications of the Acts". Working Draft (February 2005), available online at http://www.oxfam.org.uk/resources/learning/landrights/east.html#Tanzania

Suzman, James

2002   *Minorities in Independent Namibia*. Minority Rights Group International Report. London: MRG.

Swepston, Lee

1990   "A New Step in International Law on Indigenous and Tribal Peoples: ILO Convention No. 169 of 1989". *Oklahoma City University Law Review*, 15 (fall 1990).

Syagga, Paul Maurice

2006   "Land Ownership and Use in Kenya: Policy Prescriptions from an Inequality Perspective". In *Readings on Inequality in Kenya: Sectoral Dynamics and Perspectives*. Nairobi, Kenya: Society for International Development, Eastern Africa Regional Office. Available online at http://www.sidint.org/files/focus/Chapter8.pdf

Symonides, Janusz

1998   "Cultural Rights: A Neglected Category of Rights". *International Social Science Journal*, Vol. 50 (1998).

Swynnerton, R. J. M.

1955   *A Plan to Intensify the Development of African Agriculture in Kenya*. Nairobi: Government Printer.

Taylor, Michael

2004   "The Past and Future of San Land Rights in Botswana". In *Indigenous Peoples' Rights in Southern Africa*, edited by Robert K. Hitchcock and Diana Vinding. IWGIA Document No. 110. Copenhagen: IWGIA.

Tenga, Ringo

1992   *Pastoral Land Rights in Tanzania: A Review*. Pastoral Land Tenures Series. London: IIED Drylands Programme.

1998a   "Legislating for Pastoral Land Tenure in Tanzania: The Draft Land Bill". Available online at http://www.whoseland.com/paper8.html

1998b   "Processing a Land Policy: The Case of Mainland Tanzania". Available online at http://www.whoseland.com/paper7.html

1999   "Legitimizing Dispossession: The Tanzanian High Court's Decision on the Eviction of Maasai Pastoralists from Mkomazi Game Reserve". *Cultural Survival Quarterly*, Issue 22.4, 31 January 1999.

2008   "Experiences in the Defense of Pastoralist Rights: Current Legal Issues and Statutory Reforms". In *A Study on Options for Pastoralists to Secure their Livelihoods in Tanzania*, Vol. 2

(Case Studies). Arusha, Tanzania: CORDS, PWC, IIED, MMM Ngaramtoni Centre, TNRF and UCRT. Available online on the Web site of Tanzania Natural Resource Forum http://www.tnrf.org/node/7487?group=57

Tenga, Ringo, A. Mattee, N. Mdoe, R. Mnenwa, S. Mwungi and M. Walsh
2008   "Current Policy, Legal and Economic Issues". In *A Study on Options for Pastoralists to Secure their Livelihoods*, Vol. 1 (Main report). Arusha, Tanzania: CORDS, PWC, IIED, MMM Ngaramtoni Centre, TNRF and UCRT. Available online on the Web site of Tanzania Natural Resource Forum http://www.tnrf.org/node/7487?group=57

Thornberry, Patrick
1991   *International Law and the Rights of Minorities.* Oxford: Clarendon Press.
2002   *Indigenous Peoples and Human Rights.* Manchester: Manchester University Press.
2005   "The Convention on the Elimination of Racial Discrimination, Indigenous Peoples and Caste/Descent-based Discrimination". In *International Law and Indigenous Peoples,* edited by Joshua Castellino and Niamh Walsh. Boston: Martinuus Nijhoff Publishers.

Tignor, R.L.
1976   *The Colonial Transformation of Kenya.* Series East African Studies. Princeton, N.J.: Princeton University Press.

Tjombe, Norman
2001   "The Applicability of the Doctrine of Aboriginal Doctrine in Namibia: A Case for the Kxoe Community in Western Caprivi, Namibia". Paper presented at the Southern African Land Reform Lawyers Workshop, 21 February 2001, Robben Island, South Africa.

Turpel, Mary Ellen
1992   "Indigenous People's Rights of Political Participation and Self-Determination: Recent International Legal Development and the Continuing Struggle for Recognition". *Cornell International Law Journal* 579 (1992).

Umozurike, U.O.
1997   *The African Charter on Human and People's Rights.* The Hague: Martinus Nijhoff Publishers.

United Nations Commission on Human Rights
2001   Summary Report, 57th session. U.N. Doc. E/CN.4/2001/SR.15, 2 April 2001. http://www.unhchr.ch/huridocda/huridoca.nsf

UNDP
2007   *UNDP and Indigenous Peoples: A Practice Note on Engagement.* Available online at http://www.undp.org/biodiversity/pdfs/CSODivisionPolicyofEngagement.pdf

UNESCO
1981   Meeting of Experts on Ethno-Development and Ethnocide in Latin America: Final Report and Declaration of San José, San José, Costa Rica (7-11 December 1981). Available from http://www.unesdoc.unesco.org/images/0004/000499/049951eo.pdf
1983   Meeting of Experts on the Study of Ethno-Dvelopment and Ethnocide in Africa: Final Report, Ouagadougou, Upper Volta, 31 January – 4 February 1983. http://unesdoc.unesco.org/images/0005/000557/055780EB.pdf
2001   Universal Declaration on Cultural Diversity. Available online at http://www2.ohchr.org/english/law/diversity
2005   Convention on Cultural Expressions. Available online at http://www.unesco.org/culture/en/diversity/convention

United Nations Human Rights Committee
1981   Communication No. 24/1977, *Sandra Lovelace v. Canada.* Thirteenth session (1981). U.N. Doc. CCPR/C/OP/1 at 83 (1984) Available online at http://hrlibrary.ngo.ru/undocs/session13-index.html
1984   General Comment 12, Article 1 (Twenty-first session, 1984). Reprinted in Compilation of General Comments and General Recommendations Adopted by Human Rights Treaty Bodies, U.N. Doc. HRI/GEN/1/Rev. 1 at 134 (2003). Available online at http://hrlibrary.ngo.ru/gencomm/hrcomms.htm
1988   Communication No. 197/1985, *Ivan Kitok v. Sweden* (Thirty-third session, 1988). U.N. Doc. CCPR/C/33/D/197/1985, (1988). Available online at http://hrlibrary.ngo.ru/undocs/session33-index.html

1989 General Comment 18, Non Discrimination (Thirty-seventh session, 1989). Reprinted in Compilation of General Comments and General Recommendations Adopted by Human Rights Treaty Bodies U.N. Doc. HRI/GEN/1/Rev. 6 at 146 (2003). Available online at: http://hrlibrary.ngo.ru/gencomm/hrcomms.htm

1990 Communication No. 167/1984, *Chief Bernard Ominayak and the Lubicon Lake Band v. Canada* (Thirty-eigth session, 1990). U.N. Doc. CCPR/C/38/D/167/1984 (1990). Available online at http://hrlibrary.ngo.ru/undocs/session38-index.html

1994a General Comment 23, Article 27 (Fiftieth session, 1994). Reprinted in Compilation of General Comments and General Recommendations Adopted by Human Rights Treaty Bodies, U.N. Doc. HRI/GEN/1/Rev. at 158 (2003). Available online at http://hrlibrary.ngo.ru/gencomm/hrcomms.htm

1994b Communication No. 511/1992, *Länsman et al. v. Finland* (Fifty-second session, 1994). U.N. Doc. CCPR/C/52/D/511/1992 (1994). http://hrlibrary.ngo.ru/undocs/session52-index.html

1999 Concluding Observations, Canada. U.N. Doc./CCPR/C/79/Add.105 (1999). Available online at http://hrlibrary.ngo.ru/hrcommittee/canada1999.html

2000a Communication No. 760/1997, *J.G.A. Diergaardt (late Captain of the Rehoboth Baster Community) et al. v. Namibia.* Sixty-ninth session (2000). U.N. Doc. CCPR/C/69/D/760/1997 (2000). Available online at http://hrlibrary.ngo.ru/undocs/session69-index.html

2000b Concluding Observations, Gabon. U.N. Doc. CCPR/CO/70/GAB, (2000). Available online at http://hrlibrary.ngo.ru/hrcommittee/gabon2000.html

2000c Concluding Observations, Republic of the Congo. U.N. Doc. CCPR/C/79/Add.118 (2000). Available online at http://hrlibrary.ngo.ru/hrcommittee/congo2000.html

2000d Communication No. 547/1993, *Apirana Mahuika et al. v. New Zealand.* Seventieth session (2000). U.N. Doc. CCPR/C/70/D/547/1993 (2000). Available online at http://hrlibrary.ngo.ru/undocs/session70-index.html

2006 Concluding Observations, Democratic Republic of the Congo. U.N. Doc. CCPR/C/COD/CO/3 (2006). Available online at http://hrlibrary.ngo.ru/hrcommittee/congo2006.html

United Nations Office for the Coordination of Humanitarian Affairs (OCHA)

2005 "Minutes of Information Exchange meeting, February 2005". Regional Support Office for Central and East Africa. Available at http://www.internal-displacement.org/8025708F004CE90B/(httpDocuments)/.../$file/Rapport+Final+HOA-IEM+-+09-02-05.doc

United Nations Office of the High Commissioner for Human Rights (OHCHR)

2002 *OHCHR Draft Guidelines: A Human Approach to Poverty Reduction Strategies.* Geneva: Office of the High Commissioner for Human Rights. Available online at http://www2.ohchr.org/english/issues/poverty/guidelines.htm

United Nations Organization (U.N.)

1945 The Charter of the United Nations. Available at http://www.un.org/aboutun/charter.

1949 General Assembly Resolution 275 (III) of May 11, 1949 (on the Social Problems of the Aboriginal Populations and other Underdeveloped Social Groups of the American Continent). Available online at http://www.un.org/documents/ga/res/3/ares3.htm

1960 General Assembly Resolution 1514 (XV) of December 14, 1960 (on the Granting of Independence to Colonized Countries and Peoples). Available online at http://www.un.org/documents/ga/res/15/ares15.htm.

1992 Declaration on the Rights of Persons belonging to National or Ethnic, Religious and Linguistic Minorities. U.N. Doc. A/47/135 Available online at http://www2.ohchr.org/english/law/minorities.htm

2007 General Assembly Resolution of September 13, 2007 (on The Declaration on the Rights of Indigenous Peoples). U.N. Doc. A/61/295. Available at http://www.un.org/esa/socdev/unpfii/en/declaration.html

United Nations Permanent Forum on Indigenous Peoples Issues (UNPFII)

2007 Report of the Sixth Session (14-25 May 2007). U.N. Doc. E/2007/43, E/C.19/2007/12. Available at: http://daccessdds.un.org/doc/UNDOC/GEN/N07/376/75/PDF/N073-7675.pdf?OpenElement

United Nations Working Group on Indigenous Populations (U.N.WGIP)

1997   Report of the WGIP on its fifteenth session (July-August 1997). U.N. Doc. E/CN.4/ Sub.2/1997/14.

2000   Report from Seminar on "Multiculturalism in Africa: Peaceful and Constructive Group Accommodation in Situations Involving Minorities and Indigenous Peoples". Seminar co-organized with the U.N. Work Group on Minorities and held in Arusha, United Republic of Tanzania on 13-15 May 2000. U.N. Doc. E/CN.4/Sub.2/AC.5/2000/WP.3.

United Republic of Tanzania

1994   *Report of the Presidential Commission Inquiry into Land Matters* (Shivji Report). Vols. 1 & II. Dar es Salam and Uppsala, Sweden: Government of the United Republic of Tanzania (Ministry of Lands, Housing and Urban Development), and the Nordiska Afrika Institutet.

1995   *Tanzania National Conservation Strategy for Sustainable Development (NCSSD).* Dar es Salaam: National Environment Management Council, Republic of Tanzania.

2005   *Strategic Plan for the Implementation of the Land Laws, SPILL.* Dar es Salaam: Ministry of Lands and Human Settlements Development.

2008   *Draft Wildlife Act of 2008.* Dar es Salaam: Ministry of Natural Resources.

Urban Morgan Institute for Human Rights et al.

1998   "The Maastricht Guidelines on Violations of Economic, Social, and Cultural Rights". *Human Rights Quarterly,* 20, no. 3.

Useb, Joram

2001   "One Chief is Enough! Understanding San Traditional Authorities in the Namibian Context". In *Africa's Indigenous Peoples: "First Peoples" or "Marginalized Minorities",* edited by Alan Barnard and Justin Kenrick. Edinburgh: Centre of African Studies, University of Edinburgh.

Vollmann, Tim

2002   "Recognition of Traditional Forms of Ownership of Land and Natural Resources by Indigenous Peoples in the Jurisprudence and Legislation of the U.S.A.". Presentation for the Panel on Traditional forms of ownership in the legislation and practices of the Region, Organization of American States, Washington, D.C., November 7, 2002. http://www.oas.org/consejo/CAJP/docs/cp10445e04.doc

Walsh, Martin T.

2008   "Study on Options for Pastoralists to secure their Livelihoods: Pastoralism and Policy Processes in Tanzania. Mbarali Case Study." In *A Study on Options for Pastoralists to Secure their Livelihoods in Tanzania,* Vol.2 (Case studies). Arusha, Tanzania: CORDS, PWC, IIED, MMM Ngaramtoni Centre, TNRF and UCRT. Available online on the Web site of Tanzania Natural Resource Forum http://www.tnrf.org/node/7487?group=57

Wamba-dia-Wamba, Ernest E.

1991   "Discourse on the National Question". In *State and Constitutionalism: An African Debate of Democracy,* edited by Issa G. Shivji. Harare Zimbabwe: Southern Africa Political Series.

Wanjala, Smokin C.

1990   *Land Law and Disputes in Kenya.* Nairobi: Oxford University Press.

Weeramantry, Christopher and Nathaniel Berman

1999   "The Grotius Lecture Series". 14 *American University International Law Review* 1515.

Weissbrodt, David S., Shinobu Garrigues and Roman Kroke

1998   "An Analysis of the Forty-ninth Session of the United Nations Sub-Commission on Prevention of Discrimination and Protection of Minorities". 11 *Harvard Human Rights Journal* 221 (1998).

Whitaker, Benjamin

1985   "Revised and Updated Report on the Question of the Prevention and Punishment of the Crime of Genocide". Report prepared by the Special speaker, B. Whitaker for ECOSOC. U.N. Doc. E/CN.4/Sub.2/1985/6).

Wiessner, Siegfried

1999   "Rights and Status of Indigenous Peoples: A Global Comparative Legal Analysis". 12 *Harvard Human Rights Journal* 57 (1999). Available online at http://www.law.harvard.edu/students/orgs/hrj/iss12/wiessner.shtml

Woodburn, James
  1979   "Minimal Politics: The Political Organisation of the Hadza of North Tanzania". In *Politics in Leadership: A Comparative Perspective*, edited by W.A. Shack and P.S. Cohen. Oxford: Clarendon Press.
  1997   "Indigenous Discrimination: The Ideological Basis for Local Discrimination against Hunter-Gatherers Minorities in Sub-Saharan Africa". *Ethnic and Racial Studies*, 20, no. 2 (1997).
  2000   "The Political Status of Hunter-Gatherers in Present Day and Future Africa". In *Africa's Indigenous Peoples: "First Peoples" or "Marginalized Minorities"?*, edited by Alan Barnard and Justin Kenrick. Edinburgh: Centre of African Studies, University of Edinburgh.

World Bank
  1991   Operational Directive 4.20 on "Indigenous Peoples". Available as Attachment III at http://www.austlii.edu.au/au/journals/AILR/2003/14html
  2004   Operational Policies (OP) and Bank Procedures (BP).4.10 on "Indigenous Peoples". Available at http://www.worldbank.org

Wøien, Halvor and Lewis Lama
  1999   *Market Commerce as Wildlife Protector? Commercial Initiatives in Community Conservation in Tanzania's Northern Rangelands*. Pastoral Land Tenures Series. London: International Institute for Environment and Development (IIED).

Yeager, Rodger and Norman N. Miller
  1986   *Wildlife, Wild Death: Land Use and Survival in Eastern Africa*. Albany: State University of New York Press.

Zaninka, Penninah
  2003   "The Impact of (Forest) Nature Conservation on Indigenous Peoples: The Batwa of South-Western Uganda; A Case Study of the Mgahinga and Bwindi Impenetrable Forest Conservation Trust". In *Indigenous Peoples and Protected Areas in Africa: From Principles to Practice*, edited by J. Nelson and L. Hossack. Moreton-in-Marsh, UK: Forest Peoples Programmes.

Zayas, Alfred de
  1995   "The Right to One's Homeland, Ethnic Cleansing and the International Criminal Tribunal for the Former Yugoslavia". *Criminal Law Forum* 6 (2) (1995).

USEFUL WEB SITES

This list is by no means exhaustive but is meant to group some of the main Web sites used in this book and which may be of use for further research.

U.N. System

UN General Assembly documents
   http://www.un.org/ga
Charter based bodies' documents
   http://www.unhchr.ch/Huridocda/Huridoca.nsf/
Office of the High Commissioner for Human Rights
   http://www.ohchr.org/EN/Pages/WelcomePage.aspx
U.N. Permanent Forum
   http://www.un.org/esa/socdev/unpfii
Mechanism of the Special Rapporteur on the situation of human rights and fundamental freedoms of indigenous people
   http://www2.ohchr.org/english/issues/indigenous/rapporteur/

Core human rights documents, including human rights treaties and other primary international human rights instruments can also be accessed at the two Web sites of the University of Minnesota Human Rights Library
   http://hrlibrary.ngo.ru/google/localsearch.html & http://www1.umn.edu/humanrts

Global and regional organizations

ILO database on International Labour Standards, including Conventions.
   http://www.ilo.org/ilolex/
Convention on Biological Diversity
   http://www.cbd.int
UNESCO (general)
   http://www.unesco.org/

UNESCO Conventions
   http://portal.unesco.org/en/ev.php-URL_ID=12025&URL_DO=DO_
   TOPIC&URL_SECTION=-471.html
International Committee of the Red Cross, with a section on international humanitarian law
   http://www.icrc.org
African Commission on Human and Peoples' Rights
   http://www.achpr.org
Inter American Commission on Human Rights
   http://www.cidh.oas.org/DefaultE.htm
European Union
   http://europa.eu/index_en.htm
EU cooperation on indigenous peoples
   http://europa.eu/legislation_summaries/development/sectoral_development_policies/r12006_en.htm

Multilateral Development Banks

World Bank
   http://www.worldbank.org
Inter American Development Bank
   http://www.iadb.org
Asian Development Bank
   http://www.adb.org
African Development Bank
   http://www.afdb.org

Global, regional and national legal databases

The International Court of Justice
   http://www.icj-cij.org
Worldwide Legal Database
   http://www.worldlii.org/
Database on (most) constitutions grouped by country (Richmond University, USA)
   http://www.confinder.richmond.edu/
Legal databases from South Africa and other Southern African countries (Southern African Legal Information Institute)
   http://www.saflii.org/

The Privy Council, UK
> http://www.privy-council.org.uk/

Database on Commonwealth and International Human Rights Case Law (The International Centre for the Legal Protection of Human Rights)
> http://www.interights.org/search/index.htm

Kenya Law Reports
> http://www.kenyalaw.org/update/

Database on U.S. Supreme Court (since 1805) and Federal Appellate case reports (since 1950)
> http://www.altlaw.org

Database on U.S. state and federal laws (including resources pertaining to constitutions, statutes, cases, etc.)
> http://www.findlaw.com/casecode/

U.S. Code, e.g., Title 25 – Indians
> http://www.gpoaccess.gov/uscode/

Canadian Legal Information Institute (CANLII) (Canadian legislation, case laws, etc.)
> http://www.canlii.org/en

Australasian Legal Information Institute (AustLII) (Australian legislation and court judgments)
> http://www.austlii.edu.au/

New Zealand Legal Information Institute (Case law, legislation, etc.)
> http://www.nzlii.org/databases.html

Web sites specialized in indigenous issues

Australian Institute for Aboriginal and Torres Strait Islanders (AIATSIS)
> http://www.aiatsis.gov.au

The Native Title Research Unit (NTRU) is part of AIATSIS and specialized in native title legislation and case law
> http://www.ntru.aiatsis.gov.au/index.html

Indigenous Rights in Aotearoa (New Zealand)
> http://www.converge.org. nz/pma/indig.htm

The Agreements, Treaties and Negotiated Settlements (ATNS) project provides information, historical detail and published material relating to agreements made between indigenous people and others in Australia and overseas
> http://www.atns.net.au/default.asp

National and international NGOs

Community Research and Development Services—CORDS (Tanzania)
http://www.cordstz.org
Community of Rwandese Potters/Communauté des Potiers Rwandais (formerly Caurwa)
http://www.coporwa.org/batwa.html
Forest Peoples Programme—FPP (UK based NGO)
http://www.forestpeoples.org
Indigenous Peoples of Africa Coordinating Committee—IPACC (based in South Africa)
http://www.ipacc.org.za
Legal and Human Rights Centre (Tanzania)
http://www.humanrights.or.tz
Les Heritiers de la Justice (DRC).
http://www.heritiers.org
Maasai Association (Kenya)
http://www.maasai-association.org
MPIDO-Mainyoito Pastoralist Integrated Development Organisation (Kenya)
http://www.mpido.org
Ogiek Welfare Council (Kenya)
http://www.ogiek.org
Tanzania Natural Resource Forum
http://www.tnrf.org
International Work Group for Indigenous Affairs (IWGIA) (international NGO based in Denmark)
http://www.iwgia.org
Survival International - the movement for tribal peoples (UK)
http://www.survivalinternational.org/
World Rainforest Movement (international NGO based in Uruguay)
http://www.wrm.org.uy

INDEX OF CITED COURT CASES AND INTERNATIONAL JURISPRUDENCE

Adeyinka Oyekan v. Mussendiku Adele
[1957] 1 WLR 876 [PC/Nigeria], p. 192n664
Ako Gembul and 100 Others v. Gidagamowd and Waret Farms Ltd and NAFCO
[1989] HC – Arusha CV#12/1989 [Tanzania], p. 124n403
Alexkor Ltd and Government of the Republic of South Africa v. Richtersveld Community and Others
2003 (12) BCLR 1301 (CC) [South Africa], pp. 158-163, 195
Amodu Tijani v. Secretary, Southern Provinces, Nigeria
[1921] 2 A.C. 399 [PC/Nigeria], pp. 159n523, 192, 195
Apirana Mahuika et al. v. New Zealand
U.N. Human Rights Committee, Communication No 547/1993 (2000), pp. 242-243
Calder v. Attorney General of British Columbia
[1973] S.C.R. 313 (1973) [Canada], p. 196
Chetankumar Shantkal Parekh v. The People
[1995] SCZ/11a (unreported). (SCZ Judgment No. 11a of 1995) [Zambia], pp. 193, 193n673
CKGR case – **see** *Sesana and Others*
Delgamuukw v. British Columbia
[1997] 3 S.C.R. 1010 [Canada], pp. 52n140, 162, 197
East Timor Case (Portugal v. Australia)
I.C.J. Judgment, June 1995, pp. 241, 241n871
Fletcher v. Peck
[1810] 6 Cranch 87 [U.S.A.], p. 200n700
Francis Kemei and Others v. The Attorney General and Others
Miscellaneous Civil Application No. 128 of 1999 [Kenya], pp. 95-99
Gove Land Rights [Milirrpum v Nabalco Pty Ltd]
(1971) 17 FLR 141 [Australia], p. 185
Guerin v. The Queen
[1984] 2 S.C.R. 335. (1984) [Canada], p. 197

Hong Leong Equipment Sdn Bhd v. Liew Fook Chuan & Anor
[1996] 1 MLJ 481 (Mal CA) [Malaysia], p. 59n175

Indian Council for Enviro-Legal Action v. Union of India and Or
[2000] 2000(5) SCALE 286, p. 59

Ivan Kitok v. Sweden
U.N. Human Rights Committee, Communication No. 197/1985, pp. 213, 246-247

J.G.A. Diergaardt et al. v. Namibia
U.N. Human Rights Committee, Communication No. 760/1997, p. 247

Johnson v. M'Intosh
[1823] 8 Wheat. 543 [U.S.A.], p. 200n700 & n703

Joseph Letuya and Others v. The Attorney General and Others
Miscellaneous Civil Application No. 635 of 1997 [Kenya], pp. 91-95

Karuk Tribe of California et al. v. United States
[2000] 209 F.3d 1366 (Court of Appeals for Federal Circuit 2000) [U.S.A.], p. 201n706

Kerajaan Negeri Johor & Anor v. Adong bin Kuwau & Ors
[1998] 2 MLJ 158, (1998) 2 CHRLD 281 [Malaysia], p. 59

Kerajaan Ngeri Selangor and 3 others. v. Sagong bin Tasi and 6 Others
[2005] 2 MLJ 591. [Malaysia], p. 211

Kopera Keiya Kamunyu and 44 Others v. The Minister for Tourism, Natural Resources and Environment and 3 Others
HC – Moshi, CV# 33/1995 [Tanzania], pp. 133-135

Länsman et al. v. Finland
U.N. Human Rights Committee, Communication No.511/1992, p. 246

Lekengere Faru Parutu Kamunyu and 16 Others v. The Minister for Tourism, Natural Resources and Environment and 3 Others
HC-Moshi, CV# 33/1994 [Tanzania], pp. 233-235, 149n496, 193, 286-288

Lekengere Faru Parutu Kamunyu & Others v. Minister of Tourism, Natural Resources and Environment & Others
CA-CVA#53/1998, unreported, (1999) 2 CHRLD 416 [Tanzania], pp. 136-137, 286-288

Lubicon Lake Band v. Canada
U.N. Human Rights Committee, Communication No. 167/1984, pp. 52n147, 57, 238-239, 245

Mabo and Others v. The State of Queensland
(No. 2) [1992] 175 CLR 1 [Australia], pp. 46, 53, 98-100, 137, 162, 168-169, 172-173, 178, 185, 187, 187-190, 192-193, 207, 207n237, 283, 288

Mashpee Tribe v. New Seabury Corp.
[1979] 592 F.2d 575 (1st Cir. 1979) [U.S.A.], p. 203n719

Mkomazi cases
see *Kopera...*, *Lekengere...CV#33*, and *Lekengere...CA-CVA#53*

Mulbadaw Village Council and 67 Others v. National Agricultural and Food Corporation
    HC – Arusha - CV# 10/1981 [Tanzania], pp. 53, 124-126
Narragansett Tribe v. Southern R.I. Land Dev. Corp.
    [1976] 418 F.Supp. 798 (D.R.I. 1976) [U.S.A.], p. 203n719
National Agricultural and Food Corporation (NAFCO) v. Mulbadaw Village Council and 66 Others
    CA – Dar es Salaam, CA#3/1986 [Tanzania], pp. 53, 126-127, 192-193
Ol le Njogo and 7 Others v. The Honorable Attorney General and 20 Others
    Civil Case No. 91 of 1912 (E.A.P. 1914), 5 E.A.L.R. 70 [East Africa/Kenya], pp. 36, 86-90, 181, 181n599, 187, 190
Olga Tellis v. Bombay Municipal Corporation
    [1996] AIR 180 (S;) [India], p. 93
Organización Indígena de Antioquía v. Corporación Nacional de Desarrollo del Choco & Madarien
    [1993] Círculo Judicial de Antioquía [Colombia], p. 59
Otoe and Missouria Tribe of Indians v. United States
    [1955] 131 F. Supp. 265, 272 (Ct. Cl. 1955) [U.S.A.], p. 200n702
Pratt and Morgan v. Attorney-General for Jamaica
    [1993] 4 All E.R. 769 [PC/Jamaica], p. 193n671
R. v. Adams
    [1996] 3 SCR. 101 [Canada], p. 194n674
R. v. Côté
    [1996] 3 SCR 139 [Canada], p. 194n674
R. v. Symonds
    [1847] N.Z.P.C.C. 387 [PC/New Zealand], p. 209
R. Rama Chandran v. The Industrial Court of Malaysia & Anor
    [1997] 1 MLJ 145 (Mal FC) [Malaysia], p. 59n175
Re Southern Rhodesia
    [1919] AC 211 [PC/Southern Rhodesia], p. 191
Richtersveld Community and Others v. Alexkor Ltd and Another
    2001 (3) SA 1293 (LCC) [South Africa], pp. 13, 154-156
Richtersveld Community and Others v. Alexkor Ltd. and Another
    2003 (6) BCLR 583 (SCA) [South Africa], pp. 157-158, 194-195
Sesana and Others v. the Attorney General (CKGR Case)
    (No. 52/2002) [2006] BWHC 1 [Botswana], pp. 164-173, 224, 285-288
Sandra Lovelace v. Canada
    U.N. Human Rights Committee, Communication No. 24/1977, pp. 176-177
Sobhuza II v. Muller and Others
    [1926] AC 518-19 (PC/Swaziland), p. 192
South Carolina v. Catawba Indian Tribe, Inc.
    [1986] 476 U.S. 498 [U.SA], p. 203n719

Tan Tek Seng v. Suruhanjaya Perkhidmatan Pendidikan & Anor
    [1996] 1 MLJ 261 (Mal CA) [Malaysia], p. 59n175
Tee-Hit-Ton Indians v. United States
    [1955] 348 U.S. 272 [U.S.A.], p. 200, 200n704 & 705
Tellis and Others v. Bombay N Municipal Corporation and Others
    [1987] LRC (Const) 351 [India], p. 97
United States v. Dann
    [1985] 470 US 39 [U.S.A], p. 202n714
United States v. Shoshone Tribe of Indians
    [1938] 304 US 111 [U.S.A.], pp. 200n702, 202-203
Western Sahara: Advisory Opinion of 16 October 1975
    International Court of Justice (I.C.J.), pp. 85, 187, 191, 282
William Arap Ng'asia & 29 Others v. Baringo County Council and Koibatek County Council
    HC – Nakuru, Civil suit No. 522 of 1998 [Kenya], p. 101-105, 105n301, 271, 288-289
Wi Parata v. Bishop of Wellington
    [1877] 3 NZLR 72 [New Zealand], p. 209
The Wik Peoples v. The State of Queensland & Ors; The Thayorre People v. The State of Queensland & Ors
    [1996] HCA 40 [Australia] , p. 208
Wisconsin v. Yoder
    [1972] 406 U.S. 219 [U.S.A.], p. 175
Yoke Gwaku and 5 others v. NAFCO and Gawal Farms Limited
    HC – Arusha, CV#52/1988 [Tanzania], pp. 128-132, 193, 287, 289

APPENDICES

1. ADVISORY OPINION OF THE AFRICAN COMMISSION ON HUMAN AND PEOPLES' RIGHTS ON THE UNITED NATIONS DECLARATION ON THE RIGHTS OF INDIGENOUS PEOPLES

Adopted by the African Commission on Human and Peoples' Rights at its 41st Ordinary Session held in May 2007 in Accra, Ghana.

Introduction

1. At its 1st Session held on the 29th June 2006 in Geneva, the United Nations Human Rights Council (UNHRC) adopted the United Nations Declaration on the Rights of Indigenous Peoples (the Declaration). This Declaration is the result of a process of negotiation, which began in March 1995, under the auspices of the former United Nations Commission on Human Rights (UNHRC), during which an inter-session working group prepared the draft.

2. During its consideration by the 3rd Committee of the United Nations General Assembly (UNGA) in New York, the adoption of this resolution was brought before a certain number of countries as well as the group of African States which expressed a number of concerns which had been submitted to the State Parties in the form of an aide-memoire of the African Group dated 9th November 2006.

3. Having been seized of the issue, the Assembly of Heads of State and Government (AHSG) of the African Union (AU), meeting in Addis Ababa in January 2007, took a decision aimed at requesting the deferment of the consideration by the UNGA of the adoption of the said Declaration with a view to opening negotiations for making amendments, in order to take

into consideration the fundamental preoccupations of the African countries, namely:

    a. The definition of indigenous peoples;
    b. The issue of self-determination;
    c. The issue of land ownership and the exploitation of resources;
    d. The establishment of distinct political and economic institutions
    e. The issue of national and territorial integrity

4. Seized of this matter during its 41st Ordinary Session (Accra, Ghana, 16 – 30 May 2007), the African Commission on Human and Peoples' Rights (ACHPR), deliberated on the issue and on the recommendation of its Working Group on Indigenous Populations/Communities (WGIP), passed a Resolution which underlined the fact that the concept of indigenous populations in the African Continent had been the subject of extensive study and debate resulting in a report adopted by the ACHPR in November 2003 at its 34th Ordinary Session. [Report of the African Commission's Working Group of Experts on Indigenous Populations /Communities, adopted at the 34th Ordinary Session in November 2003, which fact was included in the 17th Annual Activity Report of the African Commission later noted and authorized for publication by the 4th Ordinary Session of the AHSG of the AU held in January 2005 in Abuja, Nigeria (Assembly/AU/Dec.56 (IV))].

5. Following its adoption of the said report, the ACHPR in its jurisprudence has interpreted and shed some light on matters similar to the concerns voiced by the AHSG of the AU on the draft UN Declaration and to that end, decided to ask, at its 41st Ordinary Session held in Accra, Ghana, its WGIP to draft an Advisory Opinion on the various concerns expressed by the African States on the UN Declaration for submission to and discussion with key AU organs concerned with the matter before and during the AU Summit scheduled to take place in Accra, Ghana, from 1st to 3rd July 2007.

6. The ACHPR has interpreted the protection of the rights of Indigenous Populations *within the context of a strict respect for the inviolability of borders and of the obligation to preserve the territorial integrity of State Parties,* in conformity with the principles and values enshrined in the Constitutive Act of the AU, the African Charter on Human and Peoples' Rights (the African Charter) and the UN Charter.

7. Within this context, the present Advisory Opinion is being submitted on the basis of the relevant provisions of **Article 45(1)(a) of the African Charter** which gives mandate to the ACHPR to:

    Collect documentation, carry out studies and research on African problems in the field of Human and Peoples' Rights ... and, if need be, submit opinions or make recommendations to the Governments.

8. In providing this Advisory Opinion, the ACHPR also relies on its well established jurisprudence in interpreting the provisions of the African Charter, which is one of its mandates under Article 45 (3) of the African Charter:

    Interpret all the provisions of the present Charter at the request of a State Party, an institution of the OAU or an African Organization recognized by the OAU.

I. On the lack of a definition of indigenous populations

9. The lack of a definition of the notion of indigenous populations in the draft UN Declaration is considered as likely to create major juridical problems for the implementation of the Declaration. The aide-memoire of the African Group of November 2006 even indicates that this "would be not only legally incorrect but could also create tension among ethnic groups and instability between sovereign States".

10. From the studies carried out on this issue and the decisions it has made on the matter, **the ACHPR is of the view that, a definition is not necessary or useful as there is no universally agreed definition of the term and no single definition can capture the characteristics of indigenous populations. Rather, it is much more relevant and constructive to try to bring out the main characteristics allowing the identification of the indigenous populations and communities in Africa.**

11. Thus, the major characteristics, which allow the identification of Africa's Indigenous Communities is the favored approach adopted, and it is the same approach at the international level. [See the Report of the ACHPR's WGIP, adopted by the ACHPR].

12. The concept in effect embodies the following constitutive elements or characteristics, among others [See page 93 of the Report of the ACHPR's WGIP, adopted by the ACHPR]:
   a. Self-identification;
   b. A special attachment to and use of their traditional land whereby their ancestral land and territory have a fundamental importance for their collective physical and cultural survival as peoples;
   c. A state of subjugation, marginalisation, dispossession, exclusion, or discrimination because these peoples have different cultures, ways of life or mode of production than the national hegemonic and dominant model.

13. Moreover, **in Africa, the term indigenous populations does not mean "first inhabitants" in reference to aboriginality as opposed to non-African communities or those having come from elsewhere.** This peculiarity distinguishes Africa from the other Continents where native communities have been almost annihilated by non-native populations. Therefore, the ACHPR considers that any African can legitimately consider him/herself as indigene to the Continent.

II. On the question of self-determination and territorial integrity

14. In its preamble, the UN Declaration on the Rights of Indigenous Peoples states *"the fundamental importance of the right of all persons to self-determination and considers that no provision of the present Declaration can be invoked to deny a people, whatever they may be, of their right to self-determination exercised in conformity with international law."*

15. Article 3 of the Declaration specifies that Indigenous Peoples *"freely determine their political status and freely pursue their economic, social and cultural development." Article 4 states that "in the exercise of their right to self-determination, the indigenous peoples have the right to autonomy or self-government in everything that concerns their internal and local affairs as well as ways and means to finance their autonomous activities."*

16. In reaction to these provisions, the aide-memoire of the African Group of November 2006 re-affirms: *"To implicitly recognize the rights of indigenous peoples to self-determination in paragraph 13 of the preamble and in Articles 3 and 4 of the Declaration may be wrongly interpreted and understood as the granting of a unilateral right to self-determination and a possible cessation to a*

specific section of the national population, thus threatening the political unity and territorial integrity of any country".

17. The ACHPR advises that articles 3 and 4 of the Declaration should be read together with Article 46 of the Declaration, which guarantees the inviolability of the integrity of Nation states. Article 46 of the Declaration specifies *"that nothing in this Declaration may be interpreted as implying for any State, people, group or person any right to engage in any activity or to perform any act contrary to the Charter of the UN".*

18. In the opinion of the ACHPR, Articles 3 and 4 of the Declaration can be exercised only in the context of ***Article 46 of the Declaration which is in conformity with the African Commission's jurisprudence on the promotion and protection of the rights of indigenous populations based on respect of sovereignty, the inviolability of the borders acquired at independence of the member states and respect for their territorial integrity.***

19. **In Africa, the term indigenous populations or communities is not aimed at protecting the rights of a certain category of citizens over and above others.** This notion does not also create a hierarchy between national communities, but rather tries to guarantee the equal enjoyment of the rights and freedoms on behalf of groups, which have been historically marginalized.

20. In this context, Article 20(1) of the African Charter is drafted in similar terms: *"all peoples shall have the right to existence. They shall have the unquestionable and inalienable right to self-determination. They shall freely determine their political status and shall pursue their economic and social development according to the policy they have freely chosen".*

21. It is true that the decision of the AU Summit of January 2007 on the subject re-affirms in its preamble the reference to the UNGA Resolution 1514(XV) of 14 December 1960, which recognizes the rights to self-determination, and the independence of the populations and territories under colonial domination or under foreign occupation.

22. The fact remains however that **the notion of self-determination has evolved with the development of the international visibility of the claims made by indigenous populations whose right to self-determination is exercised within the standards and according to the modalities which are compatible with the territorial integrity of the Nation States to which they belong.**

23. In its jurisprudence on the rights of peoples to self-determination, the ACHPR, seized of Communications/Complaints claiming for the enjoyment of this right within State Parties, has constantly emphasized that these populations could exercise their right to self-determination in accordance with all the forms and variations which are compatible with the territorial integrity of State Parties. [See Communication 75/92 of 1995 - the Katangese People Congress vs. Zaire, reported in the 8th Annual Activity Report of the ACHPR].

24. In this respect, the report of the ACHPR's WGIP states that, "the collective rights known as the peoples' rights should be applicable to certain categories of the populations within Nation States, including the indigenous populations but that ... the right to self-determination as it is outlined in the provisions of the OAU Charter and in the African Charter should not be understood as a sanctioning of secessionist sentiments. The self-determination of the populations should therefore be exercised within the national inviolable borders of a State, by taking due account of the sovereignty of the Nation State" (Experts' Report of the ACHPR, p. 83/88).

25. Several States in Africa and elsewhere share this meaning of the right to self-determination taken either from its perspective of identity for the preservation of the cultural heritage of these populations, or from its socio-economic perspective for the enjoyment of their economic and social rights within the context of the specificities of their way of life.

26. However, if it is taken from the political perspective, the right of Indigenous Populations to self-determination refers mainly to the management of their "internal and local affairs" and to their participation as citizens in national affairs on an equal footing with their fellow citizens without it leading to a total territorial break up which would happen should there be violation of the territorial integrity of the State Parties. Therefore this mode of attaining the right to self-determination should not at all be confused with that which issued from the Resolution 1514(XV) of the 14th December 1960 which is applicable to the populations and territories under colonial dominance or foreign occupation and to which the UN Declaration, which is the objective of this Advisory opinion, does not refer to at all.

27. In consequence, the ACHPR is of the view that the right to self-determination in its application to indigenous populations and communities, both at the UN and regional levels, should be understood as encompass-

ing a series of rights relative to the full participation in national affairs, the right to local self-government, the right to recognition so as to be consulted in the drafting of laws and programs concerning them, to a recognition of their structures and traditional ways of living as well as the freedom to preserve and promote their culture. It is therefore a collection of variations in the exercise of the right to self-determination, which are entirely compatible with the unity, and territorial integrity of State Parties.

28. From another angle, the question is also raised in terms of determining the exact meaning and scope of Article 9 of the UN Declaration, which stipulates:

> *"Indigenous peoples and individuals have the right to belong to an indigenous community or nation, in conformity with the traditions and customs of the community or nation concerned. No discrimination of any kind may arise from the exercise of such a right."*

29. On this point, the document representing the aide-memoire of the African Group of November 2006 states that there is: *"a real danger that the tribal communities may interpret this clause as meaning that they can chose to belong to a country whilst they live in the territory of another".*

30. **The ACHPR observes that trans-national identification of indigenous communities is an African reality for several of the socio-ethnic groups living on our Continent and which co-habit in perfect harmony with the principle of territorial integrity and national unity.** Furthermore it would be erroneous to think that certain trans-border cultural activities anchored in the ways of life and the ancestral productions of these communities can imperil the national unity and integrity of the African countries.

31. **In this regard, trans-border identification of indigenous communities or nations has not resulted in any challenge to the question of citizenship or nationality being governed by the internal laws of each country.**

III. On the right of indigenous peoples to land, territories and resources

32. The UN Declaration states in its preamble that: *"the control by indigenous peoples over developments affecting them and their lands, territories and resources will enable them to maintain and strengthen their institutions, cultures*

and traditions and to promote their development according to their aspirations and needs."

33. In the comment relating to the provision contained in the draft aide-memoire of November 2006 by the African Group, it is stated that the said provision "is impracticable within the context of the countries concerned. In accordance with the constitutional provisions of these countries, the control of land and natural resources is the obligation of the State".

34. On this issue, Article 21(1) of the African Charter states that: *"all peoples shall freely dispose of their wealth and natural resources. This right shall be exercised in the exclusive interest of the people. In no case shall a people be deprived of it."*

35. Similar provisions are contained in many other instruments adopted by the AU such as the African Convention on the Conservation of Nature and Natural Resources whose major objective is: *"to harness the natural and human resources of our continent for the total advancement of our peoples in spheres of human endeavour"* (preamble) and which is intended *"to preserve the traditional rights and property of local communities and request the prior consent of the communities concerned in respect of all that concerns their access to and use of traditional knowledge,"* which is similar to the provisions of Article 10, 11(2), 28(1) and 32 of the UN Declaration.

36. With regard to Article 37 of the UN Declaration on the rights of indigenous peoples, it states: *"the indigenous populations have a right to the effect that treaties, agreements and other constructive arrangements signed by the States or their successors be recognized, honored, respected and applied by the States"*. In its aide-memoire the African Group states having "serious reservations" on the possible repercussions of this article.

37. On this point, the UN report on treaties and agreements signed between the States and indigenous peoples shows that apart from the case of the Maasai in East Africa where the agreement with the British Colonial administration went through a judicial procedure, there is nowhere on the African continent where other indigenous communities have signed a historic agreement or treaty with a State. Moreover, these agreements have never resulted in the emergence of entities that have the characteristics of international sovereignty.

38. Consequently, it seems that this concern is predicated on fears relating to the reality of other continents, e.g., North America, where countries rec-

ognize its validity and implement agreements signed with indigenous communities and people living on their territories.

IV. On the right of indigenous peoples to establish separate political and economic institutions

39. This concern was expressed by referring to Article 5 of the UN Declaration on the rights of indigenous peoples which states that: *"indigenous peoples have the right to maintain and consolidate their separate political, legal, economic, social and cultural institutions, by maintaining the right, if that is their choice, to fully participate in the political, economic and cultural life of the State"*.

40. In its comments on the issue, the aide-memoire of the African Group of November 2006 is of the view that this article "contradicts the constitutions of a number of African countries which, if adopted, would create constitutional problems for the African Countries".

41. In this context, it is pertinent to reiterate the provision of Article 46 of the UN Declaration which guarantees the inviolability and integrity of Member States: *"that nothing in this Declaration may be interpreted as implying for any State, people or group or person any right to engage in any activity or to perform any act contrary to the Charter of the UN."*

42. Moreover, Articles 5 and 19 of the Declaration appears to merely restate the right to culture and development and the duty of the state to take into account cultural rights while fulfilling its obligations to guarantee the right to development similar to the provisions of Article 22(1) and (2) of the African Charter.

43. It is appropriate in this regard to recall the definition given to the notion of culture by the Southern African Development Community (SADC) which means "...The totality of a people's way of life, the whole complex of distinctive spiritual, material, intellectual and emotional features that characterize a society or a social group, and include not only arts and letters, but also modes of life, the fundamental rights of the human being, value system, traditions and beliefs", as well as the pertinent provisions of the African Cultural Charter that make reference to it as "a balancing factor within the nation and source of enrichment among the different communities."

Conclusion

44. On the basis of this Advisory Opinion, the ACHPR recommends that African States should promote an African common position that will inform the United Nations Declaration on the rights of indigenous peoples with this African perspective so as to consolidate the overall consensus achieved by the international community on the issue.

45. It hopes that its contribution hereof could help allay some of the concerns raised surrounding the human rights of indigenous populations and wishes to reiterate its availability for any collaborative endeavor with African States in this regard with a view to the speedy adoption of the Declaration.

2. LIST OF TREATIES, CONVENTIONS, ETC., ADOPTED, SIGNED AND/OR RATIFIED BY AFRICAN COUNTRIES

TABLE 1

Status of Ratification of ICERD, ICCPR, UNDRIP, ILO C107, ILO C169, CBD and CRC

Treaties, Conventions, etc. Year of adoption/ entry in force Countries /Year ratification	ICERD[a] 1966/1969	ICCPR[b] 1966/1976	UNDRIP[c] 2007	ILO C 107[d] 1957/1959	ILO C 169[e] 1989/1991	CBD[f] 1992/1993	CRC[g] 1989/1990
Algeria	1972	1989	2007	1976	Not party	1995	1993
Angola	Not party	1992	2007	Not party	Not party	1998	1990
Benin	2001	1992	2007	Not party	Not party	1994	1990
Botswana	1974	2000	2007	Not party	Not party	1995	1995
Burkina Faso	1974	1999	2007	Not party	Not party	1993	1990
Burundi	1977	1990	Abstained	Not party	Not party	1997	1990
Cameroon	1971	1984	2007	Not party	Not party	1994	1993
Cape Verde	1979	1993	2007	Not party	Not party	1995	1992
Central African Republic	1971	1981	2007	2010	Not party	1995	1992
Chad	1977	1995	Not present	Not party	Not party	1994	1990
Comoros	2004	S[1]/ not ratified	2007	Not party	Not party	1994	1993
Congo	1988	1983	2007	Not party	Not party	1996	1993
Côte d'Ivoire	1973	1992	Not present	Not party	Not party	1994	1991
Dem. Rep. Congo (DRC)	1976	1976	2007	Not party	Not party	1994	1990
Djibouti	2006	2002	2007	Not party	Not party	1994	1990
Egypt	1967	1982	2007	1959	Not party	1994	1990
Equatorial Guinea	2002	1987	Not present	Not party	Not party	1994	1992
Eritrea	2001	2002	Not present	Not party	Not party	1996	1994

a   International Convention on the Elimination of All forms of Racist Discrimination: http://www.unhchr.ch/Huridocda/Huridoca.nsf

b   International Covenant on Civil and Political Rights: http://www.unhchr.ch/Huridocda/Huridoca.nsf

c   United Nations Declaration on the Rights of Indigenous Peoples: http://www.un.org/News/Press/docs/2007/ga10612.doc.htm

d/e ILO Convention 107 and ILO Convention 169: http://www.ilo.org/ilolex

f   Convention on Biological Diversity: http://www.cbd.int

g   Convention on the Rights of the Child: http://www.unhchr.ch/Huridocda/Huridoca.nsf

Table 1 (continued)

Treaties, Conventions, etc. Year of adoption/ entry in force Countries /Year ratification	ICERD[a] 1966/1969	ICCPR[b] 1966/1976	UNDRIP[c] 2007	ILO C 107[d] 1957/1959	ILO C 169[e] 1989/1991	CBD[f] 1992/1993	CRC[g] 1989/1990
Ethiopia	1976	1993	Not present	Not party	Not party	1994	1991
Gabon	1980	1983	2007	Not party	Not party	1997	1994
Gambia	1978	1979	Not present	Not party	Not party	1994	1990
Ghana	1966	2000	2007	1958	Not party	1994	1990
Guinea	1977	1978	2007	Not party	Not party	1993	1990
Guinea Bissau	S[2]/ not ratified	1992	Not present	1977	Not party	1995	1990
Kenya	2001	1972	Abstained	Not party	Not party	1994	1990
Lesotho	1971	1992	2007	Not party	Not party	1995	1992
Liberia	1976	2004	2007	Not party	Not party	2000	1993
Libyan Arab Jamahiriya	1968	1970	2007	Not party	Not party	2001	1993
Madagascar	1969	1971	2007	Not party	Not party	1996	1991
Malawi	1996	1993	2007	1965	Not party	1994	1991
Mali	1974	1974	2007	Not party	Not party	1995	1990
Mauritania	1988	2004	Not present	Not party	Not party	1996	1991
Mauritius	1972	1973	2007	Not party	Not party	1992	1990
Morocco	1970	1979	Not present	Not party	Not party	1995	1993
Mozambique	1983	1993	2007	Not party	Not party	1995	1994
Namibia	1982	1994	2007	Not party	Not party	1997	1990
Niger	1967	1986	2007	Not party	Not party	1995	1990
Nigeria	1967	1993	Abstained	Not party	Not party	1994	1991
Rwanda	1975	1975	Not present	Not party	Not party	1996	1991
Sao Tomé and Principe	S[3]/ not ratified	1995	Not present	Not party	Not party	1999	1991
Senegal	1972	1978	2007	Not party	Not party	1994	1990
Seychelles	1978	1992	Not present	Not party	Not party	1992	1990
Sierra Leone	1967	1996	2007	Not party	Not party	1994	1990
Somalia	1975	1990	Not present	Not party	Not party	2009	S4/not ratified
South Africa	1998	1998	2007	Not party	Not party	1995	1995

Table 1 (continued)

Treaties, Conventions, etc. Year of adoption/ entry in force Countries /Year ratification	ICERD[a] 1966/1969	ICCPR[b] 1966/1976	UNDRIP[c] 2007	ILO C 107[d] 1957/1959	ILO C 169[e] 1989/1991	CBD[f] 1992/1993	CRC[g] 1989/1990
Sudan	1977	1986	2007	Not party	Not party	1995	1990
Swaziland	1969	2004	2007	Not party	Not party	1994	1995
Togo	1972	1984	Not present	Not party	Not party	1995	1990
Tunisia	1967	1969	2007	1962	Not party	1993	1992
Uganda	1980	1995	Not present	Not party	Not party	1993	1990
United Rep. of Tanzania	1972	1976	2007	Not party	Not party	1996	1991
Zambia	1972	1984	2007	Not party	Not party	1993	1991
Zimbabwe	1991	1991	2007	Not party	Not party	1994	1990
TOTAL COUNTRIES 53[i]							
TOTAL PARTIES	50	52	35	6	1	53	52

Notes

1   Signed in 2007;
2   Signed in 2000;
3   Signed in 2000;
4   Signed in 2002;
5   There are 53 independent African states

Next page:

TABLE 2
Status of Ratification of UNESCO, Geneva and Hague Conventions,
The African Charter and its Protocol on the establishment of
the African Court on Human and Peoples' Rights

Treaties, Conventions, etc.	UNESCO	4th Geneva Convention		Hague Convention		African	Union
	C.CULT. EXP.[a]	Convent.[b]	Protocols I/II[c]	C. & Protocol I[d]	Protocol II[e]	Charter[f]	Afr. Court[g]
Year of adoption/ entry in force	2005/2007	1949/1950	1977	1954/1956	1999/2004	1981/1986	1998/2004[i]
Countries /Year ratification							
Algeria	Not party	1960	1989/1989	Not party	Not party	1987	2003
Angola	Not party	1984	1984/1984	Not party	Not party	1990	Signed 2007
Benin	2007	1961	1986/1986	Not party	Not party	1986	Signed 1998
Botswana	Not party	1958	1979/1979	2002/ Not party	Not party	1986	Signed 1998
Burkina Faso	2006	1961	1987/1987	1969/1987	Not party	1984	1998
Burundi	2008	1971	1993/1993	Not party	Not party	1989	2003
Cameroon	2006	1963	1984/1984	1961/1961	Not party	1989	Signed 2006
Cape Verde	Not party	1984	1995/1995	Not party	Not party	1987	Not party
Central African Republic.	Not party	1966	1984/1984	Not party	Not party	1986	Signed 2002
Chad	2008	1970	1997/1997	2008/ Not party	Not party	1986	Signed 2004
Comoros	Not party	1985	1985/1985	Not party	Not party	1986	2003
Congo	2008	1967	1983/1983	Not party	Not party	1982	Signed 1998
Côte d'Ivoire	2007	1961	1989/1989	1980/ Not party	Not party	1992	2003
Dem.Rep.Congo (DRC)	Not party	1961	1982/2002	1961/1961	Not party	1987	Signed 1999
Djibouti	2006	1978	1991/1991	Not party	Not party	1991	Signed 2005
Egypt	2007	1952	1992/1992	1955/1955	2005	1984	Signed 1999
Equatorial Guinea	Not party	1986	1986/1986	2003/ Not party	2003	1986	Signed 1998
Eritrea	Not party	2000	Not party	2004/ Not party	Not party	1999	Not party
Ethiopia	2008	1969	1994/1994	Not party	Not party	1998	Signed 1998
Gabon	2007	1965	1980/1980	1961/1961	2003	1986	2000
Gambia	Not party	1966	1980/1989	Not party	Not party	1983	1999
Ghana	Not party	1958	1989/1989	1960/1960	Not party	1989	2005
Guinea	2008	1984	1984/1984	1960/1961	Not party	1982	Signed 2003
Guinea Bissau	Not party	1974	1986/1986	Not party	Not party	1985	Signed 1998
Kenya	2007	1966	1999/1999	Not party	Not party	1992	2004
Lesotho	Not party	1968	1994/1994	Not party	Not party	1992	2003
Liberia	Not party	1954	1988/1988	Not party	Not party	1982	Signed 1998
Libyan Arab Jamahiriya	Not party	1956	1978/1978	1957/1957	2001	1986	2003
Madagascar	2006	1963	1992/1992	1961/1961	Not party	1992	Signed 1998
Malawi	Not party	1968	1991/1991	Not party	Not party	1989	Signed 1998

Table 2 (continued)

Treaties, Conventions, etc.	UNESCO C.CULT. EXP.[a]	4th Geneva Convention Convent.[b]	Protocols I/II[c]	Hague Convention C. & Protocol I[d]	Protocol II[e]	African Charter[f]	Protocol Afr. Court[g]
Year of adoption/ entry in force	2005/2007	1949/1950	1977	1954/1956	1999/2004	1981/1986	1998/2004[i]
Countries /Year ratification							
Malawi	Not party	1968	1991/1991	Not party	Not party	1989	Signed 1998
Mali	2006	1965	1989/1989	1961/1961	Not party	1981	2000
Mauritania	Not party	1962	1980/1980	Not party	Not party	1986	2005
Mauritius	2006	1970	1982/1982	2006/ Not party	Not party	1992	2003
Morocco	Not party	1956	Not party	1968/1968	Not party	Not Member of AU	Not Member of AU
Mozambique	2007	1983	1983/2002	Not party	Not party	1989	2004
Namibia	2006	1991	1994/1994	Not party	Not party	1992	Signed 1998
Niger	2007	1964	1979/1979	1976/1976	2006	1986	2004
Nigeria	2008	1961	1988/1988	1961/1961	2005	1983	2004
Rwanda	Not party	1964	1984/1984	2000/ Not party	Not party	1983	2003
Sao Tomé and Principe	Not party	1976	1996/1996	Not party	Not party	1986	Not party
Senegal	2006	1963	1985/1985	1987/1987	Not party	1982	1998
Seychelles	2008	1984	1984/1984	2003/ Not party	Not party	1992	Signed 1998
Sierra Leone	Not party	1965	1986/1986	Not party	Not party	1983	Signed 1998
Somalia	Not party	1962	Not party	Not party	Not party	1985	Signed 2006
South Africa	2006	1952	1995/1995	2003/ Not party	Not party	1996	2002
Sudan	2008	1957	2006/2006	1970/1970	Not party	1986	Signed 1998
Swaziland	Not party	1973	1995/1995	Not party	Not party	1995	Signed 2004
Togo	2006	1962	1984/1984	Not party	Not party	1982	2003
Tunisia	2007	1957	1979/1979	1981/1981	Not party	1983	2007
Uganda	Not party	1964	1991/1991	Not party	Not party	1986	2001
United Rep. of Tanzania	Not party	1962	1983/1983	1971/ Not party	Not party	1984	2006
Zambia	Not party	1966	1995/1995	Not party	Not party	1984	Signed 1998
Zimbabwe	2008	1983	1992/1992	1998/ Not party	Not party	1986	Signed 1998
TOTAL COUNTRIES 53							
TOTAL PARTIES	27	53	50/50	27/16	6	52	24

a   Convention On the Protection and Promotion of Cultural Expression: http://portal.unesco.org/la/convention.asp?KO=31038&language=E&order=alpha

b   4th Geneva Convention: http://www.icrc.org/ihl.nsf

c   Protocol I on Protection of Victims of International Armed Conflicts; Protocol II on Protection of Victims of Non-International Armed Conflicts:Both at http://www.icrc.org/ihl.nsf

d   The Hague Convention for the Protection of Cultural Property in the Event of Armed Conflict, and its Protocol I were signed on the same date. Both at http://www.icrc.org/ihl.nsf

e   Protocol II to the Hague Convention at http://www.icrc.org/ihl.nsf

f   The African Charter on Human and Peoples' Rights: http://www.achpr.org/english/ratifications/ratification_african%20charter.pdf

g   Protocol to the African Charter on Human and Peoples' Rights on the Establishment of an African court on Human and Peoples' Rights:
http://www.achpr.org/english/ratifications/ratification_court.pdf.

Note

1   50 out of 53 African states have signed the Protocol on the Establishment of an African Court, but so far, it has only been ratified by 24.